European cities

Manchester University Press

European cities

Modernity, race and colonialism

Edited by Noa K. Ha and Giovanni Picker

MANCHESTER UNIVERSITY PRESS

Published by Manchester University Press
Oxford Road, Manchester M13 9PL

www.manchesteruniversitypress.co.uk

British Library Cataloguing-in-Publication Data
A catalogue record for this book is available from the
British Library

The book cover is taken from the painting *Chafariz d'el Rey
in the Alfama District* (*View of a Square with the Kings
Fountain in Lisbon*), ca. 1570–88, Museu Colecção Berardo
in Lisbon. The name of the author is unknown. This is one
of the first figurative representations of an urban space in
Europe where whites and 'non-white Others' are side by
side. Distinguishable here are Jewish, white and Black
people.

ISBN   978 1 5261 5843 7   hardback
ISBN   978 1 5261 7871 8   paperback

First published 2022

Typeset
by New Best-set Typesetters Ltd

For our students and all critical learners from anywhere outside academia

Contents

Part III: Provincialising the (urban) political

Figures

Contributors

Ana Rita Alves is an anthropologist and a PhD student at the Centre for Social Studies, University of Coimbra (Portugal). She was one of the 2020–21 Black Studies Dissertation Scholars at the University of California, Santa Barbara. Over the past decade, Ana Rita has been producing critical academic knowledge on institutional racism, urban segregation, housing and public policies, working with several grassroots movements of peripheral self-produced and rehousing neighbourhoods. She is the author of the book *When Nobody Could Stay: Racism, Housing and Territory* (Tigre de Papel, 2021). She has been involved in several research projects, including RAP – 'Race' and Africa in Portugal: A Study on History Textbooks, COMBAT – Combating Racism in Portugal: An Analysis of Public Policies and Anti-discrimination Law and AFRO-PORT – Afro-descendance in Portugal: Sociability, Representations and Sociopolitical and Cultural Dynamics. A Study in the Lisbon Metropolitan Area.

Mahdis Azarmandi is a Senior Lecturer in Educational Studies and Leadership at the University of Canterbury. After obtaining her PhD from the National Centre for Peace and Conflict Studies at the University of Otago, she held a position as Assistant Professor at DePauw University. She has also taught in Germany and Denmark. Her research looks at anti-racism and colonial amnesia in Aotearoa New Zealand and Spain. She has published on the politics of memorialisation in Spain as well as on the absence of race critical research in the field of Peace Studies. She is one of the editors of the book *Decolonize the City! Zur Kolonialität der Stadt – Gespräche | Aushandlungen | Perspektiven* (Unrast, 2017). Her research interests are anti-racism, critical race and whiteness studies, memorialisation and decolonisation.

Antonio Carbone is a post-doctoral researcher in Modern History at the German Historical Institute in Rome. In his current project, he works on the emergence of global concepts of South and their influence on ideas of

European integration in the post-war period. He previously worked as a lecturer in the department of Global History at the Freie Universität Berlin and taught at Technische Universität Berlin as well as at the Europa-Universität Viadrina. For his dissertation research, he spent extended periods in the archives of Buenos Aires and at Columbia University in New York and received his PhD with a thesis on the influence of epidemics on urban imaginaries in nineteenth-century Buenos Aires. He is the author of two forthcoming books, *Epidemic Cities* (Cambridge University Press, 2021) and *Park, Tenement, Slaughterhouse* (Campus Verlag, 2022). With a regional focus on Europe and Latin America, his interests range from global and urban history to the history of science and ideas.

Julie Chamberlain is Assistant Professor in the Department of Urban and Inner-City Studies at the University of Winnipeg, on Treaty 1 territory, the traditional territory of the Anishinaabeg, Cree, Oji-Cree and Dakota peoples, and the homeland of the Métis. She aspires to activist scholarship in both Canada and Germany, with a focus on the intersections of anti-racism, urban development, planning, discourse and the self-determination of racialised communities. She is from Toronto.

Stoyanka Eneva holds a BA and MA in Social and Cultural Anthropology and a PhD in Political Science from Universidad Autónoma de Madrid. Her academic background has been acquired in different areas of the Social Sciences and Humanities with the aim of achieving a transdisciplinary education. Specifically, her training has focused on the fields of Linguistics, Social and Cultural Anthropology, with special emphasis on the public orientation of Anthropology, and, finally, on Political Science, the main area in which she has developed her PhD research.

Noa K. Ha has taught and researched in the areas of Historical Urbanism, Urban Sociology and the Sociology of Space at TU Berlin, Center for Metropolitan Studies, the Humboldt-Universität and TU Dresden, and now at weißensee academy of art berlin. Her research investigates processes of urban production from decolonial, critical race theory, feminist and queer theory perspectives. She has published on urban informality, racism and public space in the neoliberal city Berlin, and has written extensively about decolonisation, the European city and the coloniality of urban space. She is a founding member of the Critical Race, Postcolonial and Decolonial Studies Association – FG dekolonial, and is active in several grassroots community organisations and initiatives.

Tania Mancheno has taught at the University of Hamburg in the field of Social Sciences on postcolonial theory and decolonial thought since 2009.

She studied Sociology, Political Science and Social Anthropology in Quito, Hamburg and Paris. Her research is focused on urban space and violence, colonial history and the analysis of its local and transnational consequences from a feminist perspective from the Global South, with a special focus on Black Caribbean political thinking. In 2019, she obtained her PhD with a dissertation on the politics of translation and the debate on multiculturalism. She is an associate scholar at the Hamburg's (post)colonial heritage research centre.

Aidan Mosselson is currently a Chancellor's Fellow in the Edinburgh School of Architecture and Landscape Architecture, University of Edinburgh. His research agenda focuses on diverse forms and experiences of social and spatial inequality and marginalisation, and works to overcome conceptual divides separating the Global South and Global North. He has undertaken research that analyses processes of urbanisation and development in the Global South as well as socio-material infrastructures of migration, labour, race and care in Britain. He has previously held a Newton International Fellowship (2018–20) as well as an Urban Studies Foundation International Fellowship (2017–18).

Manuel Peters works as academic assistant to the Chair of Intercultural Studies / UNESCO Chair in Heritage Studies at BTU Cottbus-Senftenberg. Research interests include Cultural Studies, Critical Migration Studies, Heritage Studies, Educational Studies and Post-/De-colonial and Post-Socialist Studies. Manuel's doctoral thesis was in Educational Sciences with a focus on Critical Race and Migration Studies.

Giovanni Picker is Lecturer/Assistant Professor of Sociology at the University of Glasgow (UK). After obtaining his PhD in Urban Studies (2009), he held a number of research positions in Italy, Romania, Russia, Hungary, Germany and the UK. His current research and teaching centre on the articulations of Urban Studies and Critical Race Studies, and empirically focus on Europe. He is the author of *Racial Cities: Governance and the Segregation of Romani People in Urban Europe* (Routledge, 2017) and co-editor, with Enikő Vincze, Norbert Petrovici and Cristina Raţ, of *Racialized Labour in Romania: Spaces of Marginality at the Periphery of Global Capitalism* (Palgrave, 2018).

Piro Rexhepi holds a PhD in Politics from the University of Strathclyde. His research focuses on decoloniality, sexuality and Islam. His recent work on racism and borders along the Balkan Refugee Route has been published in a range of mediums in and out of academia including the *International*

Journal of Postcolonial Studies, Ethnic and Racial Studies, Critical Muslim and *The Guardian* among others.

Anke Schwarz is a lecturer in Human Geography at Technische Universität Dresden's Institute of Geography. Her recent publications include 'Hydraulic standby: anticipating water in Mexico City' (*ephemera*, 2021) and the 2020 *Geographica Helvetica* special issue 'Contested urban territories: decolonized perspectives' (co-edited with Monika Streule). Anke specialises in Urban Studies and is particularly interested in the social production of space and territory, urban infrastructures and everyday practices. Among her present projects, she is conducting comparative research on future geographies and identitarian territorialisations in postfascist societies, and serves as one of the coordinators of the scientific network Territorializations of the Far Right, funded by the German Research Foundation.

AbdouMaliq Simone is Senior Professorial Fellow at the Urban Institute, University of Sheffield and Visiting Professor of Urban Studies at the African Centre for Cities, University of Cape Town. Key publications include *For the City Yet to Come: Urban Change in Four African Cities* (Duke University Press, 2004), *City Life from Jakarta to Dakar: Movements at the Crossroads* (Routledge, 2009), *Jakarta: Drawing the City Near* (University of Minnesota Press, 2014), *New Urban Worlds: Inhabiting Dissonant Times* (with Edgar Pieterse; Polity, 2017), *Improvised Lives: Rhythms of Endurance for an Urban South* (Polity, 2018) and *The Surrounds: Urban Life Within and Beyond Capture* (Duke University Press, 2022).

Pieter Troch teaches History of Southeast Europe at Ghent University. He is trained as a Slavist and worked in civil society in Kosovo and Serbia. In his research, he focuses on modernisation politics in the former Yugoslavia. His doctoral research dealt with Yugoslav nation-building programmes in education during the interwar period. In his ongoing research, he looks at socialist development politics in Albanian-populated parts of the former Yugoslavia, in particular through the prism of urbanisation and industrialisation.

Miriam Friz Trzeciak works as a post-doctoral researcher at the Chair of Intercultural Studies at the Brandenburg University of Technology Cottbus-Senftenberg. Their doctoral research focuses on social worlds of leaving and staying in indigenous communities in the southern Mexican borderland. They have carried out ethnographic and collaborative research. Their teaching and research interests include critical migration and border regime studies, gender studies and queer theory, de- and postcolonial studies, postsocialist studies, qualitative research and activist/dialogical research practice.

Acknowledgements

When a global pandemic strikes in the middle of an ongoing project, the efforts to continue and eventually finalise the project exponentially increase. That's what we have learnt during this editorial work, most of which was carried out during the COVID-19 pandemic. Hence, our gratitude expressed here to everyone who contributed, in one way or another, to the making of *European cities* should be multiplied several times.

All authors who contributed to the process of exchange, discussing, writing and revising have been our main source of strength, with their truly amazing perseverance in possibly the hardest of working conditions in a lifetime. Sincere gratitude to you all.

Some people have been closer to this project than others and gave us the kindest of supports. Michael Keith has believed in the project since the start and provided thoughtful and careful advice. AbdouMaliq Simone has given us inspiring and precious insights before and after generously accepting our invitation to offer a closing reflection for the volume. Fatima El-Tayeb provided us with valuable encouragement and thoughtful guidance, in particular to illuminate the porous and complex racial formation of Europe, and Jin Haritaworn provokes our thinking to rearticulate the knowledge production perspective and inspires us in so many ways – thanks so much to both of them for their support!

We would also like to thank the organisers of the 2019 RC21 Annual Conference in Delhi, where we launched the first global dialogue on 'Provincializing European Cities'; this volume is largely the result of that conference session. Sincere thanks to Tom Dark, our editor, and Humairaa Dudhwala, Editorial Controller, at Manchester University Press, for providing us with careful support and guidance. We are also grateful for the financial support we received: the ZEIT-Stiftung Ebelin und Gerd Bucerius generously funded part of the project, and the Technische Universität Dresden provided funding for a workshop, which we sadly had to renounce because of pandemic-related restrictions and then turned into an online workshop.

Giovanni wishes to thank Dasha and Lilia for their caring support and encouragement.

Near the end of the editorial work, when we sent each other our respective list of acknowledgements, our reciprocal names were on them. So we would like to thank each other as editors and companions, for the support and the commitment, the care and the patience, the clarity of communication and the continuous stimuli to push critical thinking further. It is our privilege to experience and practise collaborative and supportive knowledge production.

In that spirit, we dedicate our work to our students in universities, learning institutions and to those who learn primarily from lived experience, for their inspiring questions and engagement to always more emancipatory forms of knowledge and practice. And we extend our dedication to all critical learners who, in times of increasing global, regional, national and urban disparities, are fearless and stubborn in satisfying their hunger to learn and understand more about the world we inhabit.

Introduction: rethinking the European urban

Noa K. Ha and Giovanni Picker

The European city is not the prolongation of the native city. The colonisers have not settled in the midst of the natives. They have surrounded the native city; they have laid siege to it.

> Frantz Fanon, *A Dying Colonialism* (1965), 51.

… which version of European modernity?

> Stuart Hall, 'Culture, community, nation' (1993), 358.

As Paul Gilroy has insisted, racial terror lies at the very heart of innocent modernity. I do not think we have acknowledged this enough in urban studies, steeped as we are in Eurocentrism.

> Ananya Roy, 'Urban Studies in the age of Charlottesville' (2018).

Europe is not affirmative. It is always contingent on a negative dialectic, on a negation, on an omission, on lack – Europe is what its others are not.

> Hamid Dabashi, *Europe and Its Shadows: Coloniality After Empire* (2019), 49.

This book is a multidisciplinary collection which sets out to contribute to debates on European cities and, more broadly, on global geographies of knowledge production. Two wide-ranging aspects of Social Sciences scholarship on urban Europe appear to us as remarkable limitations: first, the relative lack of a broad focus on the history of colonialism and the centrality of race and, second, the comparative relegation of Central and Eastern European cities to area studies. Analyses that theoretically and historically outline major common properties across European cities seem to gloss over the role played by five centuries of circulation between colonies and metropole of technologies of governance, wealth, knowledge, and affect. Relatedly, yet increasingly less pronounced, state socialism seems to be the only foregrounded feature for placing certain European cities in the Central and Eastern Europe 'area-study box', outside Europe 'proper'. In this Introduction we are going to discuss these two limitations before outlining the ten chapters, with a view to contribute to a renewed understanding of urban Europe.

The multiple biographical, geographical, historical and professional locations from which we as editors inhabit and analyse urban Europe shaped our intention to launch this project. Based in Berlin, Noa K. Ha is an urban scholar and anti-racist activist, whose family history extends to the East Indies (now Indonesia), the Netherlands, Germany and Vietnam, a history which reflects colonial and postcolonial migration between Europe and its colonies; Giovanni Picker is a Glasgow-based urban scholar from Milan, whose several Hungarian-Jewish relatives were deported and exterminated under Nazi rule, a regime which learnt significantly from German colonial ruling.[1] We see our biographical trajectories, in Lisa Lowe's words, as 'intimacies [...] in a residual sense' – 'scenes of close connection in relation to a global geography that one more often conceives in terms of vast spatial distances' (2015: 18). These historical and spatial proximities reach back to the genesis of transatlantic capitalism, which coincided with the birth of what became known as *modernity*, and the beginning of colonialism. We see racial and racialist dispositions that drove and variously organised the numerous imperial projects of colonial subjugation as crucial in organising contemporary societies globally, while being contextually diversified. Our biographical trajectories hence continue to reverberate across European urban life and beyond, crystallising in varying formations of racial injustice and anti-racist expressions.

Coming from these residually intimate biographies, when we met in 2015 in Berlin, our common intellectual grounds were laid bare; over the subsequent years, they continued to stimulate our conversations on the multiple, complex and unfinished entanglements of the European urban. The 2019 'Provincializing European Cities' session that we organised at the annual International Sociological Association RC21 conference in New Delhi provided a fertile ground for the germination of critical insights on the European urban. In spring 2020, during the early stages of the COVID-19 pandemic and against the odds of imposed lockdown, three days of online discussions with the contributors to this volume further expanded those epistemic provocations and empirical clues toward critically (un)learning from and engaging with urban worlds in and beyond Europe. We are all the more grateful to the authors for their multiple efforts and care in making this volume possible.

Inspired by these connections and conversations, we would like to start our discussions here by interrogating the main paradigms within which the Social Sciences have studied European cities.[2] One of the most classic and influential of those paradigms has been 'developmentalism' (Dussel, 1998), meaning the understanding that European cities are among the most significant expressions and drivers of what is generally intended as 'modern'. From Georg Simmel's (1971 [1903]) study of Berlin to the more comprehensive investigations of Max Weber (1958 [1922]) and Lewis Mumford (1963),

European urban contexts have primarily been depicted as sites of modern structures and lifestyles, politics and social organisation, steered by innovatively reformist agendas.[3] In the early 2000s, these influential analyses prompted the formation of a significant body of Social Sciences scholarship, primarily in Sociology, which proposed a renewed 'European City' model, or ideal type (Häußermann and Haila, 2005). While acknowledging, and at times foregrounding, the presence of urban poverty and inequalities, this scholarship's understanding of the modern/European city is primarily associated with accessible prosperity as well as progress, openness, tolerance, growth and democracy.

This dominant narrative of European cities seems to us significantly partial – not only because it discloses a rather hagiographic understanding of modernity whereby 'progress' is viewed as largely uncontested, but also and primarily because it reproduces a developmentalist understanding of the world, as differentiated between more and less 'developed' cities.[4] Put otherwise, since 'modernity', as any other evaluative concept, can only be defined in relation to its opposite – i.e. that which is considered unmodern – it seems necessary to ask what this 'unmodern' is and how it is conceived of in the scholarship of European cities. The answer to this question emerges both explicitly and implicitly, but overall 'the European City' scholarship tends to overlook the relations through which the very caesura modern/unmodern is produced. This point relates to Dabashi's (2019) idea of 'negative dialectic', which we offered as an epigraph to this text, and suggests an epistemic concealment of the terms in relation to which the universal of 'modernity', including its extensions such as 'progress', 'cohesion' and 'development', is deployed to characterise various urban arrangements across Europe.

This epistemic erasure is part of 'Eurocentrism' (Dussel, 1998) – peculiar dispositions to knowledge that we are going to discuss in this Introduction. At the start of our discussion, we find it important to consider that such dispositions to knowledge tend to reproduce a certain hierarchical understanding of the urban by differentiating between two extremes: the allegedly disordered and 'underdeveloped', so-called megacities – primarily located in the southern hemisphere – that are described as having defective infrastructures; and the allegedly ordered and 'developed' metropolises – mostly cities of the (post-) industrialised West – which by way of opposition come to appear as a sort of normative ontology of the urban (Ong and Roy, 2011; Robinson, 2006). One of the most noteworthy implications of this binary paradigm is that categories of analysis become split in the same way. For instance, while poverty and social exclusion feature as chief problems in analyses of European cities megacities, tend primarily to be seen as suffering from urban informality and a lack of infrastructures, two phenomena which, in turn, tend to be overlooked in studies of urban Europe.

Such a developmentalist paradigm becomes perhaps even more explicit when considering an additional caesura, which that paradigm encourages – that between Western European and Central and Eastern European cities. As we are discussing in this Introduction, Social Sciences scholarship tends to define Europe by reference to Western European cities while classifying Central and Eastern European cities primarily, if not exclusively, as postsocialist. Curiously, then, while the twentieth century is usually taken as the only defining dimension of Central and Eastern European cities, Western European cities seem to find their most significant and enduring historical references in the Weberian High Middle Ages. And for the sake of clarity, we want to stress that we do not question the fact that European cities may be viewed as 'modern'; what we do, instead, is point at the lack of a reflexive attention to specific aspects of the 'modernity' that those cities are deemed to embody. These specific aspects primarily concern the role of race as a quintessentially European modern formation.[5] Hall's (1993) question in the epigraph to this text, then, becomes our guide quote.

In our endeavour, we are inspired by Chakrabarty's *Provincializing Europe: Postcolonial Thought and Historical Difference* (2000). The reason why we decided to draw on Chakrabarty's seminal study is not just because it proved influential in rethinking European global hegemony, but also because it did so during a period of strong enthusiasm for the 'finally' reunited Europe. The book's critique of historicism as a form of teleological constructivism seems particularly well tailored for looking at the post-1989 euphoria, during which many (Western) European cities, for example Berlin and Vienna, regained their 1910s and 1920s aura as epitomes of 'European modernity'.

The historian starts by considering that '[i]n Europe itself, [historicism] made possible completely internalist histories of Europe in which Europe was described as the site of the first occurrence of capitalism, modernity, or Enlightenment' (Chakrabarty, 2000: 7), and sets out to 'rethink two conceptual gifts of nineteenth-century Europe that are integral to the idea of modernity. One is historicism – the idea that to understand anything it has to be seen as both a unity and in its historical development – and the other is the very idea of the political' (2000: 6). In addition to following this twofold line of enquiry – by centring a critique of both 'historicism' and 'the political' – we welcome Keith's (2005: 193, n.60) on-point invitation to add the spatial dimension to Chakrabarty's (2000) analytic of the historical one: 'the contextualising of a language of urbanism, a making problematic the street, the tower block, the neighbourhood, the ghetto, the cultural quarter and the whole city identifies a problematic that is spatial in precisely the sense that Chakrabarty's project is historical'.

Hence, we decided to organise this volume in three sections – 'Provincialising historicism', 'Provincialising (urban) geography' and 'Provincialising the (urban) political'. Our attention to the temporal (urban-historical), the spatial (urban-geographical) and the urban-political reflects a long intellectual tradition of reflexivity that interrogates the analytical categories with which Western Social Sciences operate. It does so in order to encourage the study of largely overlooked processes, silences and subjectivities that have more or less direct connections to the various European colonial projects. In doing that, our aim is 'not to reject social science categories', such as those typically used to look at European cities (for example 'cohesion', 'inclusion' and 'equality'), but rather 'to release into the space occupied by particular Euro histories sedimented in them, other normative and theoretical thought enshrined in other existing life practices and their archives' (Chakrabarty, 2000: 13).

We are aware of the immensity of this task. Our effort here, we want to stress, is not intended to be a definitive critique of European urban formations as we know them today, nor a univocal theorisation of them. Rather, we offer points of departure, angles and opportunities for identifying generative venues of critical thought about past and contemporary European urbanities. Such sought-after plurality emerges also from the multiplicity of the chapters' theoretical references – from postcolonial perspectives, to decolonial approaches, to more comprehensive race critical theories – and triggers our ultimate hope of achieving 'decentred poetics that may help us imagine geohistorical categories for a non-imperial world' (Coronil, 1996: 52).

Provincialising the European City

When Chakrabarty's *Provincializing Europe* was published in 2000, scholarly conversations on various aspects of European societies were burgeoning. After the Maastricht (1992) and Lisbon (2000) treaties, there were debates on the EU enlargement; debates on the increasing global migration flows; on changing labour markets; and debates on rights and liberties in the context of emerging virtual connectivities. Despite their global breadth, these debates tended to ignore what Chakrabarty (2000) vividly analysed at the dawn of a new global world order after the end of the Cold War: the very making and legacies of Europe's global hegemony, that is, the almost five centuries of imperial colonial projects.

Along with debates on European societies, conversations on 'The European City', also emerging in the early 2000s, inaugurated significantly influential ways of looking at European urbanities by centring the model of 'The European City' as a peculiar ideal type and an ontological plausibility. On the wave of 1990s planning debates on Berlin's post-1989 reconstruction (Molnar, 2013), and substantially drawing on the Weberian (1958 [1922])

historical sociology of medieval European urban formations, these conversations posited that 'the diminishing significance of nation-states (as a consequence of globalisation) in Europe (and promoted by the European Union)
has created a "power vacuum" that has provided new opportunities for
local and regional action' (Häußermann and Haila, 2005: 52). In contrast
to the recent Global City and 'urban sprawl' scholarships, as well as to the
model of 'the American city', these emerging ideas were largely based on
the perceived 'preponderance of medium-large cities', a characteristic 'intended
to exemplify [...] Europeanness' (Bagnasco and Le Galès, 2000: 15). Four
features were seen as constitutive of this urban Europeanness, namely (a)
public land ownership, (b) the legacies of the burghers, (c) relative autonomy
and (d) the prominence of public, welfare-state services. This model, it was
argued, presented outstanding similarities with the Weberian (1958 [1922])
model of 'the Occidental city' – the medieval Western European city as a
specific kind of political collective, the very first democratic one (see also
Grainger and Cutler, 2000; Häußermann, 2004; Kazepov, 2005; Le Galès,
2000; Siebel, 2006).

At the junction of these two events – the publication of *Provincializing
Europe* and the invention of the European City model (hereafter ECM) – we
identify a significant tension between voices and sensibilities addressing
Europe at the dawn of a new millennium: on one side, a postcolonial critique
of European knowledge production and global cultural hegemony; on the
other, solidly Eurocentric conversations about European urban formations,
stretching back to the High Middle Ages, and void of any reference to
global history. In light of this, while ECM was built on a series of empirically
meticulous analyses of late twentieth-century local powers (included, for
instance, in Bagnasco and Le Galès, 2000), both the analytical construction
of the model and some of its implications appear as problematically partial.
Chamberlain, in Chapter 10 of this volume, sharply articulates some of
these critical aspects. Here we would like to focus on some of the key
empirical observations, methodological choices and practical implications
of that model. In doing so, we obviously do not engage with all the empirical
and theoretical streams of research which orbit around ECM. We nonetheless
offer a hopefully useful critique of ECM's historical and epistemic grounds.

One of ECM's foundations is the Weberian observation that the central
and northern medieval Occidental City was clearly separated from the
countryside, and one of the determinants of this separation was the presence
of city-farmers. Recent historical and archaeological research on this point,
however, has shown that '[Weber] may be right, if by Medieval city we are
thinking of north Italian city states where there was a sharp division between
city (*città*) and hinterland (*contado*). But north of the Alps there were many
cities like those of ancient Greece, which had city-farmers as a group

connecting city and hinterlands' (Hansen, 2006: 93).[6] This seems to diverge from Weber's analysis, especially from his idea of freedom in Central and Northern European cities that was, for him, 'the *revolutionary* innovation which differentiated the medieval occidental cities from all others' (Weber, 1958 [1922]]: 1239) and which 'gave European cities the honour of symbolizing modernization and civilization' (Häußermann and Haila, 2005: 51). Famously, Weber (1958 [1922]: 94) hagiographically mentions the medieval slogan *Stadtluft macht frei* ('City air makes man free').

While not surprising in itself, this hagiographic tone becomes noteworthy if one asks for whom freedom was available in the European cities of the High Middle Ages and – indeed – for whom it is available in the twenty-first century. What Weber, let alone the ECM scholarship's analyses of Weber's work, either overlooks or discounts as marginal is the presence in medieval European cities of enslaved people (Bartlett, 1993: 167–191; Heng, 2018: 151–155) as well as the recurrent persecutions – including exterminations – of Jews, who were largely regarded as strange figures (Heng, 2012: S57; 2018: 15). The appearance of guilds, confraternities and political associations indeed marked a significant change from previous feudal social orders. What is often overlooked, however, is that what Weber calls freedom seems primarily if not exclusively the freedom of the emerging urban ruling class of able-bodied men – the merchants, the bankers, the traders and anyone else who was not sold, banished, enslaved or reduced to the role of servant, many of whom were Muslim women and women from the eastern parts of Europe (Heng, 2018: 143–144; Robinson, 1983: 112–133).[7]

This point not only serves to contextualise, and thus better understand, Weber's emphasis on freedom in the European medieval city; it also allows one to appreciate a very influential way in which urban Europe was imagined and represented in the Middle Ages. Through a series of meticulous discussions, the historian and literary scholar Heng (2003; 2018) has uncovered the various and complex ways in which race appeared in the European Middle Ages. The author names one of these ways 'cartographic', referring to the production of the first world maps; one of those maps, the Hereford Mappa Mundi, dated 1300, could be viewed as one of the first projects of crafting a European identity – the map represents Europe as a 'civilized territory of urban life – a web of cities' (Heng, 2018: 35). This representation of Europe was sharply contrasted by a depiction of other parts of the world as containing monstrous figures, 'global races swarm[ing] in other vectors of the world', which served as a comparator for constructing, through that representation, 'European self-identity and civilization' (Heng, 2018: 35). The fact that one of the most authoritative ways in which race was invented in the European Middle Ages was a representational alignment of Europe with urbanity and humanity, in direct opposition to rurality as the typical domain of bestiality, coinciding with non-Europe, gives a sense of the powerful medieval imaginaries surrounding European cities. Therefore, the 'urban air' which 'sets you free' might in actuality refer to a specific, racially exclusive 'air', deemed lacking outside European cities.[8] As Isin (2002a: 15–22; 2002b: 119-120) repeatedly showed, Weber's understanding of the medieval European city is highly orientalist, hence Eurocentric.[9]

Eurocentrism, urbanity and colonial epistemes

The example of the Hereford Mappa Mundi illustrates a key aspect of European knowledge production in the Middle Ages, specifically knowledge of Europe, including its cities: the construction of a hierarchical caesura between European urbanity and the deemed less-urban rest of the world. From this perspective, the ECM narrative about modernity constitutes a similar hierarchical caesura – a narrative that deceives a markedly Eurocentric standpoint. In use since the 1920s, the concept of Eurocentrism was made popular by the political theorist Amin (1989) and comprehensively theorised a decade later by the philosopher Dussel (1998).[10] The latter argued that 'modernity' is not European, but was constructed as such, not least through the European production and imposition of specific world maps. According to Dussel (1998), Eurocentrism is the product of both European colonialism and the various celebratory narratives that went along it, including the 'Enlightenment', 'Renaissance', 'Reformation' and indeed 'Modernity'. The author locates some of the conditions for these 'universals' to appear in the production of evaluative categories such as 'the West', 'the East', 'the first world' and so on. These everyday categories, ubiquitous in standard knowledge production, far from being naturally given, are flexible and emerged through Europeans' colonial expansion since the fifteenth century, building on their material and symbolic power.

Key implications of these historical processes are palpable in twenty-first-century Europe. The Eurocentric constitution of 'Europe' reflects the becoming of a supranational entity – and identity. The articulation of a shared European identity relates to two important historical events as a moral conclusion of history: on one hand the experience of National Socialism and the Holocaust, and on the other hand the end of the Cold War with its breakdown of former socialist and communist states (Böröcz and Kovács, 2001; Melegh, 2006). When a shared European identity was being formulated after 1989, the postcolonial historicity, in itself historicist, of European inception largely omitted to consider colonial violence as a feature of contemporary societies in urban Europe and normalised a nostalgic perspective on the European colonial past (Hansen and Jonsson, 2017; Boatcă, 2010). Despite that shared European history, the various national colonial histories unfold very differently

– with different colonial practices and relations. Nevertheless, one continues to see – as, for instance, in the current European debates on migration, refugees, national identity and urban living that Mosselson discusses in Chapter 5 of this volume – colonial differentiation through the construction of the European Other, the fortification of European borders and the crafting of the figure of the refugee as a threat to European identity (Bhagat, 2019; De Genova, 2018; El-Tayeb, 2011; Schierup et al., 2006).

As Wekker (2016) argues in her work *White Innocence*, Europe imagines itself as an 'innocent' project, and – as El-Tayeb (2011) argues in her book *European Others* – Europe locates racism and colonialism somewhere else and far away from its own borders. It may be that non-European territories have been colonised and even violently conquered – this is the general narrative – but this all took place outside Europe. More generally, the impact of colonial violence is not regarded as key for European societies or for the case here: metropolitan societies. European imagination establishes a narrative of the enlightened, democratic and equal Europe, while so-called ethnic inequalities within European nations are analysed in the framework of 'migration' and (national) 'integration', considering neither race nor the European postcolonial condition (Lentin, 2014; Schierup et al., 2006).

This suggests that while Europe has a long history of producing postcolonial Others in a variety of subjectivities to maintain 'the coloniality of power' (Quijano, 2000) within the colonial metropoles, it is conventionally regarded as the birthplace of humanity which is founded on the history of enlightenment as a universal value. The becoming of modern colonial Europe is often traced back to the late fifteenth century, and most notably to Christopher Columbus's voyages. The 'Berlin Conference', or 'Congo Conference', which took place in 1884–85 when European nations were hosted by Otto von Bismarck in Berlin to partition the African continent in accordance with European national interests – and the borders here established still define contemporary African nations decades after their independence – marks another fundamental moment. Europe's self-esteem, by which it persuades itself that it is 'raceless', hampers a theoretical reflection on how racism and white supremacy are constitutive to and implicit in European urban epistemologies (Goldberg, 2000; Ha, 2017; Kipfer, 2007; Picker, 2017; Simone, 2010). Eneva in Chapter 9 of this volume provides such a theoretical, critical reflection by ethnographically illustrating how pervasive Eurocentric notions of activism are, including anti-racist activism, in organising urban social movements in Madrid.

Given that these historical and contemporary processes shape the ECM, it seems important to discuss the conditions and limits of the model's Eurocentrism. As Robinson (2006: 21–40) seminally exposed, the genesis of Urban Studies on both shores of the Atlantic was already highly Eurocentric, or 'developmentalist'. From Georg Simmel's 'primitive figures' to Robert Park's 'freedom of cities' as substitution 'for the local loyalties', as well as 'the rational organization which we call civilization' for 'the sacred order of tribal custom' (quoted in Robinson, 2006: 21), the so-called 'forefathers' of Urban Studies – unanimously considered as such after removing W. E. B. Dubois from the scene (Morris, 2015: 45–54) – follow a decisively Eurocentric paradigm. Alves in Chapter 8 of this volume proposes an in-depth examination of these points with reference to urban knowledge production in the Portuguese academy.

The production of a developmentalist and Eurocentric urban order, according to which Europe is viewed as superior and by extension as the reference to which those who supposedly are less developed must adapt, establishes binaries such as developed/underdeveloped and modern/unmodern. The (re)production of these binaries seems to happen due to a lack of reflexivity in producing knowledge from the European 'centre'. An example of this is the Weber-inspired contrast between the slave-ridden, ancient city and the freedom-based medieval city: 'The classic city was governed by a sharp division between a citizenry of free men [...] and on the other hand the slaves and the foreigners. The medieval city thrived on another distinction, between town and country, between the burghers on one side and the peasants – servile or not – and the landowners on the other' (Le Galès and Therborn, 2009: 2). Such a contrasting (comparative) method leads to a developmentalist reading of the past that owes much to a Eurocentric methodological essentialism for which Weber provided an authoritative legitimation.[11] In this regard, Zimmerman's point that in Weber's Sociology 'race is superfluous: culture functions just as effectively to *reduce history to an elaboration of stereotyped identities*' resonates quite pertinently (2006: 68; our italics).[12]

Developmentalist and Eurocentric readings of European cities are pervasive. Another usually accepted binary is between megacities in the Southern hemisphere and European cities:

> Those writing on megacities, gigacities, or the rise of global urban regions [...] point to the rise of networks and governance failures related to obsolete governmental boundaries. Another way to think along the same lines relates to the idea of the end of cities and the triumph of the urban sprawl [...]. A classic argument dismisses this view, because the relatively stable core of Europe's urban system is made up of medium-sized and reasonably large cities, which are fairly close to one another, and a few metropolises. (Le Galès, 2011: 1577)

Here the author refers to European cities in order to dismiss the claim that cities are allegedly becoming 'ungovernable'. What we would like to stress here is that the rhetorical contrast between 'megacities' and European cities produces a hierarchy of governability in which European cities rank higher. The reproduction of a century-old celebratory representation of Europeanness seems particularly effective in this context because it conceals the fact that many 'megacities, gigacities' happen to be former European colonised cities, including for example Manila, New Delhi, Mumbai, Jakarta and Mexico City; unreflexively contrasting these cities with European cities is Eurocentric, and cannot but end up reproducing notions of European superiority. Indeed, one page later this appraisal emerges clearly: 'European cities make a fairly general category of urban space, relatively original forms of compromise, aggregation of interest and culture, which bring together local social groups, associations, organized interests, private firms, and urban governments'.

Overlooking the historicity of both precolonial urban orders beyond Europe and current global inequalities may affect depictions not only of the allegedly faulty postcolonial urban world but also of Europe.[13] In one of the most seminal contributions to the ECM scholarship, Le Galès (2000: 125) focused on migrants' presence in European cities by noticing that 'The decline in city-centre districts since the 1970s [...] was all the more visible because immigrants from outside these communities had settled in them during the 1960s and later [...] This concentration of vulnerable, deprived populations produces self-reinforcing effects because the immobility of such population intensifies the districts' separate cultures'. While not the only discussion on 'immigrants' in the book, this passage conveys the idea that 'immigrants' are the reason for the visibility of 'the decline in city-centre districts'; failing to acknowledge that many members of 'such population' are in Europe because of the colonial past seems to be premised on a quite fixed approach, which leads such scholarship to view 'immigrants' as the reason for urban decline. And the use of notions such as 'ethnification' (Le Galès and Therborn, 2009: 19) to refer to immigration in European cities signals a widespread assumption according to which the default, self-ascribed European condition is non-ethnic, implicitly meaning white, requiring in this way that black and brown people be positioned as exogenous to an imagined white European self (Boulila, 2019; Essed et al., 2018; Goldberg, 2006; Lentin, 2008; Wekker, 2016). This unchecked racial conception of (white) European urbanity persists by virtue of its concealment. Put differently, Eurocentrism contributes to, and is predicated on, overlooking the key global and historical connections, which are constitutive of the contemporary European urban, in both the past *and* the present.

Another example refers to racial segregation in Western continental European cities, a phenomenon largely deemed either relatively limited or non-existent (e.g. Musterd, 2005; Préteceille, 2009; Tammaru et al., 2014; van Kempen and Murie, 2009). A first seminal work in this literature mentions 'caste systems, slave-owning societies, repressed religious minorities' as cases

of politically imposed segregation, brings up South African apartheid and
Jim Crow USA, and contrasts them to 'most developed states', implying
(Western) European states, which 'have taken an unequivocal stand against
segregation' (Préteceille, 2000: 84). This premise establishes an epistemic
contrast between Europe and the USA that unreflexively overlooks the spatial
and temporal contextuality of race, its variable articulations and modalities of
concealment according to place-related, global-historical connections (Murji
and Picker, 2019: 915–918; Kipfer, 2007; Martina and Schor, 2015).

Such a contrasting strategy almost inevitably results in suggesting that in
Europe residential segregation displays dimensions other than race, such as
ethnicity and nationality. This move, which seems to have become a kind of
conventional wisdom, leads to casually erasing the possibility of adopting
race as analytical category in studies of residential segregation in Europe:[14]
'ethnicity and race are socially constructed concepts and quite contentious;
the former is more predominant in Europe, while the latter is preferred in
North America (and Anglo-Saxon world), South Africa, and Latin America'
(Arbaci, 2019: 59).[15]

Coterminous to this contrasting approach is the peculiar role reserved
to the urban East. Since Eastern Europe has historically been represented
as the 'dark other' of 'European civilisation' (Todorova, 2009 [1997]),
Central and Eastern European cities seem to remain cast in a separate and
mono-dimensional analytical camp. Indeed, Weber (1958 [1922]) never
referred to them when constructing his ideal-type. When Eastern European
cities are mentioned in the ECM scholarship (typically in passing and at
the end of an essay on 'proper' European cities), they seem to permanently
need to catch up to some kind of supposedly acceptable level of development
after the transition from socialism to postsocialism that fatally produced,
according to this view, 'losers and winners' (e.g. Le Galès and Therborn,
2009: 42; Mingione, 2005: 82).

Deep-rooted, orientalist narratives on Eastern Europe echo in Urban
Studies particularly through the notion of the 'postsocialist city', which
suggests that only in the East is the past haunting cities. As Bodnár (2018)
persuasively suggested, 'State socialism ended long ago but its importance
has lingered uncannily in "postsocialist" urbanism [...]. Fascism was
defeated in 1945, and by the sixties hardly anyone talked about postfascist
Germany or Europe'. And even in studies that purposely focus on Central
and Eastern European cities, as Ferenčuhová and Gentile (2016: 484) point
out, 'a resilient assumption [...] is that these cities are anomalous, subject to
gradual correction [...] and lagging behind'. By contrast, Troch in Chapter
4 of this volume sharply shows how the scholarship on urban Europe
typically overlooks the rich history of multireligious and multicultural urbanism in South-Eastern Europe as territories connected to the Middle East
and Asia.

What we would like to stress here is the unfortunate implication of creating a hierarchical model in which European cities viewed as 'proper' – those in the Western part of the continent – are seen as better or more 'developed' than 'other' European cities in the East. As a matter of fact, a burgeoning scholarship, primarily in urban geography, critically reviews the dominant orientalist conceptions of theories of Eastern European cities and engages key urban theorisations from the East (e.g. Ferenčuhová and Gentile, 2016; Gentile, 2018; Tuvikene, 2016). Trzeciak and Peters in Chapter 6 of the present volume, critically unearth the colonial vestiges of Cottbus, in East Germany, indicating how Europeanness emerges also in relation to the collective amnesia of colonialism across the West–East divide.

A last point concerns the role and functions of ECM, as a reference for urban policy makers and planners. As Molnar's (2013: 136–166) seminal analysis of post-World War II European architecture shows, the 'European city' ideal goes back to the early 1980s; the author specifically discusses the ways in which that idea, grounded in nineteenth-century planning principles and promoting a notion of the city as a repository of collective memory, functioned as the pivotal reference for rebuilding Berlin's Potsdamer Platz in the early 1990s. Architects, mostly from West Germany, opted to follow this model 'as a starting point of future plans and chased an idealized picture of a European city that may have never existed' (Molnar, 2013: 145), instead of starting from the ruins and fragments left by almost three decades of urban splitting.

Schwarz in Chapter 1 of the present volume articulates the implications of such an 'idealised picture' in twenty-first-century urban projects, including the Humboldt Forum in Berlin and the category of 'decorum' in Italian cities. Lawton (2017) scales up the critical analysis to the European Union's urban policy framework, in which 'The "European city" has come to be seen as representing the virtues of the "good city" [...] deeply embedded within processes of a highly neoliberalized economic terrain' (Lawton, 2017: 80–81). The author makes clear that, as a reference for urban policy makers, ECM may well encourage 'an ideal where social inclusion and all other elements of an idealized city will be led through innovative practices. [...] Embedded within such an approach is a tightly manicured urban imaginary which rolls out mantras of "innovation", "smartness" and "creativity" in an unproblematic manner as saviours of the urban future' (Lawton, 2017: 83; see also Lawton and Punch, 2014). In a similar yet more theoretical take, Novy and Mayer (2009: 108) criticise ECM as a 'blueprint to guide future urban development', especially because of its allegedly good and 'just' qualities. And stretching these processes both historically and geographically, Carbone in Chapter 3 of this volume demonstrates the global reach of the European city ideal, by discussing its impact on urbanisation debates in nineteenth-century Argentina.

So far, we have stressed some of ECM's limitations according to its historical grounding, its methodological underpinnings and some of its implications as a reference for urban practitioners. Our invitation here remains 'not to reject social science categories' (Chakrabarty, 2000: 13) but rather to identify possible venues for alternative, non-Eurocentric analyses. We are aware that Eurocentrism is not a prerogative of ECM, and features in urban scholarship which is inspired, for example, by Marxist rather than by Weberian theories.[16] It is also important to stress that our critical engagement with the ECM scholarship does not result in constructing an alternative model, but in contributing to open up a multiplicity of venues for reflexive, critical and global perspectives on urban Europe. Equally, we want to make clear that our critique does not only pertain to specific scholarship debates, be they on so-called 'urban diversity', 'urban culture' or 'residential segregation' in Europe. Rather, our approach – owing much to Dipesh Chakrabarty – is in line with Stuart Hall's, in that: 'I have never worked on race and ethnicity as a kind of subcategory. I have always worked on the whole social formation which is racialized' (1995: 53–54). With this in mind, the remainder of this Introduction will discuss the rationale for non-Eurocentric theorisations of urban Europe, before outlining the various contributions to such theorisations that are offered by the chapters included in this volume.

Introducing the racial European urban

We would like to consider three fundamental missing connections between the various scholarly literatures on the European urban. First, there seems to be no conversation between, on one side, historical and anthropological studies of the relevance of colonial urbanism for contemporary European cities and, on the other, the Sociology of European cities.[17] Various streams of anthropological and historical studies uncovered the contribution of colonial trade to the development of European port and other cities, and the various circulations between metropole and colony of forms of urban knowledge such as planning and governance (e.g. Abu-Lughod, 1980; Bigon and Ross, 2020; Bruns and Gerend, 2018; Driver and Gilbert, 1999; Fuller, 2007; King, 1990; 1992; Nightingale, 2012; Njoh, 2007; Pula, 2013; Rabinow, 1989; Wright, 1991). And yet this scholarship is largely absent from the (Historical) Sociology of urban Europe; equally, contemporary asymmetrical relations of economic dependency between cities in the postcolonial South and European cities remain out of focus. This series of missing connections signals the importance of recontextualising histories and sociologies of European cities and emphasises the hegemonic power of these cities over formerly colonised contexts. All chapters in this volume are contributions to this end – while the first three chapters take history as their object, not only their perspective, in Chapter 7 Azarmandi and Rexhepi show the dialectical plurality of historical reconstructions through migrant and queer of colour politics of reimagining the urban space de-linked from hegemonic historical/historicist narratives of Europe.

The second missing connection relates to the discrepancy between, on one side, the mounting scholarly evidence of the relevance of race and racism in contemporary European urban processes and, on the other, the relative lack of attention to critical race in theories of European urbanism. A fairly large body of scholarship has uncovered the fundamental ordering function that race plays in a number of urban processes across Europe, including, but not limited to, urban governance (e.g. Bhagat, 2019; Bruce-Jones, 2015; Fassin, 2013; Fassin et al., 2014; Gonick, 2015; Gressgård, 2019; Ha, 2016; Ivasiuc, 2021; Keaton, 2006; Kipfer, 2007; 2016; Modest and de Koning, 2016; Picker, 2016), spatial dynamics of containment, gentrification and segregation (e.g. Filčák and Škobla, 2013; Gruner, 2010; Haritaworn, 2015; Kipfer and Goonewardena, 2013; McCombs, 2018; Picker et al., 2015; Picker, 2017; Rogozen-Soltar, 2017; Schierup et al., 2018; Tissot, 2007; Vincze et al., 2018; Vincze and Zamfir, 2019), and urban cultural production and collective memory (e.g. Aldrich, 2005; El-Tayeb, 2012; Fleming, 2017; Kopp and Krohn, 2013; MacFarlane and Mitchell, 2019; Nasiali, 2016; Peralta and Domingos, 2019; Silverstein, 2018; Simone, 2010; Zwischenraum Kollektiv, 2017). These studies empirically document contextually varied and variable urban phenomena, including the racial oppression and dehumanisation recurrently experienced by Romani people, Migrant, Black and People of Colour, together with their related political and cultural responses; also addressed by these studies are urban governance logics and mechanisms, as well as identity and memory politics that are promoted by urban authorities, mediating state agencies and grassroots collectives.

These processes, scattered across the European urban, directly relate to global dynamics of racial injustice, strongly marked by the colour line, contributing to their perpetuation. One key illustration of this is the disproportionately higher rates of police stop-and-search of People of Colour, Travellers and Roma than of the majority, across all EU Member States (FRA, 2021). Systemic racial profiling in European cities emerges as indisputable by looking at the same data disaggregated in 'Stopped in a vehicle' and 'Stopped while on foot' – the latter figures ranking consistently higher than the former. For example, in France, while 18 per cent of the general population is being stopped while on foot, this figure swells to 43 per cent in the case of people with biographical connections to South Saharan African countries; in Hungary, walking while being Roma makes you almost three times more likely to be stopped and searched by the police than the average population (40 per cent v. 15 per cent); and in Germany, if you have biographical connections to South Saharan Africa, you are over three times more likely to be stopped and searched by the police while walking in the street (40 per cent v. 13 per cent) than the general population (FRA, 2021). Collected mostly in cities, these data show that racial oppression does not routinely occur only at Europe's borders (De Genova, 2018), but in its urban centres too. We think the time has come for Urban Studies to acknowledge these processes as constitutive of European urban formations.

The third and final missing connection is between two scholarly literatures – the one on theorising so-called 'postsocialist cities' and the one on the so-called 'East–West slope' (Melegh, 2006), the latter denoting how the developmentalist media and political discourses in the West, prominent since the late 1980s, construct a 'slope' in civilisational, moral terms between the allegedly superior West and the allegedly inferior East (Böröcz and Kovács, 2001). The deeply rooted tradition, widespread among European cultural elites and institutions, of analysing Eastern Europe as the dark side of its enlightened counterpart is part of Eurocentric knowledge production, which was and is primarily generated in former imperial capitals such as Paris, London and Berlin. The hierarchical order that Eurocentric representations construct, contributes to the reproduction of a 'debilitating diachronic and spatial ghettoization' (Todorova, 2009 [1997]: 202) of Eastern Europe; it furthers structural inequalities between the many 'Europes' (Boatcă, 2010) and overlooks the intensive East–West mutual exchanges and interdependencies. For example, in Berlin, the second largest nationality of foreign residents after Turkey is Poland, which is twice as large as the third largest nationality, Syria; in Rome, the most common foreign nationality is Romania, accounting for a quarter of the total number of foreign residents; in Madrid, while the sum of all former colonised Latin American nationalities make up half of the total number of foreign residents, Romanians make up the relative majority, even more numerous than any single Latin American country; and in London, while eight out of the ten most numerous nationalities are from former colonies, Poland ranks second just after India.[18]

The present volume contributes to establishing these three major connections, and offers a repertoire of empirical and theoretical interventions, merging critical urban and critical race studies. By referring to Chakrabarty's provincialising work, we want to expose the 'developmentalism' as dominant understanding of European urbanities, and simultaneously centre what that dominant understanding typically silences, namely both the various colonial projects and the racialised subjects whose biographies and voices continue to be shaped by that silencing. Since that dominant understanding primarily emerged in relation to the crafting of a 'new Europe' after 1989, the urban practices, urban space-making and urban epistemologies analysed in the chapters of this volume refer to a post-1989 Europe. As colonial epistemes and epistemologies have prospered for centuries, we see the urgency, thirty years after the establishment of Europe as a unified neoliberal capitalist system, of emphasising the conjunction of a normalisation of colonial nostalgic systems of representation and the growing research on race/racism in Social Sciences (see Ha, 2022).

By increasing and refining knowledge on European cities, we contribute to global conversations on post/colonial urban knowledge production. When Said (1993: 19) asked 'who in Britain or France can draw a clear circle around British London or French Paris that would exclude the impact of India and Algeria upon these two imperial cities?', he was referring not only to racial and ethnic traces in late twentieth-century urban Europe, but also to the active erasure of those traces and archives – many people today would probably be ready to draw that circle. The point here, as we have discussed, is not only that the colonial *past* is largely erased across analyses of European (urban) societies, but that its present *and presence* are. That is not to suggest that colonialism haunts contemporary Europe from an imagined outside – such a view would simply obliterate the historicist understanding that colonialism is ultimately an exogenous and ancient nightmare whose shadow hangs over the present. Instead, the colonial past is, as we discussed at length, constitutive to Europe as a social, political, economic and cultural formation. As Mancheno in Chapter 2 of this volume discusses with reference to the Parisian banlieues, colonial continuities are crucial aspects of European cities. To paraphrase Roy's (2018) point which we quoted in the epigraph, it is time for Urban Studies to acknowledge such continuities.

To unravel the complex dynamics which connect the colonial past to the present, the chapters in this book follow Chakrabarty's twofold line of enquiry: first, provincialising historicism by 'unlearn[ing] to think of history as a developmental process' (2000: 249) and by centring the relevance of the colonial and its contemporary racial structures; second, provincialising the political by documenting and learning from contemporary anti-racist, postcolonial and decolonial views and expressions (in both physical-political action and writing). In addition to these two lines of inquiry, and in view of our specific attention to urban space, we propose to provincialise (urban) geography by examining various instances of race–space articulations.

Provincialising historicism

European cities: Modernity, race and colonialism intends to shift the conversation on European cities toward a non-Eurocentric paradigm, away from colonial epistemes. The category of race, racism and racialised societies are produced and maintained through the urban and the understanding of the European urban, because race is not only inscribed into what is called modernity, but is constitutive of it, and by extension of urbanity. Acquiring different forms and functions across the centuries, race has remained one of the most pervasive and decisive phenomena across European knowledge production and related social structuring during the various stages into which European history is traditionally divided (Araujo and Maeso, 2015; Goldberg, 1993; Hondius, 2014). Colonies were crucial settings in which Europe experimented with many of the institutional and cultural arrangements which characterise contemporary cities – as Wright (1997) seminally and concisely put it, colonial urban and architectural praxes and forms of knowledge were 'laboratories of modernity'. It should be stressed that the category of race – which was rendered through European monarchies at the beginning of colonialism and, from the eighteenth century on, through their nation states – does not operate everywhere in the same way. As was already the case during colonialism, it has been translated and rearticulated, framing different hierarchies of embodiment (Stam and Shohat, 2012; Stoler, 1989).

In Chapter 1, Schwarz's theoretical insights on the notion of 'the European city' show that, if approached from a socio-territorial perspective, this idealised notion shows its appeal to conservative, even reactionary, sensibilities through a common reaction to global interconnections, understood as threats to established and deep-rooted identities. The author's line of argument persuasively indicates that some of the anxieties behind the ideal of the 'European city', which originated in the context of Germany's 1990 reconstruction, resonate with racist and white supremacist sensibilities. Schwarz meticulously reviews the theoretical concept of territory/*territorio* to highlight the privileged perspective it provides to detect racialising notions that are implicit within multiple instances of urban policies across Europe. Urban 'decorum' resonates particularly with the very dimension of the ideal, and acquires a criminalising and securitising function with very concrete consequences in terms of banishment and repression across Italian cities. The author's preoccupation with the European city ideal does not stop at a deconstructing analysis, but envisages possibilities of reframing, resistance and retheorising, across disciplines and actions towards strategising emancipated modalities of urban existence.

Focusing on the politics of heritage as it plays out in the UNESCO programmes in Paris, Mancheno shows, in Chapter 2, that the banlieues (Parisian peripheries), first celebrated as an architectural innovation during the Paris world fair in 1889, acquired a quite different aura once they became the residence of postcolonial subjects. The author 'countermaps' the narrative and policy on the Parisian banlieues by engaging a decolonial analysis of public memory. Building primarily on Frantz Fanon's work and the historiography of colonial urbanism, the author traces some of the most significant connections between colonial and metropolitan France. Mancheno shows that the banlieues are actually crucial sites for understanding French history, yet are totally erased from UNESCO heritage politics. The analysis of the colonial continuities embedded in the very project and function of the banlieues until the twenty-first century – as securitised urban spaces for lower-class, postcolonial urbanites – allows the author to argue that the selective nature of UNESCO heritage politics serves to deepen the urban colour line in Paris. In this light, Mancheno's analysis also calls for a rethinking of the notions of race and ethnicity that often fail to circulate among urban scholars working on Europe: a strong historical consciousness and interpretation would allow scholars to see race as firmly grounded in colonial continuities, refracted in, among other dimensions, various instantiations of the European urban, including the Parisian banlieues.

The historical contribution that Carbone provides journeys through the *longue durée* of the European city ideal and shows how the ideal functioned in structuring moral and racial hierarchies. In Chapter 3, the author discusses a very specific debate in nineteenth-century Argentina, from which the nexus of urbanisation and industrialisation emerges, and shows how European cities were considered highly positive and idealised symbols of progress to the extent that they were considered 'hyperreal', hence self-evidently positive, not even requiring any specification. Squarely and invariably embedded in these hyperrealities were the racial markers of whiteness defined as quintessentially European and superior. Carbone's analysis of the racial semantics of modernity and industry provides invaluable clues about the extent to which, in the nineteenth century, European cities' images shaped representation of humanity, morality and worth, well beyond Europe; it demonstrates not only how pervasive historicism was back then, but also how European cities were constitutive parts of European historicism.

Provincialising (urban) geography

If in Berlin you take the northern entrance to Großer Tiergarten across from the Brandenburg Gate, you bump into the Memorial to the Sinti and Roma Victims of National Socialism. Walk five minutes southbound and you arrive at the Memorial to the Murdered Jews of Europe. If you then continue eastbound on Hannah-Arendt-Straße, at the corner with Wilhelmstraße, you see the building where, during a meeting in 1884–85, European empires partitioned and appropriated the African continent for the sake of exploitative domination – with only a little information about this history at the spot. Take Wilhelmstraße southbound for ten minutes, and on your right-hand side is Topographies of Terror, the former Gestapo Headquarters, now a museum of Nazi terror.

Cast in European cities' space are countless traces of an embalmed European racial past. Other examples of these urban traces include the Warsaw ghetto; Rome's Cinema Impero (Bianchi and Scego, 2014); Amsterdam's Royal Palace and Jodenbuurt (Hondius et al., 2018); Paris's Jardin des plantes and Vélodrome (Aldrich, 2005); and the many neighbourhoods in other cities with various colonial links.[19] While these urban historical sites assemble a narrative about the past, they simultaneously intervene in the present by educating about the importance of remembering and honouring the victims of variously expressed racial rulings.[20] As emerges throughout this volume, these urban sites signal a 'post-' condition 'that is temporally *after* but not *over* that to which it is affixed' (Brown, 2010: 21). At the same time, they are reminders of outbursts of racist politics that, as such, lend themselves to being precisely pinned in time; they say something, but certainly not everything about the pervasive ways in which race routinely and variably contributes to organising urban life across the continent.

In Chapter 4, Troch looks at one of these ways, by deciphering everyday dynamics of conviviality in the divided city of Mitrovica, Kosovo. In doing this, the author critically reviews the scholarship on urban conviviality that emerged in the West and underlines its Eurocentric modalities, often mingled in scholarly literature on super-diversity, and contributes in this way to a provincialising reflection on urban theory. The Ottoman and socialist histories of the city provide a historical canvas for deconstructing what Todorova (2009 [1997]) calls 'balkanism', namely the racist view of the Balkans as morally inferior to the rest of the European peninsula, especially its Western lands. By showing how racial and ethnic boundary-making have been constitutive to convivial social relations across the two empires and until today, the chapter argues that urban forms of conviviality, rather than an antidote to exclusion, may just be its integral part. This serves as a stringent critique of the conviviality literature, which might be relevant just in Western metropolises, where analyses of existing racial divisions typically situate conviviality in opposition to structures of exclusion.

In Chapter 5 Mosselson sheds light on urban phenomena that, while often hinted at or implicitly assumed, are not often discussed as everyday realities. By discussing Sheffield's reconfiguration of urban space in relation to the UK's 'hostile environment' (i.e. the anti-migrant national policy in force since 2012), the author analyses three urban infrastructures: monuments as sites of memorialisation across the city; spatial segregation along racial lines; and asylum seekers' housing conditions. These three types of infrastructure tell stories of continuities of colonialism and racial oppression, and allow Mosselson to bring to the fore a perpetually neglected issue in debates on urban infrastructures across Europe – the imperial and colonial constitution of European urbanism, substantially built on colonial wealth, hence on the transatlantic enslavement of people from the African continent, whose nationalities correspond to very many of today's asylum seekers in the city. By looking at their urban experiences, struggles and desires for decent living conditions amidst hostile infrastructures, windows are opened into urban possibilities of alternative existence.

Trzeciak and Peters, in Chapter 6 on Cottbus, Germany, discuss a second example of the European socialist state's organisation of the urban space. The authors expose from a decolonial perspective the entangled histories of colonialism and socialism as they emerge from three urban sites – the aesthetic and architecture of a socialist cafe, the housing conditions of a group of migrant workers during socialism and the postsocialist renaming of one street. The analysis of these urban sites shows the ways in which socialist ideals and the racial underpinning of German colonialism unfolded hand in hand, and crystallised in specific urban locations whose histories are today largely forgotten. The authors contextualise their analysis within a contemporary postcolonial city tour they offer on a regular basis and discuss the ways in which these entangled histories of socialism and colonialism reverberate also in contemporary Germany through two main phenomena – the stigma placed on East Germany as the less civilised, backward part of the country, and the related steep rise of racist incidents in this part of the country. The authors' city tour aims precisely to raise awareness of racial and colonial continuities; the ultimate aim of such awareness is to provide inventive venues for countering contemporary racist manifestations and dispositions.

Provincialising the (urban) political

Urban space in postcolonial Europe is not only a space in which metropolitan society establishes a difference between itself and 'Others'; urban space is not only a space or representation of European history and national museums, not only a commodified infrastructure for globalised financial and tourist industries. It is also a space of self-organisation, of self-determination and of resistance against institutional discrimination, state violence and capitalist exploitation – seeking to disrupt colonial practices in urban Europe (Ha, 2017). The following contributions centre the political subjects seemingly not registered as European bodies but proving their being on a daily basis in urban Europe.

Chapter 7, by Azarmandi and Rexhepi, points at some of these disruptions in both Barcelona and Salonika, and engages a decolonial analysis of these two cities, viewed as 'migrant metropolises'. Barcelona's 1992 Olympics are examined as an instantiation of both whitewashing state and market narratives of Europeanisation and Catalanisation, taking the shape of massive displacements of racialised communities, as well as successful anti-racist urban struggles. Salonika is scrutinised through a similar lens, via a genealogy of its cultural policies which branded the city a European Capital of Culture in 1997. While newly arrived refugees can only find an abode in a former-toilet-factory-turned-camp, urban development aspirations refer to European multiculture and progress, by way of forcibly displacing Roma and Albanian migrant families while sidelining the Ottoman past via the art-industry repurposing of Islamic urban spaces such as mosques. Racialised and migrant urbanites' multiple forms of resistance and re-existence emerge as central forces of inventive politics, primarily memory politics, in both cities, countermapping in this way the Mediterranean city and thus showing venues for its decolonial reimagining. By reconstructing the ways in which dominant narratives of Europeanisation and 'European culture' materialise and are contested in the two Mediterranean cities, the authors propose a decolonial rethinking of Europe and its cities as allegories, myths whose power emerges in all its fragility if seen from the point of view of the racialised's dissent.

Alves in Chapter 8 enacts a kind of academic-epistemic disruption in the form of an unconventional literature review. The author takes the reader on a journey across Portuguese Urban Anthropology, to show the ways in which race and institutional racisms have been silenced throughout that scholarly literature. Across libraries and texts in the UK, Brazil and Portugal, the author engages in a quasi-autoethnography of awareness of epistemic silences. In the process, various literatures are critically reviewed, precisely through the lens of race critical theories, to reveal how epistemic silences are part of institutional racism, insofar as they reinforce hierarchies of legitimacy within the politics of knowledge production. The notion of 'epistemic apartheid' is then discussed as an intellectual refraction, which translates into an elicitation, of really existing racial segregation dynamics happening across Portugal's cities.

In Chapter 9, Eneva investigates the ways in which racism and anti-racism are reshaping twenty-first-century Madrid's urban space. As the author shows, the urban map of social vulnerability indicators directly correlates with the map of density of foreigners' residence, within the context of changing labour relations through migration policies and high levels of discrimination in accessing housing. The chapter empirically focuses on two neighbourhoods, Lavapiés and Usera, where low-income and migrant households feature significantly, and develops a critique of *barrionalismo* (the feeling of belonging to a *barrio*, meaning neighbourhood), arguing that the concept has failed to consider racialised and migrant voices and experiences as central. By focusing on the various alliances between racialised newcomers and local, white anti-racists, the chapter provides a sharp and convincing contribution to the overwhelmingly raceless urban scholarship on Europe. These themes resonate vividly across all chapters, but perhaps mostly with Schwarz's attention to the ways in which forms of 'territory' and territorial belonging are able to both assemble different kinds of voices and elicit tensions and disruptions between those very voices.

The point of 'amnesia of spatial disciplines', referring to the widespread erasure of the colonial past in urban scholarship, does not only resonate with Alves' discussion on Portugal but is also thoroughly analysed in Chapter 10. Chamberlain ethnographically and historically dissects the constitutive matrix of the racial stigma that dominates narratives on the district of Hamburg-Wilhelmsburg. It does so by contextualising Hamburg as a port city within global power structures which reach back to colonialism and its social and economic aftermath, and argues that without a race-conscious analysis, it would hardly be possible to understand both the material and the representational making of the district. The voices of racialised non-German workers emerge as the first and most important sources for theorising 'from the South', following anti-racist methodologies of social enquiry, prior to engaging with the 'Northern', dominant planning narratives. This analytical structure allows Chamberlain to offer a rare and disruptive understanding of the city, able to question not only the 'amnesia' of the scholarship but also some of the most conventional modalities of knowledge production.

AbdouMaliq Simone closes our collection by addressing its topic from the epistemological territory where the last section resides. In a propositional move, Simone invites us to critically reflect on European urbanities as nodes of urban *provisioning* yet beyond the loci of deemed race-neutral welfare *provisions*, and as combinations of social relations that converge in making racialised lives more viable emotionally, economically and socially. Ultimately, these provisionings are there, proliferating in their genericity, along with and in parallel to designs of economic calculi of extraction. These forms of provisioning invite us to contribute to an archive of encounters of care, health and schooling in which institutions and people share the urban, its spaces and opportunities. A race-conscious, reflexive archive of urban provisioning, then, is what we hope this book will encourage, because such an archive would ultimately help us – to go back to where we started – 'imagine geohistorical categories for a non-imperial world' (Coronil, 1996: 52).

Notes

1 On the German colonial lessons for Nazi racial rule, see Césaire (1972 [1955]), Baranowski (2011) and Olusoga and Erichsen (2010).

2 By Social Sciences, we primarily refer to Sociology, Political Science, Economics
   and Social Anthropology.
3 An exception to this influential scholarship is Walter Benjamin, whose critique
   of colonialism, especially in his *Arcades* project, is part of his holistic critique
   of modernity (see Bjelić, 2016: 247–267; Keith, 2005; Robinson, 2006: 28–36;
   Vandertop, 2016). The significance and limitations of Benjamin's work for the
   study of race in European cities have yet to be fully unearthed.
4 The 'European city' scholarship foregrounds the notion of 'moderated modernity'
   to establish a contrasting difference with the model of the US city, which is
   widely considered, from an equally Eurocentric angle, the epitome of urban
   modernity (Häußermann and Haila, 2005: 53 *et passim*).
5 Lack of space here prevents us from offering a theoretical discussion of the racial
   in its peculiar, variable articulations across Europe. See on this Wekker (2016);
   Essed et al. (2018); Boulila (2019). On modalities of silencing race in post-WWII
   Europe, see Goldberg (2006), Lentin (2008) and Nimako and Small (2009).
6 Hansen (2006: 94) finds that Weber (1958 [1922]) is 'unclear' about city-farmers
   as a crucial factor for differentiating between the ancient and the medieval city.
7 Weber (1958 [1922]: 200) argues that 'in the typical city of the medieval Occident
   the economics of slavery declined until it lost all importance. The powerful guilds
   could not tolerate the work of slaves, paying personal tribute to a master in
   competition with free crafts'. Phillips (1985: 99–106), in partial disagreement
   with Weber, shows the fundamental importance of slave labour and the slave
   economy in Italian cities in the early Middle Ages. On 'freedom', Stasavage
   (2014) argues that medieval European cities were able to sustain their political
   autonomy largely because they were imposing barriers to entry into markets
   and professions; hence, 'freedom' was a kind of exclusive freedom. On the
   oppression of disabled people in medieval European cities, see Gilchrist (1994).
8 The scholarly literature on race in medieval Europe is extensive. See, for example,
   the 2001 *Journal of Medieval and Early Modern Studies* Special Issue on 'Race
   and Ethnicity in the Middle Ages'. Bartlett's (2001) article in that special issue is
   particularly important for a comprehensive overview of the complex interrelations
   of ethnicity, nationhood and race.
9 Vlassopoulos' (2007) conclusion on Weber's (1958 [1922]) work aligns with
   Isin's (2002a; 2002b) analyses: 'The comparison [...] between the ancient and
   the medieval/modern economy [...] makes sense only from a certain European
   perspective. It reifies complex processes with different levels and temporal and
   spatial frameworks, in order to render them as part of the genealogy of Europe'
   (2007: 127).
10 The literature on Eurocentrism has since burgeoned. For comprehensively
   theoretical overviews, see the Duke University Press 'On Decoloniality' book
   series, edited by Catherine E. Walsh and Walter D. Mignolo, and launched in
   2018.
11 Said's (1978: 259) comment on Weber's method of 'ideal types' in relation to
   studies of the Orient is to the point here: '[Weber's] notions of type were simply
   an "outside" confirmation of many of the canonical theses held by Orientalists,

whose economic ideas never extended beyond asserting Orientals' fundamental incapacity for trade, commerce and economic rationality'.

12 On Weber's racism, imperialism and nationalism, see also Hund (2014).

13 On the importance of precolonial urban arrangements to understand cities of the Global South, see Bigon and Ross (2020) and Hull (1976).

14 Arbaci (2019: 309) importantly acknowledges the significance of colonial legacies in contemporary Southern European cities for understanding segregation in those cities yet, equally importantly, omits to view those legacies in terms of race as the foundational logic of spatial organisation of colonial rule (see on this point Nightingale, 2012: 1–18; the historian (2012, 390–393), however, fails to acknowledge works which centre race in segregation dynamics in contemporary European cities).

15 For example, see Andersen (2019) and Musterd (2020). A partial exception to this comparative conventional wisdom is Wacquant's (2008) sociology of urban marginality of Chicago and Paris, where 'ethno-racial' is one of the categories used, at times, to explain the condition of social marginality in the Parisian banlieues. The author, however, omits to theoretically clarify what that category indexes and entails, and still deploys it within the USA–Western Europe contrast, ending up foregrounding it only in the USA.

16 See, for instance, Harvey's (2004) work on Paris and Cox's (2016) USA–Western Europe comparison. More generally, one of the most important features of Eurocentrism is the silence on black and people of colour's lives. On this point, Goldberg made an incisive observation, with a focus on Britain and the Netherlands: 'It is significant then, both as a mark of urban life and of historical scholarship, that accounts of blacks in Britain and the Netherlands [...] are (regarded as) outside of – not properly belonging to – standard historical accounts of those societies, and take this exclusion as their almost exclusive motivating or inspirational focus. This exceptionalism, it should be clear, is not a product principally of self-determining "minority" separation, an infantilising celebration of ethnic self-identification. Rather, *it is a product primarily of that initial ignoring, the rendering invisible, of peoples designated black so that representational exceptionalism, an emphatic foregrounding focus, becomes the only possibility for writing Strangers and Outsiders, black people in particular, back into the historical record*' (2000: 77; our italics). Goldberg's point on exceptionalism lies at the core of our choice of the present volume's title, which reflects our invitation to attend to the constitutive contributions of blacks, people of colour and other racialised groups to European urban formations. The last section of this edited volume particularly addresses this point.

17 As we make clear above, we are not suggesting that the Urban Sociology of Europe never considers colonial urbanism, but that, when it does, it largely considers it as a thing of the past, which occurred far away from the European core, and with important legacies only in former colonial cities. See e.g. May et al., 2005; Crenshaw, 2014.

18 Data Sources. Berlin: 'Number of foreigners in Berlin in 2019, by nationality', available at https://de.statista.com/statistik/daten/studie/1094889/umfrage/anzahl-der-auslaender-in-berlin-nach-staatsangehoerigkeit/ [accessed 17 December 2021];

Rome: 'La popolazione straniera a Roma, 2018', available at www.comune.roma.it/web-resources/cms/documents/Popolazione_straniera_di_Roma_2018_DEF.pdf [accessed 17 December 2021]; Madrid: 'Población extranjera en la ciudad de Madrid: Población según Nacionalidad en la ciudad de Madrid', available at www.madrid.es/portales/munimadrid/es/Inicio/El-Ayuntamiento/Estadistica/Areas-de-informacion-estadistica/Demografia-y-poblacion/Poblacion-extranjera/Poblacion-extranjera-en-la-ciudad-de-Madrid/?vgnextfmt=default&vgnextoid=c289d54944580510VgnVCM2000000c205a0aRCRD&vgnextchannel=9ce23636b44b4210VgnVCM2000000c205a0aRCRD [accessed 17 December, 2021]; London: '2011 Census Ethnic Group Fact Sheets', available at https://data.london.gov.uk/dataset/2011-census-ethnic-group-fact-sheets [accessed 17 December 2021].

19 Fundamental for this awareness and understandings are the several city tours of postcolonial Europe, organised by grassroots groups and supported at times by academics. See, for example, Trzeciak and Peters in Chapter 6 of this volume; Bianchi and Scego (2014) about Rome, and Hondius and colleagues (2018) about Amsterdam.

20 The location of the 1884–85 Berlin Conference was not publicly marked as an urban site until 2005; since then, a minimal stele provides some information about German and European colonial history and that specific location. Since 2019 the project 'DEKOLONIALE' has its office at this address and centering the presence of colonial history in Berlin.

References

Abu-Lughod, J. L. (1980), *Rabat: Urban Apartheid in Morocco*. Princeton, NJ: Princeton University Press.

Aldrich, R. (2005), *Vestiges of the Colonial Empire in France: Monuments, Museums and Colonial Memories* (London and New York: Palgrave-Macmillan).

Amin, S. (1989), *Eurocentrism* (New York: Monthly Review).

Andersen, H. S. (2019), *Ethnic Spatial Segregation in European Cities* (Abingdon and New York: Routledge).

Araujo, M. and S. Maeso (eds) (2015), *Eurocentrism, Racism and Knowledge: Debates on History and Power in Europe* (Basingstoke: Palgrave).

Arbaci, S. (2019), *Paradoxes of Segregation: Housing Systems, Welfare Regimes and Ethnic Residential Change in Southern European Cities* (Oxford: Wiley-Blackwell).

Bagnasco, A. and P. Le Galès (eds) (2000), *Cities in Contemporary Europe* (Cambridge: Cambridge University Press).

Baranowski, S. (2011), *Nazi Empire: German Colonialism and Imperialism from Bismarck to Hitler* (Cambridge: Cambridge University Press).

Bartlett, R. (1993), *The Making of Europe: Conquest, Colonization and Cultural Change, 950–1350* (Princeton, NJ: Princeton University Press).

Bartlett, R. (2001), Medieval and modern concepts of race and ethnicity. *Journal of Medieval and Early Modern Studies* 31(1): 39–56.

Bhagat, A. (2019), Displacement in 'actually existing' racial neoliberalism: refugee governance in Paris. *Urban Geography* 42(5): 634–653.

Bianchi, R. and I. Scego (2014), *Roma negata. Percorsi postcoloniali nella città* (Rome: Ediesse).

Bigon, L. and E. Ross (2020), *Grid Planning in the Urban Design Practices of Senegal* (Basingstoke: Palgrave).

Bjelić, D. I. (2016), *Intoxication, Modernity, and Colonialism: Freud's Industrial Unconscious, Benjamin's Hashish Mimesis* (New York: Palgrave Macmillan).

Boatcă, M. (2010), Multiple Europes and the politics of difference within. In Brunkhorst, H. and G. Grözinger (eds) *The Study of Europe* (Baden Baden: Nomos Verlag), pp. 55–66.

Bodnár, J. (2018), Lay methodological regionalism to rest: posting 'postsocialism' in Urban Studies. In *Urban Studies at IJURR's 40th Anniversary*. Available at www.ijurr.org/spotlight-on/urban-studies-at-ijurrs-40th-anniversary/judit-bodnar/ [accessed 17 December 2021].

Böröcz, J. and M. Kovács (eds) (2001), *Empire's New Clothes: Unveiling EU Enlargement* (Telford: Central European Review).

Boulila, S. C. (2019), *Race in Postracial Europe: An Intersectional Analysis* (London: Rowman and Littlefield).

Brown, W. (2010), *Walled States, Waning Sovereignty* (New York: Zone Books).

Bruce-Jones, E. (2015), *Race in the Shadow of Law: State Violence in Contemporary Europe* (London: Routledge).

Bruns, A. and J. Gerend (2018), In search of a decolonial urban transformation. *GAIA-Ecological Perspectives for Science and Society* 27: 293–297.

Césaire, A. (1972 [1955]), Discourse on colonialism. In *Discourse on Colonialism* (New York: New Monthly Press), pp. 29–79.

Chakrabarty, D. (2000), *Provincializing Europe: Postcolonial Thought and Historical Difference* (Princeton, NJ: Princeton University Press).

Coronil, F. (1996), Beyond occidentalism: toward nonimperial geohistorical categories. *Cultural Anthropology* 11(1): 51–87.

Cox, K. R. (2016), *The Politics of Urban and Regional Development and the American Exception* (New York: Syracuse University Press).

Crenshaw, E. (2014), New directions in urban sociology. *International Journal of Sociology* 44(4): 3–6.

Dabashi, H. (2019), *Europe and Its Shadows: Coloniality After Empire* (London: Pluto Press).

De Genova, N. (2018), The 'migrant crisis' as racial crisis: do *Black Lives Matter* in Europe? *Ethnic and Racial Studies* 41(10): 1765–1782.

Driver, F. and D. Gilbert (eds) (1999), *Imperial Cities. Landscape, Display and Identity* (Manchester: Manchester University Press).

Dussel, E. (1998), Beyond Eurocentrism: the world-system and the limits of modernity. In Jameson, F. and Miyoshi, M. (eds) *The Cultures of Globalization* (Durham, NC: Duke University Press), pp. 3–31.

El-Tayeb, F. (2011), *European Others: Queering Ethnicity in Postnational Europe* (Minneapolis, MN: University of Minnesota Press).

El-Tayeb, F. (2012), 'Gays who cannot properly be gay': queer Muslims in the neoliberal European city. *European Journal of Women's Studies* 19(1): 79–95.

Essed, P., K. Farquharson, K. Pillay and E. J. White (2018), *Relating Worlds of Racism: Dehumanisation, Belonging, and the Normativity of European Whiteness* (Basingstoke: Palgrave).

Fassin, D. (2013), *Enforcing Order: An Ethnography of Urban Policing* (Cambridge: Polity Press).

Fassin, É., C. Fouteau, S. Guichard and A. Windels (2014), *Roms & Riverains. Une politique municipal de la race* (Paris: La Fabrique).

Ferenčuhová, S. and M. Gentile (2016), Introduction: post-socialist cities and urban theory. *Eurasian Geography and Economics* 57(4–5): 483–496.

Filčák, R. and D. Škobla (2013), Another brick in the wall: ghettos, spatial segregation and the Roma ethnic minority in Central and Eastern Europe. In Duxbury, N. (ed.) *Rethinking Urban Inclusion: Spaces, Mobilizations, Interventions* (Coimbra: Centro de Estudos Sociais, Universidade de Coimbra), pp. 413–428.

Fleming, C. M. (2017), *Resurrecting Slavery: Racial Legacies and White Supremacy in France* (Philadelphia, PA: Temple University Press).

Fuller, M. (2007), *Moderns Abroad: Architecture, Cities, and Italian Imperialism* (London: Routledge).

Fundamental Rights Agency (FRA) (2021), *Your Rights Matter: Police Stops* (Vienna: Fundamental Rights Agency). Available at https://fra.europa.eu/sites/default/files/fra_uploads/fra-2021-fundamental-rights-survey-police-stops_en.pdf [accessed 19 July 2021].

Gentile, M. (2018), Three metals and the 'post-socialist city': reclaiming the peripheries of urban knowledge. *International Journal of Urban and Regional Research* 42: 1140–1151.

Gilchrist, R. (1994), Medieval bodies in the material world. In Kay, S. and M. Rubin (eds) *Framing Medieval Bodies* (Manchester: Manchester University Press), pp. 43–61.

Goldberg, D. T. (1993), *Racist Culture: Philosophy and the Politics of Meaning* (Oxford: Blackwell).

Goldberg, D. T. (2000), Heterogeneity and hybridity: colonial legacy, postcolonial heresy. In Schwarz, H. and S. Ray (eds) *A Companion to Postcolonial Studies* (Malden, MA: Blackwell), pp. 410–427.

Goldberg, D. T. (2006), Racial Europeanization. *Ethnic and Racial Studies* 29(2): 331–364.

Gonick, S. (2015), Interrogating Madrid's 'slum of shame': urban expansion, race and place-based activism in the Cañada Real Galiana. *Antipode* 47(5): 1224–1242.

Grainger, H. and R. Cutler (2000), The European city: a space for post-national citizenship. In Harmsen, R. and T. M. Wilson (eds) *Europeanization: Institution, Identities and Citizenship* (Amsterdam: Rodopi), pp. 239–260.

Gressgård, R. (2019), The racialized death-politics of urban resilience governance. *Social Identities* 25(1): 11–26.

Gruner, M. (2010), 'The others don't want …'. Small-scale segregation: hegemonic public discourses and racial boundaries in German neighbourhoods. *Journal of Ethnic and Migration Studies* 36(2): 275–292.

Ha, N. K. (2016), *Straßenhandel in Berlin: Öffentlicher Raum, Informalität und Rassismus in der neoliberalen Stadt* (Bielefeld: Transcript Verlag).

Ha, N. K. (2017), Zur Kolonialität des Städtischen. In Zwischenraum Kollektiv (eds) *Decolonize the City! Zur Kolonialität der Stadt: Gespräche | Aushandlungen | Perspektiven* (Münster: Unrast), pp. 73–85.

Ha, N. K. (2022), Städtische Episteme dekolonisieren: die Europäische Stadt nach 1989 als neokoloniale Ordnung. In Bauriedl, S. and I. Carstensen-Egwuom (eds) *Geographien der Kolonialität. Geschichten globaler Ungleichheitsverhältnisse der Gegenwart* (Frankfurt: Transcript Verlag).

Hall, S. (1993), Culture, community, nation. *Cultural Studies* 7(3): 349–363.

Hall, S. (1995), Not a postmodern nomad [interviewed by Les Terry]. *Arena Journal* 5: 51–77.

Hansen, P. (2006), *Polis: An Introduction to the Ancient Greek City* (Oxford: Oxford University Press).

Hansen, P. and S. Jonsson (2017), Eurafrica Incognita: the colonial origins of the European Union. *History of the Present* 7(1): 1–32.

Haritaworn, J. (2015), *Queer Lovers and Hateful Others: Regenerating Violent Times and Places* (Chicago, IL: Pluto Press).

Harvey, D. (2004), *Paris: Capital of Modernity* (London: Routledge).

Häußermann, H. (ed.) (2004), *An den Rändern der Städte: Armut und Ausgrenzung* (Frankfurt am Main: Suhrkamp).

Häußermann, H. and A. Haila (2005), The European city: a conceptual framework and normative project. In Kazepov, Y. (ed.) *Cities of Europe: Changing Contexts, Local Arrangements and the Challenge to Urban Cohesion* (Oxford: Blackwell), pp. 43–64.

Heng, G. (2003), *Empire of Magic: Medieval Romance and the Politics of Cultural Fantasy* (New York: Columbia University Press).

Heng, G. (2012), England's dead boys: telling tales of Christian-Jewish relations before and after the first European expulsion of the Jews. *MLN – Modern Language Notes* 127(5): S54–S85.

Heng, G. (2018), *The Invention of Race in the European Middle Ages* (Princeton, NJ: Princeton University Press).

Hondius, D. G. (2014), *Blackness in Western Europe: Racial Patterns of Paternalism and Exclusion* (New Brunswick, NJ: Transaction Publishers).

Hondius, D. G., N. Jouwe, D. Stam, J. Tosch and A. de Wildt (2018), *Amsterdam Slavery Heritage Guide* (Volendam: LM Publishers).

Hull, R. W. (1976), Urban design and architecture in precolonial Africa. *Journal of Urban History* 2(4): 387–414.

Hund, W. D. (2014), White sociology: from Adam Smith to Max Weber. In Hund, W. D. and A. Lentin (eds) *Racism and Sociology* (Vienna and Berlin: Lit Verlag), pp. 23–67.

Isin, E. (2002a), *Being Political: Genealogies of Citizenship* (Minneapolis, MN: University of Minnesota Press).

Isin, E. (2002b), Citizenship after Orientalism. In Isin, E. and B. S. Turner (eds) *Handbook of Citizenship Studies* (London, Thousands Oaks, CA and New Delhi: Sage), pp. 117–128.

Ivasiuc, A. (2021), Race matters: the materiality of domopolitics in the peripheries of Rome. *International Journal of Urban and Regional Research* 45, 6(21): 1047–1055.

Kazepov, Y. (ed.) (2005), *Cities of Europe: Changing Contexts, Local Arrangements and the Challenge to Urban Cohesion* (Oxford: Blackwell).

Keaton, T. D. (2006), *Muslim Girls and the Other France: Race, Identity Politics and Social Exclusion* (Bloomington, IN: Indiana University Press).

Keith, M. (2005), *After the Cosmopolitan? Multicultural Cities and the Future of Racism* (London: Routledge).

King, A. D. (1990), *Urbanism, Colonialism, and the World Economy: Cultural and Spatial Foundations of the World Urban System* (London: Routledge).

King, A. D. (1992), Rethinking colonialism: an epilogue. In AlSayyad, N. (ed.) *Forms of Dominance* (Aldershot: Avebury), pp. 339–355.

Kipfer, S. (2007), Fanon and space: colonization, urbanization, and liberation from the colonial to the global city. *Environment and Planning D* 25(4): 701–726.

Kipfer, S. (2016), Neocolonial urbanism? La Rénovation Urbaine in Paris. *Antipode* 48(3): 603–625.

Kipfer, S. and K. Goonewardena (2013), Henri Lefebvre and 'colonization': from reinterpretation to research. In Moravánsky, A., C. Schmid and L. Stanek (eds) *Urban Research and Architecture: Beyond Henri Lefebvre* (Farnham and Burlington, VT: Ashgate), pp. 93–109.

Kopp, C. and M. Krohn (2013), Blues in Schwarz-Weiß. Berlins Black Community im Widerstand gegen kolonialrassistische Straßennamen. In Diallo, O. and J. Zeller (eds) *Black Berlin. Die deutsche Metropole und ihre afrikanische Diaspora in Geschichte und Gegenwart* (Berlin: Metropol), pp. 219–231.

Lawton, P. (2017), Idealizing the European city in a neoliberal age. In *The Sage Handbook of New Urban Studies* (London: Sage), pp. 78–91.

Lawton, P. and M. Punch (2014), Urban governance and the 'European city': ideals and realities in Dublin, Ireland. *International Journal of Urban and Regional Research* 23(2): 136–148.

Le Galès, P. (2000), *European Cities: Social Conflicts and Governance* (Oxford: Oxford University Press).

Le Galès, P. (2011), Urban governance in Europe: what is governed? In Bridge G. and S. Watson (eds) *The New Blackwell Companion to the City* (Oxford: Blackwell), pp. 747–758.

Le Galès, P. and Therborn, G. (2009), Cities in Europe. From city-states to state cities, and into union and globalization. *Working papers du Programme Villes & territoires*, 2009/4, Paris, Sciences Po.

Lentin, A. (2008), Europe and the silence about race. *European Journal of Social Theory* 11(4): 487–503.

Lentin, A. (2014), Postracial silences: the Othering of race in Europe. In Hund, W. D. and A. Lentin (eds) *Racism and Sociology* (Vienna and Berlin: Lit Verlag), pp. 69–106.

Lowe, L. (2015), *The Intimacies of Four Continents* (Durham, NC: Duke University Press).

McCombs, J. (2018), The class-to-race cascade: interrogating racial neoliberalism in Romani studies and urban policy in Budapest's Eighth District. *Critical Romani Studies* 1(2): 24–39.

MacFarlane, K. and K. Mitchell (2019), Hamburg's spaces of danger: race, violence and memory in a contemporary global city. *International Journal of Urban and Regional Research* 43: 816–832.

May, T., B. Perry, P. Le Galès, S. Sassen and M. Savage (2005), The future of urban sociology. *Sociology* 39(2): 343–370.

Martina, E. A. and P. Shor (2015), *White Order*: Racialization of Public Space in the Netherlands. *DEDALUS: Revista Portuguesa de Literatura Comparada* (19): 161–188.

Melegh, A. (2006), *On the East–West Slope: Globalization, Nationalism, Racism and Discourses on Central and Eastern Europe* (Budapest: Central European University Press).

Mingione, E. (2005), Urban social change: a socio-historical framework of analysis. In Kazepov, Y. (ed.) *Cities of Europe: Changing Contexts, Local Arrangements and the Challenge to Urban Cohesion* (Oxford: Wiley-Blackwell), pp. 67–89.

Modest, W. and A. de Koning (2016), Anxious politics in the European city: an introduction. *Patterns of Prejudice* 50(2): 97–108.

Molnar, V. (2013), *Building the State: Architecture, Politics, and State Formation in Postwar Central Europe* (Abingdon and New York: Routledge).

Morris, A. (2015), *The Scholar Denied: W. E. B. Du Bois and the Birth of Modern Sociology* (Berkeley, CA: University of California Press).

Mumford, L. (1963), *The City in History: Its Origins, Its Transformation and Its Prospects* (London: Secker and Warburg).

Murji, K. and G. Picker (2019), Race and place. *International Journal of Sociology and Social Policy* 39(11/12): 913–922.

Musterd, S. (2005), Social and ethnic segregation in Europe: levels, causes, and effects. *Journal of Urban Affairs* 27(3): 331–348.

Musterd, S. (2020), Urban segregation: contexts, domains, dimensions and approaches. In *Handbook of Urban Segregation* (Cheltenham and Northampton, MA: Edward Elgar), pp. 2–17.

Nasiali, M. (2016), *Native to the Republic. Empire, Social Citizenship, and Everyday Life in Marseille since 1945* (Ithaca, NY: Cornell University Press).

Nightingale, C. H. (2012), *Segregation: A Global History of Divided Cities* (Chicago, IL: University of Chicago Press).

Nimako, K. and S. Small (2009), Theorizing Black Europe and African diaspora: implications for citizenship, nativism and xenophobia. In Hine, D. C., T. D. Keaton and S. Small (eds) *Black Europe and the African Diaspora* (Urbana and Chicago, IL: University of Illinois Press), pp. 212–237.

Njoh, A. J. (2007), *Planning Power: Town Planning and Social Control in Colonial Africa* (London: UCL Press).

Novy, J. and M. Mayer (2009), As 'just' as it gets? The European city in the 'just city' discourse. In Marcuse, P., J. Connolly, J. Novy, I. Olivo, C. Potter and J. Steil, *Searching for the Just City* (London: Routledge), pp. 103–119.

Olusoga, D. and C. W. Erichsen (2010), *The Kaiser's Holocaust: Germany's Forgotten Genocide and the Colonial Roots of Nazism* (London: Faber and Faber).

Ong, A. and A. Roy (2011), *Worlding Cities: Asian Experiments and the Art of Being Global* (Oxford: Wiley).

Peralta, E. and N. Domingos (2019), Lisbon: reading the (post-)colonial city from the nineteenth to the twenty-first century. *Urban History* 46(2): 246–265.

Phillips, W. (1985), *Slavery from Roman Times to the Early Transatlantic Trade* (Manchester: Manchester University Press).

Picker, G. (2016), 'That neighbourhood is an ethnic bomb!' The emergence of an urban governance apparatus in Western Europe. *European Urban and Regional Studies* 38(3): 864–885.

Picker, G. (2017), *Racial Cities: Governance and the Segregation of Romani People in Urban Europe* (Abingdon and New York: Routledge).

Picker, G., M. Greenfields and D. Smith (2015), Colonial refractions: the 'Gypsy camp' as a spatio-racial political technology. *City* 19(5): 741–752.

Préteceille, E. (2000), Segregation, class and politics in large cities. In Bagnasco, A and P. Le Galès (eds) *Cities in Contemporary Europe* (Cambridge: Cambridge University Press), pp. 74–97.

Préteceille, E. (2009), Has ethno-racial segregation increased in the Greater Paris metropolitan area? *Revue française de sociologie* 3(50): 489–520.

Pula, B. (2013), Building the cities of empire: urban planning in the colonial cities of Italy's fascist empire. In Steinmetz, G. (ed.) *Sociology and Empire* (Durham, NC: Duke University Press), pp. 366–395.

Rabinow, Paul (1989), *French Modern: Norms and Forms of the Social Environment* (Berkeley, CA: University of California Press).

Robinson, C. (1983), *Black Marxism: The Making of the Black Radical Tradition* (London: Zed Books).

Robinson, J. (2006), *Ordinary Cities: Between Modernity and Development* (London: Routledge).

Rogozen-Soltar, M. H. (2017), Muslim Disneyland and Moroccan danger zones: Islam, race, and space. In *Spain Unmoored: Migration, Conversion, and the Politics of Islam* (Bloomington, IN: Indiana University Press), pp. 115–157.

Roy, A. (2018), Urban Studies in the age of Charlottesville. In *Urban Studies at IJURR's 40th Anniversary*. Available at www.ijurr.org/spotlight-on/urban-studies-at-ijurrs-40th-anniversary/ananya-roy/ [accessed 7 December 2021].

Said, E. W. (1978), *Orientalism* (New York: Vintage Books).

Said, E. W. (1993), *Culture and Imperialism* (London: Chatto & Windus).

Schierup, C., A. Ålund and A. Neergaard (2018), Race and the upsurge of antagonistic popular movements in Sweden. *Ethnic and Racial Studies* 41(10): 1837–1854.

Schierup, C.-U., P. Hansen and S. Castles (2006), *Migration, Citizenship, and the European Welfare State: A European Dilemma*. Illustrated edition. (Oxford: Oxford University Press).

Siebel, W. (2006), *Die europäische Stadt* (Frankfurt am Main: Suhrkamp).

Silverstein, P. (2018), *Postcolonial France: Race, Islam, and the Future of the Republic* (London: Pluto Press).

Simmel, G. (1971 [1903]), The metropolis and mental life. In *On Individuality and Social Forms* (Chicago, IL: University of Chicago Press), pp. 324–339.

Simone, A. (2010), Reclaiming Black urbanism. In *City Life from Jakarta to Dakar: Movements at the Crossroads* (London: Routledge), pp. 263–333.

Stam, R. and E. Shohat (2012), *Race in Translation: Culture Wars Around the Postcolonial Atlantic* (New York: New York University Press).

Stasavage, D. (2014), Was Weber right? The role of urban autonomy in Europe's rise. *The American Political Science Review* 108(2): 337–354.

Stoler, A. L. (1989), Rethinking colonial categories: European communities and the boundaries of rule. *Comparative Studies in Society and History* 31(1): 134–161.

Tammaru, T., M. van Ham, M. Szymon and S. Musterd (eds) (2014), *Socio-Economic Segregation in European Capital Cities* (Abingdon: Routledge).

Tissot, S. (2007), *L'Etat et les quartiers. Genèse d'une catégorie d'action publique* (Paris: Le Seuil).

Todorova, M. (2009 [1997]), *Imagining the Balkans* (Oxford: Oxford University Press).

Tuvikene, T. (2016), Strategies for comparative urbanism: post-socialism as a deterritorialized concept. *International Journal of Urban and Regional Research* 40: 132–146.

Vandertop, C. (2016), The colonies in concrete: Walter Benjamin, urban form and the dreamworlds of empire. *Interventions* 18(5): 709–729.

van Kempen, R. and A. Murie (2009), The new divided city: changing patterns in European cities. *Tijdschrift Voor Economische En Sociale Geografie* 100(4): 377–398.

Vincze, E., N. Petrovici, C. Raț and G. Picker (eds) (2018), *Racialized Labour in Romania: Spaces of Marginality at the Periphery of Global Capitalism* (Basingstoke: Palgrave).

Vincze, E. and G. I. Zamfir (2019), Racialized housing unevenness in Cluj-Napoca under capitalist redevelopment. *City* 23(4–5): 439–460.

Vlassopoulos, K. (2007), *Unthinking the Greek Polis. Ancient Greek History beyond Eurocentrism* (Cambridge and New York: Cambridge University Press).

Wacquant, L. (2008), *Urban Outcasts: A Comparative Sociology of Urban Marginality* (Cambridge: Polity Press).

Weber, M. (1958 [1922]), *The City*, trans. and ed. D. Martindale and G. Neuwirth (New York and London: The Free Press).

Wekker, G. (2016), *White Innocence: Paradoxes of Colonialism and Race* (Durham, NC: Duke University Press).

Wright, G. (1991), *The Politics of Design in French Colonial Urbanism* (Chicago, IL: University of Chicago Press).

Wright, G. (1997), Tradition in the service of modernity: architecture and urbanism in French colonial policy, 1900–1930. In Cooper, F. and A. L. Stoler (eds) *Tensions of Empire.Colonial Cultures in a Bourgeois World* (Berkeley, CA: University of California Press), pp. 322–345.

Zimmermar., A. (2006), Decolonizing Weber. *Postcolonial Studies* 9(1): 53–79.

Zwischenraum Kollektiv (eds) (2017), *Decolonize the City! Zur Kolonialität der Stadt: Gespräche | Aushandlungen | Perspektiven* (Münster: Unrast).

Part I

Provincialising historicism

1

Parochial imaginations: the 'European city' as a territorialised entity

Anke Schwarz

Introduction

The present chapter seeks to broaden our understanding of cities in contemporary Europe and their postcolonial condition through a socio-territorial lens. Two names seem to have dominated the European canon of Urban Sociology since the mid-1980s: Hartmut Häußermann and Walter Siebel. So prominent was this academic pair that, during my undergraduate studies in Urban Planning at Technical University of Hamburg-Harburg, students rarely thought of H&S as individual characters. Early on, we busied ourselves with rather clumsy attempts at applying their concepts to our urban surroundings and experiences. Living in a coal-heated municipal flat in the gentrifying Schanzenviertel neighbourhood, and working several odd jobs at a time to support my studies, I remember hacking away on my desktop computer, composing bleeping 'soundscapes of gentrification' (from intriguing poly- to tepid monotony) as a way of analysis (or rather, of illustration). As was expected from aspiring young bureaucrats and urban planners, students also drafted 'practical' proposals for ameliorating the situation. These ranged from what would now be read as a comical antecedent of the gig economy and temporal urban re-use – pop-up tents for urban pioneers on the roofs of tenements! – to the more utopian. Initially, the texts of Häußermann and Siebel, notably their 1987 classic *Neue Urbanität*, served as a template: the 'European city' – and our Hamburg neighbourhood as its incarnation – was supposed to be a place where strangers meet and diversity thrives, characterised by a 'social mix' of inhabitants. Yet somehow this did not square with what was happening in our city at the very same time. Othering formed the basis for discriminatory practices in the housing and labour market. Racialised policing and repression were rife, sometimes resulting in death. In December 2001, 19-year-old Nigerian Achidi John was arrested by police and died in custody during the forcible administration of emetics at a Hamburg hospital. (The European Court of Human Rights ruled in

2006 that even in cases where those subjected to this procedure survive, it amounts to inhuman and degrading treatment.) Was the 'European city' with its carefully balanced 'social mix' and our attempts to promote and sustain said mix with our student projects going to be of any help to grapple with and dismantle such systemic racism, brutality and discrimination?

Some two decades on, not nearly enough has changed. The May 2020 killing of George Floyd by police in Minneapolis amplified a global debate over systemic racism, colonial legacies and police brutality, with a strong response by the Black Lives Matter movement. Worldwide protests ensued, including throughout Europe. At the same time, racialised discrimination on the German housing market and elsewhere continues, as does racial profiling. Over the past years, initiatives such as KOP (Campaign for Victims of Racist Police Violence) and Death in Custody have documented numerous incidences of police brutality against People of Colour in Germany, including several unsolved cases of deaths in custody. Openly and unapologetically identitarian, nationalist, revisionist and authoritarian ideologies and politics – as exemplified by the former US president, who 'made white supremacy a pillar of his administration's domestic and international outlook' (Shatz, 2020: 4) – have been gaining considerable strength in many places. From Brazil, India and the Philippines to Italy, Germany and Poland, these ideologies also induce specific urban practices and spatialities.

Despite a dominant nationalist discourse, an idealised image of the 'European city' seems to resonate in the current political climate. In this chapter, I will outline how some of the ways in which this ideal caters to parochial imaginations of the urban become visible when a socio-territorial lens is applied. Apparent in reconstructed 'historical' facades, restrictions on 'improper' urban practices and emblematic writings, we can discern some aspects of the 'European city's' territorialised character that may appeal to identitarian actors and speak through their actions. Departing from these intersections of influential intellectual legacies and pressing political conjunctures, this chapter takes the writings of (West) German urban sociologists Häußermann and Siebel as a point of departure for the following questions: How does the idea of the 'European city' resonate with racist and white supremacist discourses? How does it speak to an emboldened far right?

The chapter is organised into five sections. After outlining the socio-territorial approach employed to pursue these questions, it reflects on three potential ways in which the 'European city' is territorialised as a self-contained entity: as a specific representation of the urban, as something materialised in urban reconstruction projects and as a particular type of urban regulation rooted in Othering. The fourth section reflects on the findings with respect to implications for the Urban Studies field, with conclusions drawn in the final section.

Relational space, relational power

To reflect upon the relational workings of society, power and space, this chapter draws on the *territorio* concept emerging primarily from Latin American literature (Haesbaert, 2013; Porto-Gonçalves, 2009; Raffestin, 2012; Santos, 2000; Saquet and Sposito, 2009). Such socio-territorial perspectives differ somewhat from dominant anglophone conceptualisations, which so far have tended to centre on the state.[1] In what follows, I will briefly outline how such an approach helps respond to the questions this chapter poses. A socio-territorial approach – as derived from what we might call, by way of approximation, a Latin American school of territoriology – allows for a transposition of analytical focus from more state-centred practices to urban contexts and dynamics in particular (Schwarz and Streule, 2016; 2020). It enables an analysis of urban practices according to their territorialising content, which involves a wide range of non-state actors and actions, thus opening up perspectives beyond the territorial nation state. It allows, in other words, scrutinisation of links between the making of space and of power on the urban scale. Grasping the urban as a realm of relational space and relational power, we can pose questions as to who dominates the creation and recreation of which kinds of space, and for whom these spaces 'work' best. Hence, the social production of territory can be understood as an ongoing de- and reterritorialisation involving the dimensions of materiality, regulation and representation. Territory, understood in this manner, is not a pre-existing place but something continuously made and remade. Practices of territorialisation are often acts of boundary-drawing that 'generate a basic discontinuity between the inside and the outside' (Brighenti, 2010: 65). By extension – and central to conceptualisations emerging from the Latin American context in particular – there is a political understanding of territory and territorialisation with intimate links to social struggles and contestations. As Carlos W. Porto-Gonçalves puts it, 'places do not exist *a priori* but are established in the shifting terrain of social struggles, which are also struggles over the attribution of meaning' (2001: 15).[2] A distinction between an analytical concept of territory and its political use was opened up as early as 1985, when Berta K. Becker wrote of 'social movements organised around a territorial base' (1985: 25). In Mexico, Colombia, Brazil and Argentina as well as the Andean region, feminist, Indigenous and Afro-descendant movements have given rise to a political framing of *territorio* in defence of urban, rural and Indigenous territories (Anthias, 2018; Colectivo de Geografía Crítica del Ecuador, 2018; Offen, 2003; Rivera Cusicanqui, 2012). None of these are understood as state spaces in the strict sense, but rather as collective products of a strong material, representational and regulatory relevance to local communities. Correspondingly, Arturo Escobar understands territory as 'subaltern strateg[ies] of localization' (2008: 52), emerging from Indigenous and Afro-descendant communities' struggles over land, nature and identities in the Colombian Pacific region. Both Bernardo Fernandes (2005) and Raúl Zibechi (2012) frame them as socio-territorial movements. Along with a relational conceptualisation of space and power, this insurgent perspective makes such socio-territorial perspectives relevant for a more decentred field of Urban Studies (Schwarz and Streule, 2020). This urban angle is essential for the present chapter, where the making of territory is understood as an urban practice mainly of non-state actors. Undeniably, practices of de- and reterritorialisation are a strong instrument and feature of essentialising spatial exclusion, whether in Germany (Bürk, 2012) or the Ecuadorian–Colombian borderland (Zaragocin, 2018). Framing 'race' with Stuart Hall as a discursive category which emerges from its enactment in social practices (Hall, 2012 [1996]: 208), territorialising practices are one of the more obvious areas where this category operates. In this sense, deterritorialisation could be framed as a manner of denying space – that is, as referring to ways in which the appropriation and use of urban space are contested as non-state actors seek to deny people access through more or less openly violent forms of Othering. Such Othering comes in many forms, whether openly racist, misogynist, transphobic, ultra-nationalistic or in a range of other nativist,[3] 'ethnopluralist' or identitarian guises. Beyond clear-cut examples of hate speech, racist violence and vigilantism, the present chapter is interested in seemingly more 'innocent' or apparently neutral, ordinary forms of de- and reterritorialisation. This work involves embracing a relational understanding of territory, as opposed to what Owen Dwyer and John Paul Jones III call the 'socio-spatial epistemology of whiteness [...] an essentialist and non-relational construction of space and identity that underwrite[s] its claims to be realized independent of an Other' (2000: 209). Specifically, it seeks to unpack the ways in which Häußermann and Siebel's 'European city' – a concept originally drafted by sociologist Max Weber – may speak to white supremacist and far-right actors and actions through parochial urban imaginations. The following sections draw from existing literature to illuminate three socio-territorial dimensions, outlining for each how it may feed into a regressive imagination of the urban, and the 'European city' in particular.

The 'European city' as a territorialised entity

Parochial imaginations

For a start, let us return to the key figures of undergraduate reading in Urban Planning, Häußermann and Siebel, and the way they have outlined the 'European city'. In one of his last texts, Zygmunt Bauman (2017a: 51) wrote of parochial imagination – a play on localised, almost insular, identitarian communities. A 2005 essay by Häußermann, entitled 'The end of the European city?', appears to exemplify this sentiment. Here, the author pits the 'European city' against an alleged 'Americanisation'. With reference to Arnaldo Bagnasco and Patrick Le Galès' 2000 volume *Cities in Contemporary Europe*, he argues that

> (a) the European urban system is different from the American (more medium-sized cities, fewer metropolises) (b) the appreciation of an urban culture never ends, and (c) cities remain strongly regulated. ... one question remains open: *what is the basis of a local identity or the formation of the city as a social, respectively political, subject?* Part of the answer should concern the way in which the impact of globalization upon the urban fabric is perceived. (Häußermann, 2005: 246; emphasis added)

Not only is globalisation presented as the first time the 'European city' ever seems to come into relation with the wider world, papering over centuries of colonial history. The argument seems to be based on an assumption of some kind of inherent or innate local identity or urban culture – a very specific kind of imagined urban community, to borrow Benedict Anderson's term (1983). Within the German-speaking Urban Studies context, it is hard to avoid drawing a link to the debate over an alleged intrinsic logic of cities (Berking and Löw, 2008; Kemper and Vogelpohl, 2011). The main claim of its proponents was that each city somehow has its own habitus, which in turn exerts an influence on social practices. John Agnew had long since cautioned against such reification of space, or as he calls it, the 'territorial trap' (1994): thinking of space as a container of social relations. Such notions of 'containers' are not only being mobilised in nationalist and white supremacist narratives, but they also work on scales beyond the nation (state). Identitarian territorialisations are often at the heart of mobilisations of 'authentic communities', as Anthony Ince argues with a view to post-2008 Britain: 'Linked to increasing social, economic and cultural insecurity surrounding the multiplicity of territorialisations taking place as part of globalised capitalism, the deployment of claims to authenticity can be a powerful political device for neo-fascist politics' (2011: 23). Organising claims of a homogeneous collective identity around a specific place or territory beyond the nation appears to be rather effective. Such parochialisms – or essentialist 'campfire' perspectives, to use Bauman's term (2017b) – play a central role and point to links between the construction of identity, difference and urban space. In part, parochial urban imaginations appear to be rooted in the kind of Eurocentrism criticised by Aníbal Quijano and others. One of its core elements is a naturalisation of cultural difference combined with a linear conceptualisation of time wherein the non-European is conceived of as the past (Quijano, 2016: 70). In what he famously defines as 'coloniality of power', such classed, gendered and racialised hierarchies stabilise hegemonic power relations. We could add that they simultaneously materialise in human bodies and objects such as buildings and the city more generally. If we shift focus to a larger scale, we might note that the figure of *Europa Nostra* ('our Europe') was used by the Identitarian Movement and also serves as the name of an EU-sponsored initiative to preserve Europe's cultural and natural heritage. For the purpose of the present chapter, there are characteristic ways in which the figure of the 'European city' may allude to white supremacist discourse. For instance, Häußermann presents it as the cradle of capitalism and modernity (2005: 241 f.), not bothering to locate it within a global network of colonial and capitalist relations of exchange and exploitation. With respect to the idea of the 'European city', and more generally to similar contemporary urban imaginations, a range of questions arises: Who is present and who is absent from such images and seemingly singular/linear historical narratives? Which urban practices are highlighted and which ones are silenced? Assuming with Noa K. Ha that multiple spatialities and temporalities are always overlapping in the coloniality of the urban (Ha, 2017: 76), which spatialities and temporalities are visible and voiced, and which ones are not? One example would be what Teresa Caldeira has termed peripheral urbanisation – a constant making of urban 'spaces that are never quite done, always being altered, expanded, and elaborated upon' (2017: 5). This logic extends to the making of a home, to street vending and to all kinds of indeterminate actions, which are global phenomena rather than specific to one particular place or city. Häußermann and Siebel, in their 1987 book *Neue Urbanität*, had highlighted such ambiguities in the DIY/self-help paradigm *en vogue* in the alternative sectors of 1980s Western Germany (1987: 246 ff.), pitching them as a contradiction between modern and pre-modern ideas at the core of urbanity:

> The city is both home (*Heimat*) and machine, single-family home and hotel. The choice between appropriation and relief, autonomy and administration, activity and passivity must be kept open for everyone, as must the choice between proximity and anonymity. [...] contradictions are constitutive for urban life. If they are suppressed, the core of urban culture is also damaged. [...] Life in cities is a contradictory life: between distance and proximity, anonymity and identification, familiar home and care device. (1987: 249)[4]

Yet somehow, such awareness of multiple temporalities and the ambiguities of self-help between empowerment and exhaustion appears to be increasingly lost in the late work of Häußermann. Instead, he leans further towards *Heimat*,[5] and appears to be fanning the flames of Bauman's campfire analogy: 'The idea of the regeneration or revitalization of the European city is based upon the notion of *a lively regional or local identity* that devotes energy to the struggle against the regimental forces of globalization' (Häußermann, 2005: 247; emphasis added). Paradoxically, this seems to imply that Europe, and by extension the 'European city', are somehow merely subject to – and not also agents of – such 'forces of globalization'. Such victimising language[6] omits uneasy questions about the role and actions of European actors, politicians and corporations in the globalisation of mercantilist and capitalist conditions from precolonial times up to the current day.

As is well known, there is a wide-ranging apparatus of literature from several schools of thought on the colonial/capitalist condition, which I cannot even begin to outline adequately here. The 'European city', or the metropolis, is key to most of this thought. European cities form a cornerstone of what Immanuel Wallerstein (1974) famously framed as the core of the capitalist world-system, with its geographically and socially differentiated division of labour. Later, research on Global Cities (Sassen, 1991) has called our attention to their role and function in a tight, hierarchical network of global economic relations. It has been argued that the key claim that 'global cities are critical places for the organisation of uneven development also holds for cities beyond "the usual suspects"' (Parnreiter, 2019: 81), including cities in the Global South. A critical stance towards the concept of development, progress and, ultimately, modernity is paramount to much of postcolonial theory (Chakrabarty, 2008 [2000]; McClintock, 1992) and the coloniality/modernity school (Lugones, 2007; Quijano, 2000). How colonialism, capitalism and the imperial project have affected and continue to affect urbanisation not only in the former colonies but in the European 'centre' itself is the key subject of Postcolonial Urban Studies since Brenda Yeoh's seminal 2001 paper. The writings of Ananya Roy and Jennifer Robinson in particular have challenged World City/Global City research in favour of what they see as a more decentred field of global urban theory (e.g. Robinson and Roy, 2016). These debates are ongoing in the fields of Geography and Urban Studies. In any case, it seems somewhat preposterous to imply that sudden forces of globalisation endanger the 'European city' while omitting any reference to its role as subject and product of colonisation and the global spread of capitalist conditions. Surely, Windhoek, Kolkata or Lima are subject to globalisation in a way that is both quite different and similar to what happens in Hamburg, London or Seville – and we would need to pay attention to these particularities while maintaining a systematic view on interdependencies, historical inequalities and exploitations. To return to our initial question of what it is that makes the idea of the 'European city' appealing to the far right, Häußermann's framing of globalisation as a threat to a localised urban identity provides a strong hint. As Gurminder K. Bhambra reminds us, 'concerns about globalisation – the movement of capital – were often euphemisms for concerns about immigration – the movement of labour – and the presence of racial and ethnic minority populations in the UK and US' (2017: 217). The contrast to and distance from the relational concept of place and space that is epitomised in Doreen Massey's 'A Global Sense of Place' (1994) could hardly be more marked. Such parochial gathering around the campfire of the 'European city' certainly seems to resonate with reactionary discourses and materialise in specific urban projects, as the following section will lay out.

Nostalgic reconstructions

Throughout Germany, there is a host of recent examples of urban (re)development and reconstructive architecture, from the new 'old towns' of Dresden and Frankfurt am Main mimicking pre-World War II appearances to Berlin's much-debated recreation of an imperial palace. Inaugurated in December 2020 on the former site of the GDR parliamentary building, the newly-built Humboldt Forum – a museum complex behind a neo-Prussian facade – and some of the artefacts exhibited there are subject to criticism from activists and academics alike (e.g. Appadurai, 2017; Heller and AfricAvenir, 2017; Savoy, 2017). The partial replica of a palace not only refers to a potent symbol of the German Empire; it also houses one of the biggest ethnological collections in the country, containing numerous artefacts of colonial provenance. What seems to link these examples is a prominent discourse built around the wish to reconcile with a hegemonic point of view of the past, effectively rendering a fascist and/or colonial history invisible: deterritorialising post-war ideals of urban development, replacing them with outlived architectural forms such as cathedrals and imperial palaces. Anna Yeboah identifies these revisionist projects as 'reconstructions of spatialisations of German colonialism' (2019: 225). Similarly, Stephan Trüby (2019), in his analysis of the ideological roots of the reconstruction of Frankfurt's historic downtown between 2008 and 2018, argues that reconstructive architecture serves as a key medium and backdrop for reactionary and far-right ideas. What is progressive or reactionary, he argues, is not architecture itself but rather the politics and social processes behind each construction (Trüby, 2020). In the Berlin case, the end of state socialism and the subsequent reunification of both German states returned the city to centre stage as the national capital. Francis Fukuyama's much-quoted 'end of history' (1992) evidently provided momentum to reorganise Berlin's urban image, thus rehabilitating German *Gründer-* and *Kaiserzeit*.[7] From 1990 onwards, in particular, urban planning in Germany was prone to grand gestures meant to symbolise and represent an emboldened capitalist state and, perhaps equally important, a dramatically recharged national identity. The narrative figure of the 'European city' underpinning Berlin's urban development plans

(*Planwerk Innenstadt*) at the turn of the twenty-first century is pertinent (Lanz, 2002: 64 f.). This narrative caters to an idealised (neo)bourgeois citizen-as-homeowner – as opposed to the tenants who still make up the majority of urban inhabitants. More often than not, it is represented in reconstructive urbanism and architecture in the form of phantasmatic facades and ornaments with a vaguely 'historical' air that speak to an imagined European heritage. The emphasis on form and appearance is no coincidence. In their study of urban development plans for Dublin, Philip Lawton and Michael Punch found that the 'European city' discourse was 'largely design- and image-driven' (2014: 881), with 'authentic' urbanism mobilised as a selling point in neoliberal inter-urban competition. The target audience was composed of middle-class residents and investors, who were to be lured back to downtown areas. According to Lawton and Punch, 'it could be that the leading contribution of the ideal of the 'European city' was to obfuscate to some degree the class character of urban development priorities in the transformation of the city' (2014: 881). While Lawton and Punch do not address questions of race and racism, the ideological impetus that they found the 'European city' ideal gained from its focus on urban form speaks directly to the case of Berlin. In the post-reunification years, nostalgic architecture citing an imagined national past in gestures and names often replaced post-war prefabs in the more lucrative inner-city locations in both East and West Germany. This 'retrospective construction' (Hartbaum, 2019: 219) or imagineering of, say, upper-scale apartment blocks as *Kronprinzengärten* continues to the present day and was given further impetus by the ongoing Berlin real estate boom. A desire to take unreserved pride in an imagined, straightforward national and bourgeois past is displayed in the reconstructions of both Potsdam's Church of the Garrison, a symbol of German militarism (Yeboah, 2019: 226), and Dresden's Church of Our Lady. As Jason James puts it with respect to Dresden: 'The appeal of narrative fetishism in this case lies in the possibility of exchanging culpability for innocence and trauma for wholeness, rather than constructing a narrative that refuses such totalized alternatives in favour of a less satisfying, more ambivalent memory' (2006: 265). All in all, the crafting of a 'European city' seems not only to address a homogenised European ideal, but also – in the German case at least – to cater to the reinforcement of a supposedly homogeneous and clear-cut bourgeois national identity that has somehow overcome the imperialist, fascist and genocidal ghosts of the past.

Moralistic Othering

An idealised 'European city' is implemented not only through urban reconstruction projects but also through urban regulations. *Decoro urbano* policies popularised over the past decade in Northern Italy and given a broader legal base by a 2017 law on urban security are a case in point.[8] Setting *decoro* (dignity) against *degrado* (decay), such policies regulate the 'proper' use of public space (e.g. Comune di Parma, 2010). This discourse features a strong moralistic undercurrent and has clear parallels to 1990s 'zero tolerance' policies (Bukowski, 2019). It seems to have gained traction in municipalities governed by far-right political parties such as Lega and Fratelli d'Italia, as well as the populist Five Star Movement. What qualifies as 'proper' use of public space often remains vague. In Rome and other cities, strolls in bathing suits, the installation of 'love locks' and the consumption of food in the vicinity of historical monuments – practices typically associated with tourists – are regulated and transgressions may carry hefty fines (e.g. Coffey, 2019). At the same time, *decoro* policies throw the door wide open to classed and racialised vigilantism and policing. Venice's ban on the sale and purchase of contraband in public spaces, illustrated on an official poster by a handbag bearing the letters 'FAKE' being exchanged for paper money,[9] is only one example. A 2006 study found that most street vendors peddling counterfeit bags in Venice's tourist hotspots were Senegalese migrants. It furthermore indicated that many of these goods were effectively a by-product of the fashion industry, manufactured in the very same workshops in the south of Italy (Scheppe and IUAV, 2009: 814 ff.). By including such street vending in the list of 'forbidden behaviour', the municipality of Venice marks this interaction between vendors and tourists not only as illicit but also as somehow immoral.

The regressive aspect of *decoro urbano* seems to be rooted precisely in its vagueness. The way it leaves gaps to fill in reveal it as an empty signifier (Bukowski, 2019: 110). With decorum crudely defined as an absence of decay, a dignified 'we' is pitted against an imagined 'Other' which in turn is characterised as somehow degenerate. There are parallels in Melissa Deem's definition of decorum as 'the regulatory site of stranger sociability' (2002: 447) and the Bourdieuian concept of habitus, where the rules of the game form a kind of incorporated or subconscious knowledge. Decorum here also gains a collective quality, wherein the individual is expected to maintain social dignity by adhering to the rules. Key to Victorian morale (Hughes, 2018), the concept of *decorum* can be traced back – via *Enciclopedia Treccani*'s definition as 'a proper way to do architecture'[10] – to a pre-modern formal and moral framework concerning urban aesthetics (Kohane and Hill, 2001). The aim of current-day *decoro* policies is, in my view, a disciplining of bodies and spaces by deterritorialising certain practices in public space – these policies stem from a desire to render them invisible.[11] They point to a parochial version of localism, wherein the local is conceived of as an authentic and bounded, reified entity to be protected from the Other. Ince's critique of 'authentic communities' (2011) again comes to mind. In what appears to be a deliberately vague outlining of the Other as 'improper' or 'immoral', *decoro* policies cater to racist reflexes, mobilising stereotypes and affects via a distinction between practices which allegedly form part of an idealised European urbanity and those that do not. A recent proposal for the regeneration of Genoa's UNESCO World Heritage-protected downtown, for instance, claims that shops in one particular area 'are not characterised by virtuosity, themselves causing degradation and representing a meeting point for micro-criminality' (Comune di Genova/Università degli Studi di Genova, 2019: 26).[12] This cryptic language is decipherable as thinly veiled racialisation when taking the multi-ethnic character of Genoa's downtown population into account. Whether in Venice, Rome or Genoa, such Othering is frequently staged against the backdrop of historical buildings and monuments to be protected from what is equivocally hinted at as 'improper' acts and actors. Current debates in architecture theory seem to revolve around similar questions, with a fierce debate over what counts as a 'proper' architectural expression of the contemporary 'European city'.[13]

The 'European city' in relation

What seems to unite the material, imagined and regulated facets of the urban territorialisations outlined in this chapter are filaments woven into an allegedly authentic, self-contained identity of the 'European city'. We might ask which kinds of imagined urban communities are implicitly and explicitly conjured by this idea. What does this nostalgia reveal and occlude? The crafting of a 'European city' idea seems to cater – in the German case at least – to a supposedly homogeneous and clear-cut white bourgeois national identity that has successfully overcome and neutralised the past, mainly through urban form. Walter Benjamin's 'aestheticisation of politics' (1935) as a central tenet of fascist ideology is close at hand. The kind of collective memory mobilised through this narrative – parochial, decorous and firmly placing modernity in Europe, from where it propagates globally over time – is fundamentally opposed to what bell hooks calls for in *Yearning*: 'a politicization of memory that distinguishes nostalgia, that longing for something to be as once it was ... from that remembering that serves to illuminate and transform the present' (1990: 147). To illuminate the present, we could pause to reimagine the 'European city' as not (only) a matter of cities around the globe created in its image, but (also) the multiple ways in which coloniality continues to shape the urban in Europe and everywhere. As Stephen Small (2018: 1187) has it, 'economic and social institutions, political ideologies and moral and cultural values in Europe were created and unfolded, not in a vacuum, but in large part in opposition to "the other"'. What are the effects of a territorial lens on the myopic range of parochial imaginations of the urban? There is an undeniable normativity at play whenever it comes to analysing 'group sentiments'. It has been argued that along with a sensibility for colonial continuities, historical difference and complexity, there is also a need to distinguish between claims for majority partiality and those for minority partiality, as Bhambra emphasises:

> The difference between minorities and majorities expressing group sentiments is that the sentiments of the former arise in the context of a wish for inclusion and equality, while those of the latter are a consequence of a wish to exclude and to dominate (Allen, 2005). In the first case, what is attributed as identity politics cannot be separated from an address of inequalities, while in the second case, identity politics are an expression of a wish to maintain those inequalities. (2017: 220)

A relational conceptualisation of *territorio* as an act of resistance speaks to this perspective and is reminiscent of hooks's concept of the *homeplace* as a locale of Black resistance, renewal and self-recovery (1990: 46 ff.) – a place that is not fixed, potentially not even physically rooted, but continuously created through the work of Black women. At the same time, it can be argued that it is precisely this split between a political and an analytical dimension of territory that is not without controversy (Stienen, 2020). At times, the political reading seems to incline towards a simplification of hegemonic versus counter-hegemonic practices of territorialisation, thus risking simplifying and glossing over empirical complications. With respect to the ambivalence between a conceptualisation of territory as 'a site of radical ontological difference' (Anthias, 2019: 68) and a political technology, Penelope Anthias cautions scholars that 'narrat[ing] alternative worlds into being [may] eclipse the messy realities that Indigenous peoples are forced to navigate' (2019: 71). Notably, while proposing strategic essentialism as a manner of shifting asymmetrical power relations in favour of the subaltern, Gayatri Chakravorty Spivak herself also declares sympathy for a 'defetishization of the concrete' (Spivak, 1999: 283). In addition, straightforward claims are complicated by questions of intersectionality (Crenshaw, 1989), adding complexity and complicating attempts at a clear-cut subaltern identity (as Pulido, 2017 highlights for the chicanx/Latinx community in the US). Closely related to this, there is also an urgency to discuss residual essentialism in conceptualisations of territory itself – something that becomes particularly obvious when such essentialism is situated in its European province of origin. There, it could well appear as a remnant of a 'realist, imperialist intellectual past' (Usher, 2020: 1019), engrained in anti-urban sentiments and essentialist claims of 'blood and soil', expressed by prominent nineteenth- and twentieth-century

German geographers and intellectuals such as Karl Haushofer, Carl Schmitt and others (e.g. Michel, 2018; Minca and Rowan, 2015). All in all, it would seem that research on processes of de- and reterritorialisation would do well to keep things complicated. As Achille Mbembe reminds us, 'in order to account for both the mind-set and the effectiveness of postcolonial relations of power, we need to go beyond the binary categories used in standard interpretations of domination, such as resistance v. passivity, autonomy v. subjection, state v. civil society, hegemony v. counter-hegemony' (1992: 3).

One possible way of keeping things in perspective could be what Rogério Haesbaert (2020) calls multi-territoriality, or multiple territories. With reference to Indigenous and Afro-descendant ontologies and socio-territorial movements, he proposes thinking of territorialisations as non-bounded, non-exclusive and overlapping – thus speaking to the complexity of the urban, its diverse spatialities and temporalities. While Haesbaert's proposal offers a potential opening towards multiple subjectivities, we could also discuss the ways in which a political conceptualisation and mobilisation of territory not only potentially empowers the subaltern but may also serve to obscure unequal relations of power organised along other social categories. Between the postcolonial call to decentre knowledge and knowledge production, on the one hand, and a necessary critique of essentialisation and reification of bodies and territories, on the other, there are unresolved tensions waiting to be made productive.

Conclusions

While I am somewhat less optimistic than Angharad Closs Stephens (2013) about the potential of the urban as an anti-racist and anti-nationalist bulwark, there clearly is room to further decentre the ideal of a 'European city'. Such a move could entail highlighting social relations and differentialisations involved in the constitution of urban space, as well as continuing to unveil how race, class, gender, sexuality, nationality and other social markers are mobilised and territorialised as a form of spatially organised 'cultural' difference. Scrutinising the 'European city' through a socio-territorial lens allows us to analyse the logic, operations and actors involved in such territorialisations. As I hope to have shown, Häußermann and Siebel – the urban sociologists who coined the concept of the 'European city' – seem somehow uninterested in the way that the geographies of social inequality in urban Europe are ethnicised and racialised. By emphasising and retracing the tightly knit fabric of global relations in which any idea of a 'European city' is necessarily located, the blind spots of parochial urban imaginations become increasingly clear. It remains a task for future research to study in greater depth how the image of an allegedly harmonic, authentic and decorous 'European city' overlaps with and appeals to territorialised urban discourses, paradigms and values promoted by racist, white supremacist and other far-right movements and ideologies. The politics of a strategic territorialisation of subaltern identities as opposed to racist nativism and 'ethnopluralism' also remain a matter for further discussion. For the discipline of Geography, and others, there are tasks ahead, heeding calls to maintain complexity and complicate historical and spatial narratives. As Anne McClintock put it almost three decades ago, yet in an uncannily up-to-date manner: 'a proliferation of historically nuanced theories and strategies is called for, which may enable us to engage more effectively in ... the currently calamitous dispensations of power' (1992: 97). Interrogating the nature of the legacies of European modernity and their incarnation in the 'European city' is but one way of doing so.

Acknowledgements

I am grateful to Noa K. Ha, Giovanni Picker, Tania Mancheno, Antonio Carbone and Ana Rita Alves for their comments on earlier versions of this chapter, to Daniel C. Barber for language editing and to Cristina Mattiucci and Monika Streule for ongoing conversations.

Notes

1 Anglophone Geography has started adopting similar approaches more recently, also taking Latin American perspectives and theories into account (e.g. Clare et al., 2017).
2 Translation from Spanish by the author. Original quote: 'los lugares no están dados a priori, sino que son construidos/instituidos en el terreno movedizo de las luchas sociales, que también son luchas por atribución de sentidos'.
3 In contrast to a generic definition of nativism as a right-wing populist item, racist nativism is defined in critical race literature as 'the assigning of values to real or imagined differences, in order to justify the superiority of the native, who is to be perceived white, over that of the non-native, who is perceived to be People and Immigrants of Colour, and thereby defend the rights of whites, or the natives, to dominance' (Perez Huber et al., 2008: 43).
4 Translated from German using DeepL and edited by the author. Original quote: 'Die Stadt ist sowohl Heimat wie Maschine, Einfamilienhaus wie Hotel. Die Wahl zwischen Aneignung und Entlastung, Selbstverwaltung und Administration, Aktivität und Passivität muß für jeden offengehalten werden, ebenso wie die Wahl zwischen Nähe und Anonymität. [...] für städtisches Leben sind Widersprüche

konstitutiv. Wenn sie verdrängt werden, wird damit auch die Stadtkultur in ihrem Kern beschädigt. [...] Leben in Städten ist widersprüchliches Leben: zwischen Distanz und Nähe, Anonymität und Identifikation, vertrauter Heimat und Versorgungsapparatur'.

5   In German, *Heimat* bears a particular, nativist and partly untranslatable meaning (see also Frisch, 1979). Though commonly translated to English as *home* or *homeland*, it bears more essentialising roots related to one's place of birth, and is used to describe the place of origin of individual humans as well as entire zoological and botanical species. Collins German–English dictionary (1993: 589) consequently proposes *home (town), native country* and *natural habitat* as alternative meanings.

6   Note the militarist connotations of the 'regimental forces' that the urban is facing according to Häußermann's text. This expression is perhaps more adequately applied to (neo)colonial agressions such as the conquest and destruction of the Aztec metropolis of Tenochtitlán by Spanish troops and their allies in 1521, the early twentieth-century genocide of Herero and Nama by German colonial troops in 'German South West Africa' in present-day Nambia, or the increasingly militarised police forces operating in Black and African American communities in Brazilian and US cities today.

7   *Gründerzeit:* the epoch from 1871 onwards, at the 'peak of European imperialism' (Small, 2018: 1192), that was marked by the establishment of the German Empire as a unified nation state under Emperor Wilhelm I and Otto von Bismarck, colonial campaigns, massive industrialisation throughout the country and Historicism as the predominant architectural style in the rapidly expanding urban centres.

8   The so-called 'Minniti law', legislative decree no. 14 from 20 February 2017, entitled 'Disposizioni urgenti in materia di sicurezza delle citta', was established during Marco Minniti's time in government as interior minister for the Partito Democratico.

9   Forbidden behaviour, *Città di Venezia,* www.comune.venezia.it/en/content/comportamenti-vietati [accessed 19 June 2020].

10 www.treccani.it/enciclopedia/decoro [accessed 16 September 2020].

11 Similarily, decorum has been identified as a rhetorical strategy to delegitimize Black Lives Matter protests in the US (Banks, 2018: 715).

12 Translated from Italian using DeepL and edited by the author. Original quote: 'Le attività commerciali [...] non presentano caratteri virtuosi, sono esse stesse causa di degrado e rappresentano un punto di incontro per la micro-criminalità'.

13 S. Trüby, Positioning architecture (theory). *e-flux* (December 2017), www.e-flux.com/architecture/history-theory/159235/positioning-architecture-theory [accessed 16 September 2020].

References

Agnew, J. (1994), The territorial trap: the geographical assumptions of international relations theory. *Review of International Political Economy* 1(1): 53–80.

Anderson, B. (1983), *Imagined Communities: Reflections on the Origin and Spread of Nationalism* (London: Verso).

Anthias, P. (2018), *Limits to Decolonization: Indigeneity, Territory, and Hydrocarbon Politics in the Bolivian Chaco* (Ithaca, NY: Cornell University Press).

Anthias, P. (2019), Beyond territories of resistance. *Human Geography* 12(3): 66–72.

Appadurai, A. (2017), Museum objects as accidental refugees. *Historische Anthropologie* 25(3): 401–408.

Banks, C. (2018), Disciplining Black activism: post-racial rhetoric, public memory and decorum in news media framing of the Black Lives Matter movement. *Continuum* 32(6): 709–720.

Bauman, Z. (2017a), Symptome auf der Suche nach ihrem Namen und Ursprung. In Geiselberger, H. (ed.) *Die große Regression. Eine internationale Debatte über die geistige Situation der Zeit* (Berlin: Suhrkamp), pp. 37–56.

Bauman, Z. (2017b), *Retrotopia* (Berlin: Suhrkamp).

Becker, B. (1985), El uso político del territorio: consideraciones a partir de una visión del Tercer Mundo. *Revista Geográfica de América Central* 2: 13–26.

Benjamin, W. (1935), The work of art in the age of mechanical reproduction. In Arendt, H. (ed.) (1969), *Illuminations* (New York: Schocken Books), pp. 217–251.

Berking, H. and M. Löw (eds) (2008), *Die Eigenlogik der Städte: Neue Wege für die Stadtforschung* (Frankfurt am Main: Campus).

Bhambra, G. K. (2017), Brexit, Trump, and 'methodological whiteness': on the misrecognition of race and class. *The British Journal of Sociology* 68(1): 214–232.

Brighenti, A. M. (2010), On territorology: towards a general science of territory. *Theory, Culture & Society* 27(1): 52–72.

Bukowski, W. (2019), *La buona educazione degli oppressi: Piccola storia del decoro* (Roma: Alegre).

Bürk, T. (2012), *Gefahrenzone, Angstraum, Feindesland: Stadtkulturelle Erkundungen zu Fremdenfeindlichkeit und Rechtsradikalismus in ostdeutschen Kleinstädten* (Münster: Westfälisches Dampfboot).

Caldeira, T. (2017), Peripheral urbanization: autoconstruction, transversal logics, and politics in cities of the Global South. *Environment and Planning D: Society and Space* 35(1): 3–20.

Chakrabarty, D. (2008 [2000]), *Provincializing Europe: Postcolonial Thought and Historical Difference*, reissue with a new preface by the author (Princeton, NJ: Princeton University Press).

Clare, N., V. Habermehl and L. Mason-Deese (2017), Territories in contestation: relational power in Latin America. *Territory, Politics, Governance* 6(3): 302–321.

Coffey, H. (2019), Rome bans tourists from going topless, eating 'messy' food and leaving love padlocks. *The Independent* (10 June), www.independent.co.uk/travel/news-and-advice/rome-tourist-rules-italy-topless-ban-water-fountains-love-padlocks-fines-a8951766.html [accessed 19 June 2020].

Colectivo de Geografía Crítica del Ecuador (2018), Untangling the strategies of capital: towards a critical atlas of Ecuador. In kollektiv orangotango (eds) *This Is Not an Atlas* (Bielefeld: transcript), pp. 130–135.

Comune di Genova/Università degli Studi di Genova (2019), *Prè-Visioni: Quarderno degli appunti*, www.genovameravigliosa.com/en/portfolio/176 [accessed 16 September 2020].

Comune di Parma (2010), *Regolamento del Decoro Urbano. Approvato con deliberazione del Consiglio communale*, n.119/26 in data 07/12/2010.

Crenshaw, K. (1989), Demarginalizing the intersection of race and sex: a Black feminist critique of antidiscrimination doctrine, feminist theory and antiracist politics. *University of Chicago Legal Forum* 1989(8): 139–168.

Deem, M. (2002), Stranger sociability, public hope, and the limits of political transformation. *Quarterly Journal of Speech* 88(4): 444–454.

Dwyer, O. J. and Jones III, J. P. (2000), White socio-spatial epistemology. *Social & Cultural Geography* 1(2): 209–222.

Escobar, A. (2008), *Territories of Difference: Place, Movements, Life, Redes* (Durham, NC: Duke University Press).

Fernandes, B. M. (2005), Movimentos socioterritoriais e movimentos socioespaciais: contribuição teórica para uma leitura geográfica dos movimentos sociais. *Observatorio Social de América Latina* 6(16): 273–283.

Frisch, M. (1979), *Tagebücher 1966–71* (Frankfurt am Main: Suhrkamp).

Ha, N. K. (2017), Zur Kolonialität des Städtischen. In Zwischenraum Kollektiv (eds) *Decolonize the City!* (Münster: Unrast), pp. 73–85.

Haesbaert, R. (2013), A global sense of place and multi-territoriality: notes for dialogue from a 'peripheral' point of view. In Featherstone, D. and J. Painter (eds) *Spatial Politics: Essays for Doreen Massey* (Malden, MA: Wiley-Blackwell), pp. 146–157.

Haesbaert, R. (2020), Territory/ies from a Latin American perspective. *Journal of Latin American Geography* 19(1): 258–268.

Hall, S. (2012 [1996]), *Rassismus und kulturelle Identität*, reedition (Hamburg: Argument).

Hartbaum, V. (2019), Rechts in der Mitte. Hans Kollhoffs CasaPound. *ARCH+* 235: 217–229.

Häußermann, H. (2005), The end of the European city? *European Review* 13(2): 237–249.

Häußermann, H. and W. Siebel (1987), *Neue Urbanität* (Frankfurt am Main: Suhrkamp).

AfricAvenir (ed.) (Heller, M. and 2017), *No Humboldt 21! Dekoloniale Einwände gegen das Humboldt-Forum* (Berlin: International).

hooks, b. (1990), *Yearning: Race, Gender and Cultural Politics* (Boston, MA: South End Press).

Hughes, K. (2018), *Victorians Undone: Tales of the Flesh in the Age of Decorum* (Baltimore, MD: Johns Hopkins University Press).

Ince, A. (2011), Contesting the 'authentic' community: far-right spatial strategy and everyday responses in an era of crisis. *ephemera* 11(1): 6–26.

James, J. (2006), Undoing trauma: reconstructing the Church of Our Lady in Dresden. *Ethos* 34(2): 244–272.

Kemper, J. and A. Vogelpohl (eds) (2011), *Lokalistische Stadtforschung, kulturalisierte Städte: Zur Kritik einer 'Eigenlogik der Städte'* (Münster: Westfälisches Dampfboot).

Kohane, P. and M. Hill (2001), The eclipse of a commonplace idea: decorum in architectural theory. *Architectural Research Quarterly* 5(1): 63–77.

Lanz, S. (2002), Mythos europäische Stadt: Fallstricke aktueller Rettungsversuche. In Bukow, W. D. and E. Yildiz (eds) *Der Umgang mit der Stadtgesellschaft. Interkulturelle Studien 11* (Heidelberg: Springer), pp. 63–77.

Lawton, P. and M. Punch (2014), Urban governance and the 'European city': ideals and realities in Dublin, Ireland. *International Journal of Urban and Regional Research* 38(3): 864–885.

Lugones, M. (2007), Heterosexualism and the colonial/modern gender system. *Hypatia* 22(1): 186–209.

McClintock, A. (1992), The angel of progress: pitfalls of the term 'post-colonialism'. *Social Text* 31/32, *Third World and Post-Colonial Issues*: 84–98.

Massey, D. (1994), A global sense of place. In *Space, Place and Gender* (Cambridge: Polity Press), pp. 147–156.

Mbembe, A. (1992), Provisional notes on the postcolony. *Africa. Journal of the International African Institute* 62(1): 3–37.

Michel, B. (2018), Anti-semitism in early 20th century German geography: from a 'spaceless' people to the root of the 'ills' of urbanization. *Political Geography* 65: 1–7.

Minca, C. and R. Rowan (2015), The question of space in Carl Schmitt. *Progress in Human Geography* 39(3): 268–289.

Offen, K. H. (2003), The territorial turn: making Black territories in Pacific Colombia. *Journal of Latin American Geography* 2: 43–73.

Parnreiter, C. (2019), Global cities and the geographical transfer of value. *Urban Studies* 56(1): 81–96.

Perez Huber, L., C. Benavides Lopez, M. C. Malagon, V. Velez and D. G. Solorzano (2008), Getting beyond the 'symptom,' acknowledging the 'disease': theorizing racist nativism. *Contemporary Justice Review* 11(1): 39–51.

Porto-Gonçalves, C. W. (2001), *Geo-grafías: Movimientos sociales, nuevas territorialidades y sustentabilidad* (Mexico City: Siglo XXI).

Porto-Gonçalves, C. W. (2009), De Saberes y de Territorios – diversidad y emancipación a partir de la experiencia latino-americana. *Polis* 22 [online], http://journals.openedition.org/polis/2636 [accessed 9 March 2020].

Pulido, L. (2017), Geographies of race and ethnicity II: environmental racism, racial capitalism and state-sanctioned violence. *Progress in Human Geography* 41(4): 524–533.

Quijano, A. (2000), Coloniality of power and Eurocentrism in Latin America. *International Sociology* 15(2): 215–232.

Quijano, A. (2016), *Kolonialität der Macht, Eurozentrismus und Lateinamerika* (Wien and Berlin: Turia + Kant).

Raffestin, C. (2012), Space, territory, and territoriality. *Environment and Planning D: Society and Space* 30(1): 121–141.

Robinson, J. and A. Roy (2016), Global urbanisms and the nature of urban theory. *International Journal of Urban and Regional Research* 40(1): 181–186.

Rivera Cusicanqui, S. (2012), Ch'ixinakax utxiwa: a reflection on the practices and discourses of decolonization. *South Atlantic Quarterly* 111: 95–109.

Santos, M. (2000), El territorio: Un agregado de espacios banales. *Boletín de Estudios Geográficos* 96: 87–96.

Saquet, M.A. and E. S. Sposito (eds) (2009), *Territórios e territorialidades. Teorias, processos e conflitos* (São Paulo: Editora Expressão Popular).

Sassen, S. (1991), *The Global City: New York, London, Tokyo* (Princeton, NJ: Princeton University Press).

Savoy, B. (2017), Das Humboldt-Forum ist wie Tschernobyl [interview by Jörg Häntzschel]. *Süddeutsche Zeitung* (20 July 2017), www.sueddeutsche.de/kultur/benedicte-savoy-ueber-das-humboldt-forum-das-humboldt-forum-ist-wie-tschernobyl [accessed 2 April 2021].

IUAV Class of Politics of Representation (Scheppe, W. and 2009), *Migropolis. Venice / Atlas of a Global Situation* (Stuttgart: Hantje Cantz).

Schwarz, A. and M. Streule (2016), A transposition of territory: decolonized perspectives in current urban research. *International Journal of Urban and Regional Research* 40(5): 1000–1016.

Schwarz, A. and M. Streule (2020), Introduction to the special issue 'Contested Urban Territories: Decolonized Perspectives'. *Geographica Helvetica* 75(1): 11–18.

Shatz, A. (2020), America explodes: Adam Shatz on Trump's domestic war. *London Review of Books* 42(12): 4.

Small, S. (2018), Theorizing visibility and vulnerability in Black Europe and the African diaspora. *Ethnic and Racial Studies* 41(6): 1182–1197.

Spivak, G. C. (1999), *A Critique of Postcolonial Reason: Toward a History of the Vanishing Present* (Cambridge, MA: Harvard University Press).

Stephens, A. C. (2013), *The Persistence of Nationalism* (London: Routledge).

Stienen, A. (2020), (Re)claiming territory: Colombia's 'territorial-peace' approach and the city. *Geographica Helvetica*, 75(3): 285–306.

Trüby, S. (2019), Altstadt-Opium fürs Volk. *ARCH+* 235: 160–167.

Trüby, S. (2020), Rechte Räume: Politische Essays und Gespräche. In *Bauwelt Fundamente* 169 (Gütersloh and Basel: Birkhäuser), pp. 7–36.

Usher, M. (2020), Territory incognita. *Progress in Human Geography* 44(6): 1019–1046.

Wallerstein, I. (1974), *The Modern World-System I: Capitalist Agriculture and the Origins of the European World-Economy in the Sixteenth Century* (New York: Academic Press).

Yeboah, A. (2019), Blackout Berlin-Brandenburg: Die Rekonstruktion der Potsdamer Garnisonskirche und des Berliner Stadtschlosses und andere Spatialisierungen des deutschen Kolonialismus. *ARCH+* 235: 225–230.

Yeoh, B. S. (2001), Postcolonial cities. *Progress in Human Geography* 25(3): 456–468.

Zaragocin, S. (2018), Gendered geographies of elimination: decolonial feminist geographies in Latin American settler contexts. *Antipode* 51(1): 373–392.

Zibechi, R. (2012), *Territories in Resistance. A Cartography of Latin American Social Movements* (Oakland, CA: AK Press).

2

Countermapping colonial amnesia in Parisian landscapes

Tania Mancheno

European cities are composed of landscapes of world heritage and, at the same time, are urban registers of colonial amnesia.[1] Thereby, I mean with Françoise Vergès that the agency of those who built them and those who keep them clean today (2019: 3) is not part of the 'official' urban history. Neither are their identities or biographies commemorated in the urban space. The European city is thus constituted by two histories: one of them is known, commemorated and celebrated worldwide, while the other is omitted from collective memory and the narrative of national identity.

The 'heritage regime' (Berliner, 2012) put into place by UNESCO is crucial in the institutionalisation of such fragmented memory at the global scale. By 'collecting' cultural monuments and adding sections of urban landscapes into the World Heritage Convention, UNESCO treats urban space as a museological object. Similar to the colonial de-contextualisation of non-European artworks that takes place in European ethnographic museums,[2] this heritage regime alters the economic and symbolic value of tangible objects and raises questions about the authorship of, ownership of and public accessibility to urban sites of cultural heritage (Bendix et al., 2012; Rico, 2008).

The benevolent impulse to protect and conserve 'humanity's cultural richness' (Bendix et al., 2012: 14) that drives the World Heritage Convention shifts the global politics of history and memory. It delimits the way in which the city is remembered and experienced (Rico, 2008: 344). The heritage regime also affects the lives of citizens insofar as the sacral zones cannot be altered or readapted into new social requirements. The aesthetic and historical significances of urban space are valued more highly than the adaptability of that space to local needs (Bendix et al., 2012: 18). In this sense, the heritage regime restrains the possibilities for local and international visitors to interact spontaneously with the city, as well as to resignify the past.

The UNESCOisation (Berliner, 2012) of urban landscapes, which set in motion drastic changes in the productive uses of space, can be traced back to 1972 when the first World Heritage Convention with regard to urban materiality was signed.[3] Almost fifty years later, this convention is a powerful mechanism for increasing the real estate value and publicity of a city. In Paris, there are more than fourteen monuments and places marked as sites of world heritage (UNESCO, 2020a). Among them, the Eiffel Tower is probably the best known. The metallic phallus at the bourgeois centre is recognised worldwide as a Parisian symbol. However, the history of the world fair in 1889, at which the Tower was inaugurated, remains widely ignored. In this sense, the urban history that is transmitted as the world's heritage is a partial, selective one.

This chapter deals with the colonial politics that guide the selective memory of the city, or the colonial amnesia in the post-imperial French capital, and proposes a decolonial analysis of the world heritage regime. By countermapping[4] the amnesia veiling the colonial history in Parisian landscapes, I situate the meaning of heritage in the history of its urban margins. The reconstruction of the city beyond its official historicity means to recentre the historical significance of the banlieues.[5] Built at the end of the nineteenth century, the banlieues were first presented to the public as an urban model during the aforementioned Parisian world fair of 1889 (Young, 2008: 339). At that time, this was the world's largest housing project. This 'coincidence' raises questions with regard to the 'glocality' of world fairs and their role in framing global/colonial cultural heritage. Moreover, it intertwines the category of heritage with local and international projects of infrastructure that were designed to 'urbanize the world' (Mbembe, 2016: 24) and to administer the habitat of Indigenous, immigrant and displaced peoples in colonial and postcolonial times.

The critical attentiveness to the politics of selective memory, or what Françoise Vergès (2018) calls the 'politics of forgetfulness', allows countermapping the systematic exclusion of racial violence from national and global history. Vergès' (2013: 9) decolonial critique of heritage visualises the colonial governmentality administering the uses and misuses of history and memory in the urban space.[6] This political selection of memories responds to Aníbal Quijano's (2000: 533) concept of coloniality, which refers to 'the model of power that is globally hegemonic today' and which 'expresses the basic experience of colonial domination and pervades the more important dimensions of global power, including its specific rationality: Eurocentrism'.

My analysis links Frantz Fanon's (1965) and Vergès' (2018) decolonial and feminist critiques of the heteronormative and heteronationalist institutional modalities of modern nation states in remembering, commemorating and dealing with the history of colonial violence in the city with Reinhart Koselleck's (2010) critique of national memory, which suggests that no politics of memory can be neutral. In this context, I ask: How does colonialism frame the category of heritage in the city? Following this question, I will redescribe urban history beyond methodological nationalism and then resignify the category of global heritage by highlighting some entanglements in the urban history between the French former colonies and the metropole. By tracing urban history through a critical-decolonial approach, I attempt to recontextualise the category of heritage in its colonial/modern history and relate it to the transnational cartographies of racialised urban space. Hence, I shall countermap Paris's colonial amnesia by intersecting the role of world fairs, the meaning of heritage and the postcolonial significance of the banlieues.

The chapter is structured in five sections. I will first introduce Fanon's and Koselleck's urban analyses. In the second section, I will analyse the world fair of 1889 as an event that intersects urban and colonial history, as well as the colonies and the metropole. Thirdly, I will map the travelling history of heritage by describing some of the connections between the urban planning of Algiers, Rabat and the Parisian banlieues. The last section discusses the world heritage regime in relation to the colour line[7] in the city, or the cartographies of racialised urban space that will have been reconstructed through the examples presented in the previous sections. In the conclusion, Paris's urban history will be intertwined with French colonial history to situate the banlieues as a monument of (post)colonial legacy and decolonial urban memory.

Mapping the transatlantic wounds of a fragmented city with Fanon

In her creolising approach to the European city, Fatima El-Tayeb (2014: 11) suggests that the reconstruction of the many facades of coloniality, which create and sediment urban segregation, requires tracing the migration of people and of cultural meaning that converged in the city. The trajectories encountered in Paris bring diasporic histories and historicities of singular and collective anti-colonial resistances,[8] which either contradict or challenge the homogeneity of the European nation state. These counter-narratives and subterranean veins are traditionally banished from the official urban history.[9]

Paris is described as 'the city of lights', as capital of the colonial empire, but also as *Paris-Noir* (Blanchard et al., 2001a) and as *Black Paris* (Keaton et al., 2012). These definitions converge in the monumental city, which is constantly in motion. The metro system is an essential component of its urban geography. A primarily ethnographic fieldwork in the subterranean corridors shows a microcosmos of the heterogeneous composition of society.[10] Blackness, Indigeneity[11] and whiteness compose the textuality of the city.

Fanon's reflections on urban space visualise multiple identities that inhabit the city and localise nodes of historical intersections in which the existential 'passing' and 'crossing' are decided and performed. As Nalini Natarajan (2005: 89) suggests: 'reading Fanon's texts, with reference to the specific city he observes' enables a discussion on 'the coexistence of class, gender and race'. Fanon criticises everyday racism as an alienating spatial relation (2008: 84) and deals with the city from a transnational and decolonial perspective. He defines colonialism through the 'zones of being and non-being' (Grosfoguel, 2017: 59) that it creates and describes how these are mirrored in urban/colonial planning (Fanon, 1963: 37). The division between the 'white-European', colonial (part of the) city and the 'Oriental', colonised Casbah sediments a racialised order, which Fanon characterises as the coloniser's city, 'the town of white settlers and foreigners' (1963: 38). The Casbah or Medina is defined as the space occupied by *Indigènes*. In his words: 'The town belonging to the colonized people' is the 'native town, the Negro village, the medina, the reservation' (1963: 38). To this racialisation of space, he adds that this 'is a place of ill fame, peopled by men of evil repute. They are born there, it matters little where or how; they die there, it matters not where, nor how. It is a world without spaciousness; men live there on top of each other, and their huts are built one on top of the other. The native town is a hungry town, starved of bread, of meat, of shoes, of coal, of light'.

He further suggests that racialised spatialities immobilise non-white bodies, who are considered 'foreign' and who occupy a position of existential dependency, which is translated into their habitat (Mancheno, 2011: 18). According to Achille Mbembe (2016: 43), the city's colonial fracture between the white and non-white neighbourhoods is embedded in the genealogy of segregation that was planned in the plantation. For example, in the Caribbean, the mobility of enslaved people was controlled by a wide range of forms of cruelty that had as a common target the punishment, mutilation and death of undisciplined bodies (Mbembe, 2016: 36), and which included numerous technologies of surveillance, appointed guards and dogs. In the city, the various checkpoints created by the colonial power to restrain circulation among racialised compartments (Fanon, 1963: 36) replicate this logic. The racialised planning or, in Mbembe's words, the 'form of government of bodies, behaviours and affects with the purpose of the pacification of social spaces' is today found in the creation of 'disposable populations' (2016: 32; own translation). This reconstruction of the racial making of the city culminates in the spaces created by apartheid, the prison and the suburban ghetto (Mbembe, 2016: 59).

Fanon's depiction of the city, which connects the social history in the colonies and the metropole, also illustrates the coloniality inscribed in the urban space and resignifies the ontological permeability achieved by the movement of racialised bodies. By intersecting urban and social mobility, he explains that the movements of Black and Indigenous people challenge the whiteness governing the racialised urban/social order (1963: 38). He identifies a political significance in the circulation of non-white bodies and defines decolonisation as a 'form of reappropriating and transforming spatial relations in the colonial city and through the construction of nationwide sociospatial alliances' (Kipfer, 2007: 701). In this sense, he counteracts the static urban and ontological order by focusing on the socio-spatial linkages created by the visible and invisible subversions which are caused by non-white bodies crossing the colour line between the white city and the non-white Casbah (Fanon, 1965: 53). Localising the transgression of the racial/urban order at its checkpoints, he shows that the movement of racialised bodies enables the writing of another (urban) history.

The transgression of militarised nodes in the occupied city is the alteration of an internalised immobility or an ontic mobility. Fanon (1965: 52) describes the crossing of an Algerian woman into the white-European part of the Casbah in colonial Algiers and notes that she must 'consider the image of the occupier lodged somewhere in her mind and in her body, remodel it, initiate the essential work of eroding it, make it inessential, remove something of the shame that is attached to it, devalidate it'. He also notes that the collective mourning of colonised peoples breaks down the checkpoints between the Western (colonial) and 'Oriental' (colonised) urban spaces. Yet, these transgressions remain exceptional as they occurred only in 'rare occasions' of collective commemoration such as festivals or funerals (1965).

There is, however, another kind of public mourning, which is not exceptional and transgressive but is rather central to the selective politics of memory. In Fanon's view, the city is an artificial extension of the coloniser's memory and history. He reflects on the French war memorial monument and the Central Hotel, in Fort de France, Martinique's capital, which he saw every day on his way back from school, and concludes that in the urban planning of this former colony and now French overseas territory (*France d'outre-mer*), French national memory is as present in the public space as in Paris (2008: 13–14).[12] In the Antilles, Fanon states: the 'view of the world is white, because no black voice exists' (2008: 118). He defines the colonised city as a 'world divided into compartments, a motionless, Manicheistic world, a world of statues: the statue of the general who carried out the conquest, the statue of the engineer who built the bridge; a world which is sure of itself, which crushes with its stones the backs flayed by whips: this is the colonial world' (1963: 50–51).

The crossing of Algerian women from the racialised periphery of the city into its white centre, as well as the migration of Martinique's inhabitants to the metropole, are movements that render tangible the violence caused by the racialisation of the urban space. Fanon describes both the local and the transcontinental journey through an affective memory, or what he calls 'that feeling which pervades each new generation of students arriving in Paris: It takes them several weeks to recognize that contact with Europe compels them to face a certain number of problems that until their arrival had never touched them. And yet these problems were by no means invisible' (2008: 118). The cultural estrangement and physical petrification of the immigrant in the metropole explain how racism causes an inversion in 'the line of self-esteem'. In Fanon's words: 'the Antillean who goes to France pictures this journey as the final stage of his personality. ... [T]he Antillean who goes to France in order to convince himself that he is white will find his real face there' (2008: 118 n.16).[13]

Fanon entangles the colonial ordering of urban space in the three-continental zone by describing the similar experiences of estrangement in the European white city (Paris), the colonised Casbah (Algiers) and the Caribbean capital (Fort de France). In these transcontinental landscapes, the transgressions of racialised compartments are, at the same time, local and global.

Koselleck's critique of the artificiality of war memorials

Koselleck's (2010: 21) critique of the way in which national history[14] is manifested in the urban space is neither anti-colonial nor anti-racist, but rather guards against the totalitarian politics of memory, which, in his view, characterises modern nation-building. He criticises the meaning of public statues and monuments in European cities and their fetishist significance for national identity (2002: 287–288). According to the conceptual historian, monuments are expressions of a collective artificial identity due to the inherent fragmentation of memory and identity at a national scale (2010: 17). Koselleck suggests that there is no homogeneous identity, nor uniform memory (2010: 19). Instead, there are transnational forms of remembrance, which are transversally linked through the common public expressions of memory in the public space.

Koselleck identifies in monuments the spatialisation of modern history; yet, he criticises their timeless representation. War monuments hypostatise the past. These urban 'places of memory' not only keep memory alive; they also forge citizens' duty to remember (Koselleck, 2002: 286, 291). Furthermore, he notes that the sites of national memory are highly restrictive. In his words: 'dying happens alone; killing another takes two' (2002: 288). Describing the religious function of monuments, or what he calls the mediation between the life and death of the political community, Koselleck suggests that next to churches and cemeteries, war memorials are sites in the modern urban landscapes that claim to establish a timeless link between the living and the dead (2002: 287). Therefore, these are secular places, which are still embedded in the Christian-patriarchal tradition of religious institutions (Kattago, 2009: 152).

According to Koselleck, 'war memorials appearing in almost every community in Europe' exemplify the artificiality of a unified national memory that commemorates the individual death of an unknown (or even fictive) male white soldier. In his words, 'the only identity, which is conserved by war monuments is the identity of the dead with themselves' (2002: 289). Since their meaning cannot be automatically transmitted to new generations, these places of memory require constant resignifications. Otherwise, old and new victims remain invisible, while a nameless dead soldier continues to be commemorated in the city.

Koselleck's view of war monuments and memorials as sites of an artificial national memory challenges both the sacrality and the universality of heritage. Sites of heritage are epistemic spaces that forge and affirm an invented national identity worldwide. Yet their function of commemorating the past in the present, and in establishing a common and artificial culture of remembrance, is not free from violence. As Vergès describes in the postcolonial city, the heritage regime is manifested in the selective national memory that sacralises monuments without addressing their colonial legacy (2019: 13). Linking Koselleck's critique on monuments to the colonial history of the city allows mapping of the affective landscapes in a transnational manner. Thereby, the fragmentation of memory performed by the sites of heritage can be identified in modern urban planning of a city, which is always two: the 'native's town' or the medina, and the European settlers' city or 'the white city'. Framed within this racialised order – that is, in the continuity between the colonial cartography of the world fairs and the colour line in the city – the category of heritage converges with the colonial amnesia celebrating the racialisation of urban space.

The world on display in the city

Almost no other event brought together the European city and the colony in such a close manner as the world fairs did (Young, 2008: 339).[15] Their unique design caused a sort of 'joyful' state of emergency because the circulation within the city changed dramatically.[16] Blurring the frontiers between fiction and reality and reinventing urban space to the point that 'it was not always easy in Paris to tell where the exhibition ended, and the world itself began' (Mitchell, 1989: 224), these spectacles framed the narratives of national identity (Blanchard et al., 2001b). Moreover, the affective and virtual landscapes created for these monumental events, which took place in Paris between the nineteenth and twentieth centuries, were central in framing the national and global uses of heritage.

World fairs functioned as catalysers of rapid urban transformation, in which 'past and present mingled inextricably, and to each other's advantage' (Swenson, 2006: 1). Astrid Swenson (2006) describes the urban arrangement during the world fair in 1889 in the following manner: people could 'meander through the Rue des Nations along the Seine', where colonial powers had constructed 'pavilions in "national styles", be mesmerised by the reconstructions of the Vieux Paris and numerous rural idylls, or view the entire history of human housing in a single place'. In short, the world was on display at the city centre. In this intersection of past and future, and of the local and the global, the events deeply shaped the idea of cultural heritage. Exemplarily, in 1889, the Eiffel Tower was criticised as an enemy of the Parisian and French *patrimoine*. One year later, it was already considered national heritage.

Also called universal expositions, world fairs were major celebrations of imperial achievements (Regourd, 2008: 121), in which colonial violence was romanticised. At the world fair of 1889 that celebrated the centenary of the French Revolution, visitors could see war-horses at the esplanade des Invalides or immerse themselves in so-called 'ethnographic displays'. This section was composed of 'human exhibitions' of non-white people, mostly from the French colonies, who were turned into 'curiosities' and presented as objects of public attraction (Tran, 2007: 151). The 'exhibition sites' displaced Black and Indigenous people in fictive towns and cages for visual consumption by the white populations. The biggest site in this section was called the 'negro village', which was composed of four hundred Black persons (Young, 2008: 351). In this section, inhabitants from the French colonial West African territories, mostly from Senegal, were exhibited next to people from Cochinchine (southern Vietnam) and from New Caledonia (Young, 2008: 351). The racist exhibition and exotic promenade culminated with the night event known as the *Danse Canaque* (the Kanak dance) performed by dancers from the Dutch colony of Java (Young, 2008: 339).

Between the nineteenth and the twentieth centuries, Paris was regularly transformed into a plantation of colonial fantasies that produced racist stereotypes. Even after the first official abolition of slavery was signed in 1827, the celebrations of colonial expansionism and public exhibitions of wealth remained common cultural events (Blanchard et al., 2008: 5). Between 1877 and 1912, there were at least thirty human exhibitions in Paris alone (Blanchard et al., 2001b). Their magnitudes are proportionally comparable to today's mass tourism since around 30 million people travelled (without aeroplanes) to these places/events.[17] Pascal Blanchard (2006: 26) notes that human exhibitions were regularly held in zoological gardens, botanic gardens, museums and during public festivals. In this sense, even though no plaque, monument or street name provides a critical reminder of these colonial events, these marked the affective memory of the city and still determine the way in which we orient ourselves in it.

World fairs pursued the education and cultivation (*Bildung*) of the colonial society (Young, 2008: 340) by reframing the uses of *souvenir* (memory). The colonial design of world expositions and their dehumanising rituals known as 'human zoos' altered the conception of the city as a place of remembrance (Blanchard, 2006: 26). The universalist celebration, which was paradoxically used by the organising country for the deployment of nationalism, brought together geographies and worldviews that were in principle opposed. The exhibition was a microcosm of human experience in colonial contexts and a symbolic and temporary resolution of the contradictions between the universalism in French republicanism and the colonial essentialisation of differences (Tran, 2007: 147). The spatial grid dividing and ordering the pavilions of the French colonies allowed for the reappropriation of the metropolitan space presented in the unity of the French Empire (Tran, 2007: 149).

The pavilions devoted to European architecture, which included illustrations, pictures and drawings of representative monuments in selected cities, were built in opposition to the 'natural habitats' of the colonies. In this section, the glorification of the past was oriented towards the future. Experts and non-experts discussed the protection and restoration of selected buildings and planned urban projects. Visitors were informed about the visions for the city and the housing market, in a setting that has been described as 'propaganda' (Dumont, 1991: 108). These pavilions condensed the double endeavour of forging heritage and keeping a certain memory alive in the city (Koselleck, 2002: 291).

In one of these settings during the world exposition in 1889, congress member Jules Siegfried created the Société française des Habitations à Bon Marché (French Society for Affordable Residences; HBM). His aim was to solve the housing crisis that for over a century had been haunting the flourishing private housing market in Paris (Shapiro, 1982: 507). The buildings were planned as the biggest European urban project, which began one year later and was carried out without official competition until 1906 (Dumont, 1991: 151). The construction of several rows of tall buildings covering an area approximately ten miles long at the peripheral northern regions of the city was followed by the adaptation of further suburban areas into identical public housing projects, which were renamed in 1950 as *habitations à loyers modérés* (moderate rent residences; HLM) (APUR, 2017: 9).

The Parisian banlieues, which were the result of the HLM project, were planned according to a uniform and massive architecture. The homogeneous habitats, known as *Grands Ensembles*, were (and still are) characterised by the lack of individual and public space (Mancheno, 2011: 27). Moreover, their infrastructure was driven by a Fordist logic that privileged functionality over design and control over privacy and safety. This suburban territory precariously housed people who were marginalised from the city centre for reasons of religion, class and/or behaviour (Mancheno, 2011: 11). Among the structurally disadvantaged populations were members of European minorities such as Sinti, Romani (Picker, 2017: 30) and Jewish communities, as well as white workers, peasants or daily traders.[18] Land prices in St Denis were much lower than in the centre, yet the prices for basic needs such as food and transportation were much higher (Vieillard-Baron, 2016: 77).

In the twentieth century, the history of this particular urban complex experienced a radical transformation as immigrants from the French colonies and their descendants became the majority of the population (Mancheno, 2011: 25). The banlieues were reconceived as the temporary housing 'solution' to the 'colonial presence' (Blanchard, 2006: 29) of the second great migration movement from the French colonies to Paris, during which its population increased by almost 50 per cent (Shapiro, 2015: 42). This development suits Mbembe's observation that: 'Space became both a social and a racial relationship, one that was additionally inherent to the notion of property' (2004: 380). In other words, race was added as a category to the intersectional marginalisation of the banlieues' inhabitants.

In reference to Fanon, Léopold Lambert (2017) describes the fracture of the city embodied in the banlieues as the space outside the city walls, where 'the street formed by the newly built urbanism is organized to be penetrable to the various colonial policing forces, while inside, the social hierarchization and division between colonizers and colonized (servants, for instance), or between colonized male subjects and their female counterparts, is materialized through the apparatus of architecture'. The racialised spaces in the city are designed to control and to regulate the mobility of colonised peoples, as well as to prevent anti-colonial movements and possible insurrections (House, 2012: 78). As Fanon explains, both the 'native's town' and the suburb are 'caught in the conqueror's vise' (1965: 52). To get an idea of this power, it is necessary to investigate their common colonial geography: 'one must have in one's hands the plans according to which a colonial city has been laid out' (Fanon, 1965: 52) and compare the colonial strategies of the occupation forces.

The celebration of colonialism in the city during the world fairs and the 'postcolonial urban apartheid' (Tschukam, 2020: 103) that is established in the banlieues visualise the continuity of the colour line in the city: both are colonial devices that deal with the (post)colonial difference in the metropole. Whilst human exhibitions and the imperial arrangement of the pavilions transformed the city into the stage of colonial imagination, modern urban planning sedimented racialised segregation. In the banlieues, the coloniser's gaze still controls the movement of non-white and Black citizens. Hence, the banlieues are living archives of the way in which the presence of the postcolonial difference is spatially governed. Entangled with the history of human exhibitions, the Parisian banlieues are monuments of the tactics and the rigour with which (post)colonial populations are socially petrified. In Mbembe's words, this means that the national and global heritage that is condensed in these landscapes and simultaneously ignored by the official narratives nevertheless continues 'to determine today, if not the language of the city, then at least part of its unconscious' (2004: 375). The banlieues may be described as monuments of colonial amnesia, but also as catalysers of diasporic habitats and archipelagic urban historicities, which remain subterranean yet central for the localising of the coloniality of heritage that was planned and performed during the world fairs and is today inhabited in the banlieues.

From Paris to Rabat: intertwining coloniality and heritage

The racial division of the city that was planned during colonial world fairs and afterwards adapted to the planning of modern Paris was exported, during the twentieth century, to the French colonies. The Parisian planning of the port-cities Algiers and Rabat registers the entangled history among the three capitals. Used as a model for the colonial function of the urban space, the Parisian 'mimicry' created European quarters, in which colonial settlers 'did not experience a sense of having genuine ties with the world surrounding them' (Mbembe, 2004: 375–376). Moreover, this model framed a selective conservation and preservation of heritage in the colonies. The French endeavour of building an 'authentic' and civilised city – 'clean' of any tradition or premodern past – links the history of the cities, which were constructed after the destruction of the non-European urban space and the disassociation of the non-European from the urban space (Bonnett, 2002: 354). This travelling history illustrates the connection between colonialism and urban planning and allows for the countermapping of the category of heritage transnationally.

The European metropole and the north African capitals were modernising projects carried out through aggressive and invasive military tactics. Their large boulevards were designed to connect hospitals with casernes and to avoid barricades (Lambert, 2017). In Africa, the Parisian model was adapted in a process cynically called 'pacification' (Lambert, 2017). In Algiers, the lower parts of the Casbah were completely demolished. In an act of colonial commemoration, the remaining streets in the higher parts of the precolonial old city were renamed after French male figures (Lambert, 2017). The reconstruction followed the racist housing politics that were previously implemented in the metropole (Nightingale, 2012: 215).

Haussmann's architecture in the Parisian city centre was the outcome of the political denial of private and public financing to mixed social housing projects (Shapiro, 1982: 505). Since the uniform buildings were planned for housing an economically and culturally homogeneous community (Nightingale, 2012: 204–205), the city isolated whiteness.[19] In order to adapt this model in Morocco, the French architect Henry Prost was called to Rabat in 1912 by colonial officer Lyautey to build the white *villes nouvelles* (new neighbourhoods). Prost planed a *cordon sanitaire* (sanitary belt) separating the new neighbourhoods from the Medina (Nightingale, 2012: 25) and adapted Haussmann's discourses on hygiene to carry out expropriations (Nightingale, 2012: 205). The 'white fear' manifested towards the density and pollution in indigenous settlements provided French colonialists with boundless support for the implementation of segregating, authoritarian and sanitary measures that culminated in a divided city, which Janet Abu-Lughod (2014: 275) describes as an 'apartheid model'. By the beginning of the twentieth century, the 'ethnic segregation' expressed in a white city centre and its non-white banlieues was common to Paris (Mancheno, 2011: 37), Algiers and Rabat (Picker, 2017: 24–25). In short, the Haussmannian facades that in the metropole hosted the world exposition also isolated white colonial settlers from indigenous populations (Picker, 2017: 205).

French authorities justified forced displacements and ghettoisation by claiming that indigenous peoples could not take care of their city and, therefore, were unable to preserve their own history. However, the destruction of the Casbah (Algiers) and the Medina (Rabat) was followed by the endeavour to 'protect' what was left (Picker, 2017: xvii). The conservation of the old city became a French priority. This 'new mission', which was defined in terms of 'historical preservation' (Nightingale, 2012: 215), reframed the colonial occupation of the city as the benevolent impulse to 'protect' urban heritage.

Whilst the precarity of 'native' neighbourhoods was explained through a supposedly 'natural lack of civility' among the inhabitants (Picker, 2017: 24), the cultural richness of the old city had to be protected from them, and for the sake of history. In 1913, Lyautey stated: 'The problem we envisage is to let modern civilization with all its progress and economic exploitation penetrate, while preserving what … is of the greater interest' (in Picker, 2017: 24).

In the colonial uses of urban space, heritage is detached from Indigeneity, Blackness and the non-European. In other words, heritage is ascribed to the creation of white spaces. Heritage becomes a privilege for the exclusive usage of white settlers, who are entitled to take care of its historical signifi-cance. In this racialised arrangement, heritage is defined in opposition to the 'native's village' – a space found in the world fairs, in the planning of Algiers and Rabat, as well as in the Parisian banlieues. The police who keep non-white bodies in *their* marginal place and punish unexpected transgressions of the highly organised compartments also maintain the urban/ontological order, i.e. the colour line separating the racialised zones (Fanon, 1963: 38). In short, the police 'protect' the segregation (Fanon, 1963: 54).

The coloniality of the heritage regime links the politics of selective memory already performed during the world fairs to the racialisation of the space at 'the other side of the city-walls' (Morestin, 1950: 68). Crystallised in the strategies of surveillance and authoritarian measures for controlling and restricting the mobility of racialised bodies, the colonial uses of urban space reproduce an order in which the police builds the frontier between the citizens and the *Indigènes*. This order creates an affective geography that isolates heritage from the 'native's village' or the territoriality associated with a 'legal exception', in which the experience of sub-citizenship is the rule (Iveković, 2006: 67–68). This inhabited experience is articulated in the regular controls of identity or checkpoints that take place in these 'zones of exception'. The violent displacement and silencing, i.e. the 'so-called "pacification", and then counter-insurrection' (Lambert, 2017) are among those colonial tactics that continuously 'turn demands into mere noises' (Dikeç, 2002: 93). These tactics also limit access to indigenous (urban and suburban) histories.

Throughout the twentieth and twenty-first centuries, members of the French government have accused young, male, non-white citizens who live in the banlieues of causing barbaric violence by using pejorative analogies and zoological concepts (Tschukam, 2020: 101), thereby, as Fanon (1963: 41) notes, reinforcing the racialisation of the urban space. During urban protests in response to police brutality in Seine-Saint-Denis,[20] non-white masculinities have been regularly condemned as dangerous and incapable of protecting the city (Mancheno, 2011: 37). Political discourses, which suggest that racialised minorities cannot inhabit the city in a civil manner, justify the constant police presence in neighbourhoods characterised by 'high-density housing within a low-density urban fabric' (Lambert, 2017). As Vergès points out, colonial amnesia legitimises the exclusion and persecu-tion of 'foreign bodies' (2013: 2).

Within this transcontinental history of urban and ontological segregation, the Parisian banlieues are archives of French colonial history and sites of urban heritage from which the politics of selective memory, together with the frontiers of citizenship, are continuously retraced and contested. The banlieues, as a place from which demands of historical reparation are literarily raised to the centre, are a site from which to write another history of Paris and a decolonial history of the city.

Mapping the decolonial margins of global heritage

The travelling history of heritage has been attached to white spaces, from the world fairs' pavilions to the selected areas in the Casbah of Algiers and the Medina of Rabat that are today protected by UNESCO.[21] This selective memory, or colonial amnesia, deepens the wounds of the racialised city. In other words, the world heritage regime reinforces the politics that keep alive the colonial uses of the urban space because it omits the history that transgresses the site's locality. The postcolonial strategy that memorialises historical monuments while ignoring their historical context suits Koselleck's description of heritage as the preservation of an artificial and fragmented memory. In a similar view, Vergès notes that 'it is necessary to retrace new cartographies and to interrogate the role of memory as a social practice' (2013: 5; own translation). Otherwise, used as a historical compass for creating sacral areas, the UNESCOisation of heritage continues to honour the beneficiaries of colonialism and to omit the victims. This violent form of commemoration, which reinforces the opposition between memory and history (Vergès, 2013: 10), also justifies the apparent irreconcilability between national heritage and the banlieues. Through the selective politics of memory, the Parisian banlieues are associated with 'lawless zones' (Tschukam, 2020: 107).

The colonial violence in urban planning fractures the city into antagonistic compartments that are ideal-typically 'characterized by the contrast between the grim slave-quarters and the elegant houses of the slave traders' (UNESCO, 2020b).[22] This design does not serve 'as a reminder of human exploitation and as a sanctuary for reconciliation' (UNESCO, 2020b), but rather as a memorial site of the economy of exploitation, extraction and exhaustion (Vergès, 2019: 13). The rebranding of colonial landscapes as touristic sites detaches heritage and the politics of memory from their colonial legacy. Moreover, the heritage regime reinforces the racial frontiers in the city precisely by redefining sites of heritage as the property of humanity.

World heritage sites selected by UNESCO, such as the Eiffel Tower, the Notre Dame Cathedral[23] – a deeply Christian icon that is currently being reconstructed in a secular republic – as well as the selected sites in the Casbah and the Medina, are historical monuments of the selective politics of memory, in which heritage is detached from the inherited responsibility in altering the coloniality in the urban landscapes. As Vergès suggests, the fracture in the conception of heritage illustrates that 'while the condemnation of slavery causes no problem, the comprehension of this phenomenon remains challenging' (2019: 4; own translation).

On the contrary, the recognition of the banlieues as places of colonial memory takes into consideration the merging of official memory with the living archives of the French citizens of African heritage who inhabit these places (Vergès, 2019). The value of places of memory for our present, such as the Parisian colonial landscapes, resides in the fact that these are registers of the inheritance of colonialism and of immigration as a lived experience. This reorientation of the meaning of heritage resignifies the shared history in opposition to the national narrative and positions the banlieues as landscapes of transcontinental living memory. From this perspective, urban violence ceases to be understood as a disturbance to the civil order and instead becomes an expression of grief at the coloniality of the city and at its postcolonial frontiers of citizenship, memory and national identity.

Conclusions

Reconstructing the category of heritage through its circulation and migration within French transcontinental geographies, in this chapter I have sought to countermap the colonial amnesia in the Parisian landscapes. I have suggested that the world fairs and the banlieues are components of the Parisian landscapes and sites of urban history, which are entangled with urban planning in the French colonies. I have attempted to link the urbanisation of the South (colonised world) with the creation of urban heritage in the North (colonial world), and so to trace a transversal politics of remembrance and colonial amnesia in the public space. I have thereby suggested that an analysis of the colonial frontiers established in the city since the nineteenth century offers a transcontinental approach to urban history, but also that the critical reconstruction of ritualised events of colonial violence in the city allows the transgression of its racialised order. The histori-city becomes a junction of narratives which, while explaining the textuality of urban landscapes, also contests the universal definition of heritage and therefore the white order of the city.

A global heritage from below entangles urban history with colonial history, i.e. with the ontological distortion caused by the colour line in the city, and it emphasises the requirement that the histories of its transgressions circulate beyond the native's villages. This reorientation allows us to deal with heritage through a 'glocal' approach and to write a decolonial urban history from the city's margins. The colonial events and postcolonial places of memory that compose the landscapes of Paris allow mapping of the colonial administration and policing of life in the city and, thereby, they unveil the subterranean but transcontinental landscapes of colonial heritage. This countermapping replaces the homogeneity of memory condensed in sites of heritage with the spatial/racial divisions of humanity, which are (in) visible in the city.

Notes

1 In the German context (where I am based), the term has been coined by Jürgen Zimmerer (2013). In the French, I identify an equivalent of this term in Françoise Vergès' 'politics of forgetfulness' (2018) and Achille Mbembe's uses of the surgical metaphor of an 'ablation of French [imperial, TM] history' (2006: 24) for referring to the absence and estrangement of the colonies in French national history. See also Ann Stoler, who notes that 'French colonialism ... has been assiduously circumvented, systematically excluded from the pedagogic map' (2011: 230).

2 The latest critique of the European postcolonial museological regime is articulated in the report prepared for the French government by Felwine Sarr and Bénédicte Savoy (2018), in which they emphasise the feasible restitution of art objects in possession of French museums to African countries.

3 The UNESCO Convention of 1972, which established the 'Recommendation concerning the Protection, at National Level, of the Cultural and Natural Heritage', was signed in Paris.

4 My understanding of countermapping is inspired by Léopold Lambert's decolonial urban analysis of Paris disseminated in the journal *The Funambulist*. Fanon's critical lens is central to Lambert's contributions and to my analysis of this city in this chapter and in my previous article (Mancheno, 2019).

5 The first Parisian banlieues were built in the northern region of Île-de-France, at the *département* Saint Denis. I focus my research on this municipality, which is central to the history of labour, so as to trace the entanglements between modern urban planning and colonialism. Note for example the travelling history of the Christian name St Denis from France to Algeria, then to Martinique and back to France.

6 See also Noa Ha (2017), Grada Kilomba (2016) and the mapping of the diasporic/urban art industries in Fatima El-Tayeb's work (2014).

7 I use this term, which was coined by W. E. B. Du Bois in the nineteenth century in his book *The Philadelphia Negro* (1899), to a Fanonian analysis of urban space.

8 To name just a few Black activists, artists and intellectuals who should be commemorated in Paris: Josephine Baker, W. E. B. Du Bois, Léopold Sédar Senghor and Alioune Diop. For a short description of their presence in Paris see Blanchard et al. (2001a).

9 Solely one passage in the whole city centre is named after an anti-colonial hero: Louis Delgrès, who fought against Napoleon's reinstitution of slavery in Martinique. I am thankful to the Haitian historian Jean Waddimir Gustinvil for this observation.

10 Field notes were gathered in the Parisian metro (northern region) from 2014 to 2015 and again in 2019. For a reconstruction of the contemporary demographic constitution of French society, see the introduction to the edited volume *Paris-Noir* (Blanchard et al., 2001a), which explains that already throughout the twentieth century, two out of ten citizens were considered Afro-descendant.

11 I use this term in relation to the decolonial feminist Houria Bouteldja (2016), co-founding member of the French political party Indigènes de la République. In the French context, Indigenous does not make reference to First Nations, but it rather refers to the colonial history of this name. *Indigènes* are French citizens and undocumented inhabitants of France, who identified themselves as descendants from colonialism (in opposition to the designation of immigrants). Following Fanon, Bouteldja (2016: 117–118) uses the name *Indigènes* as a political positioning of non-white people in the postcolonial metropole.

12 It is worth noting that Fanon's description of Fort de France coincides with the urban arrangement in a central Parisian neighborhood: the Shoah monument (originally highly controversial among Jewish minorities for being a martyr monument) was built in front of the Hôtel de Ville. The difference lies in the uses of the space in between the buildings. While in Paris there are streets, houses and the church Saint-Gérvais, in Fort de France, Fanon's description of 'three or four hundred' Black young men 'walking up and down, greeting one another, grouping – no, they never form groups, they go on walking' on 'a miserable tract of uneven cobbles, pebbles that roll away under one's feet' (2008: 14) recalls both the anonymity of the city and the impossibility of creating community among enslaved Black men in the plantation.

13 Fanon's analysis of the journey from the colony to the colonial metropole is an autobiographic introspection and a source of insights on his psychiatric theories on the psyche and body of the colonised.

14 Following the tradition of the Enlightenment, Koselleck dates modernity to 1780, but decolonial thinking contests this view by dating modernity back to 1492 (Quijano, 2000: 574).

15 According to Fanon (2008: 15), the social composition of the French military in colonial times created a similar proximity between colonisers and colonised.

16 For example, in 1889, fifty Egyptian drivers of donkeys came to Paris with their animals to be part of the 'Egyptian exhibit', which was organised by French Orientalists (Mitchell, 1989: 217).

17 The Paris Exhibition attracted an average of 175,000 visitors per day (Young, 2008: 341). Solely during the first six months of the colonial exposition of 1931, 33 million tickets were sold (Blanchard, 2006: 29). In 1900, 50 million people attended the event (Blanchard et al., 2001b).

18 In 1568 the census counted fifty habitations only in the suburb Saint Ouen, which is located next to Saint Denis; in 1717 there were 122 habitations and in 1921 the census counted 2,800 habitants (Derainne, 2012).

19 Haussmann's buildings brought different classes under a single roof, however, following the 'logics' of eugenics, in which differentiated spaces of intimacy and privacy responded to a social model of racialised necessities. He built more

than 100,000 rooms for domestic servants across the inner city. The so-called *chambres de bonne* (maids' rooms) had neither bathrooms nor running water and were as tiny as 85 square feet (O'Sullivan, 2020).

20 From the 1980s onwards, there have been protests in this Parisian department, the latest being in April 2020. The unemployment rate is more than double the national average and more than one in three inhabitants between 15 and 24 years old are unemployed (Morrow, 2020). For a deeper analysis of the so-called riots see Mancheno (2011; 2019).

21 The selected zones are briefly described in the articles 'Kasbah of Algiers' (inscription in 1992) and 'Rabat, Modern Capital and Historic City: a Shared Heritage' (inscription in 2012) at the UNESCO's official site (https://whc.unesco.org). None of the articles mentions the colonial occupation and the history of the cities.

22 Quoted from the UNESCO description of the island Gorée as a site of World Heritage. Lying on Senegal's coast, opposite Dakar, Gorée was from the fifteenth to the nineteenth century the largest deportation centre on the African coast. Yet the official description euphemistically notes that it was '[r]uled [sic!] in succession by the Portuguese, Dutch, English and French' (UNESCO, 2020b).

23 For a comparison of these two Parisian symbols see Young (2008).

References

Abu-Lughod, J. (2014), *Rabat. Urban Apartheid in Morocco* (Princeton, NJ: Princeton University Press).

Atelier Parisien d'urbanisme (APUR) (2017), *Les Habitations à Bon Marché de la ceinture de Paris: étude historique* (Paris: APUR).

Bendix, R., A. Eggert and A. Peselmann (eds) (2012), *Heritage Regimes and the State* (Göttingen: Göttingen University Press).

Berliner, D. (2012), The politics of loss and nostalgia in Luang Prabang (Lao PDR). In Daly, P. and T. Winter (eds) *Routledge Handbook of Heritage in Asia* (New York: Routledge), pp. 234–246.

Blanchard, P. (2006), L'exposition coloniale, lieu de mémoire du XX siècle. In Mairie de Paris (eds) *75 ans après, regards sur l'exposition coloniale de 1931*. Programme de Manifestations. L'exposition coloniale (Paris: Mairie de Paris), pp. 25–36.

Blanchard, P., E. Deroo and G. Manceron (eds) (2001a), *Paris-Noir. Présence afro-antillaise dans la capitale* (Paris: Hazan).

Blanchard, P., N. Bancel and S. Lemaire (eds) (2001b), From human zoos to colonial apotheoses: the era of exhibiting the Other. *Journal Africultures* 43, www.ces.uc.pt/formacao/materiais_racismo_pos_racismo/From_human_zoos_to_colonial_apotheoses_the_era_of_exhibiting_the_Other.htm [accessed 20 April 2021].

Blanchard, P., N. Bancel, G. Boëtsch, E. Deroo, S. Lemaire and C. Forsdick (eds) (2008), *Human Zoos: Science and Spectacle in the Age of Colonial Empires* (Liverpool: Liverpool University Press).

Bonnett, A. (2002), The metropolis and white modernity. *Ethnicities* 2(3): 349–366.

Bouteldja, H. (2016), *Les Blancs, les Juifs et nous: vers une politique de l'amour révolutionnaire* (Paris: La Fabrique).

Derainne, P. (2012), *Le Vieux-Saint-Ouen. Du village au quartier* (Paris: Archives municipales de Saint-Ouen), www.saint-ouen.fr/fileadmin/user_upload/fichiers/SIP/Culture_et_patrimoine/Histoire_Patrimoine/livret-quartiers-Vieux-Saint-Ouen.pdf [accessed 20 April 2021].

Dikeç, M. (2002), Police, politics, and the right to the city. *GeoJournal* 58: 91–98.

Du Bois, W. E. B. (1899), *The Philadelphia Negro* (New York: Schocken).

Dumont, M. (1991), *Le Logement social à Paris. 1850–1930; les habitations à bon marché* (Liège: Mardaga).

El-Tayeb, F. (2014), Creolizing Europe. *Manifesta Journal around Curatorial Practices* 17: *Future(s) of Cohabitation*: 9–12.

Fanon, F. (1963), *The Wretched of the Earth* (New York: Grove Weidenfeld).

Fanon, F. (1965), *A Dying Colonialism* (New York: Groove Press).

Fanon, F. (2008), *Black Skin, White Masks* (Sidmouth: Pluto Press).

Grosfoguel, R. (2017), Was ist Rassismus? Die 'Zone des Seins' und die Zone des 'Nicht-Seins' in den Werken von Frantz Fanon und Boaventura de Sousa Santos. In Zwischenraum Kollektiv (eds) *Decolonize the City! Zur Kolonialität der Stadt* (Münster: Unrast), pp. 56–74.

Ha, N. K. (2017), Zur Kolonialität des Städtischen. In Zwischenraum Kollektiv (ed.) *Decolonize the City! Zur Kolonialität der Stadt* (Münster: Unrast), pp. 75–87.

House, J. (2012), L'impossible contrôle d'une ville colonial? Casablanca, décémbre 1952. *Genèses* 1: 78–103.

Iveković R. (2006), Le retour du politique oublié par les banlieues. *Lignes* 1(19): 64–88.

Kattago, S. (2009), War memorials and the politics of memory: the Soviet war memorial in Tallinn. *Constellations* 16(1): 149–165.

Keaton, D., D. Sharpley-Whiting and T. Stovall (eds) (2012), *Black France/France Noir. The History and Politics of Blackness* (Durham, NC: Duke University Press).

Kilomba, G. (2016), *Plantation Memories. Episodes of Everyday Racism* (Münster: Unrast).

Kipfer, S. (2007), Fanon and space: colonization, urbanization, and liberation from the colonial to the global city. *Society and Space* 25: 701–726.

Koselleck, R. (2002), War memorials: identity formations of the survivors. In *The Practice of Conceptual History. Timing History, Spacing Concepts* (Stanford, CA: Stanford University Press), pp. 285–326.

Koselleck, R. (2010), *Vom Sinn und Unsinn der Geschichte* (Berlin: Suhrkamp).

Lambert, L. (2017), Colonialism as a continuous process, architecture as a spatial apparatus. *The Funambulist: Politics of Space and Body* 1(10), https://archinect.com/features/article/149994523/uncovering-the-architecture-of-colonialism-with-the-funambulist [accessed 21 April 2021].

Mancheno, T. (2011), *Raum und Gewalt: Eine Geo-Ethnologische Analyse über die Pariser Banlieues*. Working Paper No. 2 (Hamburg: Institute of Political Sciences, University of Hamburg).

Mancheno, T. (2019), Behind the walls of Paris: the inhabited history of the space in the Parisian banlieues. In Varela, M. and B. Ülker (eds) *Doing Tolerance. Democracy, Citizenship and Social Protests* (Leverkusen: Barbara Budrich), pp. 115–135.

Mbembe, A. (2004), Aesthetics of superfluity. *Public Culture* 16(3): 373–405.

Mbembe, A. (2006), L'histoire de la France et de son empire reste à écrire. In Blanchard, P. et al. (eds) *75 ans après, regards sur l'exposition coloniale de 1931. Programme de Manifestations. L'exposition coloniale* (Paris: Mairie de Paris), p. 24.

Mbembe, A. (2016), *Politiques de l'inimitié* (Paris: La découverte).

Mitchell, T. (1989), The world as exhibition. *Comparative Studies in Society and History* 31(2): 217–236.

Morestin, H. (1950), Les faubourgs indigènes de Rabat. *Les Cahiers d'Outre Mer* 3(9): 66–79.

Morrow, W. (2020), Unrest spreads in France in response to police brutality. *World Socialist* (23 April), www.wsws.org/en/articles/2020/04/23/unre-a23.html [accessed 23 April 2020].

Natarajan, N. (2005), Fanon as 'metrocolonial' flaneur in the Caribbean post-plantation/Algerian colonial city. In Isfahani-Hammond, A. (ed.) *The Masters and the Slaves. New Directions in Latino American Cultures* (New York: Palgrave Macmillan), pp. 89–102.

Nightingale, C. H. (2012), *Segregation: A Global History of Divided Cities* (Chicago, IL: University of Chicago Press).

O'Sullivan, F. (2020), Before Paris's modern-day studios, there were chambres de bonne. *Bloomberg CityLab* (16 January), www.bloomberg.com/news/articles/2020-01-16/the-history-of-paris-s-chambres-de-bonne [accessed 20 April 2021].

Picker, G. (2017), *Racial Cities: Governance and the Segregation of Romani People in Urban Europe* (London: Routledge).

Quijano, A. (2000), Coloniality of power, Eurocentrism, and Latin America. *Nepantla: Views from South* 1(3): 533–580.

Regourd, F. (2008), Capitale savante, capitale coloniale: sciences et savoirs coloniaux à Paris aux XVIIe et XVIIIe siècles. *Revue d'histoire moderne & contemporaine* 55–2(2): 121–151.

Rico, T. (2008), Negative heritage: the place of conflict in world heritage. *Conservation and Management of Archaeological Sites* 10(4): 344–352. DOI: 10.117 9/135050308X12513845914507 [accessed 20 April 2021].

Sarr, F. and Savoy, B. (2018), *Rapport sur la restitution du patrimoine culturel africain. Vers une nouvelle éthique relationnelle*, www.loniya.org/achat/livre/62 [accessed 20 April 2021].

Shapiro, A. (1982), Housing reform in Paris: social space and social control. *French Historical Studies* 12(4): 486–507.

Shapiro, A. (2015), Paris. In Daunton, M. J. (ed.) *Housing the Workers, 1850–1914: A Comparative Perspective* (London: Bloomsbury), pp. 33–66.

Stoler, A. (2011), Colonial aphasia: race and disabled histories in France. *Public Culture* 23(1): 121–156.

Swenson, A. (2006), 'Heritage' on display: exhibitions and congresses for the protection of ancient monuments at the world's fairs 1855–1915. In O'Carroll, E. (ed.)

Reflections (Vienna: IWM Junior Visiting Fellows' Conferences 19), www.iwm.at/publications/5-junior-visiting-fellows-conferences/vol-xix/astrid-swenson/#text10 [accessed 20 April 2020].

Tran, V. T. (2007), L'éphémère dans l'éphémère: la domestication des colonies à l'Exposition universelle de 1889. *Ethnologies* 29(1–2): 143–169. DOI: https://doi.org/10.7202/01874ar [accessed 27 April 2021].

Tschukam, H. (2020), Banlieues. In Achille, E., C. Forsdick and L. Moudileno (eds) *Postcolonial Realms of Memory: Sites and Symbols in Modern France* (Liverpool: Liverpool University Press), pp. 101–108.

UNESCO (1972), *Recommendation Concerning the Protection, at National Level, of the Cultural and Natural Heritage*, http://portal.unesco.org [accessed 20 April 2020].

UNESCO (2020a), *Paris, rives de la Seine*, https://whc.unesco.org/fr/list/600 [accessed 21 April 2021].

UNESCO (2020b), *Island of Gorée*, https://whc.unesco.org/en/list/26 [accessed 20 April 2021].

Vergès, F. (2013), Mémoires et patrimoines vivants de la traite négrière et l'esclavage. *In Situ* 20: 1–13. DOI: 10.4000/insitu.10265 [accessed 20 April 2021].

Vergès, F. (2018), Politics of forgetfulness. Conference at Transmediale [online], https://transmediale.de/program/event/politics-of-forgetfulness [accessed 20 April 2021].

Vergès, F. (2019), Capitalocene, waste, race, and gender. *E-fluxjournal* 100: 1–13, www.e-flux.com/journal/100/269165/capitalocene-waste-race-and-gender/ [accessed 10 May 2020].

Vieillard-Baron, H. (2016), Die Geschichte der Banlieues in Frankreich. Von der Mehrdeutigkeit der Definitionen zu den heutigen Besonderheiten. In Weber, F. and O. Kühne (eds) *Fraktale Metropolen, Hybride Metropole* (Wiesbaden: Springer), pp. 75–90.

Young, P. (2008), From the Eiffel Tower to the Javanese Dancer: envisioning cultural globalization at the 1889 Paris Exhibition. *The History Teacher* 41(3): 339–362.

Zimmerer, J. (2013), Kolonialismus und kollektive Identität: Erinnerungsorte der deutschen Kolonialgeschichte. In Zimmerer, J. (ed.) *Kein Platz an der Sonne. Erinnerungsorte der deutschen Kolonialgeschichte* (Frankfurt am Main: Campus-Verlag), pp. 9–38.

3

Provincialising industry: hyperreal urban modernity in nineteenth-century Buenos Aires

Antonio Carbone

This chapter discusses the ideological nexus of industrialisation and urbanisation with modernity through the analysis of debates among elites in the 1860s and 1870s in Buenos Aires. It scrutinises a pivotal controversy concerning industry that occurred on the occasion of a series of cholera and yellow fever outbreaks that dramatically hit Buenos Aires between the late 1860s and the beginning of the 1870s. These epidemics triggered a debate on the presence in the city of meat-salting factories, which represented the most important economic branch but were also considered among the possible causes of disease. As the chapter shows, by discussing these meat factories, elites of mid-nineteenth-century postcolonial Buenos Aires debated more generally the role of industry in cities and its connection with imaginaries of urban modernity, especially as it was articulated through the opposition of progress and backwardness. The analysis of this discussion provides indications of how, in the second half of the nineteenth century, white Latin American settler-colonial urban elites conceived of urbanisation and indus-trialisation, two phenomena that historiography has traditionally deemed core elements of European urban modernity.

Contributing to an 'entangled history of uneven modernities' (Randeria, 2002), this chapter aims at combining insights from postcolonial studies and global history with dependency theory (Kapoor, 2002). Deconstructing dependency theory's inclination to consider Latin American elites as entirely subjugated to European and North American imperialism, this analysis underlines their ambivalent position vis-à-vis the discourses of European modernity. The chapter emphasises the independent agency of Buenos Aires' elites, whose desires and projects were deeply rooted in the local context. At the same time drawing inspiration from dependency theory, the chapter highlights how, with regard to the idea of urban modernity, the imagination of Buenos Aires' elites nevertheless developed within the constraints of the symbolic hegemony of what I designate a 'hyperreal' European urban modernity. By focusing on the specific case of industry, the chapter shows both the locally rooted character and the Eurocentrism of the desires that local elites had for their city. With the intent of *provincialising European cities*, the chapter shows the ambiguous and non-linear character of Eurocentrism and questions one of the arguably main features of the Eurocentric discourse of urban modernity, the nexus of industrialisation and urbanisation.

In the first part of the chapter, I analyse how urban historians have conceived of the role of industry in nineteenth-century urbanisation. This first part does not provide a comprehensive overview of an otherwise gigantic corpus of literature but rather reconstructs episodically some major post-1945 positions concerning the connection between industry and the rise of 'modern' urbanism. This section focuses on how historiographic positions on the correlation between industry and urbanism have changed in response to impulses coming from different theoretical and historiographic approaches, such as world-systems and dependency theory as well as postcolonial studies and global history. In a second step, I reconstruct the discussion that occurred in Buenos Aires between the mid-1860s and 1871, when cholera and yellow fever hit the city and literally decimated the population. Beyond the historiographic analysis carried out in the first part of the chapter, this second part aims at conveying the nineteenth-century actors' perspective on the question of industry and urban modernity. Through the analysis of different positions in this debate, I identify how *porteños* – as the inhabitants of Buenos Aires are called – referred to industry and in which ways these references were connected to European cities and to multiple, partially conflicting imaginaries of urban modernity. In a final step, combining the results from the two preceding parts, I suggest a critical perspective on the connection between industrialisation and urban modernity, which mainly rests on the idea of modernity as an uneven and entangled history.

Industry and urban modernity: episodes of historiography on cities

Throughout the second half of the twentieth century, some of the strongest voices among urban historians, irrespective of their ideological positioning, deemed nineteenth-century industrialisation and urbanisation to be inextricably intertwined. For instance, Lewis Mumford, the controversial stepfather of anglophone urban history, borrowing the expression from Charles Dickens's *Hard Times*, named the nineteenth-century city 'Coketown' (Mumford, 1961). He argued that: 'up to the nineteenth century, there had been a rough balance of activities within the city' and that 'the change from ... urban handicraft to large scale factory production transformed the cities into dark hives' (Mumford, 1961: 446). Besides Mumford, the intellectual tradition equating nineteenth-century city and industry has a major initiator in Friedrich

Engels, who in *The Condition of the Working Class in England* diagnosed a structural correlation between the birth of the proletariat, the modern city and industrial capitalism (Engels, 2009 [1891]). Apart from having progenitors rooted both in the liberal and in the Marxist traditions, the equation of industry and the modern city has had numerous descendants. For instance, in 1985 the influential *The Making of Urban Europe* by Lynn H. Lees and Paul Hohenberg proposed a periodisation of urban Europe entirely revolving around industrialisation. Even though in this case the hellish imaginary of Mumford's 'Coketown' gave way to a fascinating social historical analysis, the authors situated industry as the defining feature in the history of European urbanism. Engendering a proper teleology of industry, Lees and Hohenberg not only described nineteenth-century cities as industrial, but also proposed a periodisation of European urbanism from the eleventh to the twentieth century divided into three phases: preindustrial, protoindustrial and properly industrial (Hohenberg and L. Lees, 1985).

Apart from producing an equation between industry and the modern city, these historiographic examples also share in an attempt to abstract from single cities and postulate a universalised concept of 'City.' This effort to narrate the history of the 'City' is certainly part of urban history's constitutive attempt to overcome the fragmentation and compartmentalisation of local urban biographies (Ewen, 2016; Jansen, 1996). However, this effort tends to create, as in the case of Mumford but also more recently in *The City: A World History* by Andrew Lees, a narrative that downplays the contemporaneity of different kinds of cities, thus preferring a diachronic comparison of universal 'model cities' (A. Lees, 2015; Mumford, 1961). If Mumford imagines the city of the nineteenth century as 'Coketown,' Lees sees urban history as a temporal succession of urban models functioning as universal 'leader of urban life' of a certain epoch (A. Lees, 2015: 19). This principle entails the imposition of a single or a few urban models on the entirety of Europe – in the case of Lynn H. Lees's work with Hohenberg – or even on the whole world – in the case of Andrew Lees's study. This involves the problematic tendency of abstracting from the specificity of the historical experiences of a few cities – such as the industrial cities – and transforming them into a universal yardstick of comparison for cities across the world. Concerning the nineteenth century, if London and Paris, for instance, are taken as examples of a universal model of urban modernity, as Jennifer Robinson denounces in *Ordinary Cities*, then the history of all other cities cannot but be produced as a history of lack compared with these allegedly universal models (Robinson, 2006).

A chronologically parallel but nonetheless different intellectual tradition in urban history has attempted to solve the problematic tension between the singularity of specific cities and the universality of urban history through the construction of urban typologies. Examples of this typological urban history are conceptualisations that contrast, for instance, the industrial city with the capital or the port city. In this case, the industrial city is not considered as a universal epochal model for the nineteenth century but rather one among several possible urban typologies. Social urban historians such as H. J. Dyos and Asa Briggs were pioneers in the practice of this typological urban history. For instance, in *Victorian Cities* Briggs theorised different urban typologies, which allowed a comparison of contemporary cities across space. He thus compared various urban centres and highlighted different typologies of cities and urban growth in the British empire (Briggs, 1993 [1963]). This typological tradition has helped increase the attention given to the simultaneity of multiple and diverse processes of urbanisation and to the vast range of different kinds of cities around the world, without, however, preventing comparisons between them.

The typological approach not only offers the possibility of conceiving functional typologies – such as the industrial or the port city – but also enables the imagination of, for instance, regional categories, such as the Latin American or the European city. Concerning the Latin American case, Jorge E. Hardoy, one of the pioneers in Latin American urban history, put forward the Latin American city as a regional typology (Morse and Hardoy, 1992). Generally, as in any typological system, the construction of types is based on a scheme of comparisons. Thus, the Latin American typology derives from the implicit or explicit contrast with, for instance, the North American or the European city. Concerning the issue of industrialisation and urbanisation, Hardoy stated that 'most Latin American cities, including most capital cities, are not industrial cities' (Morse and Hardoy, 1992: xiv). However, as Richard Morse added in the same book, the comparison between different typologies does not exclude the possibility that different types of cities could influence each other. In fact, he argued that, even though most Latin American cities were not industrial, the 'U.S. city (and by extension the city of the industrial West) ... [was] once a model for emulation in Latin America' (Morse, 1992: 4; 1975). In spite of being a merely comparative model that risks compartmentalising the objects of comparison, Richard Morse underlined that the city of the 'industrial West' had been an influential model for urban administrators and scholars in Latin America.

Morse and Hardoy's arguments echoed the theses that the emergence of dependency and world-system theory from the 1960s had strongly brought into the Humanities and the Social Sciences, especially for Latin American intellectuals (Almandoz Marte, 2008: 163–168). A group of scholars including Manuel Castells, Martha Schteingart, Aníbal Quijano and the aforementioned Jorge Hardoy published in 1973 two edited volumes that articulated Latin American urban history within the framework of dependency theory (Castells,

1973; Schteingart, 1973). In the volume *Imperialismo y urbanización en América Latina*, edited by Castells, the argumentative thread of most contributions consists of the idea of Latin American cities as the result of 'dependent urbanisation'. This narrative presents a central difference from the typological approach as practised by Dyos and Briggs. In the context of 'dependent urbanisation', the conceptual tension between individual cities and universal urban history is reconciled by conceiving of cities as epiphenomena of wider world-spanning phenomena, namely industrial capitalism and imperialism. Industry plays a central role in this narrative: urban history shaped by dependency theory sees the development of an industrial 'core' in the North Atlantic region as inextricably tied to the creation of a proto-industrial 'periphery' in the rest of the world. According to this framework, Latin American cities could never develop an urban industrial modernity because European and US imperialism had determined another role for them. This narrative has two major consequences concerning the correlation of industrialisation and urbanisation. Firstly, scholarship inspired by dependency theory tends to go beyond the compartmentalisation that comparisons and typologies potentially imply – in fact, it is inclined to think of the emergence of 'dependent urbanism' as a constitutive condition for the simultaneous rise of industrial cities in the imperial centres. Secondly, urban historians inspired by dependency theory nevertheless conceive of the industrial city as a universal yardstick that 'dependent' cities cannot achieve because they are pushed by the interplay of capitalism and imperialism into a position of subalternity.

Dependency and world-systems theory were pivotal in introducing the idea that constitutive connectivity was the central element in the history of modern cities and more generally of the modern past. Comparisons tend to compartmentalise the objects of comparison, whereas, in the case of cities, these objects deeply influenced each other. 'Dependent urbanisation' was the outcome of globally asymmetric power relations that saw the hegemony of industrial cities, located in the imperial core, as the cause constraining urban centres of the 'periphery' to lag. From the 1980s post-colonial studies have attempted to elaborate the intricacies of the connectivity initially highlighted by dependency theorists. Inspired by poststructuralism and the linguistic turn, postcolonial scholars have focused on discourse and representation rather than on what they perceived as a tendency to 'econ-omicist' reductionism in dependency theory (Chakrabarty, 2000; Kapoor, 2002). The outcome of their scholarship is a complex and multi-dimensional nuancing of the asymmetries in power relations between different centres of the world and an attempt at deconstructing the Eurocentrism that stood invariantly at the core, for instance, of dependency theory's conviction that industrialisation was the universally valid path to modernity.

Partially related to postcolonial studies (Conrad, 2016: 53–57), global history has also contributed in the last two decades to the study of cities by highlighting and criticising the constitutive Eurocentrism of the universal correlation of urbanisation and industrialisation. Urban historians embracing the global historical agenda as well as global historians dealing with cities have differentiated between the worldwide impact of urbanisation in the nineteenth century and the regionally limited impact of industrialisation. Jürgen Osterhammel, a global historian who also granted cities a major role in his global historical narrative, pointed at this very gap and inferred that 'urbanization is a truly global process, industrialization a sporadic and uneven formation of growth centres' (Osterhammel, 2014: 250). More generally, Christopher Bayly has added that 'historians of the last third of the twentieth century tended to downplay the importance of industrialisation in their accounts of the nineteenth century' (Bayly, 2004: 171; O'Brien, 2000).

Not only historians focusing on vast global historical narratives but also historians of Europe have highlighted the problematic generalisation of industrialisation as a key phenomenon in the emergence of modernity. Especially historians dealing with so-called peripheral European regions have underlined the shortcomings that a generalisation of North Western European categories, processes and phenomena can cause. For instance, Holste et al. argue that if the typical Western path to modernity, made of the triad *Bürgertum*, industry and nation, is applied to Eastern Europe, the result is a distorted picture that produces part of Europe as characterised by failure and deficiency (Holste et al., 2009). Consequently, accounts of the urban history of Western Europe have also grown more careful in equating nineteenth-century industrialisation and urbanisation. For example, in *European Cities in the Modern Era*, Friedrich Lenger writes: 'for one thing, urbanisation was underway long before industrialisation; for another, even in the nineteenth century, industrialisation preceded significant urbanisation, and urban expansion preceded significant industrialisation' (Lenger, 2012: 45).

In this section, I have sketched some central positions regarding the correlation between urbanisation and industrialisation in urban history from the mid-twentieth century. Historians such as Lewis Mumford, Lynn H. Lees, Paul Hohenberg and Andrew Lees considered industrialisation as a defining feature of modern urbanisation. In the attempt to abstract from the history of individual cities to the history of urbanism, they tended to equate industrialisation and urbanisation. This equation, however, is at risk of transforming the history of an exceedingly small group of 'industrialised' cities into a universally valid yardstick. Responding to the same need to draw a history of urbanism rather than of individual cities, historians such as Asa Briggs and H. J. Dyos proposed a typological study of cities, which enabled them to compare and convey the diversity and multiplicity within urban history: against this backdrop, the industrial city is just one among a variety of possible urban typologies. Differently from the study of urban typologies, urban historians inspired by dependency theory highlighted the constitutive connectivity in the history of cities and especially the relationship of power between industrial cities in the 'core' and the dependent cities on the 'periphery'. If historians inspired by dependency theory recognised, on the one hand, the constitutive relation between central and peripheral cities, they also suggested, on the other hand, a singular notion of the modern city: the industrial city in the 'core' is deemed modern whereas 'peripheral' cities are forced by economic constraints to lag behind. Starting from the idea of constitutive connectedness, postcolonial scholars and global historians have criticised and partially deconstructed the binary categories of core/ periphery that dependency theory postulated and instead highlighted the independent agency and also the strength of 'peripheral' modernities and the consistent exchanges between core and periphery.

Industry and urban modernity in nineteenth-century Buenos Aires: the case of the meat-salting factories

Starting from the contributions of both dependency theory and global history concerning the correlation between industry and urban modernity, this analysis adds to the narration of an entangled history of uneven modernity (Randeria, 2002). The following sections underline the original way in which *porteño* elites related to industry and industrial modernity, showing their independent agency and the relevance of the specific local setting. Yet the analysis illustrates, at the same time, how their way of relating to European models implied a system of asymmetric and uneven power relations, in which an idealised image of white European civilisation – that, following Chakrabarty (2000), I name 'hyperreal' – represented the indefinite and nonetheless nearly unchallenged model to be followed.

In the years between 1867 and 1871, a series of dramatic epidemics hit Buenos Aires. From 1867 to 1869, cholera plagued the city in recurring waves, killing people in the order of thousands. In 1871, just two years after the end of the cholera epidemics, yellow fever broke out, claiming the lives of almost 14,000 *porteños* (Alvarez, 2010; Alvarez et al., 2004; Armus, 2000; 2003; 2011; Bordi de Ragucci, 1992; Carbone, 2022; Recalde, 1993; Scenna, 2009 [1974]). Informed by the medical and hygienic theories of the time, urban elites largely interpreted these outbreaks as crises caused by the structure of the city. Mixed opinions and emotions were especially engendered by the *saladeros*, the meat-salting factories that mainly produced cowhides, jerked beef and tallow for the export market and represented the major manufacturing branch in Buenos Aires. These factories were associated with key economic and political interests, yet they were also the cause of dramatic pollution levels that inspired a vast array of fears and concerns. Supported by hygienic arguments, many urbanites perceived the pollution caused by the *saladeros* as a threat to public health and questioned the *saladeros*' right to pollute and consequently to endanger the lives of the city's inhabitants. Most notably, the dramatic yellow fever epidemic of 1871 triggered a controversial discussion on the *saladeros* that eventually resulted in the decision to ban meat-salting factories from the city and to impose a resettlement 50 km south of their original location on the outskirts of Buenos Aires.

The discussion concerning the *saladeros* was never only a debate on the factories themselves, and it soon developed into a discussion about industry and, more generally, the future of Buenos Aires. The epochal value of the *saladero* question was also widely felt by *porteño* elites. For instance, a contributor to *La Tribuna* – one of the major daily newspapers of Buenos Aires' elites – argued that the issue involved 'all big principles: the principle of order, the principle of justice, the principle of administration, the principle of science, and the principle of commerce' (Vazquez, 16 July 1871). Future President of Argentina Nicolás Avellaneda, in an article in which he compared London to Buenos Aires, viewed the problem concerning the meat-salting plants as a question of honour and morality, in his opinion the very foundations of a civilised society. He argued that the problem of the *saladeros* was both 'an issue of health and an issue of honour for the people of Buenos Aires, because a city cannot allow the existence of such an ongoing focus of disease, without being a distressing example of guilty improvidence or moral decay' (Avellaneda, 26 February 1871). Observing that the discussion was not only highly relevant but also involved quite a large part of the urban population, another contributor to *La Tribuna* added that 'few times has a town been shaken by such a vital question, such as our city is shaken right now by the *saladero* issue. It is comparable to a civil war, which also involves the lowest classes, because directly or indirectly it concerns the individual interests of virtually all residents of the city. Therefore, this issue is currently on everybody's lips' (Hoffmann, 23 September 1871).

The *cuestión saladeros* – the *saladero* question – was discussed in several media and institutions. This analysis focuses on the most important elite newspaper of the time, *La Tribuna*, and on the discussions held in the institutional context of the Chamber of Deputies of the Province of Buenos Aires, where the law banning the meat and cowhide factories was eventually passed. The discussion in the press and in the Chamber of Deputies unfolded in two rather distinct phases. In the first phase, which roughly corresponds to the cholera outbreaks of 1867–68, the discussion mainly revolved around the elaboration of a technical solution to the problem of pollution. The ruling elites placed trust in various committees of experts, hoping to prevent the outbreak of a controversial political discussion. However, with the outbreak of a further epidemic in 1871, trust in scientists and technicians faltered. In the second phase of the discussion, on which the present analysis concentrates, a wide group of journalists and politicians denounced the pollution that meat and leather factories caused and consequently questioned the legitimacy of industry to operate in the immediate vicinity of the city. Another group of journalists, politicians, and technicians argued, instead, in favour of the *saladeros* and advocated for their permanence in the city.

The relevance of race and ethnicity

Criticism, as well as approval for the saladeros, was often argued along the lines of a contraposition between civilisation and barbarism conceived of as a conflict between cities and countryside. This interpretation of Argentine history as confrontation between cities, which represented European civilisation and modernity, and the cattle-raising countryside, which stood instead for the alleged barbarism and backwardness of the gauchos, found its most powerful interpreter in Domingo Sarmiento, who in the analysed timeframe was President of Argentina (Amante, 2012; Halperín Donghi et al., 1994; Sarmiento, 1998). It is therefore not surprising that the second phase of the discussion tended to categorise *saladeros* as either urban and modern or rural and backward. The discussants viewed modernity and urbanity as dimensions that Buenos Aires should strive to obtain. Those in favour of the *saladeros*' continued position in the city argued that these establishments represented modern industry, whereas those opposing the *saladeros* deemed them barbaric, backward and rural places.

Intimately connected with claims concerning the modernity or the backwardness of the meat factories were considerations about the race and ethnicity of their workers. Of special importance was the question regarding the identification of the *saladero* workers as gauchos; gauchos were mostly mestizo descendants of mixed relations between the indigenous populations and Iberian settlers. Even though the nationalist elites in power in the last decades of the nineteenth century resurrected gauchos as national heroes, at the moment analysed here the urban elites of Buenos Aires deemed gauchos to be dangerous, undesirable and ultimately as the very origin of Argentina's turmoil (De la Fuente, 2000; Lehman, 2005; Ludmer, 2002; Slatta, 1983). In the debate on the *saladeros*, references to Europe often entailed a racial connotation: in this phase of Argentine history and among the upper class of Buenos Aires, correlating *saladeros* with mestizo gauchos was meant as an argument to discredit the factories and demonstrate their barbarism and backwardness. At the same time, affirmations underlining the workers' European origin were used as means to show that *saladeros* were a modern and civilised branch of industry.

An example for this latter argument is provided by Charles Pellegrini, an influential commentator who supported the thesis that *saladeros* had nothing to do with gauchos and instead represented industrial progress, which he connected with the workers' European descent. He described *saladero* workers as 'a male population of eight thousand agile, strong and diligent foreigners'. He saw the white European 'diligent foreigners' as 'the steady mass that will neutralise the disturbing inclinations of the idle people … and serve as a counterweight to their equestrian customs, in order to transform us [the people of Buenos Aires] into hard-working and sedentary people'. When describing the 'equestrian customs' Pellegrini referred to gauchos as semi-nomadic horse-riding cowboys and considered instead European immigrants as a corrective in order to 'whiten' Buenos Aires' population (Pellegrini, 1853). Although this chapter mainly focuses on how discussants in the *saladero* controversy substantiated their claims through references to a network of cities, the reader should keep in mind that considerations of race were a central component of the discussion on industry and modernity. In fact, even though not always explicitly expressed, the reference to North Atlantic cities, which represented the most common rhetorical tool to demonstrate either the progressiveness or backwardness of the *saladeros*, constantly involved the conception that these cities were constructed and inhabited by and for white people. Additionally, ideas of a clear hierarchy among cities were traced following a system of imagined racial hierarchies, in which 'whites' occupied the highest position.

References to European and American cities

In the discussion concerning the *saladeros*, commentators referred mostly to North Atlantic cities to argue both in favour of and against the permanence of the meat factories in Buenos Aires. For instance, one commentator, José Francisco López, used a reference to Europe as a key element in demonstrating the hazardous backwardness of the meat industry in Buenos Aires. In an article that appeared during the yellow fever epidemic of 1871, López argued that 'any English jury would have ordered the *saladeristas* [*saladero* owners] to compensate the families of the victims … of the plague, manufactured by the *saladero* sewer'. López thought that if the public authorities of Buenos Aires were of similar standing to their English counterparts, the misuse of the public waters of the Riachuelo, where *saladeros* dumped their waste, would have already been severely punished. Besides his reference to England, López also pointed to the neighbouring city of Rio de Janeiro and to Buba, in West Africa. He argued that the epidemics caused by the *saladeros* 'place us – in the eyes of the European ports, which were once attracted by the charm of our name Buenos Aires [good airs] and used to send us ships and migrants – at the same level of Buba and Rio de Janeiro' (López, 18 March 1871). In his statement, López implicitly affirmed a global hierarchy of port cities, in which the *saladeros* and the epidemics they caused degraded Buenos Aires to the level of cities in the tropics such as Rio de Janeiro and Buba that were allegedly infested with disease. In his opinion, the *saladeros* were responsible for the regression of Buenos Aires to a lower standing in the global hierarchy of port cities. Similarly, Jorge Dupuis, thinking that eastern Mediterranean cities occupied a lower position in the rank of the hygienic cities, argued that due to the *saladeros*, 'in a short time, Buenos Aires will equal the health standards of Aleppo or any other of the port cities of the Levant' (Dupuis, 22 March 1871).

Discussants in the Chamber of Deputies often presented the *saladeros* and the diseases they caused as a national embarrassment that degraded Buenos Aires and its inhabitants to the bottom of an imagined hierarchy of global port cities. Following this argument, the *saladeros* brought shame on Buenos Aires in the eyes of foreign observers and thus condemned the city to a position of subalternity, especially with regard to Western European cities. For example, the Deputy Irigoyen, drawing a comparison with England, argued: 'I wonder if you could see there [in England] something similar to our *saladeros* near their cities, which are not only disturbing but noxious. In France, Prussia, Austria, Bavaria, and among well-organised people, other systems rule' (*Diario de sesiones de la Cámara de Diputados de la Provincia de Buenos Aires 1871*, 1872: 208). According to Irigoyen, many European people were more organised than the Argentines, and the presence of the *saladeros* in Buenos Aires was proof of this deplorable situation.

However, opponents of the *saladeros* did more than just resort to affirmations of subalternity and self-deprecation. Some were instead engaged in thinking and formulating alternative imaginaries. One of the main aims of such projects was to raise the city to the heights of its contemporary modern counterparts. For instance, Nicolás Avellaneda, future President of Argentina, proposed a plan for the city that he articulated as an imaginary for the entire region. He endorsed the banning of the *saladeros* from Buenos Aires and mentioned the 'manufacturing and commercial cities of Europe' as a point of reference. Comparing Buenos Aires with the alleged common consensus of European best practice, he argued that 'sanitary progress, which can be seen today in the manufacturing and commercial cities of

Europe, came about through preventing the operations of dangerous and noxious industries in cities' (Avellaneda, 26 February 1871).

Commentators who argued in favour of the *saladeros* remaining in the city interpreted these factories and the role of urban industry in a completely different way. For instance, Cambaceres, one of the most important representatives of the *saladeristas*, argued that 'the Municipality of Paris, after being informed on the methods [of the *saladeros*], which were outlined and created for the first time in Buenos Aires, decreed the foundation ... of an identical factory to process dead or unserviceable horses' (Cambaceres, 3 December 1867). In his argument, Cambaceres inverted the idea according to which Buenos Aires should look to Europe when constructing modern and rational factories. Cambaceres affirmed, in fact, that Buenos Aires had been a model of inspiration for slaughterhouses in Paris with regard to the exploitation of livestock. Nevertheless, his arguments, as those of other commentators arguing in favour of the *saladeros*, shared the discursive frame of their anti-*saladero* contemporaries, in which the dichotomy of progress and backwardness and clear references to other cities, especially European cities, represented the main cornerstones. Whereas the anti-*saladero* faction considered the *saladeros* as backward and disturbing, those in favour of the meat-salting factories regarded them as modern industrial spaces.

A further commentator, A. Vázquez, who presented himself as the inventor of a new system of meat conservation, also defended the position of the *saladeristas* and the meat industry in Buenos Aires. He argued that public institutions should support the development of industry, as the institutions of industrial nations regularly did, instead of siding with those who sought to destroy it. Thus, Vázquez stated that only industry could grant people the opportunity to 'obtain health, wealth, morality, and honest pleasures. Industry is the only thing that can reduce the evils, which afflict the poor humanity'. In his opinion, industry provided positive outcomes not only for industrialists but also for workers. He affirmed that a supportive public policy towards industry would create 'hundreds of factories' in Buenos Aires, through which 'thousands of workers, who currently work for evil forces, could find honest employment' (Vázquez, 21 July 1871). Vázquez proposed an entirely positive imaginary connected with industry. The path to reach wealth passed through industry and thus, in the case of Buenos Aires, through the *saladeros*, which he considered as modern industrial spaces. Vázquez disagreed with the imaginary of the city full of smoking chimneys as a place of infectious contamination, violence and moral decay. He instead envisioned industrialisation as a positive representation of the city's prosperity, one which fostered wealth and morality among its workers. In his view, the *saladeros* were part of a positive process of industrialisation that the state had to support and strengthen in order to ensure Buenos Aires and Argentina a brighter future.

Another important contribution in favour of the *saladeros* came from the chemist Miguel Puiggari. In a pamphlet published in 1871, he interpreted industrial pollution as a normal consequence of the positive process of modern urbanisation. In other words, he interpreted pollution as a sign that Buenos Aires had chosen the right path, which the major industrial cities in America and Europe had previously followed. He did not deny the dramatic pollution caused by the *saladeros* but simultaneously contextualised it, in what he considered the natural teleology of industrial cities. He affirmed, 'our Riachuelo [a small river, where most *saladeros* disposed of their waste] has been converted into an impure stream' and wondered, 'what would we say then of the River Thames, of the Seine and of many other rivers, which carried a stream a thousand times filthier?' Imagining Buenos Aires as playing catch-up to its European and American contemporaries, he added, 'what has happened in all major cities such as Paris, London, Berlin, Vienna, Brussels and New York … is happening now to us'. Furthermore, Puiggari provided a brief reconstruction of what he identified as the natural stages in the urbanisation process. 'The same phenomenon is happening here: rapid population growth; the same cause: fast means of transportation; the same effect: the epidemics; the same consequences: the necessity of transforming the old cities and putting them in condition to be able to withstand large masses of people that penetrate their bodies' (Puiggari, 1871: 45–46).

According to Puiggari, industrial pollution – along with population growth, faster means of transportation and the epidemics – were all disturbing but nonetheless necessary ingredients of urban modernity. He pointed out that the right path was not the banning of industry but rather a hygienic transformation of the factories and of the whole city, which would also lay the foundations to embrace the rapidly increasing population that industry would draw into the city. In confronting these epochal tasks of reform and transformation, Puiggari accused his fellow *porteños* of possessing an over-delicate sense of smell. In this instance, he argued, 'aren't the first industrial cities in the world giving us an example of tolerance of the smells of vapours and gases, which in their case are even more unpleasant and perhaps more harmful than the smoke of the *saladeros*? Let us not be that fussy, for God's sake, let us not take our sense of smell too seriously, especially in the presence of national interests that concern all of the inhabitants of Buenos Aires so very much, from the most respectable to the most humble!' (Puiggari, 1871: 66).

Puiggari saw the pollution caused by the *saladeros* as proof that Buenos Aires was catching up with the world's most influential industrial cities. These phenomena, which had already occurred elsewhere, would, in his opinion, also come to pass in Buenos Aires. Central for this chapter's analysis is the finding that Puiggari saw his city as moving in a good direction because, even though delayed, the city was proceeding on the path already experienced by industrial cities in Europe and North America. Puiggari accused the anti-*saladero* party of placing its sense of smell and desire for an enjoyable city before the interests of the people, jeopardising Buenos Aires' magnificent industrial and therefore modern future.

Puiggari's irony undoubtedly arose from his surprise at the subsequent victory of the opponents of the *saladeros*. From a position of little support, the anti-*saladero* party had been able to win in parliament, even if only by one vote, and could thus enforce the ban of the *saladeros*. The trauma and fear unleashed by the endless series of epidemics and their alleged connection with the pollution that *saladeros* caused were among the most powerful elements in this unexpected victory. Furthermore, by seizing on the mood of fear and anxiety in the city, the opponents of the *saladeros* were able to promote their desire for a clean and enjoyable city that they deemed modern, even though it differed from the imaginary of urban modernity as outcome of industrialisation.

Industry and urban modernity: entangled history of unevenness

The analysis of the discussion about the *saladeros* shows that the reference to the semantics of modernity and backwardness was pivotal in constructing arguments both in favour of and against the permanence of these factories in the city. All discussants were united in arguing in favour of modernity and their distinctive rhetorical tool was the placing of *saladeros* either on the side of progress or on that of backwardness. One of the most important discursive devices used both by supporters and detractors was assessing *saladeros*' progressiveness or backwardness by putting them in relation to North Atlantic or to Mediterranean and African cities as respectively positive or negative models. Even though, as the Argentine historian of industry Fernando Rocchi implicitly suggests, Buenos Aires' meat-salting plants shared possibly few common features with British, French or Central European steel-and-coal or textile industry (Rocchi, 2006), *saladero* supporters considered them as being a local instance of the same kind of industrialisation process that had taken place in Europe. Furthermore, *saladero* opponents imagined the modernity of Western and Central European cities not necessarily as industrial but rather as a pleasant, unpolluted and healthy urbanity.

Both parties in the *saladero* controversy referred to European cities in a way that constructed an image of, for instance, Paris and London as cities that had solved the issues of pollution caused by industrialisation. *Porteño* elites were not interested in looking into the fact that discussions on industry, in some cases even more controversial and dramatic than in Buenos Aires, were taking place in Western and Central Europe as they spoke (Barnes, 2006; Halliday, 2001). The way *porteño* elites referred to London and Paris was also, for instance, irrespective of the huge differences between the two cities. *Porteño* elites, despite having different positions on the matter of industrialisation, sought to legitimise their positions by using European cities as a 'hyperreal' reference – that is, as a figure 'of imagination whose geographical referents remain somewhat indeterminate' (Chakrabarty, 2000: 27). The references to a somewhat undetermined imaginary of the European city did not constitute a univocal idea of urban modernity. Instead, it was configured as an empty signifier – a mere reference that lacked a precise and shared meaning and therefore enabled a discursive legitimation in the local context. On the one hand, the 'hyperreal' urban Europe and its connection with a colonial imaginary of a race-determined and white-centric global hierarchy played a pivotal role in shaping the hopes and desires of elites. On the other hand, local economic interests, fears and aesthetic conceptions played a great role in providing the rationales in which positions for or against industry were grounded.

The idea of the correlation between industrialisation, urbanisation and Europe was therefore at once central and irrelevant for elite *porteños*. In fact, the decisions that the elites of Buenos Aires took regarding the *saladeros* were rather independent of the actual European models, as the indifferent use by both parties of these references shows. However, local interests, fears and hopes were certainly not completely independent from what was happening in other contemporary cities across the world, which were facing in some cases similar challenges. Certainly, the abstract reference to 'hyperreal' European cities, even though not necessarily influencing the specific way in which the decision on the *saladeros* was taken, was both the explicit symptom and the motor of the production of a hierarchical system of global cities, in which North Atlantic cities represented the model that Buenos Aires had to emulate.

The analysed case confirms what Shmuel Eisenstadt argues, namely that the semantic of modernity, of which industrialisation is a part, is not a homogeneous and universally applicable model but rather a set of 'multiple institutional and ideological patterns ... carried forward by specific social actors ... pursuing different programs of modernity, holding very different views on what makes societies modern' (Eisenstadt, 2000: 2; see also Boatcă and Spohn, 2010; Preyer and Sussman, 2016). In fact, *porteño* elites referred to modernity and debated its controversial and contingent local declination. The semantic of modernity – and especially industry – functioned as a malleable concept that the elites of Buenos Aires appropriated in order to legitimate their positions in the local context. However, as their reference to European cities illustrates, the multiplicity of 'modernities' is structured as a system of hierarchies, in which the 'hyperreal' modernity of European cities is imagined as the pinnacle of civilisation. What appears through the analysis of the discussion about the *saladeros* is, as Shalini Randeria defines it, the existence of an entangled history of uneven modernities (Boatcă, 2016; Randeria, 2002). In fact, the discussion concerning industry as a part of the semantic of 'modernity' is independent of yet nevertheless implicitly entangled with contemporary European discussions and, furthermore, is based on a system of asymmetrical and uneven power relations.

In conclusion, the analysis of the discussion about industry in Buenos Aires has shown that, when it comes to discourses of urban modernity, the reference to the industrial cities of Europe (and North America) is not only a bias of Eurocentric historiography: these cities were, in fact, a central reference for Buenos Aires' elites in the analysed timeframe. However, the ways in which these references were used does not allow one to conceive of the modernity that *porteño* elites discussed as a mere surrogate of European modernity. The controversial decisions that were made in 1871 with the ban of the meat-salting factories were mostly based on locally developed rationales, which were, nonetheless, not completely independent from the discourses and hierarchies that European modernity implied. Therefore, if postcolonial studies and global history have correctly highlighted the problematic Eurocentrism of narrating the history of Latin American cities as 'dependent urbanisation', global historians can draw from scholarship inspired by dependency theory both a warning against conceiving of the world as a smooth sphere crossed by networks of reciprocal and symmetrical relations and an encouragement to comprehend global history as an entangled history of unevenness.

References

Almandoz Marte, A. (2008), *Entre libros de historia urbana: Para una historiografía de la ciudad y el urbanismo en América Latina* (Caracas: Editorial Equinoccio).

Alvarez, A., I. Molinari and D. Reynoso (2004), *Historias de enfermedades, salud y medicina en la Argentina de los siglos XIX–XX* (Mar del Plata: Editorial Universitaria de Mar del Plata).

Alvarez, A. (2010), *Entre muerte y mosquitos: El regreso de las plagas en la Argentina – Siglos XIX y XX* (Buenos Aires: Editorial Biblos).

Amante, A. (ed.) (2012), *Sarmiento* (Buenos Aires: Emecé Editores).

Armus, D. (2000), El descubrimiento de la enfermedad como problema social. In Lobato, M. Z. (ed.) *Nueva historia argentina, tomo 5: El progreso, la modernización y sus límites (1880–1916)* (Buenos Aires: Sudamericana), pp. 507–552.

Armus, D. (2003), Tango, gender, and tuberculosis in Buenos Aires, 1900–1940. In Armus, D. (ed.) *Disease in the History of Modern Latin America* (Durham, NC: Duke University Press), pp. 101–129.

Armus, D. (2011), *The Ailing City: Health, Tuberculosis, and Culture in Buenos Aires, 1870–1950* (Durham, NC: Duke University Press).

Avellaneda, N. (1871), Higiene pública: Saladeros. *La Tribuna* (26 February).

Barnes, D. S. (2006), *The Great Stink of Paris and the Nineteenth-Century Struggle Against Filth and Germs* (Baltimore, MD: Johns Hopkins University Press).

Bayly, C. A. (2004), *The Birth of the Modern World, 1780–1914: Global Connections and Comparisons* (Malden, MA: Blackwell).

Boatcă, M. (2016), *Global Inequalities Beyond Occidentalism* (New York: Routledge).

Boatcă, M. and W. Spohn (eds) (2010), *Globale, Multiple und postkoloniale Modernen* (München: Hampp).

Bordi de Ragucci, O. N. (1992), *Cólera e inmigración, 1880–1900* (Buenos Aires: Editorial Leviatán).

Briggs, A. (1993 [1963]), *Victorian Cities* (Berkeley, CA: University of California Press).

Cambaceres, A. (1867), Cuestión saladeros. *La Tribuna* (3 December).

Carbone, A. (2022), *Park, Tenement, Slaughterhouse: Elite Imaginaries of Buenos Aires (1852–1880)* (Frankfurt am Main: Campus).

Castells, M. (ed.) (1973), *Imperialismo y urbanización en América Latina* (Barcelona: Gil).

Chakrabarty, D. (2000), *Provincializing Europe: Postcolonial Thought and Historical Difference* (Princeton, NJ: Princeton University Press).

Conrad, S. (2016), *What Is Global History?* (Princeton, NJ: Princeton University Press).

De la Fuente, A. (2000), *Children of Facundo: Caudillo and Gaucho Insurgency during the Argentine State-Formation Process (La Rioja, 1853–1870)* (Durham, NC: Duke University Press).

Diario de sesiones de la Cámara de Diputados de la Provincia de Buenos Aires 1871 (Buenos Aires: Imprenta de La Tribuna, 1872).

Dupuis, J. L. (1871), Medidas urgentes. *La Tribuna* (22 March).

Eisenstadt, S. N. (2000), Multiple modernities. *Daedalus* 109(1): 1–29.

Engels, F. (2009 [1891]), *The Condition of the Working Class in England* (Oxford: Oxford University Press).

Ewen, S. (2016), *What Is Urban History?* (Cambridge: Polity).

Halliday, S. (2001), *The Great Stink of London: Sir Joseph Bazalgette and the Cleansing of the Victorian Metropolis* (New York: The History Press).

Halperín Donghi, T., I. Jaksic, G. Kirkpatrick and F. Masiello (eds) (1994), *Sarmiento: Author of a Nation* (Berkeley, CA: University of California Press).

Hoffmann, T. (1871), Los nuevos saladeros. *La Tribuna* (23 September).

Hohenberg, P. M. and L. H. Lees (1985), *The Making of Urban Europe 1000–1950* (Cambridge, MA: Harvard University Press).

Holste, K., D. Hüchtker and M. G. Müller (2009), Aufsteigen und Obenbleiben in europäischen Gesellschaften des 19. Jahrhunderts. Akteure – Arenen – Aushandlungsprozesse. In Holste, K., D. Hüchtker and M. G. Müller (eds) *Aufsteigen und Obenbleiben in europäischen Gesellschaften des 19. Jahrhunderts: Akteure – Arenen – Aushandlungsprozesse* (Berlin: Akademie Verlag), pp. 9–19.

Jansen, H. S. J. (1996), Wrestling with the angel: on problems of definition in urban historiography. *Urban History* 23(3): 277–299.

Kapoor, I. (2002), Capitalism, culture, agency: dependency versus postcolonial theory. *Third World Quarterly* 23(4): 647–664.

Lees, A. (2015), *The City: A World History* (Oxford: Oxford University Press).

Lehman, K. (2005), The gaucho as contested national icon in Argentina. In Geisler, M. E. (ed.) *National Symbols, Fractured Identities: Contesting the National Narrative* (Middlebury, VT: Middlebury College Press), pp. 149–171.

Lenger, F. (2012), *European Cities in the Modern Era, 1850–1914* (Leiden: Brill).

López, J. F. (1871), El Riachuelo, la peste y el derecho de envenenar al pueblo. *La Tribuna* (18 March).

Ludmer, J. (2002), *The Gaucho Genre: A Treatise on the Motherland* (Durham, NC: Duke University Press).

Morse, R. M. (1975), El desarrollo de los sistemas urbanos en las Américas durante el siglo XIX. In Schaedel, R. P. and J. E. Hardoy (eds) *Las ciudades de América Latina y sus áreas de influencia a través de la historia* (Buenos Aires: SIAP), pp. 263–290.

Morse, R. M. (1992), Cities as people. In Morse, R. M. and J. E. Hardoy (eds) *Rethinking the Latin American City* (Washington: Woodrow Wilson Center Press), pp. 3–19.

Morse, R. M. and J. E. Hardoy (eds) (1992), *Rethinking the Latin American City* (Washington: Woodrow Wilson Center Press).

Mumford, L. (1961), *The City in History: Its Origins, Its Transformations, and Its Prospects* (New York: Harcourt Brace & World).

O'Brien, P. K. (2000), The reconstruction, rehabilitation and reconfiguration of the British Industrial Revolution as conjuncture in Global History. *Itinerario* 3/4: 117–134.

Osterhammel, J. (2014), *The Transformation of the World: A Global History of the Nineteenth Century* (Princeton, NJ: Princeton University Press).

Pellegrini, C. (1853), Saladeros y fábricas de grasa. *Revista del Plata* 1(3): 32–33.

Preyer, G. and M. Sussman (2016), Introduction on Shmuel N. Eisenstadt's sociology: the path to multiple modernities. In Preyer, G. and M. Sussman (eds) *Varieties of Multiple Modernities: New Research Design* (Leiden: Brill), pp. 1–31.

Puiggari, M. (1871) *Sobre la inocuidad de los saladeros: La refutación de los cargos hechos a estos establecimientos como instrumentos de insalubridad y prueba de las preocupaciones que dominan sobre las condiciones sanitarias de las industrias análogas* (Buenos Aires: Imprenta de La Tribuna).

Randeria, S. (2002), Entangled histories of uneven modernities: civil society, caste solidarities and legal pluralism in postcolonial India. In Elkana, Y., I. Krastev, E. Macamo and S. Randeria (eds) *Unraveling Ties: From Social Cohesion to New Practices of Connectedness* (Frankfurt/Main: Campus), pp. 284–311.

Recalde, H. (1993), *Las epidemias de cólera (1856–1895): Salud y sociedad en la Argentina oligárquica* (Buenos Aires: Corregidor).

Robinson, J. (2006), *Ordinary Cities: Between Modernity and Development* (New York: Routledge).

Rocchi, F. (2006), *Chimneys in the Desert: Industrialization in Argentina During the Export Boom Years, 1870–1930* (Stanford, CA: Stanford University Press).

Sarmiento, D. F. (1998), *Facundo, or Civilization and Barbarism* (New York: Penguin Books).

Scenna, M. Á. (2009 [1974]), *Cuando murió Buenos Aires, 1871* (Buenos Aires: Cántaro).

Schteingart, M. (ed.) (1973), *Urbanización y dependencia en América Latina* (Buenos Aires: SIAP).

Slatta, R. W. (1983), *Gauchos and the Vanishing Frontier* (Lincoln, NE: University of Nebraska Press).

Vázquez, A. (1871a), Sobre la inocuidad de los saladeros. *La Tribuna* (16 July).

Vázquez, A. (1871b), Sobre la inocuidad de los saladeros. *La Tribuna* (21 July).

Part II

Provincialising (urban) geography

4

Provincialising conviviality: convivial boundary-making in post-Ottoman, socialist and divided Mitrovica

Pieter Troch

Introduction

One of the essential urban paradoxes is that cities are sites of large-scale multicultural interactions and mixing, yet they are also characterised by structural segregation and conflict based on fixed cultural categories (Back, 1996; Nightingale, 2012: 10–11). Departing both from Urban Sociology focused on the ecology of sociospatial segregation and from top-down or macro-theoretical approaches to identity and rights-based multiculturalism, recent scholarship thematises the everyday practices of urban mutuality that navigate, negotiate and accommodate sociocultural difference. Alongside related notions of everyday multiculturalism (Wise and Velayutham, 2009), everyday cosmopolitanism (Noble, 2009), and living multiculture (Neal et al., 2018), the concept of conviviality applies to the spontaneous, unpanicked and quotidian practices of muddling through and living with diversity in the micro-spaces of everyday contact. These are situations in which 'different metropolitan groups dwell in close proximity but where their racial, linguistic and religious particularities do not … add up to discontinuities of experience or insuperable problems of communication' (Gilroy, 2006: 40). Studies of conviviality ascribe transformative potentials to such practices. Conviviality disrupts fixed identities and cultural assumptions and thus offers an alternative to the structural segregation that characterises urban societies (Nowicka and Vertovec, 2014; Wise and Noble, 2016).

Critical accounts caution against the overtly positive take on amicable convivial encounters set against backgrounds of sociocultural inequality. They argue that research on conviviality actually risks obscuring the structural inequalities and racism that shape and are reproduced at the everyday level of convivial practices (Back and Sinha, 2016; Lapiṇa, 2016; Valentine, 2008). To be sure, studies of conviviality do not boil down to a romanticised view of living together happily (Vertovec, 2019: 128). Recognition of both structural racism and the flaws of top-down multiculturalism lies at the heart of studies of conviviality and related concepts. Paul Gilroy, who inspired much of the literature on conviviality, situates it within a broader anti-racist critique of British post-imperial melancholia (2004: 48). Gilroy suggests that vernacular conviviality serves as a counternarrative with 'emancipatory possibilities' (2004: 161), and provides 'an opening onto the multicultural promise of the postcolonial world' (2004: 157). Gilroy and others, however, do not develop analytically how conviviality and racial and ethnic exclusion function together to reach emancipatory ends (Back and Sinha, 2016: 521; Lapiņa, 2016).

Recent studies have developed the concomitant nature of conviviality and exclusion in more detail. They highlight the agonistic nature of conviviality, which operates in the face of everyday racism and marginalisation and is messy, unstable, pragmatic and precarious (Heil, 2014; Karner and Parker, 2011; Landau, 2014; Nayak, 2017; Nowicka, 2020: 20–27). As Neal et al. put it: 'conviviality insists that multiculture is not a narrative of either entrenched antagonistic division or celebratory collaborative identities but more often gradations of and convergences between these polarising binaries' (Neal et al., 2018: 29; see also Vertovec, 2015: 256). Shared spaces and the routinised practices they generate are crucial elements in explaining the strength of habitual multiculture in the face of structural division. The place-based and communal character of everyday conviviality allows urban communities to manage, negotiate and translate racialised divisions, although it occurs alongside social and spatial segregation (Georgiou, 2017; Neal et al., 2018; Vertovec, 2015). Another important element includes the tools, skills and effort that people put into creating convivial multiculture in the midst of the ruins of racism (Back and Sinha, 2016: 523; Neal et al., 2018).

This chapter contributes to ongoing efforts to outline and comprehend the concurrent processes of convivial encounter and racialised division. It argues that some of the difficulties related to analysing the presence of conflict and exclusion in conviviality speak to the Eurocentric character of the subtexts in conviviality studies of super-diverse cities in the Global West. In a historicist and Eurocentric understanding of modern urban development (Chakrabarty, 2000), super-diverse cities of the Global West appear as the first sites of truly convivial management of racialised divisions and thus set the global norm. In a recent intervention that provincialises conviviality, Gutiérrez Rodríguez (2020) analyses the concept not from a Eurocentric point of view but from and within the perspective of creolisation. This implies accounting for the structural context of modern racial hierarchisation and compartmentalisation while engaging with social processes and practices of transformation in everyday culture that surpass this racial categorisation by relying on multiple roots.

In a more sobering take on the matter, this chapter suggests how conviviality may be provincialised from the perspective of the Balkans. As Maria

Todorova (2009) made clear, the Balkans are the dark side of Europe, as they serve as a repository of negative characteristics against which the European norm is constructed. In urban contexts, Balkanism takes the form of laments for the allegedly distinctive and not-quite-European destruction of urban multiculturalism and structural urban division in Southeast Europe, which 'absorb conveniently a number of externalised political, ideological, and cultural frustrations' and exempt the West 'from charges of racism, colonialism, eurocentrism, and Christian intolerance against Islam' (Todorova, 2009: 188). Balkanising tendencies are also evident in stereotypical depictions of cities such as Sarajevo, Mostar, Mitrovica or Skopje, which have entered the canon of divided cities and become synonymous with a seemingly permanent post-conflict state of ethnic division (for a critique, see Carabelli et al., 2019).

This chapter's case study is the city of Mitrovica in Kosovo, an exemplary divided city in the Balkans. Instead of approaching the Southeast European city as a regionally distinctive and not-quite European case of urban division, the chapter identifies sociospatial patterns of conviviality and exclusion that work together across the city's modern history to support a call for the provincialisation of urban theorising on conviviality and related concepts. The Southeast European perspective invites urban scholars to consider conviviality not as a counterweight to structural exclusion or an advanced stage in urban development, but as a constituent part of urban boundary-making, and thus to investigate the modes in which urban conviviality and exclusion are not only sporadically related but co-constituted.

The chapter is organised into five sections that are not ordered chronologically. The first section presents the case study. It briefly outlines the sociospatial composition of post-Ottoman, socialist and divided Mitrovica. The second zooms in on the contemporary divided city. It presents a critical reading of conviviality and connects it to some of the silences in studies of bottom-up transgressive practices in divided cities. The chapter then elaborates on this critical assessment by analysing the co-constitutive nature of conflictual situations and conviviality in Mitrovica's development from a small Ottoman town to a Yugoslav industrial city. The third section of the chapter engages with memories of post-Ottoman conviviality in Mitrovica. In dialogue with studies of Ottoman cities, it develops a number of critical tools for addressing boundary-making, inequality and exclusion in practices of conviviality. The fourth section of the chapter applies these critical tools to memories of tolerance in socialist Mitrovica and situates conviviality and conflict within the structural context of socialist urbanisation. The final part of the chapter brings in temporality through a study of the layered memories of living with diversity in Mitrovica's multi-ethnic neighbourhoods. The conclusion links the findings of the study to the issue of Eurocentrism in conviviality research.

Presenting the case study: post-Ottoman, socialist and divided Mitrovica

Mitrovica is a product of the unstable times that characterised the late Ottoman Empire. It developed into a regional centre in the last quarter of the nineteenth century. The town's economic position boomed as it became the terminus of the railway that connected the Southeast European interior with Skopje and Thessaloniki. The town's status was further elevated with the building of large army garrisons and consulates at what had become the northern frontier of the empire. At the same time, some of the Muslim families fleeing southward with the retreating Ottoman Empire settled in Mitrovica. Sources from the middle of the nineteenth century refer to 300 houses (approximately 2,000 inhabitants), a number that grew to around 10,000 inhabitants on the eve of the Balkan Wars of 1912–13. The town itself was predominantly Muslim, with Orthodox Christian and Jewish minorities (Urošević, 1953–54).

Alongside the rise of the city, the Ottoman urban system crumbled under the weight of geopolitical nationalism. The building of the Orthodox Church of St Sava with a bell tower, for example, challenged the traditional Muslim dominance over the cityscape and reflected the growing confidence of the local Orthodox Christian community under Russian and Serbian patronage. During the Balkan Wars, Mitrovica was integrated into the Kingdom of Serbia, which after the First World War merged into the Kingdom of Serbs, Croats and Slovenes (later Yugoslavia). Symbolising the transfer of power, in 1926 the local authorities destroyed the central mosque and clock tower. The development of mining activities that were under British ownership and management turned the town into an industrial centre in the underdeveloped southern areas of Yugoslavia (Urošević, 1953–54). In addition, the state pursued a policy of internal colonialisation, discrimination and emigration with the aim of rebalancing the demographic structure of the area to the advantage of the South Slavic element (Jovanović, 2015).

After the Second World War, Mitrovica underwent a significant transformation and became the model industrial city of the autonomous region (later province) of Kosovo in socialist Yugoslavia. As the seat of the mining, metallurgy and chemical industry conglomerate Trepča, which attracted substantial state investments, the city was a privileged locus of socialist urban development. Trepça financed the construction of prestigious housing, schools and monuments on the left bank of the river Ibër. The reason for concentrating construction in this part of the city was mostly pragmatic, as the area was less densely built-up than the city centre on the other side of the river. What functioned as the city centre during the Ottoman and interwar periods decayed owing to limited public investment before being largely demolished and reconstructed in the 1970s and 1980s (Troch, 2018). The enormous rural-to-urban migration in combination with the limited investment in social-sector housing pushed rural-to-urban migrants to pursue informal building strategies on the urban peripheries (Troch, 2019b).

The city's population grew strongly, from 13,901 in 1947 to 52,866 in 1981. Its ethnic composition – a novel categorisation introduced by the Yugoslav state – changed considerably during this process. The share of Turks fell from around one third in the early interwar period to less than 2 per cent in the 1980s. The number of Serbs increased until the 1960s but then dropped relatively and absolutely. On the other hand, the number of Albanians grew exponentially from the 1960s, largely owing to rural-to-urban migration. The combined effect of these patterns was that the share of Albanian urban residents increased from 51 per cent in 1961 to 61 per cent in 1981, while the share of Serbs fell from 31 to 17 per cent. The categories of Roma and Slavic-speaking Muslims appeared only in 1961, and their appearance reflects changes in Yugoslav categorisation-related politics (Luković, 2005: 31–33).

Since the war in Kosovo of 1998–99, Mitrovica may be considered a model for an ethnopolitically divided city. Different scales of conflict come together in the urban space (Castan Pinos, 2016; Cattaruzza and Dérens, 2015; Gusic, 2019). On the local level, the city is partitioned along the river Ibar, with a Serb-dominated north and an Albanian-dominated south. At the state level, Mitrovica is a prominent locus in the ethnopolitical conflict between the Republic of Kosovo and the Republic of Serbia. While the southern part of the city is firmly integrated into the Republic of Kosovo, in the northern part Serbia continues to carry out crucial state functions and enjoys legitimacy. Finally, the city is a 'geopolitical fault-line city' (Gentile, 2019) at the interface between global-level geopolitical spheres of interest, roughly pitting the North Atlantic Treaty Organization against Russia. These divisions are also reflected in the spellings of names. I use the Albanian and Serbian spellings of place names interchangeably, in an effort to cut across the ethnic partitioning of the linguistic landscape. In almost all cases, differences in spelling are orthographic and not etymological. To clarify this with the example of the mining enterprise and river given above, I use the Serbian (Trepča; Ibar) and Albanian spellings (Trepça; Ibër) interchangeably.

Convivial transgressions in divided Mitrovica

This section scrutinises practices of sociospatial transgression in the contemporary divided city. It engages with recent studies of divided cities, which show that quotidian urban sociability disrupts spatial partitioning and ethnic fixation. These studies examine the cracks that undermine the overpowering logics of partition and the potentially transformative power of associational networks, public spheres of debate and alternative uses of space (Carabelli et al., 2019; Nagle, 2013; Véron, 2017). Although these studies do not use the term conviviality, the focus on everyday mutuality across fixed ethnic communities and the normative aim of countering dominant narratives of bounded communities resonate strongly with studies of conviviality. Drawing on critical readings of convivial practices, I bring to the fore two alternative readings of habitual mutuality in the divided city. I argue that transgressive practices are constitutive of the ethnopolitical division of the city and reflect uneven positions.

Transgressive sites and practices indicate that everyday life in Mitrovica does not abide by strict patterns of ethnospatial segregation. The physical border between the two parts of the city is much more porous than the notion of a divided city suggests. While the central bridge over the Ibër River has been closed off since the end of the war, alternative crossings have continued to exist; these crossings have facilitated movements that relate to daily convivial practices of working, buying and selling, and socialising (Castan Pinos, 2016: 132; Gusic, 2019: 53; Jarstad and Segall, 2019: 245–247). The EU-brokered dialogue between Serbia and Kosovo led to the reconstruction and opening of the central bridge. Although protracted construction works on the northern side continue to block movements and physically mark the boundary between both parts of the city, many people cross the bridge (Alternative Dispute Resolution Center and Mediation Center Mitrovica, 2017: 22). Civil society creates convivial networks and public spheres of debate (Jarstad and Segall, 2019: 248; Pavlović, 2015). Mixed apartment blocks and neighbourhoods in the northern, Serb-dominated part of the city circumvent the overwhelming logic of ethnic segregation (Jarstad and Segall, 2019).[1]

In line with arguments made by critical studies of conviviality, these transgressive practices and sites should not be taken at face value, as disruptions of fixed ethnopolitical communities. As long as sites and practices of conviviality remain socially meaningful as transgressions, they are a functional component of the ethnically divided city. Let me give two examples to substantiate this claim. First, although crossing the bridge has become increasingly habitual, the very act of crossing produces the city's ethnopolitical division. A public opinion poll of 2017 indicates that only 15.7 per cent of the respondents never cross the central bridge. However, almost 60 per cent of the respondents felt uncomfortable, threatened or exposed when doing so, while only 24.3 per cent felt normal (Alternative Dispute Resolution Center and Mediation Center Mitrovica, 2017: 22). This also explains why the central bridge remains the prime symbolic site for ethnic violence, unrest and smaller incidents (Alternative Dispute Resolution Center and Mediation Center Mitrovica, 2017: 5–7).

Second, multi-ethnic neighbourhoods in the northern part of the city are sites of simultaneous conviviality and boundary-making. The Bosniak *mahalla*, for example, is a hub of convivial permeability on the northern side of the Ibar. Drivers change their number plate in order to enter the other side unnoticed, and taxis on both sides drop off and take travellers from one side to the other. The neighbourhood is also home to a multi-ethnic non-governmental higher education institution and the Republic of Kosovo's administration office for the north of Kosovo. At the same time, however, the area has suffered the most serious violence and has a reputation for being unsafe; it is marked by rivalling ethnopolitical signs – such as flags, licence plates and graffiti – and a pronounced international security presence (Gusic, 2019: 53–54; Jarstad and Segall, 2019: 245–247).

A second element that emerges clearly in the Mitrovica case study is that conviviality reflects uneven norm-setting (Lapiņa, 2016). Ethnopolitical positions in the city are asymmetric, as the Albanian position is rather offensive and the Serbian defensive. In making this simplifying claim my point is not to take sides, but to indicate how these asymmetric positions affect local understandings of living with diversity. Hegemonic accounts on both sides present the other side as intolerant, lawless and dangerous, as opposed to the convivial tolerance, order and security apparently present on their own side (Gusic, 2019: 51–52). However, the Albanian side is much more confident about its superiority in setting the norms for convivial encounters. In the aforementioned 2017 opinion poll, over 60 per cent of Albanian respondents stated that the central bridge should be opened for traffic and pedestrians, compared with only 14.6 per cent of the Serbian respondents (Alternative Dispute Resolution Center and Mediation Center Mitrovica, 2017: 10–13). Local hegemonic Albanian accounts inscribe their demands – including the return to the north of Albanian persons who have been internally displaced, the administrative unification of the city and the freedom of movement of goods and people – within a discourse of tolerance and human rights. Reflecting an inferior position in local conviviality debates, the local Serbian community rejects these demands as an attempt to establish Kosovo Albanian hegemony and points out – as a way of undermining Albanian claims of tolerance – that no Serbs have been able to return to the southern part of the city (Braem, 2004: 90–97; United Nations Mission to Kosovo, 2019: 4). The Serbian state and local politicians address and foment these fears through ambitious plans to build housing estates intended for returning refugees and thus preserving the Serbian character of the northern part of the city, and through protracted public works projects that effectively block the movement of people and goods across the central bridge.

The unevenness of conviviality also plays out in time. While hegemonic Albanian accounts are eager to situate everyday practices of urban tolerance in the present and future, dominant Serb accounts of tolerance and conviviality resort to the past, when the norms for tolerance were set by the dominant Serb community (Pavlović, 2014: 310–311). In the remainder of the chapter, I analyse the temporalities of conviviality in more detail through an analysis of memories of tolerance in post-Ottoman and socialist Mitrovica.

The afterlives of Ottoman conviviality

This section returns to the city during the time of its integration into the Serbian, and later Yugoslav, nation state. Contemporary Serbian histories emphasise the tolerance that characterised the interwar city: 'On this road of development and progress, along with the majority Serb population there were Turks, Albanians, Jews, Russians, and English, ... which gave Mitrovica the peculiar character of a homogeneous cosmopolitan community' (Frtunić, 2010: 7; my translation). Urban cosmopolitanism is framed in Ottoman terms and located in the *čaršija*, the commercial centre of the Ottoman city, where 'Serbs, Turks, and Jews' abided by the 'unwritten rule of respect and mutual trust' (Frtunić, 2010: 98; my translation).[2] A number of critiques, which mirror critical accounts of conviviality, apply to such uncritical evocations of the legacy of Ottoman tolerance. These evocations originate from a concern to inscribe oneself in the global and European language of tolerance and human rights, and they operate as a reflex that denies the horrendous religious and ethnic violence that destroyed Ottoman urban pluralism (Bryant, 2016; Mills, 2011). Claims of post-Ottoman tolerance also often have a weak factual basis. Local governance in interwar Mitrovica was fraught with discrimination, police terror and violence. The genesis of post-Ottoman cityscapes with churches, mosques and synagogues, often cited as evidence of urban tolerance, rather displays communitarian competition for space and outright destruction in the context of late Ottoman and post-Ottoman urban instability (Hayden, 2016).

Critical studies of living with diversity in Ottoman cities develop an understanding of the links between conflict and conviviality in post-Ottoman Mitrovica. The term conviviality draws on the Spanish term *Convivencia*, used to describe the relatively peaceful coexistence of Muslims, Jews and Christians in the medieval Islamic kingdoms on the Iberian peninsula (Gutiérrez Rodríguez, 2020: 107–109; Hayden, 2016: 5–6). It is unsurprising, then, that scholars of Ottoman cities have used the concept of conviviality to analyse living with difference (Freitag, 2014). Their understanding of conviviality and related concepts, however, differs considerably from that found in studies of super-diverse cities in the Global West. This section highlights three elements of difference: (a) the function of conviviality in the making of urban boundaries, (b) the close entanglement of conviviality and conflict and (c) the patterns of exclusion inherent to conviviality.

First, studies of Ottoman cities situate conviviality within an urban system of hierarchised communities and spatial segregation, in contrast to the role of a disruptive 'counterhistory' (Gilroy, 2004: 161) ascribed to convivial relations in super-diverse cities in the Global West. The *çarşi* – the commercial and social centre of Ottoman cities – is a good starting point for understanding the political rules and social norms that regulate Ottoman conviviality. The *çarşi* served as the public space for negotiating difference across the various alliance groups that structured the spatial, political and socioeconomic organisation of Ottoman urban life on the basis of intersecting categories of religion, ethnicity, origin, profession and kinship (Freitag, 2014: 381–383; Raymond, 2008: 59–64; for particular case studies in the Balkans, see Frantz, 2016: 237–247; Lory, 2011: 688–695, 736–744; Stanoeva, 2013: 210–215). The crucial point to take from Ottoman Urban Studies is that the convivial function of the *çarşi* does not disrupt or silence fixed communitarian boundaries, but is embedded within and reproduces the urban system of social, institutional and spatial hierarchies, and as such is conducive to the Ottoman city's functioning and stability (Raymond, 2008: 67–68). Sociospatial patterns of convivial intercommunality concurred with communal delineation, insulation and even violence (Doumanis, 2012; Eldem, 2013: 217; Lessersohn, 2015). Nicosia, to give another example of a divided post-Ottoman city, 'worked as a mixed city because of a spatial structure and communal understanding of the city as one that was divided into areas with differing levels of public access and private exclusivity' (Bakshi, 2016: 119; see also Charalambous, 2020). This resonates with Wessendorf's claim (2014) that practices of conviviality in a super-diverse neighbourhood of London take place in public and semi-public realms, while group-based boundaries define the private realm. Ottoman Urban Studies, however, stress that the processes of conviviality and boundary-making constitute one another; one cannot function without the other.

Second, Ottoman Urban Studies take into account structural inequalities that are reproduced in convivial practices. They show that the dominant Muslim community set the norms for toleration and that social interactions in the *çarşi* reproduced hierarchical power relations and patterns of inclusion and exclusion based on religion, ethnicity, origin and social status (Frantz, 2016: 76–93; Lory, 2011: 687–776). This implies that there is potential conflict in convivial practices. Indeed, the *çarşi* was typically the site for the most effective urban conflict in the late Ottoman Empire, often in the form of arbitrary violence or economic boycotts against non-Muslim communities (Frantz, 2016: 246; Lory, 2011: 548–550). The model of antagonistic tolerance (Hayden, 2016) is useful to understand the potentiality of conflict in Ottoman cities. In a context of clear hierarchies, such as during the long period of stable Ottoman rule, communities live in tolerance and conviviality appears in the interest of all involved. This convivial toleration, however, remains asymmetric and antagonistic since communities continue to define themselves according to diverging interests that mark their separation from one another. When the urban hierarchy destabilises, conviviality therefore quickly gives way to conflict.

Third, conviviality implies exclusion and marginalisation, as illustrated by the reification of Turks as a convivial minority in competing Serb–Albanian claims to Mitrovica's multicultural tradition. Both Kosovo Albanian and Serb hegemonic accounts readily refer to the Turkish minority (and to the Ottoman-era urban heritage) as a means of substantiating claims of superior tolerance. Serb historical accounts, for example, point to the role of urban Turks and the Ottoman urban legacy in interwar Mitrovica's cosmopolitan heyday (Frtunić, 2010: 97–100). Contemporary Kosovo Albanian hegemonic narratives proudly refer to the convivial use of Turkish in urban settings as a sign of urbane civility and tolerance (Gold, 2019: 179–183). International observers have also taken on these kinds of accounts. The OSCE, for example, notes that the Kosovo Turk community 'has contributed significantly to multi-ethnic dialogue and tolerance' (Organization for Security and Co-operation in Europe, 2010: 3).

Such narratives, however, silence the history of marginalisation, expulsion and immobilisation of the Muslim, Turkish-speaking urban elite in Kosovo and elsewhere in Southeast Europe. For the Ottoman Empire, ethnic categories within the dominant Muslim bounded community were meaningless at the policy level, which explains the difficulties historians face in tracing Turkish, Albanian or Slavic-speaking Muslim communities prior to the rise of nation states, as well as the continued fluidity of these categories (Ellis, 2003: 65–120). The Yugoslav state politics of ethnic enumeration created the distinct ethnocultural categories of Turks, Albanians and, after the Second World War, Muslims in an 'ethnic' sense – that is, Slavic-speaking. A substantial part of the Muslim community serving as urban elite in the Ottoman period self-identified as Turks in this system. Against the background of the homogenisation of national territories and an overwhelming Serb–Albanian ethnopoliticisation, they emigrated or became immobilised as well as marginalised – much like the Ottoman-era urban heritage with which they became associated. The relative share of Turks in Mitrovica decreased from approximately one third in the interwar period to less than 2 per cent by the late socialist period.[3] According to the most recent estimates, the number of Turks in Mitrovica is around 740 (Organization for Security and Co-operation in Europe, 2018b; 2018a).

Memories of socialist Mitrovica as a convivial space of displacement?

In what appears to contradict the asymmetric memories of post-Ottoman tolerance outlined in the previous section, popular memories in the contemporary divided city to a large extent agree over the habitual mutuality across ethnic boundaries that characterised social life in the city in socialist Yugoslavia. During interviews conducted in the framework of my own research on socialist urban development in Mitrovica, I heard statements from both Serb and Albanian interlocutors along the lines that 'north and south were meaningless in those days' and 'we got along very well'. These evocations are reminiscent of common notions of transethnic peoplehood lingering in memories and practices of ordinary citizens across war-divided ethnicities in urban environments in the former Yugoslavia (Hromadžić, 2013). Research on present-day Mitrovica has uncritically taken on these views when contrasting the contemporary divided city with the allegedly well-functioning, multicultural socialist city (Gusic, 2019: 50).

Does the memory of everyday cosmopolitanism in socialist Mitrovica among Albanians and Serbs alike imply that the radical restructuring of the city into a socialist industrial city functioned as a 'moment of cultural destabilisation' that offered individuals the chance to break with fixed relations (Amin, 2002: 970)? In this section, I argue that the potential that socialist urban transformation had to destabilise ethnic fixities should not be overestimated. I rather suggest contextualising conviviality within the structural inequalities of socialist urbanisation. I make this argument through an analysis of convivial and conflictual situations that took place across the sociospatial division between the new socialist part of the city on the northern bank of the Ibar and the pre-socialist part, south of the river.

Let me first scrutinise the sociospatial division along the Ibar that characterises Mitrovica's urban development during socialism. Remember that socialist urban development primarily took place north of the Ibër, while the Ottoman-era city centre south of the river decayed. The division between the new socialist neighbourhood on the northern bank and the old city centre on the southern bank of the river carried temporal, ideological and ethnic connotations. The residential neighbourhood on the northern bank of the Ibër River originated as a site of socialist modernity as well as of socio-occupational and ethnic (Serb) segregation. In the internal colonial conditions of development in Kosovo, employment policies attracted trained professionals from outside the region, leading to a formidable overrepresentation of Serbs and South Slavs in management and among experts in industry and public services (Troch, 2019a). If we consider the priority access that management and specialists had to enterprise housing in a context marked by under-urbanisation, we can deduce that Serbs were overrepresented in the prestigious new residential neighbourhood north of the Ibar. Memories of those living in the city confirm that the new flats in the high-rise buildings in the city's northern part were primarily allocated to doctors, engineers and school teachers, who were mostly Serb. There is thus a clear legacy element at work in the contemporary Serbian ethnopolitical stronghold in the northern part of the city.

It is tempting to project the current ethnopolitical partitioning of the city back onto the sociospatial division between the 'Serb' new socialist part of the city and the 'Albanian' Ottoman-era neighbourhoods. Contemporary Albanian accounts of socialist urbanisation in Kosovo's capital Pristina, for example, interpret the deterioration and demolition of Ottoman-era neighbourhoods after the Second World War as an act of colonial aggression and control over the subjugated Albanian population (Jerliu and Navakazi, 2018). However, the superposition of Serb–Albanian ethnopolitical division on socialist urban development requires attention to nuance.

A closer look at the development of the new socialist part of the city reveals dynamic features of inclusion and exclusion. Shifts in nationality-related policies in Kosovo from the mid-1960s had an impact on patterns of ethnic segregation in housing. Positive discrimination in education and employment led to the upward social mobility of Albanians in higher education and upper management positions, while many Serb specialists left Kosovo (Troch, 2019a). As part of this process, the nascent Albanian elite received flats in the prestigious residential area in the northern part of the city. Intraurban statistics are not available, but the International Crisis Group (2005: 3) estimates that by the late 1980s the population of the northern part of Mitrovica was roughly divided into 10,000 Serbs and 10,000 Albanians, although these numbers include peripheral individual houses and settlements as well, where Albanians were particularly well represented. Residential mixing led to patterns of habitual sociability, which along with their superior position for norm-setting inform the popular memory among Serbs in the northern part of the city of good neighbourly relations and well-functioning daily encounters during socialist times. However, popular memory indicates that Albanian upward social mobility at the same time generated resentment among the formerly dominant Serb urban elites (Pavlović, 2014: 295–308). The new socialist neighbourhood in the north of the city was thus a site of both conviviality and conflictual situations at the same time, and this became dramatically clear in the aftermath of the Kosovo War, when an estimated 1,500 to 2,000 Albanian residents from the socialist-built housing blocks in the northern part of the city were expelled to the city's south. Internally displaced persons with a Serb background from Mitrovica and Kosovo moved into the vacant apartments.[4]

The simple equation of the Ottoman-era urban neighbourhoods with Albanian ethnic space is also problematic. There is no evidence of residential or political domination of one particular ethnic community in the city centre south of the Ibar River. In fact, local Serb histories, as well as memories, refer with great nostalgia to the pre-socialist town centre as a place of close-knit Serbian communal life. They distance themselves sharply from the disruptive impact – and, in their view, anti-Serb character – of socialist urbanisation (Frtunić, 2010: 225–237; Radimirović, 2013).[5] They see socialist urban destruction as part and parcel of a process of increasing Albanian domination and Serbian discrimination in urban governance.

Rather than thinking of the socialist city in terms of clear ethnospatial division or conviviality, it is more fruitful to consider contingent and dynamic patterns of conviviality and conflict in relation to the sociospatial dynamics inherent to the transformation of the socialist city. The example of Mitrovica's *korzo* – the name for the traditional late afternoon and evening stroll in the main street of the city centre – illustrates the processes of conviviality and boundary-making that take place alongside one another against the background of socialist urbanisation. Anthropological studies show that the *korzo* is a sociospatial practice of integration *and* differentiation. Particular social groups, based on age, gender, social origin, class, subculture and ethnicity, all participate in the *korzo* but take different paths, stand in different places and join at particular times (Vučinić Nešković, 2018). The *korzo* thus brings people together across sociocultural divides at the same time that it reifies urban divisions. In contexts of ethnopolitical tension, it becomes a sociospatial practice of ethnicised differentiation (Vučinić Nešković, 2018: 385). As elsewhere, Mitrovica's *korzo* is a shared social practice among various population groups. As such, it holds a prominent position in memories of urban tolerance (Pavlović, 2014: 298–299). In the early 1970s, against the background of rising ethnopolitical division in Kosovo (Ströhle, 2016a), the city's *korzo* turned into a sociospatial practice of conviviality and ethnicised division. Local party politicians and the media worriedly reported on the division of Mitrovica's *korzo* into a new Serbian route in the northern part of the city and an Albanian stroll south of the Ibar.[6] In the context of sharp ethnopolitical tensions in Kosovo in the 1980s (Ristanović, 2019), the correlation between integration and division became even more pronounced. In the mixed residential neighbourhood in the northern part of the city, Albanians and Serbs took part in the *korzo*, but on opposing sides of the main street (Pavlović, 2014: 301–302). As one Albanian resident of Mitrovica recalls, by the late 1980s, 'there was somehow an unwritten rule about where Albanians were allowed to go and where Serbs were allowed to go'.[7]

The uneven temporalities of conviviality in the urban peripheries

Studies of urban conviviality analyse in great detail the sociospatial patterns of encounters of diversity. The historical approach applied in this chapter also advances – in line with what Vertovec calls the layered effects of the meeting of 'old' and 'new' diversities (2015) – the call to take into account the temporalities of living with diversity. It is here that the co-constituting relation between boundary-making and conviviality becomes apparent. This final section thematises this plea through an analysis of the layering of conviviality and tension in the multi-ethnic peripheral neighbourhoods of northern Mitrovica.

Mixed neighbourhoods such as Mikronaselje (Serbian) / Kodra e minatorëve (Albanian), Brđani / Kroi i Vitakut or Suvi do / Suhodoll in the northern and western peripheries of North Mitrovica disrupt the fixed boundaries of ethnopolitical partitioning. They are portrayed as the only truly multi-ethnic neighbourhoods in Kosovo and a vision of how multi-ethnic Mitrovica was before the war and how it might become in the future (European Stability Initiative, 2004; Jarstad and Segall, 2019: 4–7). A closer analysis shows, however, that these mixed neighbourhoods are characterised by the coexistence of everyday peace and conflict. The latter manifests itself in fear of changing demographic balance through (re)settlement policies, conflicts over municipal boundaries or physical and symbolic violence. These manifestations of conflict, however, do not prevent communication, cooperation over shared concerns or the sharing of space and freedom of movement across ethnic boundaries (Jarstad and Segall, 2019).

To understand fully the co-occurrence of manifestations of conviviality and conflict in these neighbourhoods, it is important to consider the layered temporalities of living with diversity. These neighbourhoods originated as informal individual house settlements for rural-to-urban migrants during the expansion of the city under socialism. The division between the perceived authentic urban environment and the apparently uncivil urban-to-rural transition zones formed an additional layer in the sociospatial composition of the socialist city, one that emerged on top of the division between the new socialist and the old Ottoman parts of the city. From the perspective of the urbanites, rural migrants radically altered the refined character of the city through their way of living and their disorderly and individualistic settlements in the urban peripheries (Troch, 2019b; for the contemporary legacy of this urban–rural division in Southeast European cities, see also Hromadžić, 2018; Jansen, 2005). In socialist Mitrovica, this rural–urban cleavage carried an ethnic meaning as well, as the Albanian rural population made up the overwhelming majority of rural-to-urban migrants (Roux, 1992: 131–133). From a Serbian urban perspective, Albanian rural-to-urban migration and informal urban sprawl undermined the ethnically framed norms of urban civility and tolerance set by the dominant Serb community (Pavlović, 2014: 307). The violent riots of March 2004, when the remaining Serb population in the southern part of Mitrovica were forced to flee (Humanitarian Law Center, 2004: 6–11), are seen as the last stage in this process. Against this background, any hint of shifting demographic or territorial balances is perceived as part of a continued Albanian attempt at urban usurpation (Radimirović, 2013: 466–467).

In Kosovo Albanian accounts, on the other hand, informal house settlements in the urban peripheries are sites of bottom-up resistance against structural discrimination. Significant local underdevelopment in the rural and mountainous areas south and east of Mitrovica is interpreted as the outcome of the Yugoslav Communists' discriminatory policy against Albanian-populated rural regions, in response to the violent resistance of the latter to the Partisans during and in the wake of the Second World War (Hajrizi, 2011: 461–464; Ströhle, 2016b). In this line of reasoning, massive rural-to-urban migration circumvented structural patterns of ethnopolitical discrimination in socialist Yugoslavia (Hajrizi, 2011: 464). Such memories of deprivation and bottom-up resistance strengthen Albanian claims to convivial norm-setting in contemporary Mitrovica.

Conclusion

This chapter has addressed the failure of Urban Studies to develop analytically how exclusionary boundary-making and conviviality work together. It argues that this failure speaks to Eurocentric subtexts in research on conviviality. Studies into the many ways in which urban populations convivially negotiate and manage structural divisions in urban spaces provide an important correction to accounts of parallel urban worlds based on categories of race, ethnicity or both. By presenting convivial encounters as counterpoints that disrupt fixed racial and ethnic boundaries in the super-diverse cities of the Global West, however, research on conviviality risks obscuring the ethnic and racial boundary-making taking place in habitual convivial encounters. It thus implicitly externalises racism and sociocultural segregation to not-quite or not-yet convivial – simply diverse, rather than super-diverse – cities of the world. The metropoles of the Global West, where convivial practices succeed in overcoming fixed boundaries, therefore stand once more at the forefront of urban development.

The Balkans are an important repository in which the not-quite-European destruction of urban multiculturalism is externalised. Seemingly permanent post-conflict cities such as Sarajevo, Mostar and Mitrovica have been framed as examples of a failure of urban coexistence that sets Southeast Europe apart from the Eurocentric norm. This chapter has opposed such a Balkanising reading through an analysis of how conviviality works in Mitrovica. The aim is neither to dismiss the elements of sociospatial division that govern social life nor to glorify tolerance in the city's past. The point is rather to show that division does not preclude conviviality and that the case study of Mitrovica can therefore contribute to Urban Studies on the co-presence of conviviality and boundary-making. Instead of placing the Southeast European urban experience at the margins of urban theories of conviviality, this chapter provincialises conviviality from the perspective of Mitrovica and Southeast Europe more generally. Drawing on Ottoman Urban Studies and an analysis of the co-occurrence of conviviality and boundary-making in post-Ottoman, socialist, and divided Mitrovica, this chapter shows that conviviality functions as a constitutive part of urban systems of inequality, hierarchy and exclusion.

To be sure, the city of Mitrovica presents an outstanding case of urban partitioning, where the legacies, social impact and potentialities of ethnopolitical conflict and division shape urban relations and memories in a pronounced manner. Recognising the particularity of the case study, however, should not lead to the entanglements between conflictual and convivial situations in Mitrovica being placed on the margins of urban theories of conviviality. These entanglements should not be discarded as evidence of the not-quite-convivial – and not-quite-European – nature of Mitrovica. Based on a thick description of the co-presence of convivial and conflictual situations against the background of urban development in Mitrovica, this chapter calls on Urban Studies to analyse various modes in which conviviality and conflict are not only sporadically related but, as in Mitrovica, co-constituted.

The chapter identifies four such modes. First, it argues that conviviality is integral to urban boundary-making. Convivial encounters appear within a structural context of urban boundaries and hierarchies and are instrumental in the reproduction of social division. Second, the entanglement of conflict and conviviality figures prominently throughout the three stages of urban development in Mitrovica. The very sites and practices of conviviality are charged with conflictual situations, and reflect the structure of inequality within which conviviality functions. A third point the chapter makes is that conviviality is norm-setting and exclusive. Dominant communities in the urban system set the norms for conviviality and marginalise non-dominant groups by positioning them as tolerable, convivial and immovable minorities. Finally, the layered temporalities of living with diversity reveal the salient presence of conflict and exclusion in apparently convivial encounters.

Notes

1 The 2011 census counted 4,900 Albanians in the northern part of Mitrovica out of an estimated total of just under 30,000 people (Organization for Security and Co-operation in Europe, 2018a).

2 Note the absence of Albanians in this reference, whom Serb hegemonic accounts generally situate outside the urban tradition. Local Albanian histories posit that the majority-Muslim population of Ottoman Mitrovica was overwhelmingly Albanian and point out that the interwar Serb local authorities burned down the most important Ottoman mosque, bell tower and library in the city centre and thus have no right to claim the city's post-Ottoman heritage (Hajrizi, 2011: 14–15, 19–21).

3 For the interwar census, see Urošević (1953–54: 203). For the censuses of the 1960s to 1980s, see Abdyli (1985: 13).

4 The UNHCR gives a number of 1,900 Kosovo Albanians having fled the northern part of the city in February 2000 due to violence and harassment (www .unhcr.org/news/updates/2000/3/3c3c0caa4/monthly-update-ethnic-minorities-kosovo-february-2000.html, accessed 16 August 2021). The International Crisis Group (2005: 3) gives a figure of 1,500.

5 Radimirović (2013) presents a collection of local Serb urban memories, based on a long-running local radio show.

6 Archives of Serbia / Fond Ð2 (League of Communists of Serbia): Speech of Bahri Oruqi at the 13th Meeting of the Regional Committee of the League of Communists of Kosovo (13 July 1971); 'Naša i vaša deca' ['Our and your children'], *Politika* (18 June 1971), p. 6.

7 Oral History Kosovo. Interview with Valdete Idrizi (2017), https://oralhistory kosovo.org/valdete-idrizi/ [accessed 16 August 2021].

References

Abdyli, T. (ed.) (1985), *Titova Mitrovica 1945–1980* (Mitrovica: Institut za istoriju Kosova/Institut za savremenu istoriju/Odbor za izdavanje monografija).

Alternative Dispute Resolution Center and Mediation Center Mitrovica (2017), *Beyond the Bridge: The Symbolism. Freedom of Movement and Safety* (Mitrovica: Alternative Dispute Resolution Center and Mediation Center), http://mediation-mitrovica.org/ wp-content/uploads/2018/06/ENG-Beyond-the-Bridge.pdf [accessed 26 March 2021].

Amin, A. (2002), Ethnicity and the multicultural city: living with diversity. *Environment and Planning A: Economy and Space* 34(6): 959–980.

Back, L. (1996), *New Ethnicities and Urban Culture: Racisms and Multiculture in Young Lives* (London and New York: Routledge).

Back, L. and S. Sinha (2016), Multicultural conviviality in the midst of racism's ruins. *Journal of Intercultural Studies* 37(5): 517–532.

Bakshi, A. (2016), Trade and exchange in Nicosia's shared realm: Ermou Street in the 1940s and 1950s. In Bryant, R. (ed.) *Post-Ottoman Coexistence: Sharing Space in the Shadow of Conflict* (New York and Oxford: Berghahn), pp. 107–128.

Braem, Y. (2004), Mitrovica/Mitrovicë: Géopolitique urbaine et présence internationale. *Balkanologie* 8(1): 73–104.

Bryant, R. (2016), Introduction: everyday coexistence in the post-Ottoman space. In Bryant, R. (ed.) *Post-Ottoman Coexistence: Sharing Space in the Shadow of Conflict* (New York and Oxford: Berghahn), pp. 1–38.

Carabelli, G., A. Djurasovic and R. Summa (2019), Challenging the representation of ethnically divided cities: perspectives from Mostar. *Space and Polity* 23(2): 116–124.

Castan Pinos, J. (2016), Mitrovica: a city (re)shaped by division. In Ciardha, É. Ó. and G. Vojvoda (eds) *Politics of Identity in Post-Conflict States* (London and New York: Routledge), pp. 128–142.

Cattaruzza, A. and J.-A. Dérens (2015), Créer une frontière dans le postconflit: le cas du Nord-Kosovo et de Mitrovica. *Hérodote* 158(3): 58–75.

Chakrabarty, D. (2000), *Provincializing Europe: Postcolonial Thought and Historical Difference* (Princeton, NJ: Princeton University Press).

Charalambous, N. (2020), Spatial forms of ethnic coexistence in Ottoman Cyprus: the role of urban form in patterns of everyday life. *Journal of Urban History* 46(3): 579–602.

Doumanis, N. (2012), *Before the Nation: Muslim-Christian Coexistence and Its Destruction in Late-Ottoman Anatolia* (Oxford and New York: Oxford University Press).

Eldem, E. (2013), Istanbul as a cosmopolitan city: myths and realities. In Quayson, A. and G. Daswani (eds) *A Companion to Diaspora and Transnationalism* (Chichester: Blackwell), pp. 212–230.

Ellis, B. A. (2003), *Shadow Genealogies: Memory and Identity among Urban Muslims in Macedonia* (Boulder, CO: East European Monographs).

European Stability Initiative (2004), Mitrovica past and future, *YouTube*, www.youtube.com/watch?v=eGn33dmfhYc [accessed 18 August 2021].

Frantz, E. A. (2016), *Gewalt und Koexistenz: Muslime und Christen im spätosmanischen Kosovo (1870–1913)* (Munich: De Gruyter Oldenburg).

Freitag, U. (2014). 'Cosmopolitanism' and 'conviviality'? Some conceptual considerations concerning the late Ottoman Empire. *European Journal of Cultural Studies* 17(4): 375–391.

Frtunić, D. (2010), *Šeher-Mitrovica pod Zvečanom* (Belgrade: Književno društvo Kosova i Metohije).

Gentile, M. (2019), Geopolitical fault-line cities in the world of divided cities. *Political Geography* 71: 126–138.

Georgiou, M. (2017), Conviviality is not enough: a communication perspective to the city of difference. *Communication, Culture & Critique* 10(2): 261–279.

Gilroy, P. (2004), *After Empire: Melancholia or Convivial Culture?* (London and New York: Routledge).

Gilroy, P. (2006), Multiculture in times of war: an inaugural lecture given at the London School of Economics. *Critical Quarterly* 48(4): 27–45.

Gold, J. (2019), *Multiethnizität in Alltag und Konflikt: Schein und Realität von Identitätskonstruktionen in der Balkanstadt Prizren* (Wiesbaden: Springer).

Gusic, I. (2019), The relational spatiality of the postwar condition: a study of the city of Mitrovica. *Political Geography* 71: 47–55.

Gutiérrez Rodríguez, E. (2020), Creolising conviviality: thinking relational ontology and decolonial ethics through Ivan Illich and Édouard Glissant. In Hemer, O., M. Povrzanović Frykman and P.-M. Ristilammi (eds) *Conviviality at the Crossroads* (Cham: Springer International Publishing), pp. 105–124.

Hajrizi, F. (2011), *Mitrovica dhe Shala e Bajgorës në fokusin e historisë* (Prishtina: Libri shkollor).

Hayden, R. M. (2016), Introduction: competitive sharing of religious sites in Europe, the Middle East, South Asia, and Latin America. In Hayden, R. M. (ed.) *Antagonistic Tolerance: Competitive Sharing of Religious Sites and Spaces* (Oxford and New York: Routledge), pp. 1–24.

Heil, T. (2014), Are neighbours alike? Practices of conviviality in Catalonia and Casamance. *European Journal of Cultural Studies* 17(4): 452–470.

Hromadžić, A. (2013), Discourses of trans-ethnic narod in postwar Bosnia and Herzegovina. *Nationalities Papers* 41(2): 259–275.

Hromadžić, A. (2018), Streets, scum and people: discourses of (in)civility in postwar Bihać, Bosnia and Herzegovina. *Anthropological Theory* 18(2–3): 326–356.

Humanitarian Law Center (2004), *March 2004: Ethnic Violence in Kosovo* (Belgrade: Humanitarian Law Center), www.hlc-rdc.org/wp-content/uploads/2014/03/HLC_Report-Ethnic-Violence_in-Kosovo-March_2004.pdf [accessed 26 March 2021].

International Crisis Group (2005), *Bridging Kosovo's Mitrovica Divide*, Europe Report 165, www.crisisgroup.org/europe-central-asia/balkans/kosovo/bridging-kosovos-mitrovica-divide [accessed 26 March 2021].

Jansen, S. (2005), Who's afraid of white socks? Towards a critical understanding of post-Yugoslav urban self-perceptions. *Ethnologica Balcanica* 9: 151–167.

Jarstad, A. and S. Segall (2019), Grasping the empirical realities of peace in post-war northern Mitrovica. *Third World Thematics: A TWQ Journal* 4(2–3): 239–259.

Jerliu, F. and V. Navakazi (2018), The socialist modernization of Prishtina: interrogating types of urban and architectural contributions to the city. *Mesto a Dejiny* 7(2): 55–74.

Jovanović, V. (2015), Land reform and Serbian colonization. *East Central Europe* 42(1): 87–103.

Karner, C. and D. Parker (2011), Conviviality and conflict: pluralism, resilience and hope in inner-city Birmingham. *Journal of Ethnic and Migration Studies* 37(3): 355–372.

Landau, L. B. (2014), Conviviality, rights, and conflict in Africa's urban estuaries. *Politics & Society* 42(3): 359–380.

Lapiņa, L. (2016), Besides conviviality. *Nordic Journal of Migration Research* 6(1): 33–41.

Lessersohn, N. (2015), 'Provincial cosmopolitanism' in late Ottoman Anatolia: an Armenian shoemaker's memoir. *Comparative Studies in Society and History* 57(2): 528–556.

Lory, B. (2011), *La ville balkanissime: Bitola 1800–1918* (Istanbul: Éd. Isis).

Luković, M. (2005), Istorijske, urbano-demografske i sociolingvističke osobenosti Kosovske Mitrovice. In Sikimić, B. (ed.) *Život u enklavi* (Kragujevac: Institute for Balkan Studies), pp. 11–87.

Mills, A. (2011), The Ottoman legacy: urban geographies, national imaginaries, and global discourses of tolerance. *Comparative Studies of South Asia, Africa and the Middle East* 31(1): 183–195.

Nagle, J. (2013), 'Unity in diversity': non-sectarian social movement challenges to the politics of ethnic antagonism in violently divided cities. *International Journal of Urban and Regional Research* 37(1): 78–92.

Nayak, A. (2017), Purging the nation: race, conviviality and embodied encounters in the lives of British Bangladeshi Muslim young women. *Transactions of the Institute of British Geographers* 42(2): 289–302.

Neal, S., K. Bennett, A. Cochrane and G. Mohan (2018), *Lived Experiences of Multiculture: The New Social and Spatial Relations of Diversity* (London and New York: Routledge).

Nightingale, C. H. (2012), *Segregation: A Global History of Divided Cities* (Chicago, IL: University of Chicago Press).

Noble, G. (2009), Everyday cosmopolitanism and the labour of intercultural community. In Wise, A. and S. Velayutham (eds) *Everyday Multiculturalism* (London: Palgrave Macmillan), pp. 46–65.

Nowicka, M. (2020), Fantasy of conviviality: banalities of multicultural settings and what we do (not) notice when we look at them. In Hemer, O., M. Povrzanović Frykman and P.-M. Ristilammi (eds) *Conviviality at the Crossroads* (Cham: Springer International Publishing), pp. 15–42.

Nowicka, M. and S. Vertovec (2014), Comparing convivialities: dreams and realities of living-with-difference. *European Journal of Cultural Studies* 17(4): 341–356.

Organization for Security and Co-operation in Europe (2010), Kosovo Turkish Community Profile. *Kosovo Communities Profile*, www.osce.org/kosovo/75450?download=true [accessed 26 March 2021].

Organization for Security and Co-operation in Europe (2018a), *Municipal Profile 2018: Mitrovicë/Mitrovica region, Mitrovica/Mitrovicë North*, www.osce.org/mission-in-kosovo/122119?download=true [accessed 26 March 2021].

Organization for Security and Co-operation in Europe (2018b), *Municipal Profile 2018: Mitrovicë/Mitrovica region, Mitrovicë/Mitrovica South*, www.osce.org/mission-in-kosovo/122118?download=true [accessed 26 March 2021].

Pavlović, A. S. (2014), Albanci u sećanjima Srba u Severnoj Kosovskoj Mitrovici u kontekstu svakodnevice pre rata 1999. godine. *Baština* 36: 289–314.

Pavlović, M. (2015), Tracer les frontières, habiter la ville: le cas de Mitrovica au nord du Kosovo. *Études Balkaniques-Cahiers Pierre Belon* 21(1): 145–162.

Radimirović, M. (2013), *Kod starog bunara: Priče o staroj Mitrovici* (Raška: Gramis).

Raymond, A. (2008), The spatial organisation of the city. In Jayyusi, S. K. (ed.) *The City in the Islamic World* (Leiden/Boston: Brill), pp. 47–70.

Ristanović, P. (2019), *Kosovsko pitanje 1974–1989* (Novi Sad/Belgrade: Prometej/Informatika).

Roux, M. (1992), *Les Albanais en Yougoslavie: Minorité nationale, territoire et développement* (Paris: Maison des sciences de l'homme).

Stanoeva, E. (2013), Interpretations of the Ottoman urban legacy in the national capital building of Sofia (1878–1940). In Ginio, E. and K. Kaser (eds) *Ottoman Legacies in the Contemporary Mediterranean: The Balkans and the Middle East Compared* (Jerusalem: European Forum at the Hebrew University Conference and Lecture Series), pp. 209–230.

Ströhle, I. (2016a), *Aus den Ruinen der alten erschaffen wir die neue Welt!: Herrschaftspraxis und Loyalitäten in Kosovo, 1944–1974* (Munich: De Gruyter Oldenburg).

Ströhle, I. (2016b), Of social inequalities in a socialist society: the creation of a rural underclass in Yugoslav Kosovo. In Archer, R., I. Duda and P. Stubbs (eds) *Socialist Inequalities and Discontent in Yugoslav Socialism* (London and New York: Routledge), pp. 112–131.

Todorova, M. (2009), *Imagining the Balkans* (Oxford and New York: Oxford University Press).

Troch, P. (2018), Socialist urban development in Kosovska Mitrovica: compressed socio-spatial duality in a medium-sized industrial city in Yugoslavia's underdeveloped South. *Godišnjak za društvenu istoriju* 25(2): 33–61.

Troch, P. (2019a), Social dynamics and nationhood in employment politics in the Trepça mining complex in Socialist Kosovo (1960s). *Labor History* 60(3): 217–234.

Troch, P. (2019b), Of private and social in socialist cities: the individualizing turn in housing in a medium-sized city in socialist Yugoslavia. *Journal of Urban History* 47(1): 50–67.

United Nations Mission to Kosovo (2019), *Report S/2019/461 to the Secretary-General* (3 June 2019), https://unmik.unmissions.org/sites/default/files/s_2019_461.pdf [accessed 26 March 2021].

Urošević, A. (1953–54), Kosovska Mitrovica, antropogeografska ispitivanja. *Glasnik Etnografskog instituta SAN* II–III: 187–210.

Valentine, G. (2008), Living with difference: reflections on geographies of encounter. *Progress in Human Geography* 32(3): 323–337.

Véron, O. (2017), Challenging neoliberal nationalism in urban space: transgressive practices and spaces in Skopje. In Erdi, G. and Y. Şentürk (eds) *Identity, Justice and Resistance in the Neoliberal City* (Basingstoke: Palgrave Macmillan), pp. 117–142.

Vertovec, S. (2019), Talking around super-diversity. *Ethnic and Racial Studies* 42(1): 125–139.

Vertovec, S. (ed.) (2015), *Diversities Old and New: Migration and Socio-Spatial Patterns in New York, Singapore and Johannesburg* (London: Palgrave Macmillan).

Vučinić Nešković, V. (2018), The past and the future of ritualized sociality in open urban spaces. In Low, S. (ed.) *The Routledge Handbook of Anthropology and the City* (London and New York: Routledge), pp. 377–391.

Wessendorf, S. (2014), 'Being open, but sometimes closed'. Conviviality in a super-diverse London neighbourhood. *European Journal of Cultural Studies* 17(4): 392–405.

Wise, A. and G. Noble (2016), Convivialities: an orientation. *Journal of Intercultural Studies* 37(5): 423–431.

Wise, A. and S. Velayutham (2009), Introduction: multiculturalism and everyday life. In Wise, A. and S. Velayutham (eds) *Everyday Multiculturalism* (London: Palgrave Macmillan UK), pp. 1–17.

5

Urban infrastructures, migration and the reproduction of colonial forms of difference

Aidan Mosselson

Sheffield A is a healthy, wealthy and leafy mix of greens, golf courses and gastropubs stretching from Fulwood and Ranmoor in the west to Nether Edge, Meersbrook and Dore in the south. This is the city that made international headlines in recent months with a campaign to protect its street trees from an incompetent and complacent council. Sheffield B is an adjacent but almost entirely unconnected city running down the Don from Upperthorpe to Hillsborough, up to Ecclesfield in the north and stretching to Tinsley, Attercliffe, Darnall and Gleadless Valley in the east. It is a place economically characterised by poverty, lack of opportunity, low-skilled work, poor quality housing stock and even poorer public transport.

Sam Gregory, *CityMonitor* (2018)

there was something ephemeral about the black community in Sheffield. It was never as solid or as sure of itself as London's, and everything connected with it was underground and clandestine.

Johny Pitts, *Afropean* (2020), 19

Introduction

This chapter exposes the roles various urban infrastructures play in reproducing racialised identities and patterns of segregation in postcolonial European cities. It contributes to new ways of knowing European cities (see Introduction) by reinscribing colonial histories into daily urban life. In so doing, it contributes to the effort to reinsert European cities into global histories marked by racism, European exploitation and the marginalisation and oppression of groups racialised as inferior to white Europeanness. It consequently emphasises the fact that colonial oppression was and remains central to the making of European urbanity.

Based on research into asylum seekers' and refugees' experiences of settling in Sheffield, a city located in the UK's midlands, it highlights the ways in which infrastructures – urban spaces, the built environment and housing systems in this case – are inscribed into and reproduce colonial forms of difference and contribute to the ongoing marginalisation of national and ethnic groups within contemporary Europe. To counter the predominantly exclusionary narrative and governance regime at work in the UK, the chapter also describes some of the spaces and practices in Sheffield that challenge the hostile approach to managing migration. Through these spaces, alternative forms of belonging and identities are formed, which directly contest and alter the colonial hierarchies that make up everyday life. In doing so, they provide potential pathways to a reimagined sense of European urbanity and identity.

Infrastructure provides a helpful lens through which colonial relations and processes of racial marginalisation can be critiqued. Infrastructure has been understood as a series of provisioning systems that underpin and facilitate everyday life (Amin, 2014; Angelo and Hentschel, 2015). Drawing on this body of work, the chapter discusses how everyday life in Sheffield is made possible but also conditioned by material infrastructural systems, systems that, as will become clear, are formed on the basis of histories and recreate contemporary realities of racial domination and exclusion. I explore three types of infrastructure to highlight the ongoing salience of colonialism and racism in the UK: firstly, by scrutinising the politics of urban space in Sheffield, I illustrate how the built urban environment serves as an infrastructure of memorialisation that heralds White British histories, whilst occluding and denying the presence and contributions of other racialised groups in the city. Secondly, adopting a topological approach, I show how the spatial configuration of cities in the UK maintains patterns of segregation along racial and national lines. Finally, I expose the cumulative effects that the British government's hostile approach towards migration has on experiences of and in urban space. I utilise an infrastructural lens to emphasise both the structural and structuring nature of racism in the UK, and to highlight the ways in which Othering processes operate through discursive, socio-material and affective processes and relations.

Methodology

This chapter draws on research carried out in Sheffield and the wider Yorkshire region over a period of 12 months. The Yorkshire region is home to the largest population of forced migrants in England. As of March 2018, 5,258 asylum seekers had been settled there, and the number has grown since. The majority of asylum seekers arriving in the UK originate from Iran, Iraq, Pakistan, Albania, Somalia, Sudan, Eritrea, Sri Lanka, Zimbabwe, Afghanistan and China. Asylum seekers are thus predominantly Black and brown people who are racialised as 'Other' and different to white Britishness. Sheffield is the first City of Sanctuary in the UK, has a long history of migration and is home to an ethnically diverse population (Darling, 2010). At the same time, the city's residents harbour contrasting attitudes towards difference and migration, as illustrated by the fact that 51 per cent of the population voted Leave in the 2016 referendum on European Union membership. Furthermore, Black and Minority Ethnic (BAME) communities living in the city experience some of the most severe levels of deprivation in the entire country (Platts-Fowler and Robinson, 2013).

Fieldwork consisted of in-depth, semi-structured interviews with refugees, conversations with refused asylum seekers, action research involving volunteering at a charity supporting refused asylum seekers, and ethnographic observations of drop-in centres and support networks catering to forced migrants. Participants in my research hail from numerous countries in the Global South, including Eritrea, Sudan, Nigeria, Zimbabwe, Central African Republic, the Philippines, Iran, Afghanistan and Syria, and are all racialised as People of Colour. When referring to interviewees in the text I use pseudonyms to protect their identities. I also make use of research reports compiled by activist organisations working in the Yorkshire region. The research involved people with different statuses, including those who have gained refugee status, some who are still waiting for final decisions on their asylum applications and some whose claims have been refused. When necessary I distinguish between these different groups, but in other cases I use the term 'forced migrants' to refer collectively to people who have been forced to leave their countries of origin for reasons beyond their control, usually owing to conflict or threats of violence.

Urban infrastructure as a lens for provincialising European cities

In addition to underpinning everyday life and providing for the needs of complex urban societies, infrastructure has also been characterised as a set of socio-material arrangements that condition people's abilities to move (Lin et al., 2017; Xiang and Lindquist, 2014). As emerging work on 'migration infrastructures' shows, infrastructural systems govern mobility, dictating who can move and under what conditions, who qualifies for particular migration statuses and what these entitle people to, and what happens to people once they are granted rights to reside (Lin et al., 2017; Meeus et al., 2019). Migration infrastructures in the UK both displace and emplace migrant communities, designating some people unwelcome, criminal or 'illegal' whilst simultaneously determining how those who are able to stay inhabit urban spaces (De Genova, 2002; Hall et al., 2017).

Both of the perspectives on infrastructure that I utilise are united in their understanding that all infrastructural forms and systems are inherently social. As numerous scholars have demonstrated, material infrastructures are products of social relations as well as key mechanisms through which these relations are sustained, enacted and reproduced (Cowen, 2020; Graham and McFarlane, 2015; Larkin, 2013). As such, they are also affective, not only establishing and reproducing the material basis of sociality but shaping the immaterial relations between and feelings and perceptions of different groups of people. For these reasons, a process of provincialising European cities means drawing attention to the historical relations and hierarchies infrastructural systems rest upon, and interrogating the ways in which these relations are reproduced through the materiality, affectivity and sociality of everyday life. It is from this point of recognition that we can begin dismantling these systems and structures and moving towards creating more equitable, open and inclusive spaces and cities.

A growing body of scholarship is already attending to the entanglement of infrastructure and legacies of colonialism and empire. Many stately homes in Britain were built out of profits derived from the slave trade (Dresser and Hann, 2013). Additionally, compensation payments received upon the abolition of slavery were reinvested into numerous properties in Fitzrovia and Bloomsbury, two wealthy, architecturally distinctive areas of London (Hall et al., 2014). Research has also uncovered how infrastructural systems – bridges, roads, dockyards, waterways, pipelines – that are central to sustaining everyday life in Britain were partially funded through the proceeds of slavery (Casbeard, 2010; Draper, 2008; Dresser, 2000). These examples make it clear that contemporary Britain's materiality rests on foundations of enslavement and racialised exploitation. There is thus an urgent need to recast British history and the formation of its cities as closely linked to and shaped by transatlantic slavery (Olusoga, 2016).

Similarly, the proceeds of colonial domination were central to making contemporary Britain, as profits from taxation in the colonies helped fund post-war reconstruction, house building projects and the welfare state (Bhambra, 2009). Labour from the colonies also contributed significantly to the expansion of industries in Britain. Today, spaces in British cities are altered, adapted and maintained by migrant communities, many of whom originate from and retain links with countries that were part of the British Empire (Hall, 2015a; 2015b). Thus, it is not possible to accurately narrate the history and contemporary reality of Britain without foregrounding the roles of enslavement, colonialism, migration and the exploitation and Othering of African, Caribbean and Asian populations.

The politics of memorialisation in Sheffield – methodological whiteness in practice

One of the biggest obstacles to provincialising European cities and recognising the legacies and continuing realities of slavery, racism and colonial domination comes in the form of 'methodological whiteness'. Bhambra (2017) uses this term to foreground the deliberate acts of obfuscation and misremembering that are central to British and American national narratives. Through media reporting and political campaigns, the British and American working classes are portrayed as homogeneously white, and the needs, ideologies, grievances and interests of these imagined populations are naturalised, presented as common sense and stripped of their racist underpinnings. Methodological whiteness also plays out through forms of memorialisation and in the construction of national heritage. Mediums like statues and curated landscapes portray idealised images of the British national community, foregrounding the experiences and identities of white people whilst occluding or denying other groups' histories and experiences (Crang and Tolia-Kelly, 2010; Hall, 1999). Methodological whiteness thus draws attention to the ways in which white identities and political concerns become hegemonic and uncontested, and shape the exclusionary framing of citizenship and belonging in contemporary Britain.

Examples of methodological whiteness can be found throughout Sheffield. When I first arrived in the city,[1] one of the first things that struck me was the prominence of statues commemorating soldiers who died during the First World War. Two large monuments take pride of place in the park near my house and in the city centre, directly outside the City Hall. These monuments are frequently visited and have wreaths laid at their bases all year round. Groups also gather regularly on Sundays around the statues. The war is therefore central to everyday life and plays a prominent role in establishing the sense of place and affective experience of the city.

The war took a toll on many families and communities in Sheffield. For example, 495 soldiers from the York and Lancaster Regiment, which included hundreds of recruits from Sheffield, were killed in a single day of fighting in the Somme.[2] These forms of memorialisation are therefore important and draw attention to the sacrifices and contributions ordinary people made to a conflict provoked by and serving the interests of elites. They also give relatives and descendants places to pay respect, form connections and commune with the departed and those who remain. At the same time, these monuments reify and recreate a nationalist form of history that continues to negate the experiences of other groups. This is made explicit by white nationalists, who use the statues as rallying points and often lay their own wreaths at the statues' bases.

Stuart Hall (1999: 3) explains that heritage is the 'material embodiment of the spirit of the nation', a collective representation of the traditions, values and virtues that certain groups want to convey and solidify. The war memorials dotted around Sheffield thus serve two purposes: firstly, they are material representations that honour the memory of those who died, and secondly, they inscribe the city's people and experiences into the broader national narrative of British history, particularly its struggles, sacrifices and, ultimately, its triumphs. Seeing the war memorials, one is clearly reminded that people in and from Sheffield have been and are committed to serving the national cause, and that the national cause owes a debt of gratitude and thanks to people from the city. They create an identification between individuals and collective national life and help ensure that certain people are able to locate themselves in the British story, both historically and as it continues to unfold in the present.

However, when it comes to matters of memorialisation, the stories, people and norms that are excluded or silenced are as significant as those that are included. As Tolia-Kelly explains: 'Exclusionary landscapes and representations of national culture within Britain also continue to be crucial in dis-placing and excluding those who cannot, or will not, identify with them' (2016: 343). The construction of memorials to those who served in the First World War takes place within a larger narrative of exclusion and methodological whiteness. Whilst popular memories of the war in Britain centre the Western Front and the British soldiers who fought and died there, First World War fighting also took place in Africa and the Middle East, with brief excursions into Central Asia and the Far East (Das, 2011). Hundreds of thousands of people from colonies also fought and died on European soil and continue to be excluded from popular histories and discounted in official commemorations (Killingray and Plaut, 2012; Lunn, 1999). The memorials erected in Sheffield thus play into an incomplete narrative and locate the city within a larger colonial history and present that is premised on forgetting or discounting the politics of empire and experiences of subjugated populations. Whilst not necessarily a deliberate strategy, the war memorials act as an infrastructure that reflects local experiences and affects. However, this infrastructure also exists in a wider geopolitical context. When viewed from the standpoint of those who are excluded, it creates a different affective experience of the city. It helps to portray the city as quintessentially British – where British is read as homogeneously white and experiences of migration, diversity and hybrid forms of belonging are written out of popular and official narratives.

Methodological whiteness thus renders the city and population residing in it as a stable, uniform entity. This process unfolds further through memorialisation relating to Sheffield's industrial heritage. Sheffield is famous for being the 'Steel City' and was at the centre of British steel processing and manufacturing, industries that helped secure Britain's position as a dominant economic force in the nineteenth century. The steel industry is central to the city's identity and branding and is commemorated in several important civic locations. A frieze on the outer facade of the Town Hall (shown in Figure 5.1) displays steelworkers hard at work, forging a strong identification between the civic life of the city, the labour that it owes its origins and (relative) wealth to, and the people who performed these tasks. In the city centre, a statue portraying two feminine figures, called the *Women of Steel*, pays homage to women who worked in steel factories during both World Wars (Figure 5.2 below).

These forms of commemoration are important and honour the working class, particularly women, and their role in shaping the life and economic fortunes of the city. However, they again play a part in the politics of forgetting and creating a homogeneous representation of the city and its people.

Sheffield has long been a destination for migrants, and many relocated to the city to work in the steel industries. Large populations from Yemen, Pakistan, the Caribbean and, latterly, Somalia moved to the city and were vital in sustaining the steel factories, particularly in the period of post-war

Figure 5.1 Frieze of steelworkers on the facade of Sheffield Town Hall.

Figure 5.2 *Women of Steel.*

reconstruction (Alzouebi, 2014; Holland, 2017; Robinson, 2010). Thus, just as the construction of the post-war welfare state owes much to the wealth and taxes generated from colonies, the reconstruction of British industry, which helped fuel booms in manufacturing and housing construction, owes debts to the labour of migrants from across the colonial and postcolonial world. However, despite their seminal contribution to these industries, the histories and experiences of these groups are largely omitted from official commemoration and memorialisation. They are given space in certain times and places. For instance, in 2018, during Black History Month, an exhibition about Windrush-era migrants and their experiences of working in Sheffield was put on display for two weeks at a site in the city centre. Also in 2018, an exhibition documenting the experiences and reminiscences of Yemeni steelworkers was hosted by the Kelham Island Museum, a museum dedicated to the steel industry. These exhibitions, important as they are, are temporary and do not represent prolonged efforts to recast the history and heritage of the city. They remain brief intrusions and disruptions in an otherwise settled and homogeneous account.

These memorial practices combine to render the city a space in which whiteness is naturalised and other populations are cast as new arrivals, outsiders, interlopers or curiosities. It is therefore a whitewashing of an imperial heritage and downplays the ways in which the city, like the nation itself, was built through colonial encounters and flows of people and resources. Efforts to provincialise European cities therefore need to challenge these selective depictions of British and European heritage and identity and reinscribe them into more accurate and representative accounts. In order to do so, we need to draw attention to the ways in which selective accounts are materialised through infrastructure, and thus to critique infrastructure itself as a technology of racialisation and exclusion.

Everyday spaces and the urban landscape in Europe's racialised cities

Exclusion and racial Othering are further entrenched by other infrastructures and spatial processes too. Contrary to monolithic depictions of Sheffield, the city is ethnically diverse. According to the 2011 Census, around 19 per cent of Sheffield residents are from BAME backgrounds.[3] BAME communities in Sheffield experience significant deprivation and socio-economic marginalisation. This has a distinct spatial pattern; the neighbourhoods Darnall, Burngreave and Firth Park, in the east of the city, have the highest proportions of BAME communities. These neighbourhoods also have higher rates of unemployment, higher proportions of residents who are either long-term sick, disabled or looking after someone and lower life expectancies than the rest of the city. Overall, more than a third of BAME residents in Sheffield live in areas that are amongst the 10 per cent most deprived in all of the UK (Sheffield City Council, 2015).

Forced migrants, the majority of whom are Black or brown adult men, originating from African and Middle Eastern countries, come to be part of this broader geography of inequality. The majority live in the aforementioned deprived parts of the city, through no choice of their own. Since 1999 the UK government has operated a dispersal system for regulating and housing forced migrants. Under this system, once people have claimed asylum, they are resettled throughout the country, at the Home Office's discretion. The policy was originally intended to 'spread the burden' of accommodating forced migrants across councils throughout the country (Robinson, 2003) and to ease housing and social pressures in Southeast England, where the majority of asylum seekers were concentrated (Stewart, 2012).

Despite recommendations that the location of housing provided to asylum seekers should be informed by the availability of support services, employment opportunities, existing networks and the ethnic composition of areas, in practice none of these factors has come into consideration; dispersal policy has been determined, above all else, by the availability of cheap housing (Dwyer and Brown, 2008; Stewart, 2012). As a result, asylum seekers in Sheffield and elsewhere around the UK have been concentrated in deprived areas, where they are cut off from community organisations and social networks and often experience exclusion, isolation and racism (Phillips, 2006; Phillips and Robinson, 2015; Spicer, 2008). As Mohamed, a refugee from Sudan, replied, when asked if he knew anybody living in Sheffield before he came to the city, 'Most of the people I know are living in other cities. I didn't know anyone – it's the government's decision, they put you anywhere.' Tesfaye, a refugee from Eritrea, described being settled in Barnsley and the apprehension he felt when first arriving in a predominantly white working-class city: 'I was scared. Everyone, people, before us, we don't find people [like us] staying here, so I thought everyone looks at me ... maybe they wasn't think to see people like us, it seems like they see only me.'

The 'no choice' basis on which housing is allocated exemplifies and exacerbates forced migrants' vulnerability. During my research, a story was shared with me about a forced migrant who had been living in Sheffield for over a year. She was eight months pregnant and suddenly relocated by the Home Office to Rotherham, a city which she had no experience of or social network in. Moving also meant leaving the healthcare service where she had received all her antenatal treatment, resulting in her feeling vulnerable and discarded, and demonstrating the callous and arbitrary nature of the dispersal and housing system. Another person I befriended explained how, when he first arrived in Sheffield, he was sent to live in a neighbourhood located at the top of one of the city's prominent hills. He has a physical disability and reduced mobility (caused by injuries from an attack he suffered in his home country, which prompted him to seek asylum in the UK) and found leaving his house and moving around the city extremely difficult. This left him feeling isolated and he developed mental health problems as a result. He was subsequently relocated and received treatment for depression, but his experience demonstrates the cruel way extremely vulnerable people are treated within the UK's migration infrastructure. It also shows how forced migrants are marginalised in decision-making processes and lose a range of abilities and agencies, including opportunities to choose where they live and how they inhabit the city.

Whilst activists and volunteers have worked hard to create a culture of welcome and provide support services to forced migrants in Sheffield (see Darling, 2010; 2011; Squire, 2011; Squire and Bagelman, 2012), many asylum seekers still experience the housing dispersal programme as alienating, oppressive and traumatic. In 2012, the Home Office awarded a contract to the global security conglomerate G4S to provide housing for asylum seekers across the Yorkshire region. They were also given the contract to run the initial accommodation centre, Urban House, located in Wakefield, and several Immigration Detention Facilities across the country. To fulfil this contract, G4S subcontracted a series of private landlords to provide the required housing. In numerous cases, this housing has been found to be inadequate and often dangerous. Local activists organised under the South Yorkshire Migration and Asylum Action Group (SYMAAG) have worked with people forced to live in these houses, documenting lack of fire or emergency exits (see Figure 5.3 below), rodent and insect infestations, mould, leaking ceilings, flooded rooms, exposure to asbestos and debilitated and unsafe structures (Grayson, 2012; 2015a; Perraudin, 2017).

Scholarship on infrastructures draws attention to the importance of constant maintenance and repair (Graham and Thrift, 2007). Once laid down, infrastructural systems have to be monitored, powered, fixed, extended, managed and looked after. This array of activities gives infrastructure its social character and ensures that the defining feature of infrastructural systems is that they are processual and emergent (Amin and Cirolia, 2018; Lawhon et al., 2018). However, in the housing forced upon asylum seekers, it becomes apparent how lack of maintenance and repair is a defining feature instead. The problems documented above – mould, rodent infestations, decayed and faulty wiring, crumbling structures – are all caused through persistent, active neglect. This negligence is therefore a spatial practice that signals the place and significance of the people forced to live in these conditions, and the ways in which they are discarded, neglected and expected to tolerate suffering (Canning, 2019).

Spatial arrangements are key vehicles through which racial orders are materialised. The ghettoisation of Black communities in America and Europe (Lancione, 2016; Wacquant, 2008); red-lining practices that cause community and economic decay, whilst making areas ripe for gentrification (Bledsoe, 2020); violent policing, constant surveillance and entrenched logics and

Figure 5.3 Bars covering front windows of house used for asylum seeker accommodation.

geographies of incarceration (Byfield, 2019; Shabazz, 2009); spatial partition-ing and exclusionary planning practices (Clarno, 2008; Picker, 2017) – all of these systems create racialised spaces and cities, and provide the material and corporeal foundations through which racism is enacted and embodied. The housing in which asylum seekers in Sheffield are made to live sits within the spectrum of racialised spatial practices and serves as a powerful infra-structure that conveys and solidifies their place in the city.

Placing asylum seekers in inadequate housing located in marginalised, deprived areas exemplifies their unwanted status and reinforces their distance from the centre of urban and communal life. It is a form of racial banishment (Roy, 2019) and ensures that they are at the margins of the idealised, homogeneous community projected through the city's heritage. Instead of being treated as extremely vulnerable people with real physical and emotional traumas, asylum seekers are turned into commodities through which property owners and multinationals can extract government contracts and rent. G4S recently lost its contract to house asylum seekers in Yorkshire, and has been replaced by Mears, a company focused on social services and housing provision (Jalloh, 2019). The removal of a company that profits from running prisons and Israeli checkpoints is certainly a welcome development and represents a victory for those who campaigned to expose the conditions in G4S accommodation. However, the profiteering at the heart of the asylum housing system remains, as the contract awarded to Mears is valued at over £1bn and Mears has retained many of the sub-contractors employed by G4S. Thus, the malicious housing infrastructure remains in place and is shown to be structural – i.e. intrinsic to the social order and hierarchy – rather than the work of a particular delinquent company.

Spatialising the hostile environment

The deplorable housing people have been forced into is a physical manifestation of the 'hostile environment', the approach to governing migration that has characterised UK policy since 2012. Beginning under the leadership of Theresa May, who went on to become Prime Minister in 2016, the hostile environment is a broad range of initiatives designed to make the UK an unwelcoming, inhospitable place for supposed 'illegal' migrants (Cole, 2019). It is also intended to act as a deterrent to new migration by making people reconsider moving to the UK in the first place, or to encourage or force those who have already arrived to return home. Despite being rebranded 'the compliant environment' in 2019, at the time of writing (2020) all hostile environment policies remain in force.

The most conspicuous manifestations of the hostile environment were vans emblazoned with the text 'In the UK Illegally? Go Home or Face Arrest' that were driven around areas with large migrant populations (Cole, 2019). The policy also extends into mundane 'everyday bordering practices' that make checks on people's immigration status part of the regular course of life (Yuval-Davis et al., 2018). Doctors, employers, universities, landlords and even charities supporting homeless people are all required to check on the migration status of those attempting to access their services, and thus become part of the infrastructure regulating migration. These policies and practices have resulted in people whose immigration status has been disputed by the Home Office being deprived of welfare support, housing, medical treatment and employment opportunities. People of Afro-Caribbean descent who settled in the UK legally as Commonwealth citizens have been particularly persecuted by this system, with at least eighty-three people being wrongly deported and eleven subsequently dying. Countless others have experienced severe hardship and have died after having their welfare payments stopped or being denied access to healthcare in the UK (BBC, 2020; Gentleman, 2019).

It is important to note that the hostile environment is not new or a departure from the usual ways of governing migration in the UK. Antagonism towards racialised populations and their movement to Britain was a long-standing feature of colonial-era legislation. Successive governments took significant steps to limit migration or impose restrictions on which members of the British Commonwealth could move to Britain, with clearly stated preferences for migrants with European ancestry (in other words, white people) from settler colonial populations in Canada, Australia and South Africa (Gutiérrez-Rodríguez, 2010; Mayblin, 2014). The arrival of workers from former colonies also triggered discriminatory practices, with several industries in Britain barring People of Colour from gaining employment or restricting them to only the most menial of roles (Andrews, 2020; Kyriakides and Virdee, 2003). The current dispensation clearly builds on a series of preceding racist anti-immigration practices and pieces of legislation and increases the intensity of suspicion and hostility (Goodfellow, 2019).

The hazardous and degrading housing provided to asylum seekers thus fits into a broader pattern of banishment, degradation and hostile treatment directed towards migrants and racialised communities. The asylum process has been described as overtly adversarial and officials assessing people's claims are encouraged to adopt suspicious and antagonistic attitudes. This has created a situation in which traumatised people are forced to meet extremely high or even impossible burdens of proof, leading to approximately 75 per cent of initial asylum claims being rejected (Burridge and Gill, 2017). In addition to the poor conditions in housing provided to asylum seekers, people describe encountering surveillance cameras in initial accommodation centres and compare these facilities to prisons (Grayson, 2015b). Others have described being intimidated by G4S staff and contractors to prevent them from making complaints about the standards of their accommodation (Bulman, 2017). Hostility is therefore inscribed into forced migrants' daily infrastructural experiences and forms of habitation.

Under Vulcan's gaze: navigating the hostile city

Racial hostility also manifests in other ways and spaces and becomes a tangible atmosphere and set of affective relations between forced migrants, urban landmarks and the city itself. This is exemplified by two locations in Sheffield, both named after Vulcan, the Roman god of fire and metal. A statue of Vulcan sits atop Sheffield Town Hall, high above the frieze of steelworkers described previously. Vulcan was chosen to signify the city's steel industry and extol the virtues of hard labour in the smelters and furnaces. Again, this shows how central the steel industry is to civic life and the image the city wishes to project.

The name 'Vulcan' features again in a place that is invisible to many residents, but looms large in many migrants' lives. The headquarters for the Home Office and UK Visas and Immigration Agency are found in a building called Vulcan House. This is a place of considerable dread and anxiety for many. People registered as asylum seekers have to report regularly to the Home Office at Vulcan House. The frequency of mandated visits varies, from fortnightly, to monthly, to every six months and even only once a year, depending on individual cases. No matter their frequency, these visits are often fraught and marked by dread. In numerous cases, people have reported to Vulcan House, which has cells inside, and have been detained.

One local charity provides volunteers who accompany asylum seekers when they are reporting. They cannot prevent detentions, but can provide assurance that people are not alone and begin processes of campaigning for people's release if they are detained. Because this system disrupts the Home Office's attempts to regulate and discipline forced migrants, it has been met with anger. Volunteers recounted experiencing open hostility from staff at Vulcan House when they were present. The situation is more terrifying for those who go alone. Samuel, a refugee from Cameroon, described a harrowing experience. In 2018, a period of heavy snowfall throughout the city coincided with the time he was given to report to Vulcan House. Most of the city was shut down and there was no public transport available. He was unsure if Vulcan House would be open or not, and had no way of finding out, as his phone calls went unanswered. Not wanting to risk missing his appointment, and thus violating the terms of his asylum status, he made the two-mile journey through the snow on foot, only to find that the office was closed. He recalls how this induced more panic in him, as he had no way of telling them he had attempted to fulfil his reporting obligation, and was worried about repercussions. As he recalled,

> The worst bit was coming to the Home Office every week to sign. Even when it was snowing. The Home Office doesn't have a means of contacting you, and I would walk all the way from Page Hall [over 2 miles], until Vulcan House, and Vulcan House is shut, and I'd be like 'What should I do?! Are they going to say I wasn't here?!' And you just get confused. I started crying because you don't know what will happen.

This vivid description shows how the hostile environment is embodied and spatialised. It is not only the formal interaction with Home Office officials inside the building, but the entire journey to attempt to report that constitutes his experience. Travelling through the city in harsh weather conditions, not being able to communicate to find out if the office is actually open, standing outside a locked building, anticipating disbelief and punishment, being scared and confused about one's fate – all of these moments are means through which asylum seekers' bodies are disciplined and the harmful migration infrastructure acts on and is absorbed into their identities. There is thus an affective experience generated through the built environment. If we view it through a phenomenological lens (Ahmed, 2007), the connection drawn between a place of civic pride and another place of terror and government-administered cruelty becomes part of a larger pattern that regulates and intimidates migrants, and ultimately negates their presence in the city. In this way, the methodological whiteness of the city works through overlapping infrastructural systems and comes to condition everyday life for forced migrants and other racialised communities.

Resisting the hostile environment, contesting belonging and being at home in the racialised city

Despite the whitewashing of the city's history and heritage, a strong movement intending to support migrants, create an environment of welcome and challenge the government's hostile migration regime has developed in Sheffield. The City of Sanctuary movement has succeeded in establishing a network of support systems and services catering to forced migrants, including the accompanying measures described above (Darling, 2010; Squire, 2011; Squire and Bagelman, 2012). The most prominent space within this network is The Sanctuary. This is an office located in the city centre that offers a range of services to forced migrants. It provides a safe space where people can congregate, enjoy free tea, coffee and food and use computers. English language classes and counselling sessions are also held there, and visitors can get assistance accessing legal services, family reunification programmes and welfare support. It is thus a prominent space in the lives of many forced migrants, as well as within the community offering them support, and presents an alternative infrastructure that is based on solidarity and inclusion. However, whilst it is a significant space in many people's lives, its presence is also downplayed. The Sanctuary is in a long passageway running between two large churches and buildings hosting various shops. The entrance to this passageway is marked by a large overhanging sign informing visitors about the shops available and encouraging people to enter. However, The Sanctuary is omitted from this list, showing again that the lives of migrants are not considered important or noteworthy in the branding of the city and its spaces.

Despite the hostile environment and legacies of colonial domination, migrants have been able to create lives for themselves and find ways to connect with and belong in the city. They are aided by the networks of volunteers and activists that support them, but also draw on their own resilience and agency. In the interviews I conducted, many respondents spoke about finding community and forms of belonging in Sheffield and feeling at home in the city.

Despite not knowing anyone when he first arrived in Sheffield, Mohamed has made extensive use of the educational opportunities and social support systems that have been put in place. He attends conversation clubs, English language and maths classes and even plays football at a regular game, organised and paid for by an organisation focusing on adult education. He recounted that these experiences provide a sense of comfort and belonging:

> When someone take care about you in special ways, like treat you nicely, that makes you feel happier. When I came, they helped me a lot, by teaching me and so on. Because I used to come consistently, so when I get absent, they asked on [about] me, they asked my friend where I go, so I get care from them.

Having his absence questioned is an affirmation of his presence and existence and resonates with a sense of being part of the city. This account thus emphasises the new social relations that can be engendered through practices and infrastructures that deliberately counter the hostile environment and refuse to exclude people based on their racial and national origin.

Another research participant, Dawit, who has also been active in voluntary spaces and organisations, has similarly established a positive relationship with the city. Despite the looming threat of racism, he is still able to enjoy the urban setting. His account shows that although security and comfort cannot be taken for granted in the racialised city, discomfort is not the only affective response. As he divulged, 'Most of the time I feel actually good [walking around the city]. It never happen, bad bad thing with race, like this, but I've heard stories of that.'

Thus, even in the face of oppressive systems and a hostile climate, people are able to establish alternative forms of belonging and identification. Didier, originally from Cameroon, emphasised that, although he came to live in Sheffield through the dispersal system and wasn't given any choice in the process, he is now able to establish his own identification with the city and live in it out of choice. As he explained to me, 'You know, it is my first city, 'cause I'm come from Africa. Sometime I go back to Manchester to look [visit] some friends. They told me "Why you can't come to live in Manchester?" I told them "No, I like to live in Sheffield."'

This shows a process of empowerment and a rediscovery of agency, something that points to new possibilities for living in and reimagining the postcolonial city. Chakrabarty's original treatise for provincialising Europe came out of the recognition that teleological narratives of Euro-modernity failed to account for the range of beliefs, customs, agencies and identities that people in the colonial and postcolonial world inhabit (Chakrabarty, 1992). Instead, he introduced a framework that could bring diverse experiences, forms of knowledge and ways of being into historiographies of modernity and create more plural, representative accounts. Provincialising Europe thus entails rejecting homogenising narratives that perpetrate epistemic violence and methodological whiteness and embracing expansive, inclusive and plural bodies of knowledge and ways of being in their place.

Conclusion

In this chapter, I have demonstrated how racism and marginalisation operate through numerous infrastructural systems, including landscapes of memorialisation, spatial arrangements and housing, as well as everyday life and processes of navigating a hostile urban environment. Consequently, I have exposed the various ways in which forms of infrastructure continue to embed colonial legacies and patterns of racial domination in British cities.

Infrastructure is the stuff of everyday urban life. Rather than being a neutral background or provisioning system, it is intensely social – gendered, classed and raced – and animates the various structures that shape people's identities and life courses. This is apparent in the ways in which hostile, anti-migration practices suffuse the everyday physical and affective environments that forced migrants have to constantly navigate. As the accounts show, these environments are absorbed into people's identities and experiences of the city, and maintain processes of racialisation, marginalisation and exclusion. Taking the sociality of infrastructure seriously demands paying attention to the ways in which racial and ethnic differences (as well as other forms of exclusion based on gender, sexuality (dis)ability and/or religious identity) are perpetuated through infrastructural systems, and acknowledging the oppressive experiences infrastructural systems can and frequently do engender.

Importantly, the research I have presented here does not only point out homogeneous, exclusionary constructions of European cities. Uncovering neglected or negated histories and contemporary realities is the first step towards creating more expansive, plural and postcolonial versions of cities. Provincialising European cities does not only entail recognising those who are confined to the margins but also means building solidarity with them and actively working to create alternative infrastructures, social relations and affects. It also clearly necessitates acting against oppressive policies, state apparatuses and everyday forms of racism and discrimination. This chapter has thus sought to challenge and correct incomplete narratives and to replace methodological whiteness with more cosmopolitan, overtly anti-racist perspectives on the city. It is a small but necessary rejoinder, and one that I hope will prove helpful to others engaged in this vital task.

Notes

1 I write from the position of a privileged migrant living in the United Kingdom. Having lived and studied in London previously, my time in Sheffield was my first encounter with British life outside of the London metropolis. My position as a newcomer and relative outsider informs my reading of the city and its landscapes. However, I am aware that I am a highly privileged migrant, protected by my educational status and the fact that I am racialised as white. My experiences are therefore far removed from and insulated in comparison to the people that I engaged with during my research.

2 www.forces-war-records.co.uk/units/328/york-and-lancaster-regiment/ (accessed 1 April 2022).

3 The collection of population data that records ethnic or racial identity has a long and complicated history in the UK (Mathur et al., 2013). The 1920 Census Act recommended that 'race and national identity' be recorded during census-taking and required census-takers to assign identities to interviewees based on the categories 'White', 'Coloured' or 'Unknown'. Over time this deeply problematic approach was jettisoned in favour of allowing people to self-report their ethnic identity. The 1991 Census allowed participants to record their 'ethnic origin' by choosing from a pre-determined range of options, including 'White', 'Black Caribbean', 'Black African', 'Indian', 'Pakistani', 'Bangladeshi', 'Chinese' and 'Other'. These are the predominant categories used in the UK, although they have been refined since and allow for more variance and complexity. Notably, the categories 'Black British' and 'Asian British' were only introduced in 2001, showing that views of Britain as homogeneously, indigenously white remain deeply entrenched. Despite their dubious origins and problematic nature, statistics on ethnic origin have helped document the racialised nature of inequality in the UK, demonstrating ongoing disparities in numerous areas, including general health, labour market participation, awarding gaps in education and rates of pay.

References

Ahmed, S. (2007), A phenomenology of whiteness. *Feminist Theory* 8(2): 149–168.

Alzouebi, K. (2014), Identities and roots: a historical account of the Yemeni community in the South Yorkshire town of Sheffield, UK. *International Journal of Social Entrepreneurship and Innovation* 3(1): 1–11.

Amin, A. (2014), Lively infrastructure. *Theory, Culture & Society* 31(7–8): 137–161.

Amin, A. and L. R. Cirolia (2018), Politics/matter: governing Cape Town's informal settlements. *Urban Studies* 55(2): 274–295.

Andrews, K. (2020), Roy Hackett: the civil rights hero who stood in front of a bus – and changed Britain for ever. *The Guardian* (6 August), www.theguardian.com/society/2020/aug/06/roy-hackett-the-civil-rights-hero-who-stood-in-front-of-a-bus-and-changed-britain-for-ever [accessed 23 August 2021].

Angelo, H. and C. Hentschel (2015), Interactions with infrastructure as windows into social worlds: a method for critical Urban Studies: introduction. *City* 19(2–3): 306–312.

BBC (2020), Paulette Wilson: Windrush campaigner who faced deportation dies aged 64. *BBC News* (23 July), www.bbc.co.uk/news/uk-53521408 [accessed 23 August 2021].

Bhambra, G. (2009), Postcolonial Europe: or, understanding Europe in times of the postcolonial. In Rumford, C. (ed.) *Handbook of European Studies* (California: SAGE), pp. 69–88.

Bhambra, G. (2017), Brexit, Trump, and 'methodological whiteness': on the mis-recognition of race and class. *The British Journal of Sociology* 68(1): 214–232.

Bledsoe. A. (2020), The primacy of anti-blackness. *Area* 52(3): 472–479.

Bulman, M. (2017), G4S accused of 'culture of intimidation' against asylum seekers who complain about poor housing. *Independent* (2 February), www.independent.co.uk/news/uk/home-news/g4s-culture-of-intimidation-asylum-seekers-complain-poor-housing-refugees-public-service-private-contractor-a7557711.html [accessed 23 August 2021].

Burridge, A. and N. Gill (2017), Conveyor-belt justice: precarity, access to justice, and uneven geographies of legal aid in UK asylum appeals. *Antipode* 49(1): 23–42.

Byfield, N. P. (2019), Race science and surveillance: police as the new race scientists. *Social Identities* 25(1): 91–106.

Canning, V. (2019), Abject asylum: degradation and the deliberate infliction of harm against refugees in Britain. *Justice Power Resistance* 2(2): 37–60.

Casbeard, R. (2010), Slavery heritage in Bristol: history, memory and forgetting. *Annals of Leisure Research* 13(1–2): 143–166.

Chakrabarty, D. (1992), Provincializing Europe: postcoloniality and the critique of history. *Cultural Studies* 6(3): 337–357.

Clarno, A. (2008), A tale of two walled cities: neo-liberalization and enclosure in Johannesburg and Jerusalem. In Davis, E. and C. Proenza-Coles (eds) *Political Power and Social Theory* (Bingley: Emerald Publishing), pp. 159–205.

Cole, M. (2019), *Theresa May, the Hostile Environment and Public Pedagogies of Hate and Threat: The Case for a Future Without Borders* (London: Routledge).

Cowen, D. (2020), Following the infrastructures of empire: notes on cities, settler colonialism, and method. *Urban Geography* 41(4): 469–486.

Crang, M. and D. Tolia-Kelly (2010), Nation, race, and affect: senses and sensibilities at national heritage sites. *Environment and Planning A* 42(10): 2315–2331.

Darling, J. (2010), A city of sanctuary: the relational re-imagining of Sheffield's asylum politics. *Transactions of the Institute of British Geographers* 35(1): 125–140.

Darling, J. (2011), Giving space: care, generosity and belonging in a UK asylum drop-in centre. *Geoforum* 42(4): 408–417.

Das, S. (2011), *Race, Empire and First World War Writing* (Cambridge: Cambridge University Press).

De Genova, N. P. (2002), Migrant 'illegality' and deportability in everyday life. *Annual Review of Anthropology* 31: 419–447.

Draper, N. (2008), The City of London and slavery: evidence from the first dock companies, 1795–1800. *The Economic History Review* 61(2): 432–466.

Dresser, M. (2000), Squares of distinction, webs of interest: gentility, urban development and the slave trade in Bristol c.1673–1820. *Slavery & Abolition* 21(3): 21–47.

Dresser, M. and A. Hann (2013), *Slavery and the British Country House* (Swindon: English Heritage).

Dwyer, P. and D. Brown (2008), Accommodating 'others'?: housing dispersed, forced migrants in the UK. *Journal of Social Welfare and Family Law* 30(3): 203–218.

Gentleman, A. (2019), *The Windrush Betrayal: Exposing the Hostile Environment* (London: Faber and Faber).

Goodfellow, M. (2019), *Hostile Environment: How Immigrants Become Scapegoats* (London: Verso Books).

Graham, S. and C. McFarlane (2015), Introduction. In Graham, S. and C. McFarlane (eds) *Infrastructural Lives: Urban Infrastructure in Context* (New York: Routledge), pp. 1–14.

Graham, S. and N. Thrift (2007), Out of order: understanding repair and maintenance. *Theory, Culture & Society* 24(3): 1–25.

Grayson, J. (2012), A cockroach in the baby's bottle: asylum-seeker housing by security giant G4S. *openDemocracy*, www.opendemocracy.net/en/shine-a-light/cockroach-in-baby-s-bottle-asylum-seeker-housing-by-security-giant-g4s/ [accessed 23 August 2021].

Grayson, J. (2015a), Toddlers, rats, asbestos. G4S, asylum seekers' landlord. *openDemocracy*, www.opendemocracy.net/en/shine-a-light/toddlers-rats-asbestos-g4s-asylum-seekers-landlord/ [accessed 23 August 2021].

Grayson, J. (2015b), Neglect, contempt and hostility – how the UK government and G4S really 'welcomes refugees'. *Counterfire*, www.counterfire.org/articles/analysis/18099-neglect-and-contempt-how-the-uk-government-welcomes-refugees [accessed 23 August 2021].

Gregory, S. (2018), Uniquely, Sheffield's dividing line runs directly through the city like the Berlin Wall. *CityMonitor*, https://citymonitor.ai/economy/sheffields-dividing-line-runs-berlin-wall-inequality-two-cities4213 [accessed 8 December 2021].

Gutiérrez-Rodríguez, E. (2010), *Migration, Domestic Work and Affect: A Decolonial Approach on Value and the Feminization of Labor* (London: Routledge).

Hall, C., N. Draper, K. McClelland, K. Donington and R. Lang (2014), *Legacies of British Slave-ownership* (Cambridge: Cambridge University Press).

Hall, S. (1999), Whose heritage? Un-settling 'the heritage', re-imagining the post-nation. *Third Text* 13(49): 3–13.

Hall, S. (2015a), Migrant urbanisms: ordinary cities and everyday resistance. *Sociology* 49(5): 853–869.

Hall, S. (2015b), Super-diverse street: a 'trans-ethnography' across migrant localities. *Ethnic and Racial Studies* 38(1): 22–37.

Hall, S., J. King and R. Finlay (2017), Migrant infrastructure: transaction economies in Birmingham and Leicester, UK. *Urban Studies* 54(6): 1311–1327.

Holland, D. (2017), The social networks of South Asian migrants in the Sheffield area during the early twentieth century. *Past Present* 236(1): 243–279.

Jalloh, B. (2019), G4S loses contract to house asylum seekers in Sheffield. *Sheffield Live!* (10 January).

Killingray, D. and M. Plaut (2012), *Fighting for Britain: African Soldiers in the Second World War* (Burnley: Boydell & Brewer).

Kyriakides, C. and S. Virdee (2003), Migrant labour, racism and the British National Health Service. *Ethnicity & Health* 8(4): 283–305.

Lancione, M. (2016), *Rethinking Life at the Margins: The Assemblage of Contexts, Subjects, and Politics* (London: Routledge).

Larkin, B. (2013), The politics and poetics of infrastructure. *Annual Review of Anthropology* 42(1): 327–343.

Lawhon, M., D. Nilsson, J. Silver, H. Ernstson and S. Lwasa (2018), Thinking through heterogeneous infrastructure configurations. *Urban Studies* 55(4): 720–732.

Lin, W., J. Lindquist, B. Xiang and B. S. A. Yeoh (2017), Migration infrastructures and the production of migrant mobilities. *Mobilities* 12(2): 167–174.

Lunn, J. (1999), 'Les Races Guerrierès': racial preconceptions in the French military about West African soldiers during the First World War. *Journal of Contemporary History* 34(4): 517–536.

Mathur, R., E. Grundy and L. Smeeth (2013), Availability and use of UK based ethnicity data for health research. National Centre for Research Methods Working Paper (National Centre for Research Methods, London).

Mayblin, L. (2014), Colonialism, decolonisation, and the right to be human: Britain and the 1951 Geneva Convention on the Status of Refugees. *Journal of Historical Sociology* 27(3): 423–441.

Meeus, B., B. van Heur, and K. Arnaut (2019), Migration and the infrastructural politics of urban arrival. In Meeus, B., K. Arnaut and B. van Heur (eds) *Arrival Infrastructures: Migration and Urban Social Mobilities* (Cham: Palgrave Macmillan), pp. 1–32.

Olusoga, D. (2016), *Black and British: A Forgotten History* (London: Pan Macmillan).

Perraudin, F. (2017), UK asylum seekers living in 'squalid, unsafe slum conditions'. *The Guardian* (27 October).

Phillips, D. (2006), Moving towards integration: the housing of asylum seekers and refugees in Britain. *Housing Studies* 21(4): 539–553.

Phillips, D. and D. Robinson (2015), Reflections on migration, community and place. *Population, Space and Place* 21(5): 409–420.

Picker, G. (2017), *Racial Cities: Governance and the Segregation of Romani People in Urban Europe* (London: Routledge).

Pitts, J. (2020), *Afropean: Notes from Black Europe* (London: Penguin).

Platts-Fowler, D. and D. Robinson (2013), Neighbourhood resilience in Sheffield: getting by in hard times (Sheffield City Council, Centre for Regional Economic and Social Research, Sheffield).

Robinson, D. (2010), The neighbourhood effects of new immigration. *Environment and Planning A* 42(10): 2451–2466.

Robinson, V. (2003), *Spreading the 'Burden'?: A Review of Policies to Disperse Asylum Seekers and Refugees* (Bristol: Policy Press).

Roy, A. (2019), Racial banishment. In *Keywords in Radical Geography: Antipode at 50* (London: Wiley Blackwell), pp. 227–230.

Shabazz, R., (2009), 'So high you can't get over it, so low you can't get under it': carceral spatiality and Black masculinities in the United States and South Africa. *Souls* 11(3): 276–294.

Sheffield City Council (2015), Black and Minority Ethnic Community, Sheffield Community Knowledge Profiles (Performance and Research Team, Sheffield City Council, Sheffield).

Spicer, N. (2008), Places of exclusion and inclusion: asylum-seeker and refugee experiences of neighbourhoods in the UK. *Journal of Ethnic and Migration Studies* 34(3): 491–510.

Squire, V. (2011), From community cohesion to mobile solidarities: the City of Sanctuary network and the Strangers into Citizens campaign. *Political Studies* 59(2): 290–307.

Squire, V. and J. Bagelman (2012), Taking not waiting: space, temporality and politics in the City of Sanctuary movement. In Nyers, P. and K. Rygiel (eds) *Citizenship, Migrant Activism and the Politics of Movement* (London: Routledge), pp. 146–164.

Stewart, E. S. (2012), UK dispersal policy and onward migration: mapping the current state of knowledge. *Journal of Refugee Studies* 25(1): 25–49.

Tolia-Kelly, D. (2016), Mobility/stability: British Asian cultures of 'landscape and Englishness'. *Environment and Planning A* 38(2): 341–358.

Wacquant, L. (2008), *Urban Outcasts: A Comparative Sociology of Advanced Marginality* (Cambridge: Polity Press).

Xiang, B. and J. Lindquist (2014), Migration infrastructure. *International Migration Review* 48(1): 122–148.

Yuval-Davis, N., G. Wemyss and K. Cassidy (2018), Everyday bordering, belonging and the reorientation of British immigration legislation. *Sociology* 52(2): 228–244.

6

Decolonising Cottbus: unmasking coloniality/modernity and 'imperial difference' in post (real)socialist urban sites of remembrance

Miriam Friz Trzeciak and Manuel Peters[1]

In January 2018, Cottbus, a town of 101,000 inhabitants located on the German–Polish border in the State of Brandenburg, attracted nationwide media attention. Several media outlets portrayed the city as a hotspot for violent clashes between 'refugees' and 'Germans' (Trzeciak and Schäfer, 2021). At the same time, a far-right association named Zukunft Heimat (Future Homeland) succeeded in mobilising more and more people against the reception of refugees in the city.[2] In much of the media reporting, the local history, as well as the consistency of right-wing and racist violence, was rarely, if ever, addressed (Fröschner and Warnecke, 2019: 38). Moreover, the majority of media reporting portrayed racism and the conflict around migration as a problem mainly of a supposedly reactionary East Germany (Heft, 2018; Kollmorgen and Hans, 2011).

Even though right-wing extremism and racism indeed have a specific and, compared with West Germany, quantitatively greater manifestation in East Germany,[3] right-wing extremism and racist violence is widespread throughout the entire Federal Republic (Quent, 2019). Both the German Democratic Republic (GDR) and the Federal Republic of Germany (FRG) were and are contexts in which the experiences of colonialism, not to be reduced to the German Empire (1871–1918)[4] and national socialism (1933–45), reverberate (Messerschmidt, 2008). At the same time, the experience of real socialism (1949–90)[5] and the capitalist social-market economy after the Second World War contributed to different lived experiences in East and West Germany. In this context, today's Germany can be understood as a postcolonial, post-national-socialist and postsocialist society,[6] where various dynamics of social exclusion and Othering are powerful (El-Tayeb, 2016: 24).

We assume that current articulations of racism (e.g. in the case of Cottbus) draw on a specific history that needs to be considered in order to better understand the continuities that occur in processes of racialisation and Othering (Behrends et al., 2003; Quent, 2019). For this endeavour, we refer to 'decolonial' approaches (Lugones, 2007; Quijano, 2007). The central argument of these approaches is that the various forms of 'modernity' have emerged in ways closely interconnected with the processes of colonisation as well as with the establishment of a global capitalist mode of production. Therefore, from the perspective of decolonial studies, colonialism, Eurocentrism and capitalism are constitutively linked (Quijano, 2014: 286). The Peruvian sociologist Aníbal Quijano (2007: 171) described the after-effects of colonial relations, the legitimisation of Eurocentrism and the racial classification of the world's population as a 'coloniality of power'. He argued that this constitutive link between capitalist forms of exploitation, with their processes of racialisation, as well as other forms of social hierarchisation, have been deeply inscribed in the various socio-economic configurations of modernity since the sixteenth century and the formation of the Americas as a geocultural entity/identity (Quijano, 2014: 286; 2000: 533). The production of 'modernity' represents an extremely violent project that cannot be considered in isolation from 'coloniality'. Quijano (2014: 286–287) therefore has postulated modernity/coloniality as a mutually constituted relationship.

The 'coloniality of power' is not only significant for understanding past and present capitalist orders. As Cultural Studies scholar Madina Tlostanova (2012; 2015) has argued, colonial power relations are also inscribed in the various configurations of socialism. Using the example of Russia's leading position in the Soviet Union, she shows how the Russian state assumed an ambivalent position both vis-à-vis the countries of the 'West' and other socialist states. Tlostanova described this ambivalent position as a 'Janus-facedness', which is meant to indicate the complex coloniality of 'not-quite-Western, not-quite-capitalist empires of modernity' (Tlostanova, 2012: 134–135). On the one hand, the image of Janus-facedness refers to an imperial claim to power on the part of the Russian state. According to Tlostanova, socialist modernity was closely interwoven with a 'colonial matrix of power' (2012: 132),[7] in which social classifications such as race (Quijano, 2000) and gender (Lugones, 2007) marginalised various social groups and structured economic, epistemic and social relations. On the other hand, Tlostanova used this image to describe a condition of inferiority towards Western states. She characterised Russia as a 'second-class empire' (Tlostanova, 2012: 134) that was not (and still is not) located on top of the modern/colonial division of the world, but nonetheless longed to expand its power in competition with other states.[8] Accordingly, the nexus between modernity and coloniality structures (1) the relations between formerly socialist states (such as Russia, Poland and the GDR) and capitalist states (such as the FRG and the USA) as well as (2) the respective internal orders of difference and belonging of these individual contexts. Thus, the ambivalent field made intelligible by the bondage of modernity/coloniality entails more than just 'internal' (e.g. between Northern and Southern Europe) or 'external' (i.e. between the Global North and the Global South) demarcations. It also structured and framed imperial ambitions differently, thus providing for various kinds of 'imperial difference' (Tlostanova, 2015: 46) within and between socialist and capitalist states.

Tlostanova's reflections on the Soviet Union's ambivalent entanglements in modernity/coloniality can be used to conceptualise the coloniality of post(real) socialist urban spaces such as Cottbus. Following decolonial thinking as well as recent scholarly and activist work on the colonial roots of current racist manifestations across urban Europe and beyond (N. K. Ha, 2017; Picker et al., 2019; Zwischenraum Kollektiv, 2017), we carve out the complex ways in which (real)socialist societies such as Cottbus were embedded in the 'coloniality of power'. This is not only relevant for understanding contemporary racism, but also allows for a broader interpretation of how contemporary urban processes have been continually racialised since modernity.

This chapter stems from a decolonial city tour project that was designed to create spaces of struggle for epistemic and social justice. In the following, we uncover three different dimensions of (real)socialist urban modernity/ coloniality at local sites of remembrance in Cottbus. First, we introduce and develop strategies for mapping and analysing postcolonial and post(real) socialist sites of remembrance. Second, we present and analyse different facets of the modernity/coloniality of the post(real)socialist urban space in Cottbus, using three sites of remembrance as examples. Finally, against this background, we conceptualise the different aspects of modernity/coloniality in the urban post(real)socialist space, which resulted in an ambivalent continuity of racialised urbanities, as 'urban imperial difference'.

Making the colonial legacy of the post(real)socialist urban space visible through the project of a city tour

In summer 2018 and summer 2019, inspired by the demands of postcolonial and decolonial urban initiatives (see, for example, Aikins and Hoppe, 2011; Bernhard, 2016; Heller and AfricAvenir, 2017; Zwischenraum Kollektiv, 2017), together with students and activists we initiated a historical city tour in Cottbus (Trzeciak, 2020). The tour focused on four sites of remembrance that combined colonial and (real)socialist traces and that also seemed to be invisible in the city's collective memory.

Following Zimmerer (2013: 12), we understand sites of remembrance (*Erinnerungsorte*) as material, political, cultural or symbolic constructions that refer to multiple and dynamic relationships and constellations. The concept of 'remembrance' created here is in line with urban activist initiatives that call for rewriting the dominant histories of modernity/coloniality and

Figure 6.1 Guided City Tour Postcolonial & Postsocialist Cottbus, July 2019.

breaking with the reproduction of these forms of knowing (Bernhard, 2016). In contrast to other parts of Germany's 'undesirable' heritage (e.g. the remembrance of national socialism; Macdonald, 2006), critical discussion of remembrance regarding Germany's colonial history is poorly established, be it in science, cultures of remembrance or educational systems (Zimmerer, 2013). What does exist is mostly due to the work of activist groups who have begun to uncover colonial epistemes and histories. They have carved out the meaning of these histories to better understand the present structures of race and global inequality within the city. Although these groups have contributed significantly to the creation of anti-racist forms of knowledge and practices of resistance, the nexus between colonialism and (real)socialism, as well as the ongoing effects of post(real)socialist modernity/coloniality, remains largely unaddressed. Turning to the realm of Social Sciences and the Humanities, the interwoven histories of colonialism and (real)socialism, as well as the fields in which the GDR showed itself to be more progressive in coming to terms with its colonial legacy (see, for example, the work of historian Horst Drechsler (1966) on the struggle of the Herero and Nama against German imperialism), have remained largely unconsidered (Bürger, 2017; N. K. Ha, 2017: 114; K. N. Ha, 2017: 76). Against this backdrop, our decolonial city tour allowed us to trace places of remembrance that uncover these interconnections.

Since Cottbus is located on the territory of the former GDR, it is not only a postcolonial and post-national-socialist but also a post(real)socialist urban space. Drawing on postsocialist studies (Stykow, 2013; Todorova, 2005), we argue that (real)socialism, even though it no longer continues, still has a pervasive impact on knowledge and social relations within the city. Taking this specific post(real)socialist setting into account, we draw on the decolonial approaches introduced in the beginning in order to better understand how the colonial legacy has shaped (real)socialist discourses and socio-historical configurations in a particular way. Following Tlostanova's (2012; 2015) deliberations on the modernity/coloniality of socialism, we conclude that the forms of (real)socialist entanglements with the 'coloniality of power', i.e. the production of racial classification and hierarchisation (Tlostanova, 2012: 132), differ from those in West Germany. We take this perspective as a basis to understand the complex processes of how modern urban spaces continue to be racialised (Picker et al., 2019).

In order to initiate processes of epistemic and social justice in the city, decolonial research of urban spaces requires scrutinising the temporal (i.e. historic and contemporary) and spatial (i.e. global, transnational, regional and local) relations and entanglements bound together in dependency and inequality (N. Ha, 2017: 76). Uncovering the material traces of colonialism thus can be a *first step* to decentre Eurocentric narratives embedded in post(real)socialist urban spaces. The European colonial legacy is inscribed in particular in the architecture of European metropolises (e.g. in palaces, gardens or factory owners' villas; N. K. Ha, 2017: 77). These 'profits turned to stone' (N. K. Ha, 2017: 77) point to the history behind the ongoing unequal relationships of power between the Global North and South.

Material traces of modernity/coloniality not only refer to the accumulation and distribution of wealth within a modern World System, however (Wallerstein, 1974; Quijano, 2014: 288); the 'colonial matrix of power' has also led to 'the social classification of the world's population around the idea of race' (Quijano, 2000: 533), thus creating different experiences of domination, exploitation and inferiorisation. Hence, the *second step* of examining the modernity/coloniality of the post(real)socialist urban space lies in tracing back the different and unequal positionalities within the system of racial classification that ultimately became an integral part of both the (multiple) capitalist and socialist experiences.

Next, social division and hierarchisation within a 'colonial matrix of power' are related to forms of ontological Othering (Tlostanova, 2015: 40). As argued before, colonialism was more than a brutal form of domination and exploitation (Hall, 1996). It was also accompanied by the accumulation and generation of colonial knowledge, which secured and legitimised colonial power and the relationships of domination (Hall, 1996). This is why examining the symbolic manifestations of colonial ideology in the past and present becomes important. To expose spaces of struggle for epistemic and social justice within the scope of a city tour, the *third step* should trace the processes of Othering, e.g. by reconstructing the use of language, signs and names to demonstrate the symbolic dimensions of colonial violence (Aikins and Hoppe, 2011).

Exposing urban sites of remembrance that reflect the colonial legacy of (real)socialism in their meaning for contemporary German society means making explicit the deeply embedded processes of racial hierarchisation and exclusion in the city (Picker et al., 2019). In so doing, we attempt to oppose right-wing and racist mobilisations that seek to hide these histories and thereby reinforce the idea of a white and homogeneous urban community.

(Real)socialist modernity/coloniality in material and aesthetic remnants: the site of the socialist modern city centre

In examining the site of the bygone socialist city centre of Cottbus, we illustrate features of the material dimension of (real)socialist modernity/coloniality. These features of socialist modern architecture symbolised a claim to 'developed' modernity directed towards both capitalist and socialist states. Meanwhile, in the Kosmos mocha and milk bar, the visitors consumed products, such as hot chocolate or coffee, that were formerly known as 'colonial goods' and that thus referred to asymmetrical global production networks and power relations. Nevertheless, the ultimate demolition of most of the buildings that made up the former (real)socialist city centre highlights the degree to which, after 1990, much of the GDR's heritage was rendered worthless.

In Cottbus, the area of the former socialist-modern urban centre is now an open construction site encircled by a fence located next to a shopping mall. Traces of ventilation shafts and former buildings reveal that a grocery store, a cafe and a string of pavilions – hosting restaurants, small shops, a discotheque and a bowling lane – once stood here. Until 2007, when it was torn down despite many protests, the Kosmos bar was at the heart of this building complex. The Kosmos bar, commonly known as the Sternchen ('asterisk'), was a popular leisure destination in (real)socialist Cottbus. Built by architects Jürgen Streitparth and Gerd Wessel after Sputnik's launch (1957) and the Apollo moon landing (1969), the building was solemnly opened on the twentieth anniversary of the GDR in 1969. Designed in futuristic aesthetics showing motifs of the cosmos and of the discovery of space, and with its star-shaped, six-pointed roof construction, the bar epitomised socialist modernity (Krauß, 2012). Inscribing the socialist aspiration

Figure 6.2 Cottbus, Kosmos bar, 25 July 1972. The photo and its description are from ADN–ZB (Allgemeiner Deutscher Nachrichtendienst–Zentralbild). The ADN–ZB was the official news and photo service of the GDR. Original title: 'People in the milk-bar – the milk and mocha bar "Kosmos", residing in the new built centre of the district capital, is a famous destination for citizens and many tourists from the People's Republic of Poland' (own translation).

to progress and development into the architecture of the city centre, the Sternchen served as a material signifier for GDR's (real)socialist claim for power over other nations, both capitalist and socialist. Celebrating progress and modernity in technology and science (e.g. the motifs of aeronautics), the urban architecture became complicit in the modernity/coloniality of the (real)socialist urban space.

In addition to its architectural style of socialist modernism, the Sternchen also illustrates the GDR's involvement in asymmetrical production networks. In the bar, products from the Global South such as coffee, tea and hot cocoa were served. Enabling coffee consumption on a daily basis for the majority of the population in the GDR was both a remnant of colonial relations (i.e. products from former European colonies, such as coffee, tea and chocolate, had become integral to the living standard) and a matter of maintaining 'domestic stability' (Kloiber, 2017: 15) in the context of competitive relations with West Germany. During the Cold War period, particularly after the GDR's foreign debt skyrocketed owing to ongoing economic crises in 1975, these products became rarities (Kloiber, 2017: 22). In order to gain access to these and other commodities like black coal, the GDR engaged in unequal trade relations with socialist countries from the Global South. Economic agreements with the People's Democratic Republic of Ethiopia, the People's Republic of Mozambique, the People's Republic of Angola, Laos and Vietnam[9] also typify how extractive relations between the SED's state and other anti-imperialist states in the Global South were shaped. Not only did the GDR perceive itself as in a leading position in socialism, thus having the expertise in the field of 'modern development', but building on this self-perception, the GDR also saw itself as obliged to show other states the correct path to socialism. This 'civilising mission' (Tlostanova, 2012: 132) was directed in particular to socialist states from the Global South that allegedly had not yet 'developed' the economic conditions (e.g. in the case of subsistence farming) perceived necessary for socialist revolutions (Schilling, 2014: 94). In the name of 'anti-imperialist solidarity', the GDR could declare the exchange of raw materials such as coffee for weapons or know-how as 'solidarity aid' (Döring, 2008: 28). We suggest interpreting these relations as ambivalent practices of solidarity that fall into the realm of modernity/coloniality. As historian Ann-Judith Rabenschlag (2014) put it, this GDR policy can be understood as '*Völkerfreundschaft nach Bedarf*' ('friendship between peoples according to need').

The more recent demolition of the Sternchen and its remaining surroundings of socialist architecture can be understood as an active process of dealing with Germany's (real)socialist heritage, demonstrating the insignificance of the GDR in reunited Germany. It was on the basis of discursively positioning the former GDR as backward that West Germany could be seen as more progressive and democratic (Heft, 2018; Pates, 2013). Sociologist Kathleen Heft (2018) conceptualised these processes, in which East Germany was symbolically produced as inferior through a dialectical relationship to a superior West, as *Ossifizierung*. *Ossifizierung* can be roughly translated as 'Easternisation' and relates to the culturalisation of the East Germans, pejoratively called *Ossis*, as one of Germany's internal Others. However, in order to differentiate critically between multiple processes of difference-making in the German context, the culturalisation of East Germans cannot be compared to forms of racialised Othering (e.g. toward BPoCs). As sociologist Raj Kollmorgen has argued, the cultural devaluation of East Germany is marked by an ambivalence between recognition and contempt (2011: 340–345). The specific ways of transformation to capitalism were the result of a 'free' political decision supported by the majority of GDR citizens during the general elections of the Volkskammer (the unicameral legislature of the GDR) on 18 March 1990. What is more, the white population of East Germany indeed remains part of the imagined national community today and is also complicit in processes of racialisation, a fact that is highlighted not least by the successes of the AfD party in East Germany (Kubiak, 2018: 38).

The site of Cottbus's former (real)socialist city centre highlights the material dimension of the post(real)socialist urban space's entanglement in modernity/coloniality. The self-presentation as a modern and developed socialist nation expressed in the architecture of the Sternchen, as well as the consumption of goods from the Global South (such as coffee), contributed to the idea of (real)socialist superiority. While officially propagating anti-imperialist solidarity, the GDR profited from extractive relations with socialist states from the Global South and imagined itself as being a more developed socialism. Conversely, the demolition of the building complex showed how the FRG has dealt with (real)socialist remains, discursively positioning East Germans as the internal backward Other of West Germany.

Political-economic dimensions of (real)socialist modernity/coloniality: contract work in the Volkseigene Betriebe Textilkombinat Cottbus

Our second strategy to contribute to the decolonisation of Cottbus refers to the political-economic dimension of (real)socialist modernity/coloniality. Using the example of the structural situation of contract workers in the former textile industry of Cottbus, we show how the (real)socialist migration regime implemented a system of racial classification and social hierarchisation, resulting in very different living and working conditions.

In industrial centres like Cottbus, where 8,177 migrant workers were recorded in 1980 and the proportion of foreign workers totalled 11.3 per cent in 1987 (Strnad, 2011: 180 ff.), immigration shaped (real)socialist urban spaces in meaningful ways.[10] Nonetheless, the GDR imagined itself as an ethnically homogeneous and white society (Goel, 2013: 146). This dichotomous image is often reproduced in migration research as well as in practices of remembrance, even though both scholarly and activist projects have recently contributed to exposing the intersectional histories and positionings in and after the GDR (see exemplarily Goel, 2013; Lierke and Perinelli, 2020; Piesche, 2020; Poutrus, 2005a). The representation of the GDR as a country without a history of immigration hides the complexity of various mobility patterns that took place in and out of the GDR after World War II (Poutrus, 2005b). It also tends to impose narratives of a more 'tolerant' and 'multicultural' West Germany in comparison to the former (real)socialist regions (Goel, 2013: 146; Heft, 2018).

Cottbus, with enterprises in energy, textiles and chemical production, was one of the leading industrial centres in the GDR. Among them, the Volkseigene Betriebe Textilkombinat Cottbus (VEB TKC; 1969–90)[11] was one of the most important manufacturers of textiles, accounting for 17 per cent of the country's total textile production. As such, it was an important employer in the region. In 1977 over 16,000 people were employed at VEB TKC. Its main factory was located in Cottbus, with approximately 5,000 employees, 75 per cent of whom were female (Strnad, 2011: 174; interview with a former executive of VEB TKC, June 2018). VEB TKC was supposed to produce new products that could compete on the world market (Strnad, 2011: 174). From the mid-1970s on, because of a shortage of skilled labour, it was impossible to maintain that degree of textile production without a workforce including contract workers. After the ratification of a bilateral agreement on labour migration between Poland and the GDR, the first contract workers came to work at VEB TKC in 1972. Workers from Cuba came in the 1970s, and in the 1980s workers from Vietnam were also employed at VEB TKC. They were mostly assigned to departments characterised by monotonous and hard physical work (interview with a former executive of VEB TKC, June 2018).

Unlike the FRG, where 'guest workers' were recruited from 1953 to 1973, the GDR did not plan the employment of 'migrant' workers initially. GDR functionaries instead considered labour migration to be a vestige of forced labour from the times of national socialism (Mende, 2013: 152). This explains why the GDR initially made relatively sparse use of contract work. Contract work gained importance in the mid-1970s, mainly owing to rising mass emigration from the GDR as well as economic difficulties and labour demand. The bilateral agreements between the GDR and the countries of origin determined the specific working and living conditions for the contract workers, focusing on the economic and political needs of the involved countries instead of those of the workers (Mende, 2013: 156). At the beginning, the agreements were still based on solidarity-based claims. Although they were designed to be temporally limited from two to five years, they contained essential rights and provisions such as education and vocational training. The regulations put migrants and GDR citizens on an equal legal footing, with the exception of the immediate right of citizenship (Langner, 2020: 102; Mende, 2013: 153). By these means, the GDR was able to put its migration regime in a context of 'anti-imperialistic solidarity' as the official state doctrine seemed to suggest, and aimed to help its socialist brother states to 'develop' (Poutrus, 2005a: 129).

Thus, formally, the conditions of labour migration agreements between the GDR and other socialist countries were more egalitarian than those related to 'guest labour' in the FRG. In reality, though, and especially in the 1980s when the GDR experienced great labour shortages, regulations regarding contact work were often ignored (Strnad, 2011: 180). For example, this was the case when workers were assigned the most marginalised positions in the work hierarchy (such as hard physical and shift work) along a logic of racial classification (Poutrus, 2005a: 130). In many cases, contract workers were also unable to participate in the promised vocational training, or it did not correspond to the labour markets of their countries of origin (Langner, 2020: 102). Although the living situation in residential housing (organised by the enterprises) did not necessarily differ from those of the GDR citizens, contract workers were accommodated according to a principle of *'staatlich verordnete Abgrenzung'* (state-imposed separation) (Mende, 2013: 156–157; Poutrus, 2005a: 129–133). They had to live in separate units and were subject to strict regulations, such as registering and getting permission for external visits or overnight stays (Mende, 2013: 155). Also, their residency permits could be revoked at any time without justification, and the immigration of family members was not allowed (see the Law on the Granting of Residence for Foreigners in the German Democratic Republic 1979, §4 and §6).

Especially from the 1980s onwards, when racist violence also experienced a rise in the GDR, many contract workers increasingly experienced racist discrimination and violence at the workplace and in their places of residence (Langner, 2020: 104). GDR citizens and contract workers who engaged in relationships were formally ostracised and publicly stigmatised by the SED regime (Piesche, 2002: 43ff.; Poutrus 2005a: 132–133). For instance, if a contract worker (with the exception of Polish citizens) became pregnant, she had to choose between an abortion (a legal option in the GDR) or returning to her country of origin (Piesche, 2002: 42; Poutrus, 2005a: 132–133).

These ambivalences between the claim of implementing contract work as anti-imperialist solidarity (i.e. in order to help socialist countries from the Global South to 'develop') and the processes of social and racial division of the workforce that were implemented according to the economic needs of the GDR, illustrate the embeddedness of the (real)socialist migration regime within a 'coloniality of power'. This contradiction became even more apparent when contract workers often rejected the exploitative working conditions and fought back (e.g. by going on strike or using the possibility of petitions; Langner, 2020: 102). From the 1960s onwards and in the context of the racist attacks in Erfurt (1979), Merseburg (1983) and the death of Antonio Manuel Diogo on a railway line between Dessau and Berlin (1986), there was also continuous quantitative research on racist resentment among GDR citizens from the state-funded Zentralinstitut für Jugendforschung (Langner, 2020: 104–105). However, practices of resistance against unequal working and living conditions (such as strikes) were often suppressed with reference to an alleged *'zivilisatorische Rückständigkeit'* (backwardness in terms of civilisation) of contract workers (Schüle, 2003: 320), thus ascribing to them a supposed lack of socialist awareness (Mende, 2013: 159).

The example of contract work in VEB TKC highlights the political-economic dimensions of (real)socialist modernity/coloniality. The case of contract work in Cottbus's textile industry not only points to a (real)socialist regime of (temporal) labour migration, producing unequal living and working conditions, but also processes of social classification between GDR citizens and contract workers that highlight how the GDR's migration regime was linked to a system of racial differentiation and hierarchisation, according to a 'historicist' racial conception (Goldberg, 2010: 95).[12]

After 'reunification' in 1990, most of the industries in Cottbus were gradually privatised and dismantled, and the economic base of a large part of the population was destroyed. VEB TKC was initially sustained by companies from Germany and other Western countries but eventually closed in 1993. A series of smaller businesses took over for a while, but production was eventually outsourced to 'lower-wage countries' in Eastern Europe or to the Global South. As of 2008, only one small company with a handful of employees was still actively producing textiles in Cottbus (ACOL, 2008: 14). Today, the former VEB TKC's buildings are mostly abandoned, while some parts have been renovated as a shopping mall.

The first to lose their jobs and to be expelled from the recently 'reunited' country were contract workers, as the labour migration agreements made by the GDR were not continued by the FRG after 'reunification'. Of approximately ninety thousand contract workers in 1989, only approximately twenty-eight thousand were still staying in Germany in 1990 (Goel, 2013: 141). In 1997, when the possibility of permanent residency was finally negotiated, only fifteen thousand former contract workers still resided in Germany (Goel, 2013: 141).

Symbolic dimensions of (real)socialist modernity/coloniality: the site of Virchowstraße (Virchow Street)

The third step in the framework of our decolonial city tour in Cottbus referred to the symbolic dimension of modernity/coloniality. Uncovering the symbolic processes of Othering within the site of remembrance of the still-existing Virchowstraße, we show how the renaming of streets with reference to the German Empire (1871–1918) or German national socialism after 1945 did not necessarily entail a critical handling of colonial knowledge. Rather, the renaming of a street in Cottbus after physician and pathologist Rudolf Virchow (1821–1902), who was involved in racial phrenology, makes evident the persistence of the modernity/coloniality of the post(real)socialist urban space, which is also present in a symbolic dimension though the urban toponomy.

Places and streets that are directly related to German colonialism can be understood as symbolic manifestations of an ideology that legitimises colonialism, and therefore as signs of racism (Aikins and Hoppe, 2011: 521). In that light, colonial street names can be seen as perpetuated forms of symbolic violence, which reinscribe colonial practices of remembrance into the collective memory of the city. In both East and West Germany, there has been a political practice of renaming streets that reflected the undemocratic and undesirable heritage of national socialism and, after 1989, the SED regime. However, as the numerous streets and squares whose names continue to reference German colonialism show, this type of official historical-political intervention does not apply to the knowledge archive of colonialism. Although historians and activists in the 1950s in East Germany (and in the 1960s in West Germany)[13] initiated a critical examination of Germany's colonial past, an active and politically sustainable investigation of colonialism failed to appear (Schilling, 2014: 202).

The Virchowstraße in Cottbus received its name on 1 November 1946 (Akte Magistratssitzung, 1946) when the Soviet Occupation Zone (SOZ)[14] renamed streets that had referred to monarchy, fascism and/or colonialism in the immediate aftermath of national socialism. Louisenstraße, its former name, referred to Louise Hubert, the wife of a local politician ('Amtsrat Hubert'). However, its ambiguity seemed suspiciously similar to Louise, the Queen of Prussia (Lausitzer Rundschau, 2017). With Virchow, the SOZ instead chose to honour a politician and medical scientist of the nineteenth century who is still famous for his achievements in pathology and public health. What is less known is that Virchow was also a major proponent of racial Darwinism. He founded the Berlin Society of Anthropology (1869) and the German Anthropological Society (1970). Most importantly, he contributed to a Darwinian understanding of evolution of human 'races'. With the intention to study the stages of development from 'savagery' to 'civilisation', Virchow collected over four thousand objects, including human remains from all parts of the world (Becker, 2008: 96). Virchow also undertook extensive studies on racial characteristics of more than a million German schoolchildren, collecting their hair, eye and skin colour, as well as phrenological shapes of their heads (Becker, 2008: 95). Furthermore, he participated in the founding of Berlin's ethnological and *Völkerkunde* museum. Its opening would have been impossible without the objects from German colonies.

The fact that the SOZ renamed a street after Rudolf Virchow without addressing this history shows how (real)socialist practices of remembrance were deeply permeated by the 'coloniality of power'. On the one hand, the national doctrines of anti-fascism and anti-imperialism demanded political confrontation with the references to German Empire and national socialism in the SOZ/GDR (e.g. by tearing down monuments or renaming streets).

Figure 6.3 Cottbus, sign of Virchowstraße [Virchostreet] next to Karl-Marx-Straße [Karl-Marx-Street], street names in German and Sorbian.

On the other hand, the idea that fascism and racism had been overcome with the overturning of capitalism hindered a sustained engagement with its colonial legacy (Rabenschlag, 2014: 52–53). The externalisation of racism onto capitalist states (such as the FRG) made a political debate superfluous.[15] Racialised images and practices, however, remained powerful in the social realities of (real)socialism. As black-feminist and East German cultural scholar Peggy Piesche (2002) has exemplarily shown in her study of GDR curricular materials, racialising ideas were firmly anchored in the GDR's archive of knowledge. Piesche examined how textbooks produced images of 'different races and appearances' (2002: 44) while constructing whiteness as a social norm. Accordingly, the GDR population could be imagined on a higher level of 'development' in the global social world order than other nationalities. This form of 'socialism of difference' (Piesche, 2002: 52) not only shaped the lives of children in a decisive way but also had a great influence on cultural practices.

The example of the Virchowstraße in Cottbus highlights the symbolic dimension of post(real)socialist urban modernity/coloniality. The colonial knowledge immanent in the remembrance of Rudolf Virchow can be seen as a signifier that has rewritten forms of symbolic violence into the collective memory of the city. Although the renaming of streets during the SOZ era illustrates a critical confrontation with the regimes of German monarchy and national socialism, active confrontation with Germany's colonial history failed to appear. While the GDR removed some of the visible references to imperialism and colonialism, in some cases they were reintroduced after 1990. Such is the case with the Christopher Columbus Primary School Cottbus, which had been named after anti-fascist Ernst Thälmann in the times of the GDR. In 2004, parents, teachers and children decided in favour of the new (old) name in a competition (see Kolumbus Grundschule, 2021).

Urban colonial and imperial difference: understanding the modernity/coloniality of the (real)socialist urban space

By adopting a decolonial lens within the framework of our city tour in Cottbus, we have uncovered different aspects of coloniality/modernity that become visible in post(real)socialist sites of remembrance. The underlying assumption was that coloniality, i.e. 'the indispensable underside of modernity' (Tlostanova, 2012: 132), which is closely linked with a system of social hierarchisation and classification, not only led to forms of 'racial capitalism' (Robinson, 1983). Instead, ideas and practices related to a 'colonial matrix of power' also pervaded the various articulations of socialist modernity. As Tlostanova illustrated with regard to Russia and/or the Soviet Union: 'the racial discourse always came back to haunt socialist constructions, particularly when they referred to the internal others as well as the "brothers" outside – those socialist states that were invariably assigned a lower place on the ladder of Soviet modernity, where the Russian "superman" occupied the top position' (2012: 132). She argued that race and racism, albeit in a modified form and replaced by concepts such as 'class' or 'ideology', still shaped social relations and discourses between and within the socialist brother states. It was through the 'rhetoric of modernity' and the related 'mission of progress, development, or civilization' that coloniality continued to operate within the various spaces and temporalities of socialist socio-historical configurations (Tlostanova 2012: 132). However, while Russia was able to claim a superior position vis-à-vis its diverse internal Others (i.e. within the Soviet Union), as well as external Others (i.e. towards other socialist states, such as the GDR), it was unable to compete with the imperial ambitions from 'Western' states. According to Tlostanova (2015: 46–47), this ambivalent situation of Russia both inside and outside the socialist system had its origins in various forms of 'colonial' and 'imperial difference'.[16] Its 'Janus-faced' position within a global context of coloniality, i.e. the ambition of global supremacy while simultaneously experiencing epistemological and cultural devaluation by the Western world, caused a kind of inferiority complex, or in Tlostanova's words, 'a catching-up logic' (2015: 46).

Combining Tlostanova's deliberations on the colonial legacy socialist social-historical configurations with the framework of our decolonial city tour, we have revealed how colonial relations, classifications and forms of knowledge have shaped the urban (real)socialist space in Cottbus. Drawing on the insights from decolonial theory and Urban Studies (see the Introduction to this volume), we argue that European cities can be understood as cultural, economic and political signifiers of modernity, thus providing and maintaining processes of racialisation and social hierarchisation within the 'colonial matrix of power'. At the same time, European cities are by no means all the same. As the study of post(real)socialist cities such as Cottbus shows, East German cities not only faced different forms of modernity/coloniality than those in West Germany but also faced specific processes of devaluation and culturalisation after 1990.

Following Tlostanova's reflections on the different forms of socialism's complex, meshed embeddedness in modernity/coloniality, we conceptualise the interconnections between postcolonial and postsocialist traces as aspects of an urban 'imperial difference'. In doing so, we not only point out the traces of modernity/coloniality inscribed in the architecture, economies and/ or archives of knowledge of the city. Instead, we also highlight the ambivalent positioning of post(real)socialist urban space within the 'coloniality of power'. As we have shown, colonial as well as anti-imperialist and anti-fascist notions have shaped social realities in Cottbus. Accordingly, besides the continuities of racialised post(real)socialist urbanity, we also point out the critical potential that socialist configurations offered against colonial as well as capitalist-exploitative orders (Kušić et al., 2019). Furthermore, we highlight the processes of devaluation and culturalisation that the post(real)socialist city and its population faced after 1990.

One aspect of an internal 'imperial difference' (i.e. between socialist states) that is inscribed in the post(real)socialist urban space can be related in GDR's rhetoric to represent a 'developed socialism'. Within the competitive logic of the 'civilising mission', the GDR positioned itself directly behind the Soviet Union (Poutrus, 2005a: 124). The claim to 'progress' and 'development' is not only reflected in the aesthetics of (real)socialist architecture such as the Sternchen. It also materialised in the asymmetrical trade relations between the GDR and countries from the Global South that allowed for the daily consumption of products such as coffee or cacao. The social hierarchisation and unequal positioning that contract workers from countries such as Cuba or Vietnam experienced in Cottbus's textile industry highlight another aspect of internal 'imperial difference.' Furthermore, the site of the Virchowstraße shows how symbolic manifestations of colonial ideology were effective but undiscussed owing to the anti-fascist, yet homogeneous self-conception of the GDR.

Additionally, we have identified aspects of an external 'imperial difference' (i.e. between the GDR and the FRG) that have shaped the urban post(real) socialist space. While the GDR benefited from unequal power relations at the global level, it was in fact also characterised by a double inferiority, vis-à-vis both the Soviet Union and the FRG. In Tlostanova's words, compared with Russia as well as with Western states, the GDR politically and economically occupied a 'second [or third] class place' (2012: 134). For example, until the mid-1970s, the GDR was, on the one hand, dependent on the Soviet Union's approval for substantial decisions about its foreign policy. At the same time, until the recognition of the GDR as a sovereign state (1973), West Germany made 'development cooperation' with countries of the Global South dependent on their non-cooperation with the GDR (the so-called Hallstein Doctrine) (Döring, 2008: 27). Aspects of an external 'urban imperial difference' also become visible in the processes of deindustrialisation and the destruction of the socialist heritage after 1990, as well as in current processes of '*Ossifizierung*'.

While the focus in this chapter has been on processes of racial classification and social hierarchisation, we want to conclude by highlighting the critical potential inherent to the anti-fascist and anti-imperialist state doctrine. The point here is that the (real)socialist form of society offered spaces of possibility to fight against colonial, racist and capitalist-exploitative orders. For instance, the GDR criticised the exploitative conditions for West German 'guest workers' as a continuity with forced labour during national socialism. As a result, the bilateral migration agreements for 'contract work' between the GDR and other socialist countries, which in comparison with the FRG started comparatively late (in the 1970s and 1980s, while West Germany declared a ban on 'guest work' recruitment in 1973), were formally more egalitarian, although these rights were often not implemented in practice. Also, the GDR supported anti-colonial struggles and movements (such as in Angola, Zimbabwe, Namibia, Mozambique and South Africa)[17] and thereby situated the project of (real)socialism in systemic competition with capitalist states (Pampuch, 2018: 336). Moreover, it initiated a critical culture of remembrance in the 1950s, opposing German colonialism, imperialism and national socialism in the urban space, e.g. by renaming streets, removing the inscriptions on monuments or removing monuments entirely. We read the different facets surrounding the idea of anti-imperialism as yet another ambivalent aspect of 'imperial difference' that provided for (controversial) processes of raising decolonial and anti-imperialist awareness and recognition in the urban post(real)socialist space.

These divergent forms of urban 'imperial difference' and the diverse processes of racialisation and social hierarchisation involved provide the historical background for current debates about belonging, racist and right-wing extremist mobilisations as well as anti-fascist and anti-racist resistance in Cottbus.

In conclusion

The aim of this chapter was to uncover colonial legacies that are inscribed into three sites of remembrance in the East German city of Cottbus. Applying a decolonial perspective (Quijano, 2000; Tlostanova, 2012; 2015) to the framework of a historical city tour as developed by postcolonial and decolonial urban initiatives, we used three case studies to analyse different aspects of modernity/coloniality within the post(real)socialist urban space. Highlighting the complex ways in which (real)socialist modernity was complicit in reproducing the 'coloniality of power', we unmasked various processes of social hierarchisation and classification that have shaped the urban space in Cottbus (e.g. by exploiting and segregating contract workers, by coercing unequal trade relations or by reproducing colonial knowledge patterns in street names or educational materials). At the same time, drawing on postsocialist approaches, we reflected on the critical potential that (real) socialism offered against colonial orders and exploitative capitalist relations (e.g. by removing colonial monuments and supporting anti-colonial movements). We also pointed to contemporary processes of devaluation (e.g. the destruction of the socialist city centre or the textile industry) and culturalisation ('*Ossifizierung*') of (real)socialist practices and heritage that the East German city and its population have faced since 1990. In accordance with Tlostanova's deliberations on the modernity/coloniality of socialist social-historical configurations, we conceptualised these somewhat contradictory aspects of post(real)socialist modernity/coloniality in Cottbus as urban 'imperial difference'. As we have shown, this ambivalent meshing of modern/colonial aspirations with anti-imperialist and anti-fascist concepts during the GDR and the post(real)socialist devaluation of '*Ossifizierung*' after 1990 has not only shaped current articulations of racism but also has contributed to anti-fascist and anti-racist mobilisations and resistance in the post(real) socialist city. Furthermore, our analysis highlights how urban processes have been continually and specifically racialised since modernity.

Modernity/coloniality has profoundly structured urban realities in Cottbus and, if not addressed, will continue to be perpetuated. Making the complex colonial embeddedness of post(real)socialist space visible and creating space for epistemic and social justice thus remains an unfinished project. Accordingly, this chapter aims to contribute to more solidarity by enabling alternative, heterogeneous narratives and relations between geographical contexts and people.

Notes

1 Miriam Friz Trzeciak is a white, non-binary person with a German passport and a working-class background. They grew up in a small Catholic village located in the West German–Netherlands borderland. Manuel Peters has a white, male, middle-class background, and is a person with a German passport. He grew up in a middle-sized town in Western Germany. One of his parents fled the GDR to the FRG in the early 1960s. Both work at the Chair of Intercultural Studies at the Brandenburg Technical University Cottbus-Senftenberg.
   We thank Giovanni Picker, Noa Ha, Daniel Bendix and Reinhart Kößler for providing us with helpful and important feedback. Furthermore, we thank the participants of the study project 'Cottbus Postkolonial and Postsozialistisch'; special thanks go to: Robert Schneider, Martin Jürgens, Katharina König, Ines Krause, Andreas Lipske and Dieter Mohnhaupt.
2 At the same time, for many years, anti-racist and anti-fascist initiatives active in Cottbus have struggled for solidarity-based forms of togetherness and social participation (see, for example, Cottbus ist BUNT, 2021). It would go beyond the scope of this chapter to comprehensively describe the complex and diverse forms of anti-fascist and anti-racist resistance in Cottbus.
3 On the local level, this is reflected by the increasing number of racist attacks in the state of Brandenburg since 2015 (Opferperspektive, 2019). In September 2017 the AfD (Alternative für Deutschland) won 27 per cent of the votes during the state elections and became the strongest party in Cottbus.
4 However, the colonial history of modern Germany cannot be limited to the German Empire. For example, in 1682 Elector Friedrich Wilhelm of Brandenburg sent out an expedition to found the first Brandenburg colony in Africa.

5   The term 'real socialism' was coined by Erich Honecker, the First Secretary of the Central Committee of the Socialist Unity Party of Germany, in 1973.

6   By using the term 'postcolonialism', we refer to the 'conditions, processes and struggles of coming to terms with a presence that is imbued with the colonial past' (Bendix, 2018: 19). We use 'postsocialism' as both a political and an empirical term when we refer to the spaces that were formerly governed by socialist or communist parties (such as the GDR). Drawing on postsocialist studies (Stykow, 2013; Todorova, 2005), we assume that these contexts are politically, economically and culturally shaped by the different experiences of state socialism.

7   In decolonial theory, the term 'colonial matrix of power' is used to describe 'the imposition of a racial/ethnic classification of the world's population' (Quijano, 2014: 285) as an essential aspect of modernity/coloniality. This matrix emerged in the course of the formation of (Latin) America as a geocultural entity/identity and the establishment of Europe as a hegemonic zone beginning in the sixteenth century. According to Quijano (2014), social classification is linked to the establishment of a capitalist division of labour.

8   According to Mignolo and Tlostanova (2007: 109), coloniality is characterised as a 'specific kind of imperial/colonial relations that emerged in the Atlantic world in the sixteenth century that brought imperialism and capitalism together'. In this sense, colonialism and imperialism form a specific bond and are closely interwoven with capitalism.

9   We thank Noa K. Ha for pointing out this relation between the GDR and Vietnam.

10 The total share of employed foreign workers in the GDR's industrial sector was at 6.8 per cent. In the FRG, three million foreign workers were employed, equalling 10 per cent of the workforce (Strnad, 2011: 182).

11 People's-Owned Enterprises, Cottbus Textile Combine/Corporation (VEB TKC).

12 According to Goldberg, 'racial historicism is based on a conception that a group, broadly and long considered to constitute a racial group, is presumed less well developed in intellectual and cultural capacities than those emanating from regions supposedly representing more appealing capacities and habits. The group is taken to have coalesced from the fragments of heterogeneous dispersals in some distant past into a supposedly geographically bound coherence, with attendant physical traits and cultural habits' (2010: 95). Racial historicism, thus, is closely connected to the 'colonial matrix of power'.

13 On the differences of coming to terms with German colonial rule and genocide in Namibia (1904–08) within West and East German historiography, see for example Bürger (2017).

14 The SOZ became the GDR on 7 October 1949.

15 As the GDR constitution showed (Constitution of the GDR, Art. 6, Para. 3:1968 (1974)), GDR's anti-colonial commitment was limited to formal colonial rule (Wegener, 2019). In the constitution, the state leadership underlined its claim to support states and peoples fighting against imperialism and its colonial regime, for national freedom and independence, in their struggle for social progress (Wegener, 2019).

16 According to Tlostanova, 'colonial difference refers to the differential between the capitalist empires of modernity (the heart of Europe) and their colonies' (2012: 134). 'Imperial difference' is used to refer to a difference between imperialist powers. It describes those empires 'that failed to or were prevented by different circumstances and powers from fulfilling their imperial mission in secular modernity' (Tlostanova 2015: 46). Tlostanova renders 'imperial difference' as marked by 'internal and external variants'. The first, internal imperial difference points to 'the European losers of the second modernity which became the south of Europe'. The second, external imperial difference, describes 'the not-quite-western, not-quite-capitalist empires of modernity' (Tlostanova, 2012: 134).

17 The GDR supported various anti-colonial movements, such as the African National Congress (ANC) of South Africa, the Frente de Libertação de Moçambique (FRELIMO) and the Namibian South West Africa People's Organisation (SWAPO), which Western democracies dubbed 'terrorist organisations' (Pampuch, 2018: 323–324).

References

ACOL (Gesellschaft für Arbeitsförderung mbh Cottbus) (ed.) (2008), *Dokumentation. 50 Jahre Textilindustrie in Cottbus* (Cottbus: ACOL).

AfricAvenir International e.V. and M. Heller (2017), *No Humboldt 21! Dekoloniale Einwände gegen das Humboldt-Forum* (Berlin: AfricAVenir International).

Aikins, J. K. and R. Hoppe (2011), Straßennamen. In Arndt, S. and N. Ofuatey-Alazard (eds) *Wie Rassismus aus Wörtern spricht: Kerben des Kolonialismus im Wissensarchiv deutsche Sprache. Ein kritisches Nachschlagewerk* (Münster: Waxmann), pp. 521–538.

Akte Magistratssitzung [Magistrate Meeting File], Cottbus, 009/135, 24 September 1946.

Becker, V. (2008), *Der Einbruch der Naturwissenschaft in die Medizin. Gedanken um, mit, über, zu Rudolf Virchow* (Berlin and Heidelberg: Springer).

Behrends, J., T. Lindenberger and P. G. Poutrus (2003), Thesenpapier: Historische Ursachen der Fremdenfeindlichkeit in den Neuen Bundesländern. In Behrends, J., T. Lindenberger and P. G. Poutrus (eds) *Fremde und Fremd-Sein in der DDR: zu historischen Ursachen der Fremdenfeindlichkeit in Ostdeutschland* (Berlin: Metropol Verlag), pp. 327–333.

Bendix, D. (2018), *Global Development and Colonial Power: German Development Policy at Home and Abroad* (London and New York: Rowman & Littlefield).

Bernhard, P. (2016), Postkoloniale Spurensuche in München. Geschichtsdidaktische Reflexion eines Stadtrundgangs mit einer 'postkolonialen Initiative' im Rahmen einer kolonialgeschichtlichen Unterrichtseinheit. *Zeitschrift für Geschichtsdidaktik* 15: 101–115.

Bürger, C. (2017), *Deutsche Kolonialgeschichte(n). Der Genozid in Namibia und die Geschichtsschreibung der DDR und BRD* (Bielefeld: Transcript).

Constitution of the GDR (1974), Article 6, Paragraph 3, www.documentarchiv.de/ ddr/verfddr.html [accessed 17 July 2021].

Cottbus ist BUNT (2021), www.cottbus-ist-bunt.de/ [accessed 17 July 2021].

Döring, H.-J. (2008), Entwicklungspolitik und Solidarität in der DDR, dargestellt an Beispielen der staatlichen Zusammenarbeit mit Mosambik und Äthiopien und der entwicklungsbezogenen Bildungsarbeit unabhängiger Gruppen. PhD dissertation, Technische Universität Berlin.

Drechsler, H. (1966), *Der Kampf der Herero und Nama gegen den deutschen Imperialismus [1884–1915]* (Berlin: Akademie).

El-Tayeb, F. (2016), *Undeutsch. Die Konstruktion des Anderen in der postmigrantischen Gesellschaft* (Bielefeld: Transcript).

Fröschner, J. and J. Warnecke (2019), *Was interessiert mich denn Cottbus? Dynamiken rechter Formierung in Südbrandenburg: der Verein Zukunft Heimat,* www.rosalux.de/publikation/id/40381/was-interessiert-mich-denn-cottbus?cHash=e84afbb07629fc94a 555139c6cb8c633 [accessed 8 December 2021].

Goel, U. (2013), Ungehörte Stimmen. Überlegungen zur Ausblendung von Migration in die DDR in der Migrationsforschung. In Gürsel, D., Ç. Zülfukar and Allmende e.V. (eds) *Wer Macht Demo_kratie? Kritische Beiträge zu Migration und Machtverhältnissen* (Münster: edition assemblage), pp. 138–150.

Goldberg, D. T. (2010), Call and response. *Patterns of Prejudice* 44(1): 89–106.

Ha, K. N. (2017), Die fragile Erinnerung des Entinnerten. In Zwischenraum Kollektiv (eds) *Decolonize the City! Zur Kolonialität der Stadt: Gespräche | Aushandlungen | Perspektiven* (Münster: Unrast), pp. 108–20.

Ha, N. K. (2017), Zur Kolonialität des Städtischen. In Zwischenraum Kollektiv (eds) *Decolonize the City! Zur Kolonialität der Stadt: Gespräche | Aushandlungen | Perspektiven* (Münster: Unrast), pp. 75–87.

Hall, S. (1996), When was the post-colonial? Thinking at the limit. In Chamber, I. and L. Curti (eds) *The Postcolonial Question: Common Skies, Divided Horizons* (London: Routledge), pp. 242–260.

Heft, K. (2018), Brauner Osten – Überlegungen zu einem populären Deutungsmuster ostdeutscher Andersheit. *Feministische Studien* 2: 357–366.

Kloiber, A. (2017), Coffee, East Germans and the Cold War world, 1945–1990. Doctoral dissertation, McMaster University, Hamilton, http://hdl.handle.net/11375/22022 [accessed 11 June 2020].

Kollmorgen R. (2011), Subalternisierung. In Kollmorgen, R., F. T. Koch and H.-L. Dienel (eds) *Diskurse der deutschen Einheit. Kritik und Alternativen* (Wiesbaden: VS), pp. 301–359.

Kollmorgen, R. and T. Hans (2011), Der verlorene Osten. Massenmediale Diskurse über Ostdeutschland und die deutsche Einheit. In Kollmorgen, R., F. T. Koch and H.-L. Dienel (eds) *Diskurse der deutschen Einheit. Kritik und Alternativen* (Wiesbaden: VS), pp. 107–165.

Kolumbus Grundschule (2021), www.kolumbus-grundschule.de/50-jaehriges-schuljubilaeum-in-cottbus-sandow/ [accessed 2 May 2021].

Krauß, A. (2012), Aufstieg und Fall der Stadtpromenade Cottbus. *Arbeitshefte zur Denkmalpflege in Hamburg* 28: 179–182.

Kubiak, D. (2018), Der Fall 'Ostdeutschland' – 'Einheitsfiktion' als Herausforderung für die Integration am Fallbeispiel der Ost-West-Differenz. *Zeitschrift für vergleichende Politikwissenschaft* 12: 25–42.

Kušić, K., P. Lottholz and P. Manolova (2019), Introduction. From dialogue to practice: pathways towards decoloniality in Southeast Europe. *dVERSIA. Special Issue: Decolonial Theory & Practice in Southeast Europe* 3: 7–30.

Langner, C. (2020), 'Affen und Banditen' – über die historische Rekonstruktion von Rassismus und rechter Gewalt in der späten DDR. In Institut für Ziviligesellschaft (IDZ) (ed.) *Schwerpunkt: Kontinuitäten* (Berlin, Jena), pp. 101–109.

Lausitzer Rundschau (2017), Historische Ansicht unter neuem Namen: Die Sack'schen Häuser in Cottbus. *LR Online* (23 January), www.lr-online.de/lausitz/cottbus/historische-ansicht-unter-neuem-namen-die-sack_schen-haeuser-in-cottbus-35584304.html [accessed 11 June 2020].

Law on the Granting of Residence for Foreigners in the German Democratic Republic 1979, www.verfassungen.de/ddr/auslaendergesetz79.htm [accessed 11 June 2020].

Lierke, L. and M. Perinelli (eds) (2020), *Erinnern stören. Der Mauerfall aus migrantischer und jüdischer Perspektive* (Berlin: Verbrecher Verlag).

Lugones, M. (2007), Heterosexualism and the colonial/modern gender system. *Hypatia* 22: 186–219.

Macdonald, S. (2006), Undesirable heritage: fascist material culture and historical consciousness in Nuremberg. *International Journal of Heritage Studies* 12(1): 9–28.

Mende, C. (2013), Migration in die DDR. Über staatliche Pläne, migrantische Kämpfe und den real-existierenden Rassismus. In D. Gürsel, Z. Çetin and Allmende e.V. (eds) *Wer Macht Demo_kratie? Kritische Beiträge zu Migration und Machtverhältnissen* (Münster: edition assemblage), pp. 151–164.

Messerschmidt, A. (2008), Postkoloniale Erinnerungsprozesse in einer postnationalsozialistischen Gesellschaft – vom Umgang mit Rassismus und Antisemitismus. *Peripherie* 109/110(28): 42–60.

Mignolo, W. and M. Tlostanova (2007), The logic of coloniality and the limits of postcoloniality. In Krishnaswamy, R. and J. C. Hawley (eds) *The Postcolonial and the Global: Connections, Conflicts, Complicities* (Minneapolis, MN: University Press of Minnesota), pp. 109–23

Opferperspektive (2019), Statistics of right-wing violence in Brandenburg. www.opferperspektive.de/rechte-angriffe/statistik-brandenburg/statistik-rechter-gewalttaten-in-brandenburg [accessed 11 June 2020].

Pampuch, S. (2018), Afrikanische Freedom Fighter im Exil der DDR. In Zloch, S., L. Müller and S. Lässig (eds) *Wissen in Bewegung. Migration und globale Verflechtungen in der Zeitgeschichte seit 1945* (München: de Gruyter Oldenbourg), pp. 321–348.

Pates, R. (2013), Der 'Ossi' als symbolischer Ausländer. In Pates, R. and M. Schochow (eds) *Der 'Ossi'* (Wiesbaden: VS Verlag für Sozialwissenschaften), pp. 7–20.

Picker, G., K. Murji and M. Boatcă (2019), Racial urbanities: towards a global cartography. *Social Identities* 25(1): 1–10.

Piesche, P. (2002), Black and German? East German adolescents before 1989: a retrospective view of a 'non-existent issue' in the GDR. In Adelson, A. L. (ed.) *The Cultural After-Life of East Germany: New Transnational Perspectives* (Washington, DC: American Institute for Contemporary German Studies), pp. 37–59.

Piesche, P. (2020), *Labor 89. Intersektionale Bewegungsgeschichte*n aus West und Ost* (Berlin: Yilmaz Günay).

Poutrus, P. G. (2005a), Die DDR, ein anderer deutscher Weg? Zum Umgang mit Ausländern im SED-Staat. In Beier-de Haan, R. (ed.) *Zuwanderungsland Deutschland. Migrationen 1500–2005* (Berlin and Wolfratshausen: Deutsches Historisches Museum/Edition Minerva), pp. 120–133.

Poutrus, P. G. (2005b), 'Teure Genossen'. Die 'politischen Emigranten' als 'Fremde' im Alltag der DDR-Gesellschaft. In Poutrus, P. G. and C. T. Müller (eds) *Ankunft – Alltag – Ausreise. Migration und interkulturelle Begegnung in der DDR-Gesellschaft* (Köln: Böhlau), pp. 221–266.

Quent, M. (2019), *Deutschland Rechts Außen. Wie die Rechten nach der Macht greifen und wie wir sie stoppen können* (München: Piper).

Quijano, A. (2000), Coloniality of power, Eurocentrism, and Latin America. *Nepantla: Views from South* 1(3): 533–580.

Quijano, A. (2007), Coloniality and modernity/rationality. *Cultural Studies* 21(2–3): 168–178.

Quijano, A. (2014), Colonialidad del poder y clasificación social. In Castro-Gómez, S. and R. Grosfoguel (eds) *Cuestiones y horizontes: de la dependencia histórico-estructural a la colonialidad/descolonialidad del poder* (Buenos Aires: CLACSO), pp. 285–327.

Rabenschlag, A.-J. (2014), Völkerfreundschaft nach Bedarf: Ausländische Arbeitskräfte in der Wahrnehmung von Staat und Bevölkerung der DDR. Doctoral dissertation, Acta Universitatis, Stockholm.

Robinson, C. (1983), *Black Marxism: The Making of the Black Radical Tradition* (London: Zed Books).

Schilling, B. (2014), *Postcolonial Germany – Memories of Empire in a Decolonized Nation* (Oxford: Oxford University Press).

Schüle, A. (2003), Die ham se sozusagen aus dem Busch geholt. Die Wahrnehmung der Vertragsarbeitskräfte aus Schwarzafrika und Vietnam durch Deutsche im VEB Leipziger Baumwollspinnerei. In Behrends, J. C., T. Lindenberger and P. G. Poutrus (eds) *Fremde und Fremd-Sein in der DDR. Zu historischen Ursachen der Fremdenfeindlichkeit in Ostdeutschland* (Berlin: Metropol Verlag), pp. 309–324.

Strnad, A. (2011), Vertragsarbeiter in der Leichtindustrie am Beispiel des VEB Textilkombinat Cottbus. In Priemel, K. C. (ed.) *Transit | Transfer: Politik und Praxis der Einwanderung in der DDR 1945–1990* (Berlin-Brandenburg: Bebra Verlag), pp. 169–187.

Stykow, P. (2013), Postsozialismus. In *Docupedia-Zeitgeschichte: Begriffe, Methoden und Debatten der zeithistorischen Forschung*, https://doc-upedia.de/zg/Postsozialismus [accessed 14 June 2020].

Tlostanova, M. (2012), Postsocialist ≠ postcolonial? On post-Soviet imaginary and global coloniality. *Journal of Postcolonial Writing* 48(2): 130–142.

Tlostanova, M. (2015), Can the post-Soviet think? On coloniality of knowledge, external imperial and double colonial difference. *Intersections. East European Journal of Society and Politics* 1(2): 38–58.

Todorova, M. (2005), Spacing Europe: what is a historical region? *East Central Europe* 32(1–2): 59–78.

Trzeciak, M. F. (2020), Multidirektionale Formen des Erinnerns und Vergessens. Das Beispiel einer postkolonialen und postsozialistischen Stadtführung. *Gesellschaft – Individuum – Sozialisation (GISo). Zeitschrift für Sozialisationsforschung*, 1(2). DOI: 10.26043/GISo.2020.2.4

Trzeciak, M. F. and J. Schäfer (2021), Aggressive refugees, violent hooligans, concerned citizens: reinterpreting multiple processes of difference-making in mediatizations of migration and conflict in East Germany in the German media. *Journal of Immigrant & Refugee Studies* 19(1): 55–67.

Wallerstein, I. (1974), *The Modern World-System, Vol. I: Capitalist Agriculture and the Origins of the European World-Economy in the Sixteenth Century* (New York and London: Academic Press).

Wegener, Max (2019), Am (ost)deutschen Wesen soll die Welt genesen. Verwischte Spuren kolonialer Beteiligungen. *Ostjournal* 4: 28–33.

Zimmerer, J. (2013), Kolonialismus und kollektive Identität: Erinnerungsorte der deutschen Kolonialgeschichte. In Zimmerer, J. (ed.) *Kein Platz an der Sonne. Erinnerungsorte der deutschen Kolonialgeschichte* (Frankfurt am Main: Campus-Verlag), pp. 9–38.

Zwischenraum Kollektiv (eds) (2017), *Decolonize the City! Zur Kolonialität der Stadt: Gespräche | Aushandlungen | Perspektiven* (Münster: Unrast).

Part III

Provincialising the (urban) political

7

Decolonial migrant claims to the metropole: views from two Mediterranean cities

Mahdis Azarmandi and Piro Rexhepi

Introduction

In the summer of 2019, we attended two events in Spain that we believe illustrate the ongoing struggles for the city in the larger sense: the encuentro antirracista (anti-racist meeting) held on 22–23 June in Clua de Meià, near Lleida, and organised by the Barcelona-based transfeminist collective t.i.c.t.a.c.; and the Historical Materialism conference held on 27–30 June at Nau Bostik, a self-managed squat for cultural creation, and organised by a mix of Barcelona-based and foreign academics. In contrast to the Historical Materialism conference, which was mostly organised and attended by academics and which revolved around theoretical questions of historicity in its local and translocal forms of coloniality, the encuentro antirracista in Clua de Meià was a self-organised gathering of migrants, racialised and gendered communities whose concerns were primarily those of struggles concerning state-sanctioned racial violence, poverty and police brutality, forced evictions, community organising, the safety of sex worker and trans communities and overall questions of how to establish infrastructures of care and support in the cracks and fissures of coloniality (Mignolo and Walsh, 2018) while actively confronting the privatisation and policing of public space and making the city away from mere intellectual exercises of thinking and theorising urban space.

We think the differences between the two events illustrate not only the political climate of the city but also the possibilities that Barcelona, and many migrant cities along the Mediterranean like Salonika and Beirut, offer for reclaiming the city in ways that defy the academic abstractions of 'historical materialism' or 'capitalist realism', to borrow from Mark Fisher (2009). If in the Historical Materialism conference the city was underlined by debates around Catalan independence and the larger capitalist-colonial vestiges of Spain, the anti-racist encuentro conversations were not so much about theorising the city as they were directly involved in the praxis of making and taking the city.

Being that we find ourselves as intruders in Barcelona, we find it important to introduce ourselves as a way of situating the positions from which we are making these observations. Mahdis is a queer German-Iranian woman while Piro is a queer Albanian Muslim man raised in the Former Yugoslav Republic of Macedonia, once the Socialist Republic of Macedonia and now Northern Macedonia. We owe a great deal of gratitude to our common friend and member of the trans-feminist collective t.i.c.t.a.c., Tjaša Kancler, who introduced and invited us to the encuentro antirracista. Situated in decolonial de-linking and divesting from the ways in which Barcelona is moulded and modelled in Eurocentric epistemologies and imaginaries, we were (and remain) particularly interested in migrant and queer politics and historicity that circumvent the pressure and strengthening of ethnic, racial, national and post-national European mythologies by identifying with the city and its neighbourhoods while producing multicentred and intersectional narratives and spaces of belonging and becoming.

In conversation with the Introduction to this edited volume, our goal in this piece then is not so much to provincialise Europe, because we find Europe is already a backwater with all its isolationist vestiges of purity, racism, nostalgia and 'traditions' – from its *le bon ton* hangover all the way to its hopes that a EUropean Luftschloss will somehow save it from all its silly suspicions and the more serious responsibilities of its cruelties. Rather, we want to think about these cities through the migrant and minoritised affective and political maps and memories that make them the new Mediterranean metropoles. But here we face a contradiction. Notwithstanding our desire to push Europe off the cliff, so to speak, instead of provincialising it, the violence it continues to constitute (and has more recently intensified) on the shores of these cities is very real and erasing it altogether could relegate real reparative responsibilities to liberal studies. For us, Europe is the prize of the postcolonial migrant, the more than earned historical reward that migrants and minoritised subjects have laboured for.[1] That is just one way that we think postcolonial reparations could look in terms of decolonial praxis.

While we have both been inspired by Chakrabarty's call for 'provincializing Europe' in our earlier work as an important way of inserting modernity's 'ambivalences, contradictions, the use of force and the tragedies and ironies that attend it' (2000: 43) through the 'lack' of those historical subjects that appear inadequate to speak, we are not certain we want to narrate these processes into the canon of modernity at all. Instead, our concerns over what to do with Europe in terms of decoloniality are influenced by Dabashi (2019) who points out that, whether we want it to be or not, Europe is still not dead. Even worse, it has turned into a dead man walking, soaked and boozed as it is in its own Euthanasia, to borrow from the Bosnian artists Kurt & Plasto. That Slavoj Žižek has come to its rescue is already a sign that things have gone from far to further. The once great neoliberal projects of 'smart cities' and 'diverse cities', which defined its politics and metaphors for cities along the northern Mediterranean shores by spatially and temporally folding them into its narratives of Europeanisation and contriving them as 'European' in the 1990s, have now transformed into 'Urban Dimension[s] of the European Neighbourhood Policy' (European Commission, n.d.) – as EU externalisation of border violence is now respectably called. In other words, if the projects of urban renewal of the 1990s were marked by neoliberal entrepreneurship, in the last decade those projects have been sidelined by EU border zonification[2] – the securitisation of the southern Mediterranean borders through the externalizing of its EU-border regimes to the Mashreq and Maghreb regions (Albahari, 2015; Casas-Cortes et al., 2015; Ferrer-Gallardo, 2008). Like Barcelona, Salonika has been the recipient of these geopolitical buffer-zone measures, from the Salonika Summit of 2003 meant to seal its southeastern borders by integrating the Western Balkans into the EU to its enactment as the migrant entry gate in the Europanic over the 'refugee crisis' of 2015 (Albahari, 2015; Rexhepi, 2017, 2018a, 2018b; Romero, 2006). All of these borderisation projects and panics are being spatially and temporally historicised as belonging to 'Europe' in the larger post-Cold War 'European integration' that was supposedly borderless.

The arrival of migrants has arguably unsettled the seemingly streamlined Europeanised memories and histories. All the while, the touristification of both cities has resulted in extensive gentrification projects that have displaced mostly poor and migrant communities (Delgado and Carreras, 2008; Rexhepi, 2017). In the case of Barcelona, there is Raval, a neighbourhood that today is predominantly populated by Maghrebi and South Asian migrants; in the case of Salonika Anno, there is Poli, the historical Turkish/Muslim neighbourhood that has been 're-discovered' as a site of entertainment and adventure for tourists but is also a squatting site for migrants. Despite these urban transformations, which include the rise in museums and art spaces, tourist accommodation neighbourhoods like Raval remain largely working-class immigrant districts and sites of migrant self-organising and resistance, such as el Espacio del Inmigrante and La Tancada (López, 2019a; 2019b; Phillips, 2019) – both spaces started by migrant activists occupying abandoned spaces in Raval. La Tancada occupies a large building that used to be part of Escola Massana, an art and design school that first opened its doors in 1929. Some of the activists involved have ties to the 2001 occupations, when ten churches primarily in the city's old part were occupied by activists pressuring the government to open more legal ways of regularisation for migrants. La Tancada similarly functions as a political campaign for the rights of migrants and marginalised communities as well as educational space and housing for over thirty-five migrants, including an initiative for shared-living for elderly migrant women (López, 2019b). For the past six months, La Tancada has been under threat of eviction by the Colau government. The anti-racist trans-feminist collective of colour t.i.c.t.a.c. was the central organising body behind the weekend-long encuentro antirracista and has since its inception been working in solidarity with movements such as the ones stated above as well as with other migrant groups and initiatives.

Projects like La Tancada in Barcelona are important because they reveal the historical tensions that emerge in the process of contemporary policing and eviction processes. In the case of Salonika for instance, Mark Mazower's seminal *Salonica City of Ghosts* (2007) and more recently Aslı Iğsız's *Humanism in Ruins: Entangled Legacies of the Greek-Turkish Population Exchange* (2018) have illustrated how histories of racially organised removals of minoritised communities in the early twentieth century inform the ongoing geopolitical borderisation of the Mediterranean (Mbembe, 2019). Meanwhile, in Barcelona, the emphasis on migration in the 1990s has made invisible the memory of gitano communities and the more protracted presence of postcolonial migrant communities (Carrasco, 2012) who have formed part of the city for many decades.

Moreover, as sea cities, both Barcelona and Salonika were at the forefront of colonial and commercial 'progress', much of which was rooted in trading of bodies, the afterlives of which routes cannot be ignored in the contemporary narration of the Mediterranean Sea as the world's deadliest border (Albahari, 2015). While the sea is now conceptualised as the deadliest border for migrants, indigenous Pacific writers also highlight that thinking of the sea as part of people's living space destabilises Eurocentric-colonial understandings of territory as tied to 'terra' and solid ground. Teresia Teaiwa suggests that for Pacific Islanders, for whom the ocean makes up most of their 'home', the notion of solidarity should rather be replaced with 'fluidarity' (Teaiwa, 2005; Teaiwa and Slatter, 2013). So, if Europe is marked by territory, fortification, land and sea, it is the Mediterranean Sea that constitutes simultaneously its weakest and 'deadliest' border, its colonial ports now becoming the crucial cracks of euro-coloniality.

So, how can we think of Barcelona and Salonika as emerging Mediterranean and migrant metropolises by excavating silenced memories of solidarity and vernacular living strategies that define their contemporary socio-spatial relations? In the case of Barcelona, we'll trace the process of Europeanisation through the 1992 Olympics that required Barcelona to establish itself as a place of law and order and simultaneously as diverse and open to the world. We argue that on the one hand this whitewashing process involved large-scale displacement of particularly gitano, low-income and racialised communities for the construction of game-related sites and tourist development and the transformation, sanitisation and reimagination of neighbourhoods such as the old city and the infamous Raval. On the other hand, the process also resulted in one of the key anti-racist successes for racialised communities in the area. Such anti-racist successes and histories of resistance to sanitised versions of Europeanised and Catalanised histories are how today migrant groups and other communities of colour articulate belonging and re-existence within spaces like Barcelona. In Salonika, we will attempt to chart the revolutionary genealogy of the city to speak about ongoing ways in which those disciplined pasts come to define contemporary praxis of solidarity.

Barcelona

In order to transform, develop and 'Europeanise' Barcelona for the Olympics, low-income, migrant and gitano communities, in particular, had to be displaced. Yet in all the gentrifying violence that accompanied the Olympics, this was also a pivotal anti-racist moment. We see these moments as interruptions and fissures in 'modernity/ coloniality's matrices of power' that 'make evident concrete instances and possibilities of the otherwise' (Mignolo and Walsh, 2018: 20). Just months before the games Black and Afro-Spanish communities finally gained traction in what had been a years-long battle with the Catalan town of Banyoles and the Darder museum, founded in 1912 and the oldest museum in Girona, for displaying the human remains of an African man. Spearheaded by Afro-Spanish doctor Afonse Arcelin, the campaign to remove the human exhibit and repatriate the body to Botswana succeeded precisely because of the convergence of historical and political processes taking place in 1992. While Spain was eager to demonstrate itself as equally democratic, modern and civilised as the rest of Europe, 1992 also marked the centenary of the Bases de Manresa, a document that 'represented the starting point of Catalan claims for self-government' (Llobera, 2004: 127) and modern Catalanism. Thus, the games also became fertile ground for tensions between the Spanish central government and Catalan nationalist aspirations. While Arcelin had started his campaign years before the Olympics, it was the international public pressure and the threat of an African Olympic boycott that finally caused 'el negro' to be removed.[3] Just 100 days before the games the *LA Times* covered the controversy by describing how '[A]t the heart of the El Negro affair is Spain itself, a nation that essentially spent the last 500 years in isolation and is only now coming to grips with the modern world' (Cress, 1992). Thus, in order to modernise and Europeanise, the explicit racism of the exhibit had to be removed. However, the solutions offered did not address racism as much as the 'appearance of racism' (Azarmandi and Hernández, 2017; Tsuchiya 2019). The Olympics put Barcelona on an international stage which helped scandalise and increase pressure on the museum and the town to remove the exhibit that had now been established as 'problematic'.[4] Much as in 1992, when the exhibit was removed from sight – with little to no engagement with questions of structural and state-sanctioned racism[5] – mainly because it challenged Spain's image as democratic and cosmopolitan and potentially put at risk the 'success' of the games, in 2015 the newly elected municipal government of Ada Colau[6] rushed to remove a monument to slave trader Antonio Lopez y Lopez who now appeared incompatible with a socially progressive and multicultural Barcelona.

While the campaign to remove the racist exhibit in 1992 was primarily led by pan- Africanist and Afro-Spanish groups, the movement for the removal of the Antonio Lopez statue was also supported by white anti-racist groups and other civil society organisations. Again, despite decades-long anti-racist mobilisation it was not until the election of the progressive municipal government of Colau and a campaign to remove traces of the Francoist past that the statue was finally removed.[7] In both instances, the rationale was to promote the city's image as democratic, multicultural and open.[8] Communities of colour, for whom state-sanctioned violence is at the forefront of their activism,[9] have consistently highlighted the interconnected nature of struggles, in the past and present. When the pan-Africanists launched a petition for renaming in 2015 they pushed for the square to be renamed after Arcelin, stating

> We, Pan-Africanists of Spain, members of the African and Afro-descendant community, we are responsible actors of this historical process. Since 1985 we have led in Barcelona and the rest of Spain the process of promoting social struggles for dignity and the black reparations. During these 30 years of struggle for reparations we have had the ability to articulate ideas in a context of extreme criminalization of black immigration. (Azarmandi and Hernández, 2017: 13)

Unlike their white counterparts, whose suggestions for alternative names erased rather than acknowledged the very workings of Spanish state-racism in past and continuity (Azarmandi and Hernández, 2017), Afro-Spanish and migrant communities rallied around names such as Alfonse Arcelin and later Idrissa Diallo, an undocumented migrant who died after being held in a Barcelona detention centre. Their demand for change acknowledged genealogies of injustice as well as genealogies of resistance. As 'responsible actors of this historical process' (cited in Azarmandi and Hernández, 2017: 13) they also position themselves as collectives that shape the past and present of the city.

Here, claims to self-representation in the city directly tapped into memories and genealogies of resistance. In 2019 migrants and racialised collectives returned to moments in which the myth of Barcelona as a European city is re-narrated, exposing the colonial underside of the city but also connecting back into a continuity of migrant presence and resistance to racial violence and exclusion. Similarly, self-organised collectives such as t.i.c.t.a.c. and activists present at the encuentro antirracista counter claims of social progress and inclusion by highlighting the crackdown on undocumented migrants, the increased raids in districts such as Raval and the intensification of police brutality and surveillance (Douhaibi and Amazian, 2019). Raval, the most populated neighbourhood of the Cuitat Vella (old city) – and particularly South Raval, formerly known as the Barrio Chino,[10] with its infamous red-light district harbouring the old port – has often been described as a 'container of social problems'. Once a stronghold of the anarchist movement during the Spanish Civil War, the district became a home to internal and foreign migrants in the decades following the war.

Once described by La Vanguardia as a 'place that seems to have its own laws' (Ealham, 2004: 81), post-Olympic Raval became the site of urban intervention and development, projecting the end of 'centuries of marginalization' (Quaglieri Domínguez and Scarnato, 2017: 115). Even prior to democratisation, Raval had a large foreign migrant population. It continues to have the largest percentage of foreign migrants with approximately 46 per cent.[11] More recently coined 'Ravalistan' owing to the large influx of South Asian immigrants, the district has in fact always been a site of contention and is described as a potential hotspot for counter-terrorism intervention (Douhaibi and Amazian, 2019). Despite the public intervention, gentrification, touristification and increased police intervention Raval continues to be a predominantly working-class migrant neighbourhood.

Raval is now also site of the Barcelona Museum of Contemporary Art (MACBA), a large white modernist building, designed by American architect Richard Meier in 1990 and built between 1991 and 1995. The intention behind the architectural design was to demonstrate innovation and modernisation as well as to raise Raval out of its state of working-class lawlessness. The white monstrosity stands in clear contrast to the gothic sites, run-down buildings, hipster bars and cafes and migrant corner stores surrounding it. Just a few minutes away, activists in La Tancada divide rooms to accommodate elderly migrant women. t.i.c.t.a.c. members and other activists at the encuentro raised concerns about how these cultural sites that are aimed at 'improving' and 'developing' neighbourhoods not only exist in complete isolation from their social surroundings but actively contribute to the exclusion and expulsion of migrants, sex workers and communities of colour. While the museum hosted its first major exhibit dealing with colonialism, Undefined Territories: Perspectives on Colonial Legacies,[12] in the summer of 2019 – an exhibit with only a minor art piece featuring Barcelona (and Spain as a whole)[13] – it was under scrutiny for blocking the potential construction of a medical centre for the neighbourhood because it would take place in an area that was designed for the museum's expansion. As a result, it was suggested to build the medical centre elsewhere, in the neighbourhood's only green space.

When some of the t.i.c.t.a.c. activists and I (Mahdis) attended a concert of Krudas Cubense, an activist hip-hop group with black-feminist, queer and vegan politics, in May 2019 that was hosted by the MACBA and took place in the foyer of the sterile white space and just outside the Undefined Territories exhibit, we jokingly commented on how the space had never seen so many non-white bodies. We observed how these queer of colour bodies were carefully ushered into the confined space of the foyer, with all access to the inside and upstairs of the museum closed off. The bodies that lived and had built the social fabric around the MACBA were never meant to be inside. This is one of many occasions on which institutions like the MACBA clearly did not understand the politics of race outside its walls. In the work of the collective and the encuentro antirracista these conversations about space-making and belonging, in fact re-existence, are connected to their main goal of creating a space to share, exchange and rethink practices of solidarity and resistance through political action. The objective of the meeting is to share experiences, analysis and political-activist practices among collectives and individuals who, from different places and positions, seek to articulate associative and solidarity dynamics in the organisation of struggles against racism (encuentro antirracista, 2019).

With solidarity at the centre of politics of resistance, activists also tap into the histories of resistance and how each of these moments of modernisation and touristification, always aimed at proving the city's European identity, were accompanied by and resisted by the metropoles' postcolonial subjects. In the urban development plan of the early 2000s and the construction of the Rambla de Raval, funded by the EU, it was argued that the new promenade, a new hotel and residential blocks designed with glass fronts were aimed at bringing more light into the 'dark' streets of the old city. While the city planners might have hoped for a change in the demographic make-up of what some described as a 'gueto islamico',[14] 'the local community [...] uses the arc-lights and carefully paved surfaces to re-enact any number of floodlit test cricket matches' (McNeill 2002: 252). In the spirit of reclaiming and retaking space, the nationwide anti-racist demonstrations in November 2019 used names such as Memorias Antirracistas – Anti-racist memories, connecting past and present resistance and re-existences. In Barcelona, the convened demonstration had its own manifesto and described itself and its purpose as

[W]e racialized migrants and refugees; the trans people, sex-gender dissidents, the people who care, the domestic workers, the sex workers, the deviant, the people who disturb the order with their mere presence, the people without papers, the people who organize, the people who defend their voice, the people who remember Lucrecia Pérez Matos, the people who live and face daily this system of exclusion, denial, violence and dispossession. We leave this November 11, 2018 at 5:00 pm, simultaneously with the cities of Madrid, Valencia, Bilbao and Zaragoza to demonstrate against racism.

Places like Raval and its population – often seen as problem sites for the 'deviant', sex workers and undocumented migrants – are simultaneously the ones whose existence and creation of life in the city challenge the city-life sold by the process of touristification, the Airbnb and digital economy.

These collectives and their so-called 'dark' and run-down districts stand in contrast to EUropeanisation and cannot but speak 'contested belonging[s]' (Ferme and Ardizzoni, 2015: 10) in the Mediterranean city. The manifesto continues:

> Today we collectively celebrate the heritage of resistance of our forefathers, and twinned in the anti-racist struggle, we call on all those who confront institutional racism and its political tentacles on a daily basis. To the siblings who have stood up to the racist system of exploitation in the camps of Huelva, to the gitano siblings who after 500 years of siege and persecution, still proudly resist state integrationism. To the Manterxs who every day resist police harass-ment. To the sisters who are denied international protection by the kingdom of Spain, condemning them to illegality, and to the sisters who prove to us every day that our humanity does not depend on an identity card. To the migrant sex workers who fight against criminalisation, persecution, stigma, and for the full recognition of their rights. To the trans-migrants and refugees who fight for a name, and fight against their erasure by the Kingdom of Spain. To each and every one of the racialised collectives that white supremacy has placed on the margin of the political and human, to you, siblings, we address ourselves to initiate a process of political responsibility, living with the rage that we have accumulated over centuries. (Manifiesto contra el racismo institucional, 2019; our translation)

Again, activists return to both politics of solidarity and migrant memory to reclaim silenced and sanitised histories of the city. These dynamics are not exclusive to Barcelona but part of larger north Mediterranean cities like Salonika where migrant sex worker struggles generate new forms of solidarity and resistance that are interconnected to its histories of displacement and erasure (Rexhepi, 2021).

Meanwhile, to understand the exclusionary politics of gentrification of Ottoman sites in Salonika in the name of European multiculturalism, we examine how, in their displacement and emplacement from Ottoman sites, marginalised and immigrant communities also recruit Ottoman memory of multicultural Salonika in remaking urban spaces as sites of new urban pedagogies and futurities. We illuminate these contrasting dynamics by examining several sites of conflict designated for protection as post-Ottoman heritage sites and the displacement from there of squatting collectives that have not only come to claim these spaces to live in but who have their own emancipatory projects of remaking Salonika. Examining the convergence of queer, migrant and squatter communities in the neighbourhood of Ano Poli, the squatting collective Yfanet Fabrika, Villa Varvara and the queer and migrant collectivemassqueerraid – all operating from former Ottoman buildings marked for preservation – we want to explore how their attempts to oppose gentrification, homogenisation, displacement and the social and literal death of migrants and the marginalised have developed new geographies of being together.

Salonika

After it was declared European Capital of Culture in 1997, Salonika reclaimed derelict Ottoman buildings and neighbourhoods as national monuments – frequently by displacing squatters and migrant communities who had made them into alternative collective living, working and creative spaces. If the post-Ottoman modality of early twentieth-century Salonika becoming a European city meant leaving behind, forgetting and undoing Ottoman pasts and landscapes, contemporary forms of refashioning Salonika into a multicultural European city required unearthing, reinventing and reinscribing the disappeared Ottoman past into the public discourse in the city's branding as a mark of European progress and diversity. It seems that these forgotten sites and stories now become eligible as artefacts and museums, as time and the nation state have erased their political potency to threaten the new political order. The history of exclusion, violence, displacement and destitution becomes overwritten with the discourse of past tolerance and coexistence, potentially homogenising and further depoliticising the history of Salonika: not reclaiming the historical responsibility but summing it up in the post-colonial marketplace, where the demand for projects of recognition of minorities and unjust pasts becomes a profitable undertaking. In seeking to perhaps resolve historical tensions through the incorporation of bygone differences, however, these projects face the challenge of confronting new strategies of urban diversity that refuse to depoliticise and defer the tensions of multiculturalism to marketable politics of recognition and nostalgia located in the past. The state, EU and market demands for multicultural history have produced unintended outcomes as they have come to clash with new marginal communities, particularly migrants and squatters.

The May 1936 workers' uprisings in Salonika shook Greece. It came to be known as the Bloody May revolt (Angelis, 2016). The lament of Tasos

Tousis' mother, hovering over her son's lifeless body, left an indelible mark on the 27-year-old Greek poet Yiannis Ritsos. Retracing the anger and despair of Salonika in his poem written two days after the revolt, Ritsos foresaw the impoverished provincial future of a city once destined for revolution. His eulogy 'O Epitaphios' gave voice to the pain of degradation and death that followed Metaxas's use of the uprising to install a fascist dictatorship in the name of the monarchy and its military (Ritsos, 2014). It became the first modern Greek poetry book to be burned in public. Like the tobacco workers of Salonika who started the revolt, the workers' memory and mourning were destined to disappear in the reactionary narration of the city foreclosed under layers of coloniality.

On the seventieth anniversary of the Bloody May uprising in 2006, at a local squat in Salonika, the last survivor of the revolt, Yannis Tamtakos, retraced his memories of the murder of Tousis by the police in front of Salonika's 'Metropolis' hotel. The squat FABRIKA YFANET, a former Ottoman textile factory, fell silent, reflecting on the old and new assaults on the city from the Metaxas dictatorship to the austerity politics of becoming European. 'Ruins', as Ann Stoler (2016: 14) argues, 'can become epicenters of renewed collective claims, as history in a spirited voice, as sites that animate both despair and new possibilities, bids for entitlement, and unexpected collaborative political projects.' So, when the organisation Thessaloniki, European Capital of Culture 1997 purchased the building on Krispou str. nr. 7 near the old Kulu-Kafe quarter in Ano Poli, another squat, 'Villa Varvara', a former Ottoman school, was served a city ordinance to evict the space (Eleftherotypia, 1998). The building was now destined to become a 'cultural centre'. In order to prepare the city for being a European Capital of Culture, Roma and Albanian migrant families were thrown out through pogrom-like raids without city ordinances. The gentrification of derelict Ottoman buildings and neighbourhoods as national monuments was undertaken as a testimony to the city's newfound appreciation for multicultural pasts. It was simultaneously a process of cultural appropriation of Ottoman history into a newly curated European history, making the ongoing displacement of marginalised communities from those sites appear as signs of care and consideration for history.

Ottoman mosques opened to the public as museums and contemporary art galleries, while the abandoned toilet paper factory outside Salonika, now turned into the refugee camp Softex, became home to two thousand Middle Eastern refugees. Muslim migrants pray in a makeshift tent, while the Greek Army stands guard outside. Meanwhile, a few miles away, in Yeni Cami, an Ottoman mosque-turned-exhibition space, the Greek contemporary artist Lydia Dambassina's 2016 installation *Gini Coefficient* features an embalmed head of a large deer, spewing a piece of paper that reads, 'The 62 richest people in the world own the same wealth as half of humanity – that is, 3.5 billion people.' A toilet paper factory turned into a makeshift migrant mosque and a mosque turned into an art gallery perhaps best illustrate the ties between Greek modernity enacted in Salonika and its post-Ottoman refashioning as European.

In most Greek accounts of modernity arriving in Salonika, the fire of 1917 is considered a major turning point. The architect Ernest Hébrard, famous for designing French colonial architecture in the Maghreb and Southeast Asia, was tasked with rebuilding the city, which had just been integrated into the Greek nation state. Thus, the fire served as an opportunity to make Salonika Greek. Hébrard drew up plans for Aristotle Square, then known as Alexander the Great Square – invoking not ancient Greece, as was the case with Athens, but establishing a link between ancient Macedonia and Byzantium. The post-Ottoman imagination and production of Salonika in the French and European colonial encounter finally found its way back to Greece. As in most post-Ottoman nation states, including Kemalist Turkey, the erasure of Ottoman modernity in Greece served to project the Ottomans as an obstacle to development. The late Ottoman modernisation projects enacted in the city are generally obscured in an arrangement of history that fits the Greek national and newly Europeanised history.

Since the mid-nineteenth century, the Salonika Ottoman bourgeoisie had already started encircling the *mahallas* with cafes and storefronts, building for itself an *alla franga* neighbourhood to the east of the former city walls. Wishing to be elsewhere, they could in the new neighbourhood escape from their recent peasant past as well as from the embarrassing ailing empire that could no longer keep up. The fetishisation of those early Ottoman sites today, as traces of the splendour of pre-modern Ottoman Salonika, illuminates the absurdity of capitalist claims on a condensed and disciplined past in which the Young Turk Revolution of 1908, the population exchange of 1923, the revolt of 1936 and the deportation of the Jewish population between March and August 1943 never happened.

> The night they killed Lambrakis
> I was returning from a date.
> What's happened? Someone on the bus asked.
> No one knew. We saw policemen
> But could make out nothing more.
> (Dinos Christianopoulos, *The Splinter* in Friar, 1979: 73)

Narrating the assassination of the anti-war activist Grigoris Lambrakis by far-right extremists in 1963 in Salonika, Dinos Christianopoulos joins novelist Vassilis Vassilikos and filmmaker Costa-Gavras, not only documenting the life and death of Lambrakis but also giving voice to the growing protests against the conditions that led to his assassination. Both the novel and the movie *Zi*, which means 'he lives' in Greek, rekindle the spirits of leftist movements which had been under attack by the military dictatorship. Bringing to salience other bodies that bear the marks of violence and oppression, Christianopoulos generated a new language. He would attend to the homosexual, lesbian and transgender bodies that his friend, trans-anarchist Paola Revenioti, would later immortalise in her fanzine Kraximo in the early 1980s – the printing of which she had paid for with blow jobs (Angelidakis, 2013: 72).

Appropriating the structure and vocabulary of Greek Orthodox liturgy, which by the 1960s was widely dismissed as an instrument of state repression, his poems merge the religious with the erotic to make space for vernacular histories. Claiming kinship with his stylistic master, the Greek–Egyptian poet C. P. Cavafy, who like himself was a homosexual, Christianopoulos' poems borrow Cavafy's confessional technique to summon saints and lovers, exposing weaknesses in the lives of the saints, on which he mirrors the struggles faced by queer subjects of his generation. Cavafy was a Greek migrant from Egypt. Like the migrants of the population exchange, he embodied a sense of estrangement from the nation, in which displaced migrants become the settler oppressors who refuse the politics of the motherland once they have come to know her intimately and violently. As displaced queer subjects, both Cavafy and Christianopoulos questioned the dominant hetero organisation of time and space, seeking queer traces in a city that actively hid their ancestral songs and signs. Christianopoulos unearthed the memory of Rosa Eskenazi, who by then had fallen into oblivion in Westernised Greek mainstream culture.

Born in Istanbul in the last decade of the nineteenth century, Eskenazi grew up and came to fame in Salonika, later becoming one of the most loved performers of rebetiko among the displaced migrants from Asia Minor. Performing for members of the Greek, Turkish, Jewish and Albanian diaspora and recording in Cold War Istanbul among other collaborators with the Albanian Ayden Leskoviku, Eskenazi was the last living embodiment of late Ottoman modernity. As Christian migrants from Asia Minor brought their melancholic longing for places they had left behind, Muslims, Jewish survivors of the Holocaust and later Bulgarian, Macedonian and Slavic speaking populations deported around Eastern Europe kept Salonika in their imaginations as their home that never really was – a fallen utopia, a 'Nostalgic love' that, as Svetlana Boym remarks, 'can only survive in a long-distance relationship' (2001: xiii).

In 2014, in several prisons around Greece, inmates refused to return to their cells after their walking break. They stayed outside for one hour protesting the violent death of Ilir Kareli, an Albanian migrant who was beaten to death by the Salonika police while in custody (Halili, 2014). New migrants from former socialist states, and more recently from the Middle East, would replace the marker of the internal Other. Neoliberal restructuring of urban space replaces class with notions of culture, further racialising urban hierarchies in which the Albanian migrant is integrated with the arrival of the Syrian migrant. Chechen migrant poet Jazra Khaleed writes:

> My words are homeless,
> They sleep on the benches of Klafthmonos Square,
> covered in IKEA cartons.
> My words do not speak on the news
> They're out hustling every night.
> My words are proletarian, slaves like me.
> They work in sweatshops night and day
> (Khaleed, 2017: 157)

In *Duress: Imperial Durabilities in Our Times*, Ann Stoler suggests that '[T]he connections of colonialism and contemporary politics are not always readily available for easy grasp, in part because colonial entailments do not have a life of their own. They wrap around contemporary problems' by losing 'their visible and identifiable presence in the vocabulary, conceptual grammar, and idioms of current concerns' (2016: 1–2), insisting that 'The geopolitical and spatial distribution of inequalities cast across our world today are not simply mimetic versions of earlier imperial incarnations but refashioned and sometimes opaque and oblique reworkings of them' (2016: 5). Stoler warns against the scholarly romance with 'traces' as it 'risks rendering colonial remnants as pale filigrees, benign overlays with barely detectable presence rather than deep pressure points of generative possibilities' (2016: 5–6).

Towards decolonising Mediterranean cities

We sought to bring these two cities together here to illustrate not only the emergence of new urban becomings outside the framework of 'Europe' but also how larger geopolitical shifts are transforming these cities beyond national and postnational perspectives. This is due not just to migration and migrants as 'new' additions to these cities but also to the recovery of memories and postcolonial subjectivities that emerge in the wake of what Fred Moten (2003) calls 'the break'. It is an attempt to piece together fragmented histories and living marginalised memories to provide different, and hopefully decolonial, genealogies for the fissures and futures of these two northern Mediterranean metropoles. We understand decoloniality here as an ongoing process of de-linking and divesting from eurocentric epistemologies and the capitalist-colonial matrix with fissures and cracks constituting, as Walsh and Mignolo point out, a possibility and openings towards an otherwise (Mignolo and Walsh, 2018: 3).

Cities in the peripheries of Europe are not just undergoing epistemic provincialisation. Migrant and minoritised communities are troubling their incubator-like capitalist-colonial grids of power, redrawing and redirecting their centres of power towards their concerns and political constellations. We wanted to start with two events that reflect these politics as we find them to be important in showing how migrant and minoritised communities contribute to and challenge the established political Left – forcing them to come out of their narrow Eurocentric thinking, asking them to engage in what Catherine Walsh and Walter Mignolo (2018) call decolonial thinking-doing. The established political Left is thus called on to situate their abstractions in the city, in its neighbourhoods, in the struggles of the undercommons away from academia and anarcho-tourist industries. Perhaps we have to question the spaces of knowledge production such as the materialist conference. Who do they address and whose struggles do they centre? To whom do they relate, and to whom are they unable to relate, especially when aiming to produce emancipatory knowledge? In other words, it is not the migrants and settled minorities who need to go to the materialist historians; it is, figuratively speaking, the mountain that should go to Mohammed. What we mean by this is that new emancipatory politics for the decolonisation of cities must emerge out of the margins, in the contemporary moment but also in the revitalisation of marginalised histories of resistance and revolution. From their anarchist, anti-fascist resistances in the twentieth century to the resistance of racialised communities in the present, these histories are concealed by the standardised and branded narratives of both Barcelona and Salonika.

So, one way to provincialise European urbanity as a supposedly pristine materialisation of colonial modernity in both Barcelona and Salonika is to draw on their vernacular histories and spatialise them through migrant maps, imaginaries and memories. These various mappings and memorialisations do not imply total erasure of the European project though – as keen as we are to provincialise Europe, its forms of violence on the ground are very real and are interwoven with narratives and claims of postcolonial and racialised subjects living in these spaces (Ha, 2017; Haritaworn, 2015; Mignolo and Walsh, 2018). Europe, Frantz Fanon argued, is 'literally the creation of the Third World' (1963: 58). Hamid Dabashi (2019) returns to Fanon and expands his work by examining Europe as an allegory, and unpacks how conditions of coloniality persist even after empires collapse. Europe, as Dabashi argues, is an allegory, a myth that is told as true, which is often reproduced in the narration of its cities. Not only is colonialism relevant to the ways in which space is constructed in the European city, but the very idea and mobilisation of the notion of a/the European city give insights into entangled workings of race and space (Azarmandi et al., 2016; Bacchetta et al., 2015; Ha, 2016). Europe as allegory is also maintained and produced through the production of memory in the cityscape. For Fanon, the city is constituted by the resources and labour of the racialised world that produces and gives rise to Europe and its cities. 'The ports of Holland, the docks in Bordeaux and Liverpool owe their importance to the trade and deportation of millions of slaves' (1963: 58). The wealth of the South, its people and resources were taken to the European continent to build what tourism sites describe today as historical, architectural or cultural must-sees. Names and statues of conquistadors and businessmen who made their fortune in the colonial project are a regular sight yet the violence through which riches were produced is hidden in plain sight.

Barcelona, much like Bordeaux and Liverpool, was a key port in the trade of enslaved people and central to 'legal' and 'illegal' slave trade in the nineteenth century (Rodrigo y Alharilla, 2013).[15] Many of the city's emblematic sights are products of colonial conquest and the wealth it accumulated. However, as Dabashi would argue, it is not that Europe and its colonial Other operate in binary opposition but rather, to once again invoke Fanon, that Europe is 'literally the creation of the Third World' (1963: 58), where the colonial subjects haunt the metropole in its geopolitical and urban margins. Architectural sights and sites, such as the monument to Antonio Lopez y Lopez at Barcelona harbour, are examples of how sights that are crucial in the construction of cityscapes as 'European' always-already reveal their colonial underside. As such, the presence of Europe in any city is always-already colonial.

Looking at the mobilisation of memory in the production of cities like Barcelona and Salonika reveals how 'the European city' is always an allegory of modernity/coloniality (Dabashi, 2019). That is, not only are these sites haunted by the ghosts of their violent pasts, these cities constantly need to re-tell and mobilise memories that can constitute them as European in the first place. Yet, as Fatima El-Tayeb (2011) has argued in her seminal work, the ways in which postcolonial migrants and racialised subjects engage in space-making is not only focused on opposing the dominant colonial narratives and exposing state-sanctioned racial and gendered violence. It also focuses on actively shaping how these cities are produced and remembered. Queer of colour anti-racist organising in particular destabilises ethno-national memories and histories while simultaneously producing collective memories of belonging through the production of genealogies of resistance (Bacchetta et al., 2017; El-Tayeb, 2011).

The example of the *encuentro antirracista* illustrates how migrant and racialised communities contest Euro-histories and simultaneously reclaim Barcelona as a site of belonging. These communities claim historical memory not by virtue of their presence in and attachment to Europe – that is, not simply by wanting recognition as hyphen-Europeans – but rather by emphasising the very instability of the concept of Europe and the city's claim as inherently European themselves. Migrant claims are tied to histories of resistance and their collective memory as means of re-existence. Thus, to take Barcelona's Europeanness for granted is to miss how Spain's joining the European Union and Barcelona's winning the bid for the Olympic Games in 1986, followed by the celebration of the Olympic Games in 1992, fundamentally shifted the city's self-positioning away from the Mediterranean and towards Europe. Elsewhere in Spain, 1992 marked the year of the Seville Expo and the nationwide celebration of the 500th anniversary of Columbus' first voyage to the Americas. The making of new EU cities in Spain in the 1990s was accompanied by and tied to mobilisations of a supposed imperial and colonial past. In Barcelona, the Olympic Games in particular were key in transforming, reorienting and reimagining the city. As McNeill argues, the city was 'catalanized, globalized, informationalized, gentrified, redesigned, and Europeanized' (McNeill, 2017: 323). However, these processes of Europeanisation were always resisted and contested and it is to the memories of such contestation that migrant and racialised communities return at meetings such as the encuentro antirracista.

But margins are relevant not only for the two cities that we look at here; they are also important in the geopolitical sense. In a time of heightened EU bordering and emerging geopolitical enclosures of Euro-American spaces, cities like Barcelona and Salonika are already not so much fortressed as fugitive cities, cities that maintain the circulation of people – cities that sit on the routes that place the centres of colonial-capitalist power under siege and close in on them from the peripheries.

Notes

1 For more information see Gutiérrez Rodríguez (2018).
2 For more information on zonification see Kancler (2017).
3 The town and museum in Banyoles launched a counter-campaign to keep the remains. The man in the exhibit was soon turned into 'el negro de Banyoles'.
4 The exhibit might have been removed but no racism was ever acknowledged on the part of the town and the museum.
5 In fact, neither the museum nor the town ever acknowledged that the exhibit was racist to begin with.
6 Colau emerged out of the popular housing and anti-austerity movement.
7 The progressive municipal government of Manuela Carmena in Madrid was also part of a campaign to remove Francoist remnants. Since the Lopez y Lopez statue had been destroyed by Anarchists during the Spanish Civil War and later rebuilt, it was also connected to a fascist past.

8 The Barcelona town hall raised a banner saying 'refugees welcome' and Barcelona has, since Colau's election, been establishing the Barcelona Ciutat Refugi (Barcelona Refugee City) programme.
9 Urban development initiated by the Olympic Games was followed by increased development through private investment in expanding the brand Barcelona, followed by the punt.com development (digital city/smart city) in areas between the Olympic village towards Besos. Not only are minority communities displaced by developers but the newly built centres now have to be kept safe from supposed 'delinquents', pickpockets and businesses that might engage in sales of counterfeit FC Barça shirts. Following 2003, Raval and immigrant districts also became classified hotspots for potential 'Islamic terrorist' threats.
10 The district never had a large Chinese population but acquired the name from a journalist in the 1920s whom the red-light district reminded of San Francisco's Chinatown.
11 Foreign population in Barcelona as of 2015; see www.bcn.cat/estadistica/angles/dades/inf/pobest/pobest15/part1/t45.htm.
12 See MACBA, www.macba.cat/en/exhibitions-activities/activities/visit-undefined-territories-perspectives-colonial-legacies-0.
13 A photographic piece by Barcelona-based Peruvian artist-activist Daniela Ortiz. The frame included photographs of the Columbus monument in the port of Barcelona and a written statement about Catalunya's appropriation of Christopher Columbus.
14 In the 2015 municipal elections the conservative party Partido Popular (PP) ran a campaign and distributed flyers stating, 'Raval cannot be turned into an Islamic Ghetto'; www.publico.es/politica/pp-barcelona-pide-raval-no.html.
15 Spain was the last European country to legally abolish slavery in 1867 but did not abolish slavery in its colonies Puerto Rico and Cuba until 1873 and 1886 respectively. Trafficking of enslaved people continued illegally after legal abolition in the peninsula.

References

Albahari, M. (2015), *Crimes of Peace: Mediterranean Migrations at the World's Deadliest Border* (Philadelphia, PA: University of Pennsylvania Press).
Angelidakis, A. (2013), Candy says meet a Greek national treasure: Paola Revenioti. *Candy Magazine* (January).
Angelis, V. (2016), Change and continuity: comparing the Metaxas dictatorship and the Colonels' Junta in Greece. *Mediterranean Quarterly* 27(3): 38–52.
Azarmandi, M. and R. Hernández (2017), Colonial redux: when re-naming silences – Antonio Lopez y Lopez and Nelson Mandela. *Borderlands E-Journal* 16(1): 1–27.
Azarmandi, M., E. Laforteza and M. Ceuterick (2016), Geocorpographies of commemoration, repression and resistance. *Somatechnics* 6(1): 1–8.
Bacchetta, P., F. El-Tayeb and J. Haritaworn (2015), Queer of colour formations and translocal spaces in Europe. *Environment and Planning D: Society and Space* 33(5): 769–778.

Bacchetta., P., F. El-Tayeb and J. Haritaworn (2017), Queer-of-Color-Politik und translokale Räume in Europa. In Zwischenraum Kollektiv (eds), *Decolonize the City! Zur Kolonialität der Stadt: Gespräche | Aushandlungen | Perspektiven* (Münster: Unrast), pp. 36–52.

Boym, S. (2001), *The Future of Nostalgia* (New York: Basic Books).

Carrasco, C. (2012), Barcelona no es sólo Gaudí: representaciones cinematográficas del barrio del Raval. *Transitions* 8: 100–120.

Casas-Cortes, M. et al. (2015), New keywords: migration and borders. *Cultural Studies* 29(1): 55–87.

Cress, D. (1992), 100 DAYS TO THE OLYMPICS: El Negro Becomes Nightmare to Barcelona Games: Olympics: City of Banyoles won't put away display of stuffed bushman that many consider offensive. *LA Times* (16 April 1992), www.latimes.com/archives/la-xpm-1992–04–16-sp-1083-story.html [accessed 9 September 2021].

Dabashi, H. (2019), *Europe and Its Shadows: Coloniality After Empire* (London: Pluto Press).

Dambassina, L. (2016), *Gini Coefficient*. Art Exhibit at Yeni Cami in Thessaloniki. Retrieved from www.lydiadambassina.com/2016-gini-coefficient/ [accessed 9 September 2021].

Delgado, M. and J. Carreras (2008), Pràctiques d'exclusió als locals nocturns del centre històric de Barcelona. El dret d'admissió com a tècnica de discriminació racista. Generalitat de Catalunya. Departament d'Acció Social i Ciutadania. Collecció i Immigració n°. 1, Bloc D2, 195–216.

Douhaibi, A. and Amazian, S. (2019), *Radicalización del Racismo, La Islamofobia de Estado y Prevención Antiterrorista* (Oviedo: Editorial Cambalache).

Ealham, C. (2004), *Class, Culture and Conflict in Barcelona, 1898–1937* (Abingdon and New York: Routledge).

Eleftherotypia (1998), Police remodel in the Upper Town. *IOS Press* (9 May), www.iospress.gr/mikro1998/mikro19980509.htm [accessed 9 September 2021].

El-Tayeb, F. (2011), *European Others: Queering Ethnicity in Postnational Europe* (Minneapolis, MN: University of Minnesota Press).

encuentro antirracista (2019). Retrieved from https://encuentroantirracista.org/ [accessed 5 September 2021].

European Commission (n.d.), Urban Development, https://ec.europa.eu/regional_policy/en/policy/themes/urban-development/ [accessed 5 September 2021].

Fanon, F. (1963), *The Wretched of the Earth* (New York: Grove Press).

Ferme, V. and M. Ardizzoni (2015), Introduction – the Mediterranean, the city, and cultural encounters. In Ardizzoni, M. and V. Ferme (eds) *Mediterranean Encounters in the City: Frameworks of Mediation Between East and West, North and South* (Lanham, MD: Lexington Books), pp. 1–16.

Ferrer-Gallardo, X. (2008), The Spanish–Moroccan border complex: processes of geopolitical, functional and symbolic rebordering. *Political Geography* 27(3): 301–321.

Fisher, M. (2009), *Capitalist Realism: Is There No Alternative?* (Hants: John Hunt Publishing).

Friar, K. (1979), The poetry of Dino Christianopoulos: a selection. *Journal of the Hellenic Diaspora* 6: 68–83.

Gutiérrez Rodríguez, E. (2018), The coloniality of migration and the 'refugee crisis': on the asylum-migration nexus, the transatlantic white European settler colonialism-migration and racial capitalism. *Refuge: Canada's Journal on Refugees/Refuge: revue canadienne sur les réfugiés* 34(1): 16–28.

Ha, N. K. (2016), *Straßenhandel in Berlin: Öffentlicher Raum, Informalität und Rassismus in der neoliberalen Stadt* (Bielefeld: transcript Verlag).

Ha, N. K. (2017), Zur Kolonialität des Städtischen. In Zwischenraum Kollektiv (eds) *Decolonize the City! Zur Kolonialität der Stadt: Gespräche | Aushandlungen | Perspektiven* (Münster: Unrast), pp. 73–85.

Halili, S. (2014), E ëma e Ilir Karelit: Djali donte drejtësi jo vetëgjyqësi. *Shekulli* (29 March). Retrieved from http://shekulli.com.al/43552/ [accessed 9 September 2021].

Haritaworn, J. (2015), *Queer Lovers and Hateful Others: Regenerating Violent Times and Places* (London: Pluto Press).

Iğsız, A. (2018), *Humanism in Ruins: Entangled Legacies of the Greek-Turkish Population Exchange* (Stanford, CA: Stanford University Press).

Kancler, T. (2017), Body-politics, trans* imaginary and decoloniality. *Academia. edu*. https://www.academia.edu/31557368/Body-politics_Trans_Imaginary_and_Decoloniality [accessed 22 March 2020].

Khaleed, Jazra. (2017), Words. In Van Dyck, K. (ed.) *Austerity Measures: The New Greek Poetry* (New York: New York Review of Books), pp. 157–173.

Llobera, J. R. (2004), *Foundations of National Identity: From Catalonia to Europe* (New York and Oxford: Berghahn Books).

López, H. (2019a), Historias de la cara B de la Ciutat Refugi. *El Periodico* (5 July), www.elperiodico.com/es/barcelona/20190705/todas-las-vidas-de-la-tancada-7537397 [accessed 6 September 2021].

López, H. (2019b), Mayores, migrantes, solas y en la calle. *El Periodico* (26 November), www.elperiodico.com/es/barcelona/20191126/mayores-migrantes-solas-y-en-la-calle-7750044 [accessed 6 September 2021].

McNeill, D. (2002), Barcelona: urban identity 1992–2002. *Arizona Journal of Hispanic Cultural Studies* 6(1): 245–261.

McNeill, D. (2017), Barcelona: urban identity 1992–2002. In Bou, E. and J. Subirana (eds) *The Barcelona Reader: Cultural Readings of a City* (Liverpool: Liverpool University Press), pp. 323–346.

Manifiesto contra el racismo institucional (2019), Desde el Margen. Retrieved from http://desde-elmargen.net/manifiestacion-contra-el-racismo-institucional/ [accessed 6 September 2021].

Mazower, M. (2007), *Salonica City of Ghosts: Christians, Muslims and Jews 1430–1950*. (New York City: Vintage Books).

Mbembe, A. (2019), Bodies and borders. Lecture given at Universität zu Köln, 17 July 2019. www.youtube.com/watch?v=JqreV_1FqtU [accessed 6 December 2019].

Mignolo, W. D. and C. E. Walsh (2018), *On Decoloniality: Concepts, Analytics, Praxis* (Durham, NC: Duke University Press).

Moten, F. (2003), *In the Break: The Aesthetics of the Black Radical Tradition* (Minneapolis, MN and London: University of Minnesota Press).

Phillips, A. (2019), El Espacio del Inmigrante, reconocido por su defensa de los derechos humanos. *La Vanguardia* (16 January 2019), www.lavanguardia.com/local/barcelona/20190116/454171709302/espacio-inmigrante-reconocido-defensa-derechos-humanos.html [accessed 6 September 2021].

Quaglieri Domínguez, A. and A. Scarnato (2017), The Barrio Chino as last frontier: the penetration of everyday tourism in the dodgy heart of the Raval. In Gravari-Barbas, M. and S. Guinand (eds) *Tourism and Gentrification in Contemporary Metropolises: International Perspectives* (Abingdon: Taylor & Francis), pp. 107–133.

Rexhepi, P. (2017), Borders. *Critical Muslim* 21: 45–56.

Rexhepi, P. (2018a), Arab others at European borders: racializing religion and refugees along the Balkan Route. *Ethnic and Racial Studies* 41(12), 2215–2234.

Rexhepi, P. (2018b), The politics of postcolonial erasure in Sarajevo. *Interventions* 20(6), 930–945.

Rexhepi, P. (2021), Predatory porn, sex work and solidarity at borders. *Ethnic and Racial Studies* 44(9): 1629–1647.

Ritsos, Y. (2014), *Epitaphios* (Ripon: Smokestack Books).

Rodrigo y Alharilla. M. (2013), Spanish merchants and the slave trade: from legality to illegality, 1814–1870. In Fradera, J. M. and C. Schmidt-Nowara (eds) *Slavery and Antislavery in Spain's Atlantic Empire* (New York and Oxford: Berghahn Books), pp. 176–199.

Romero, E. (2006), *¿Quién Invade a Quién? El Plan África y la Inmigración* (Madrid: Editorial Cambalache).

Stoler, A. L. (2016), *Duress: Imperial Durabilities in Our Times* (Durham, NC: Duke University Press).

Teaiwa, T. (2005), Solidarity and fluidarity: feminism as product and productive force for regionalism in the Pacific. Colloquium presentation, University of Hawai'i.

Teaiwa, T. and C. Slatter (2013), Samting Nating: Pacific waves at the margins of feminist security studies. *International Studies Perspectives* 14: 447–450.

Tsuchiya, A. (2019), Monuments and public memory: Antonio López y López, slavery, and the Cuban-Catalan connection. *Nineteenth-Century Contexts* 41(5): 479–500.

8

Portuguese Urban Studies: between race and the absence of racism

Ana Rita Alves[1]

Disciplines have myths of origin, canonical accounts that, far from innocuous, form and mould how bodies of knowledge exist, operate and reproduce themselves today. Their (hi)stories should not be taken as given, but one should rather ask which voices are being privileged and which ones are rendered non-relevant, since past silences echo in present times and in present tensions. By examining the racial contours of urban policies in the Portuguese context, it was made evident to me how debates on race and racism were absent from academic knowledge production in Urban Studies (and particularly in Urban Anthropology). Despite the proliferation of academic studies on peripheralised territories in the Lisbon Metropolitan Area (LMA) – which are subject to the state's surveillance and repression and are mostly inhabited by black and Roma populations – there were practically no debates on institutional racism nor violence. Although these silences could be framed within broader Lusotropicalist debates in Portugal, there seemed to be no other major traces of debates on racism in the canonical history of Urban Anthropology.

This chapter is a journey through several cities, public libraries, books and authors. It is a journey to understand why Urban Anthropology has been evading race and racism as a possible lens to understand urban segregation and inequalities. As I will argue, these silences are a refraction of a more deep-rooted racist assumption about who and what is considered to be a worthwhile and pertinent subject of science. In short, I will show how epistemic silences are indeed issues that reveal the persistence of *epistemic apartheid* (Rabaka, 2010) that has been silencing both black authorship and racism, thereby leaving racial residential segregation unchallenged.

On the road: academic production, race and epistemic apartheid

Lisbon, Portugal

Back in the days when I was an undergraduate student in Anthropology, I was taught that studies on Urban Sociology were first developed by the

Chicago School (1915–45), established by scholars such as Albion Small or Robert Park. It was explained to me that, by electing the city as their quintessential social laboratory, these academics had the audacity to bring together theory and practice – developing their research through a combination of quantitative and qualitative methodologies and thereby deepening the analysis of urban space, social interaction and human nature (Bulmer, 1984; Lutters and Ackerman, 1996). For this reason, the Chicago School has been broadly recognised as the birthplace of modern Sociology, inspiring generations of scholars to this day. Considered masterpieces of sociological thought, bodies of work such as *The Polish Peasant in Europe and America* (1984 [1918–20]) by Florian Znaniecki and William Thomas, *The Ghetto* (1998 [1928]) by Louis Wirth or *Street Corner Society* (1993 [1943]) by William Foote-White became canonised, ascending to a position of what could be designated as *sociological classics*. These books became available at most academic libraries and, simultaneously, widely taught in the disciplines of Sociology and Anthropology. It must be noted that the works developed under the scope of the Chicago School of Sociology were deeply influenced by Park and Burgess's theoretical framework. By defining the city and a specific programme to study human behaviour in urban milieus (Park and Burgess, 1921; Park, 1968 [1915]) the authors set a particular theoretical and methodological framework informing further academic gazes on the territorialisation of social urban relations, which influenced countless researches until the present. Throughout my undergraduate years, I held this (hi)story as an uncontested truth.

With time, while the city started to emerge as a ground for developing research on institutional racism and the state's rationalities, I thought of reopening my old and dusty books in order to start drafting my thesis project. As I did so, I came to acknowledge that amongst the authors I knew – mostly men and white – neither the classical nor the contemporary ones have addressed race as a significant political and socio-anthropologic category in shaping contemporary urban landscapes. I remember clearly that I could not avoid asking myself, if it seemed so obvious that both black and Roma people experienced worse housing and living conditions and more segregated and ghettoised spaces than whites,[2] how could it be that Social Sciences overlooked it? How could scholars talk about space, city, periphery, migration, black youth, precarity (re)housing, poverty and social exclusion while neglecting the role of race and racism in such processes? Does only class matter? Even though I was uneasy, I was not too surprised, as over the years I had come to understand that race, as a political category, was mostly not crucial in scholarly analysis, at least in Portugal (Alves, 2016; Araújo and Maeso, 2015; 2016). I just didn't know exactly how this happened, particularly in the field of Urban Anthropology.

São Paulo, Brazil

In a second hand-bookstore in Brazil, I came across a book called *The Souls of Black Folk*, written in 1903, by an author called W. E. B. Du Bois. The book appeared to me as an unorthodox piece of sociological literature, which captured my attention. It drew upon the condition of black populations in America in the aftermath of the abolition of racial slavery. Stating that '[t]he problem of the twentieth century [was] the problem of the color-line', Du Bois (1994 [1903]: 9) claimed that black people were not only born with a *veil*, they were also *gifted with a second sight* – a *double consciousness*. After a quick read, I decided to take the book and stored it together with the older ones. Shortly after, one of my supervisors mentioned to me another volume by the same author, *The Philadelphia Negro: A Social Study* (1899). Emphasising among other things the living conditions of blacks in the city of Philadelphia, the book highlighted questions of space and race, arguing that *slums* were no exception to the urban tissue, but its by-products – the consequence of complex and entangled processes of interaction between institutional racism and urban life organisation. Later on, I learned that *The Philadelphia Negro* is 'usually depicted as the first study of an urban black community' but that 'its status as America's first major empirical sociological study has rarely been acknowledged' (Morris, 2015: 45). In the Introduction to its 1967 edition – written by sociologist E. Digby Baltzell – it is argued that there is a direct and definite link between Du Bois's work and 'a whole subsequent tradition in American sociology' as well as in the discipline of Anthropology (Baltzell, 1967: ix–xliv *apud* Green and Driver, 1976: 320; Harrison, 1988; 2012). This influence was evident in the work of the anthropologist Franz Boas when he stated the need to explain the traits of black Americans on the basis of history and social status, rejecting Darwinist theories; it reverberated in the works of Znaniecki, in the school of Urban Sociology led by Park and in W. Lloyd Warner's school of Community Studies, which inspired oeuvres such as *Black Metropolis* (Harrison, 1992). Accordingly, it could be argued that '[t]he origins, in both method and theoretical point of view of all these studies are to be found in *The Philadelphia Negro*' (Harrison, 1992). If this is so, why didn't we learn about Du Bois's work as we did about Boas's or Park's, since he seems to have applied the same methodological approaches as the Chicago School, in the same exact field of knowledge, but many years before? How was it possible that his work was disregarded in Social Sciences?

Oxford, United Kingdom

A few months later, I found this subject brought to life in a book by Aldon Morris, *The Scholar Denied: W. E. B. Du Bois and the Birth of Modern*

Sociology (2015), placed on a remote shelf at a bookstore in Oxford. The title of this recently published volume not only confirmed my then long-established suspicions; it promised some concrete responses. According to Morris (2015), Du Bois was not just forgotten; he had been denied. It was tacitly implied that he was known to the public, namely to scholars, but that he had been consistently excluded. Was this related to some degree of academic scepticism towards his work, his political position or the colour of his skin? Did racial inequality or institutional racism play a part in academic canon construction? Could this represent a case of epistemological apartheid, as pointed out by Reiland Rabaka (2010)? And what are the consequences of these silences for social analysis and the perpetuation of racialised violences and its correspondent silences across time in urban spaces?

Echoing in my mind, these were the questions that led me to further explore the works of Dan Green and Edwin Driver (1976), Faye Harrison (1988; 1992; 2012), Earl Wright II (2002a; 2002b; 2006; 2012; 2014), Reiland Rabaka (2010), Gurminder Bhambra (2014) and Aldon Morris (2015) which, among others, have been challenging this paradigmatic milestone of the history of sociological knowledge production. These authors put forward the importance of acknowledging the fundamental contributions and the pioneering role played by Du Bois in the emergence of disciplines such as Sociology and Anthropology. They argue that, in a context of pervasive institutional racism, epistemic obedience and epistemic apartheid, Du Bois's ground-breaking work has been constantly obliterated from the American sociological canon (Bhambra, 2014; Rabaka, 2010; Wright, 2012). Along with him, many other scholars, namely the ones participating in the Atlanta Sociological Laboratory (1895–1924), as well as their contributions and perspectives on social research, methodology, urban space, family or religion – more than just race and racism – have also been broadly marginalised and dismissed in the history of social thought (Wright II, 2002b; 2012). As their contributions were expunged from the whitened academic canon, these studies are absent from school curricula, debates within the classroom and, in accordance, from the shelves of university libraries. Public libraries, and particularly academic ones, are, despite their common lack of funding, the possible storefronts of the state of the art in a certain national or regional context. Their collection, in a way, establishes who and what is relevant, mirroring the canon in place and dictating what is to be academically remembered or soon to be forgotten. To be sure, the canon is not only what we learn as it has consequences in what we look for when engaging in academic knowledge production. The canon frames not only what we see but the ways in which we see what we see, with significant consequences in creating, by framing, reality.

In the library: debates on Urban Anthropology and racism

Drawing on these first *accidental* readings throughout different geographies and engaging in conversations with teachers, colleagues, activists and friends, I gathered valuable bibliographical references which could help to analyse the role of race as a political category in the construction of contemporary urban policies that, in part, determine urban landscapes. Many of the names and oeuvres I was searching for to compose my bibliographic framework were hitherto unknown to me but apparently quite important within particular anglophone latitudes of academic research focusing on racialised territories, urban segregation processes and their causes and consequences for the lives of black racialised subjects (Duneier, 2016; Harrison, 1988; 1992). Therefore, I went back to the library looking for *other* classics. The references I had managed to gather comprised mainly male African American authors.[3] I was searching for St. Clair Drake and Horace Cayton's ground-breaking sociological study on *Black Metropolis* (1945) or Kenneth Clark's psychological approach to *The Dark Ghetto* (1965). However, by then, copies of these oeuvres were not available in any of the libraries I usually go to, nor in any academic library in Portugal. Curiously, it was by this time – when I was immersed in accessing books analysing the city through the lenses of race – that I went to the preview of Raoul Peck's *I'm Not Your Negro* (2016) – inspired by James Baldwin's unfinished manuscript, *Remember This House* – exploring the history of the Civil Rights Movement in the United States. There, I recall seeing Kenneth Clark interviewing James Baldwin, Malcolm X and Martin Luther King in an excerpt of *The Negro and the American Promise* (1963). At that moment, I recall whispering to myself: 'It's Kenneth Clark, incredible!', and immediately wondering if the majority of people had recognised him from that brief archive footage so enthusiastically as I did. In fact, did people know about his work and his important contributions to academic debates on Psychology and Social Sciences? If not, what were the conditions that made him 'irrelevant' to students who are doing research on Urban Studies, namely in Anthropology? Was he only valorised by his activism, and ignored as a prominent scholar? To what extent is the recent public international debate on black intellectuals, postcolonialism, decolonisation, race and racism mirrored within Portuguese academic space and queries, specifically in Anthropology? And, finally, what can these presences and absences tell us about the state of the debate on race and racism at universities, namely in the field of Urban Anthropology? Why are these prominent US-American black scholars absent from Portuguese (and European) debates on the city and to what extent can the US African American urban experience be translated to other geographies? Why was the movie theatre packed while the bookshelves remained empty?

The absence of a lineage of black critical thought regarding the city seemed to confirm that institutional racism insists on pushing racialised black scholars away from academic spaces (Morris, 2015; Rabaka, 2010) to the point that the only black authors working on the city I could find in the shelves of Urban Anthropology were US-American sociologists Elijah Anderson and William Julius Wilson.[4] To be sure, the exclusive presence of Anderson and Wilson can be read as a symptom of how academia, as a modern institution of knowledge production, has historically marginalised black presence through systemic forms of epistemic apartheid (Rabaka, 2010). Moreover, white academia has ontologically avoided debates on institutional racism (more than just race) as a part of broader socio-anthropological discussions regarding urban spaces as the 'state-sanctioned or extralegal production and exploitation of group-differentiated vulnerability to premature death' (Gilmore, 2007: 28). The silencing of black scholars as well as of race as a colonised political category of dehumanisation urgently calls for a debate 'on various forms of social segregation, oppression, and exploitation (e.g., racism, sexism, and capitalism)' which coexist besides academia but 'illusively or inadvertently' inform and influence its interior, consolidating epistemic apartheid (Rabaka, 2010: 16).

As an anthropologist myself, at this point I was determined to grasp how the books available on the shelves of Urban Anthropology could help to disclose contemporary tendencies in Urban Studies, allowing for the identification of main historical references and debates as well as landmarks in framing contemporary urban researches in the Portuguese context. I was particularly devoted to tackling the apparent pervasiveness of a colour-blind tradition within the field of Urban Studies – even when race is present as a sociological reality – and, furthermore, to understanding its consequences in the lived experiences of black and Roma subjects in Portugal, particularly in peripheralised neighbourhoods in the Lisbon Metropolitan Area.

Take the books out of the shelf: the canonisation of race as a non-subject matter

Considering the impossibility of analysing all archives of all libraries dedicated to Social Sciences, I've chosen to map and examine existing books on Urban Anthropology in two important academic libraries. First, I went to the University Institute of Lisbon (ISCTE-IUL) and, later on, to the Faculty of Social Sciences and Humanities of the New University of Lisbon (FCSH-UNL). Other than old habits, going to these libraries had to do with the fact that these universities conjointly offer the only presently existing masters and doctoral programmes in Urban Studies.[5] Additionally, these universities host several key research centres in developing Urban Studies from within several disciplinary traditions and research contexts – therefore becoming references in the way the city is being analysed in the Portuguese academic context.[6] Even if I was aware that public libraries in Portuguese universities are normally poor in bibliographic references due to the shortage of public funds, the existent book collections, which result from purchases and donations, are a product of predominant influences within academic knowledge production and responsible for shaping future academic imaginaries.

At the library of the ISCTE-IUL, knowledge production is organised through countless bookshelves which materialise disciplines and subjects, comprising a specific place for studies on Urban Anthropology. On the other hand, the library of the FCSH-UNL is a tiny space where most of its bibliographic collection is stored, which hindered the analysis. Because of this, I decided to focus my attention particularly on the bibliographic collection of the ISCTE-IUL, having the FCSH-UNL collection as baseline and term of comparison. Little by little, I took a great majority of the books placed on the shelves of Urban Anthropology at ISCTE-IUL and compiled a list of fifty different oeuvres, which entailed book titles, authors' names, main subjects and bibliographic references quoted. By systematically charting and analysing these academic oeuvres, I aimed to map the main classic and contemporary influences in anthropological literature on cities – authors, theoretical frameworks and key subjects. The main objective of this empirical research was to ascertain possible continuities between historical and contemporary narratives of Urban Anthropology. Through this methodological approach, I intended to build a genealogy of knowledge production regarding Urban Anthropology and understand its influences and impacts on debates on contemporary Portuguese Urban Anthropology in particular. My hypothesis was that the prominence of particular international references and analytical frameworks – which historically disregarded the role of race and racism in shaping urban dynamics – could help to explain the absence of debates on race as well as structural and institutional racism in the field of Portuguese Urban Anthropology, even when race is hyper-present.

Arriving at ISCTE-IUL, my attention was immediately caught by six copies of anthropologist Ulf Hannerz's *Exploring the City: Inquiries toward an Urban Anthropology* (1980). Drawing on the work of pioneer Portuguese urban anthropologist Graça Cordeiro (2003), this significant presence could be justified by the fact that Hannerz's oeuvre has been considered a masterpiece within an intense corpus of debate on the relationship between Anthropology and the city. Moreover, the international history of Urban Anthropology was deeply influenced by a set of diverse historical, geographical and cultural approaches to the city, as well as by a corpus of sociological and ethnographical debates produced within the scope of the Chicago School of Sociology and the first 'community studies' in the USA (Cordeiro, 2003). This debate was further strengthened by contributions from British Social Anthropology, particularly by the School of Manchester, in the scope of the Rhodes Livingstone Institute (1937–64) – where urbanisation and ethnicity were analysed through innovative and interdisciplinary methodologies, favouring situation and network analysis (Cordeiro, 2003; Tembo, 2014). Furthermore, contributions from researches on urban development in Latin America, particularly in Mexico, should also be considered important to the emergence of the discipline. The birth of Urban Anthropology is understood as a direct consequence and a historical product of a series of diverse processes which led to an increasing centrality of urban spaces and urban living in anthropological studies (see Cordeiro, 2003; Eames and Goode, 1977). To be sure, the development of this recent and autonomous field of study within the discipline of Anthropology reflected the end of colonialism, the intensification of migrant flows to European cities and the emergence of a new series of problematics within cityscapes, which deserved increasing attention (Cordeiro, 2003). In this context, Urban Anthropology is said to be responsible for reshaping the discipline's epistemological approach, since it prompted an Anthropology *at home*, responsible for narrowing the (constructed) distance between the researcher and its subjects of study (when white), confirming that it was not the subject matter, but the approach which 'unwittingly [...] defined the anthropological endeavor' (Peirano, 1998).

At ISCTE there were seven bookcases dedicated to Urban Anthropology, comprising around 225 books. Besides several names engraved in the history of Urban Studies, such as Louis Wirth (1998) or Anthony Leeds (1994), the prevalence of the oeuvres of anthropologists Michel Agier and Gilberto Velho was evident. There were five different books by Agier, and six volumes written or edited by Velho. It must be noted that there were eight volumes of *Esquisses d'une anthropologie de la ville* (Agier, 2009) and its respective Portuguese translation, as well as six copies of *A Utopia Urbana* (Velho, 1989 [1973]). This wealth of repeated books pointed out the possibility that both Brazilian and French Urban Studies on Anthropology – besides classic anglophone influences – could also be predominant in the Portuguese urban anthropological context in both teaching and research.

Michel Agier is a renowned French anthropologist who initially dedicated his studies to marginalised spaces within major cities in Togo (Lomé), Brazil (Bahia) and Colombia (Cali). The author explored social, cultural, ethnic and racial mobilisations in ritualistic contexts, such as religious holidays or the Carnival. Driven specifically by his work on the neighbourhood of Agua Blanca (Cali) and the arrival of *desplazados*,[7] Agier took an interest in forced displacements, refugees and refugee camps. Engaged in an *Anthropology of the city* which departed from the study of poor and marginalised urban spaces to (re)think the city, Agier prompted innovative analytical approaches 'towards the creation of new urban contexts, particularly in vulnerable and adverse situations' (Damasceno et al., 2010: 813). Additionally, he conceptualised the importance of the city as a possible refuge and reflected upon how states invest in the management of the 'undesirables' through processes of spatial segregation (Agier, 2015). Among his far-reaching body of work, there were several titles present at the library of ISCTE (Agier, 1999; 2002; 2009; 2011; 2013). Although his earlier works revolved directly around issues such as race relations and black (urban) cultures (Damasceno et al., 2010), and even as his work continuously took place in racialised poor territories and orbited around issues such as border control regimes, dehumanisation processes and (the denial of) citizenship rights, structural or institutional racism are mostly absent from his analytical framework.

Gilberto Velho is considered the founding father of Urban Anthropology in Brazil (Bastos, 2017; Castro and O'Donnell, 2012). In his pioneering study drawing on different territorial scales to contextualise the everyday living of the inhabitants of Edifício Estrela in Copacabana (Rio de Janeiro), Velho focused on urban middle-class trajectories and expectations. This work later became a major source of inspiration for many students and researchers. *A Utopia Urbana* can be read as a milestone in the history of Urban Anthropology in the Brazilian as well as in the Portuguese context (Bastos, 2017; Castro and O'Donnell, 2012). Over the years, increasing dialogues, collaborations, movements and personal friendships have led to synergies with Velho, as testified by the edited volume *Urban Anthropology: Culture and Society in Brazil and Portugal* (1999)[8] – which epitomises epistemic, theoretical and methodological exchanges between two national contexts (Cachado, 2018), irretrievably joined by a past of (violent) colonial processes. The large number of works from Velho at the library is symptomatic of how his 'oeuvre would contribute to the ripening of the new Portuguese Anthropology, well after 1974' (Bastos, 2017: 165). It must be underlined that Velho developed most of his work in the Brazilian context, which is considered the country with the largest black-diaspora community in the world – a country which produces *anti-black cities* (Alves, 2018) where black people *were never meant to survive* (Vargas, 2010). Nonetheless, Velho has never explored the role of race or racism in the making of Brazilian cities and urban dynamics, raising the possibility that, just like him, many others have done the same, even if working on mostly black contexts. It is as if blackness is hyper-present while racism remains absent, lying underneath. According to Brazilian geographer Renato Emerson dos Santos, 'gathering articles on urban issues and racism [...] puts us face to face with a contradiction', namely 'the amplitude and multiplicity of possible thematic unfolding' or the 'dismissal of the theme in different areas' (2012: 27).

The importance of certain schools of thought and particular authors to the development of Portuguese Urban Anthropology was further echoed during an interview with anthropologist Rita Ávila Cachado who, drawing upon the work of Cordeiro, has been working on the history of Urban Ethnography in Portugal:

> [I]n Portugal, the big influences [in Urban Anthropology] are Brazil [...], and, then, the Spanish. In Brazil, Professor Gilberto Velho... he was in the US in close contact with Urban Anthropology – still under the influence of the Chicago School [...]. In the past, one of the most important references was Anthony Leeds ... and then, many others of the Chicago School: [Robert] Park of course, [Georg] Simmel and William Foote-White – compulsory reading in classes [of Urban Anthropology]. And then, more recently, Michel Agier. Then, several other references [...] [Christian] Topalov. Then, there are people in Spain, such as Joan Pujadas [...]. And, then, there's not much else. It is Spain, Brazil, the USA through the inference of the School of Chicago, some English authors who studied urban contexts, poverty, housing, vicinity, [social] networks [...]. And the French for housing .(Interview, 6 June 2018; my translation)

The prevalence of the works of Michel Agier and Gilberto Velho at the library indicates their significant influence in contemporary Portuguese Urban Anthropology. In line with preceding traditions of both the Chicago and Manchester schools, these works further testify to and reflect the extension of the influence of earlier sociological traditions up to the present, deepening continuities and particular frames through which urban spaces have been understood until the present. To be sure, Urban Anthropology was institutionalised in the United States of America with subsequent contributions from the British, Brazilian, Mexican and French contexts, among others (Cordeiro, 2003; Frúgoli et al., 2014). An attentive gaze on cityscapes and dynamics came to consolidate what is said to be a controversial and inter-disciplinary field of work, which is permeable to several disciplinary influences and which has elected Ethnography as the more adequate method to dive into cityscapes and urban living (Frúgoli et al., 2014).

Until the mid-1970s, anthropological Urban Studies were focused on rural-urban migration, urban problems (e.g., poverty, minorities and so-called deviant groups) or (transposing) classic subjects of (colonial) anthropological research, such as the study of kinship and rituals (to other urban contexts) (Cordeiro, 2003). Back then, the city was conceptualised merely as a 'locus of activity, but not the focus of research' (Cordeiro, 2003: 9). As such, between 1950 and 1970, Urban Anthropology was mostly an *Anthropology in the city*, later giving rise to an *Anthropology of the city* capable of relating microscale phenomena throughout Ethnography with macroscale structures and processes through context analysis (see Agier, 1999; Cordeiro, 2003; Eames and Goode, 1977). Besides epistemic shifts, urban matters and interests broadened in the course of the years and with them several thematic lines of study took shape. While many interests mirrored a certain anthropological and sociological tradition that continues to invest in classic lines of urban research (e.g., masculinities, poverty or migrations studies), others invested in developing new lines of enquiry by studying institutions such as the prison industrial complex or the police. Race remained, mostly, a silent matter. These major lines of enquiry reflect the impact of the aforementioned schools of thought and their direct influence/translation on/to the course of contemporary Portuguese Urban Anthropology. This becomes even more evident if we take a closer look at the fifty books selected from the shelves of Urban Anthropology and their main research subjects and themes.

Written mostly in English, French and Portuguese, and ranging from classic oeuvres to recent publications, the fifty randomly selected books evoke past and current trends on exploring the city, from Chicago to São Paulo, Paris to Lisbon. Despite the multiplicity of perspectives and approaches, the vast majority of the works engage in methodological and epistemological debates on: i) the challenges posed by Urban Anthropology as a recent field of study within the discipline; ii) the city as a new subject of research; and, iii) urban anthropologists as social scientists engaged in a new context of research (see Agier, 2011; Hannerz, 1980; Lepetit and Topalov, 2001; Low, 1999; Raulin, 2001; Southall, 1998). Neighbourhood ethnographies appear as the most appropriate methodological approach to analyse urban spaces and urban dynamics. The neighbourhood, as a porous border, appears to be a place from where it is possible to explore and analyse: i) urban lifestyles (see Sennet, 1994; Velho, 1989; Wilson, 1991); ii) social and cultural urban identities (see Agier, 2002; Signorelli, 2000; Velho, 2008); iii) urban popular cultures – namely through a series of artistic practices and sociability networks (see Biondi, 2010; Santos, 2009; Tanenbaum, 1995; Zaluar, 1985); iv) drug consumption and trafficking (see Bourgois, 2003; Chaves, 1999); v) (ethnic) ghettos and marginalised neighbourhoods (see Hannerz, 1989 [1969]; Suttles, 1968; Zaluar and Alvito, 1998); vi) violence (see Agier, 1999; Zaluar, 2004); vii) youth cultures (see Cordeiro et al., 2003; Sullivan, 1989; Velho, 2008); and, viii) migrations (see Agier, 2002; Lamphere, 1992; Repak, 1995).

The aforementioned subjects appear to be the most common research interests among urban anthropologists, according to the books available. Nevertheless, these debates overlap with those on several other issues, such as institutions, public policies, religious practices, memory, gender, class or social exclusion. Absent among these works are any bibliographic references to the intellectual W. E. B. Du Bois, except for the book edited by Frederick W. Boal (2000). There are no references to *The Philadelphia Negro* (1899). There are also practically no debates on race or institutional racism, except for Ulf Hannerz's *Soulside: Inquiries into Ghetto Culture and Community*

(1969), where several references to black intellectuals Stokely Carmichael and St. Clair Drake can be found. In this context, even if terms such as 'race', 'ethnicity, 'minorities' or 'racism' are mentioned throughout the fifty selected oeuvres, they are more descriptive than used to unveil ongoing power relations within contemporary urban milieus. The terms seem to be used more to describe and characterise particular populations and contexts than to analytically understand how historical processes of racialisation as dehumarisation have been used to create imbalances in access to citizenship or fundamental human rights. In this sense, race seems to be either invisible or rendered as 'non-relevant' in socio-anthropological debates. If this is the panorama for Urban Anthropological Studies in a general (inter)national perspective, will there be a place for critical race studies in Portuguese Urban Anthropology? Is Urban Anthropology a colonial matrix of knowledge production which urgently needs to be provincialised or decolonised, as proposed many years ago by Faye Harrison (2010 [1991])?

Portuguese Urban Studies and the silencing of institutional racism

In Portugal, Urban Ethnographies, and particularly Urban Anthropology, emerged mostly during the nineties (Cordeiro, 2003) providing an in-depth analysis of urban processes and dynamics. In fact, by using Ethnography, Urban Anthropology represented an opportunity to address microscale processes and dynamics by looking into urban living in detail. In line with previous works and debates, particularly in anglophone and Brazilian traditions, anthropologists such as Joaquim Pais de Brito (Cordeiro et al., 1983) and Graça Índias Cordeiro (1997) or sociologists such as António Firmino da Costa (1999) were responsible for developing this field of study. Electing some of the most historical and emblematic quarters of the capital, these authors conducted lengthy ethnographies in a context where cultural identities and forms of popular culture and organisation were included within the scope of analysis (see Cordeiro, 1997; 2003; Cordeiro et al., 1983; Firmino da Costa, 1999). By drawing on different disciplinary traditions to understand changing urban realities these authors were, in a way, responsible for blurring disciplinary borders and amplifying debates on the city, thus becoming references in the Portuguese context, as echoed by another part of the interview with Rita Cachado:

> [António] Firmino da Costa wrote that book that is like a bible for the Sociology students here at ISCTE – *A Sociedade de Bairro* – and has a selection of very important articles, some [of them] are in English, but very few [...] and he is one of those you can't avoid. Another [author] is Graça [Índias Cordeiro] for matters of methodology, mostly. What did she bring to Urban Anthropology?

> She was trained with other anthropologists and was almost the only one who proceeded to the field of Urban Anthropology as such. This doesn't mean there weren't others who would have worked in the urban context, they just simply (...) didn't refer to international Urban Anthropology. She used references from international Urban Anthropology and used methodologically references from Social Anthropology as researchers used to do at that time. And of course, Luís Fernandes. He's from the area of Psychology and he did long-term ethnographic research in a neighbourhood in Porto regarding drug consumption. And he is essential to the clarification of methodology and the use of fieldnotes. (Interview, 6 June 2018; my translation)

Apart from these essential references within the field of Urban Studies, mostly composed by anthropologists and sociologists, there are many other academics who inscribed their works within the context of Urban Portuguese Ethnography/Studies, such as Luís Baptista, João Pedro Nunes, Susana Durão, Miguel Chaves, Lígia Ferro, Eduardo Ascensão, Otávio Raposo or Rita Cachado (see Ascensão, 2013; Cachado, 2012; Cordeiro et al., 2003; Ferro and Gonçalves, 2018; Pereira, 2013; Varela et al., 2018), showing how, over the past few decades, ethnographic approaches became common across different disciplinary traditions, challenging disciplinary borders and prompting new approaches towards the city.

In order to put in dialogue, map and systematise the diverse approaches to urban spaces, several books and dossiers on Urban Studies were published across the years. In this context, I'd like to highlight two in particular, which are the result of conferences and academic meetings that had the city as quintessential subject. As a first attempt to map the debates on city and urban life in Portugal, I underline the *Proceedings of the Colloquium Living in/the City* (LNEC, 1991)[9] and the book *Urban Ethnographies* (Cordeiro et al., 2003)[10] – fundamental efforts in contextualising and mapping the history of Urban Ethnography. Analysing these oeuvres – present at both libraries – allows the mapping of major debates on Urban Studies within the Portuguese context. Moreover, understanding how classic references of the discipline reverberated in the way the city is placed under the gaze provides understanding of the emergence of the socio-anthropological debate on urban spaces and dynamics, and highlights its main actors.

The volume *Living in/the City* (1991) is the result of a colloquium with the same name, hosted by the Group of Social Ecology of the National Laboratory for Civil Engineering and the Group of Territorial Studies of the University Institute of Lisbon, in October 1990. This book brings into dialogue those 'who act upon the city' (e.g. architects) and those 'who think about it' (e.g. social scientists). This book reflects how most social scientists and architects attempted to keep up with the constant urban changes which characterised the past few decades. While predominantly focused on processes of urbanisation and (re)creation of sociability among lower and middle-class people, race is, again, never present as a possible lens of analysis. Even if black and Roma persons were living and building the city, race seems not to play a part in it. This happens even when racialised territories are directly addressed, as in the case of the work developed by Maria Toscano (1991) in the self-produced neighbourhood of *Fim do Mundo* (Cascais, LMA). In the chapter 'Uncovered but not "Discovery": mechanisms of (dis)integration of African migrants in the diaspora – sociological understandings of a case of intervention',[11] which focuses on precarity, poverty and social exclusion and tries to denaturalise accounts that see them as results of either identity or culture, racism is not taken into consideration even though the territory was mostly inhabited by black and Roma populations. Roma culture is portrayed as non-European, while Afro-descendants are consistently framed as immigrants, even as we can imagine that many youths of *Fim do Mundo* were already born in Portugal, therefore being black Portuguese and not migrants. Toscano's paper seems to define the borders of the neighbourhood according to the terms of Eurocentric academia. Roma and black subjects are placed outside Portuguality – a Euro-imagined fiction of a racial (white), historically and culturally (Greco-Roman and Christian) homogeneous national community (Alves, 2013). This colonial matrix of thought places non-white bodies outside the zone of being, reproducing their dehumanisation through notions of Europeanness and non-Europeanness (Fanon, 2008 [1952]; Hesse, 2007).

The book *Urban Ethnographies* (2003) is the result of a workshop organised by the Centre for Research and Studies in Sociology of the University Institute of Lisbon, that brought together different generations of anthropologists, sociologists and psychologists around the theme 'Cities and Diversity: Development Perspectives on Urban Anthropology',[12] in September 2001. The book reveals the predominance of an ethnographic approach to exploring the city, rendering it a strong area of confluence among different fields of knowledge production (Cordeiro et al., 2003). Dedicated to debating territories, images and power(s), and addressing the city both as a place and an idea, the book explores issues of migration and integration, policewomen, social control and drug consumption, the role of architecture and habitational strategies, sociability and ethnicity, belonging, youth, identity, new consumptions and psychedelic expressions. Race is not central, even when present. In the course of the paper 'Processes of integration of immigration',[13] Rui Pena Pires (2003) debates immigrants' integration in host societies and defines migration processes as disintegration processes, which demand new forms of interaction, either with Portuguese nationals or other immigrants. This results in processes of assimilation or ethnicisation which can coexist and help in understanding the formation of 'ethnic identities' (Pires, 2003).

By relying on such debates, Pires reorganises colonial categories and processes in postcolonial times. Nonetheless, the author also acknowledges that what he understood as challenges for 'systemic integration' of immigrants – related to an (in)compatibility between ethnicised identities and national ones – and the persistence of ethnicisation processes can mirror phenomena of stigmatisation and discrimination. Either way, racism is never problematised. In 'Ethnicity and sociability of Guineans in Portugal',[14] Fernando Luís Machado (2003) focuses on analysing the relationship between sociability and ethnicities which, according to him, can result in 'separatist multiculturalism' or 'irreducible individuality' (Machado, 2003). By studying the network composition of migrants from Guinea-Bissau in Portugal, he argues, among other things, that residential proximity does not always mean good neighbourhood relations – 'intercultural' conflicts can occur as they also happen in spaces without ethnic diversity (Machado, 2003). Racialised migrants are the target of research, leaving aside racial residential segregation and, most of all, the impact of whiteness through institutional and everyday racism on the living possibilities and sociability of black immigrants in Portugal. Racism is therefore absent from debates over immigrant presence and city planning, meaning that blackness is being consistently expunged from debates over nationhood, even though black people have been present in Portugal since at least the fifteenth century (Henriques, 2009).

To be sure, none of the books at ISCTE addressed issues of race and institutional racism as key research subjects while exploring cities. And the same must be said for the library of the New University of Lisbon. Consequently, the city is being analysed through several other lenses, with particular emphasis on (whitened) urban popular cultures and (whitened) urban popular sociability, space production and appropriation, tourism, gentrification, migrations or ethnicity, to mention only a few. All these studies seem to be colour blind. Nonetheless, when racism is introduced it is mostly ascribed to its moral and individual dimensions while institutions are never made accountable. This suppresses broader debates on the role of race in shaping the urban landscape of centres and peripheries through racialised urban governmentalities which make racialisation to be directly experienced as spatial (Razack, 2002). The operation of race seems to be reduced to the operation of class, in a context where racialised poverty remains unquestioned.

Concluding remarks

In the specific case of Portuguese Urban Studies – particularly in Anthropology – the absence of debates on race is pervasive, suggesting that historical and global processes of epistemic apartheid, which silenced both black scholars and discussions about institutional racism, have rendered racial segregation unquestioned, promoting the reading of urban inequalities through the lenses of migration studies and broader processes of socio-economic exclusion, mostly class. Considering the (mis)matches between academia and politics (Alves and Falanga, 2019), and particularly academia's influences on public debate, public policies and programmes, by silencing racialised residential segregation academia is, in fact, actively contributing to its perpetuation, for the persistence of academic silences around racism and the institutionalised spatialisation of blackness strongly contribute to leaving racism unchallenged. In this context, silencing W. E. B. Du Bois, St. Clair Drake, Horace Cayton, Kenneth Clark or Faye Harrison – more than a simple fact – is a symptom of a broader problem. Epistemic apartheid actively contributes to the persistence of past and contemporary racialised apartheids and violence in cities. This is even more evident if we draw on episodes of forced evictions or anti-black and anti-Roma police brutality – paradigmatic of how the colour line (Du Bois, 1899) is being constantly retraced – which reinforce racialisation as dehumanisation and enable the pervasiveness of ungrievable lives, unevenly subjected to state control, repression and death (Butler, 2009). Nevertheless, and as argued by Faye Harrison, the 'periphery, while formed in large measure by discrimination and exclusion, has historically been an important locus of critique and creativity. And it has been a significant intellectual front for anti-racist, anti-colonial, and anti-imperialist struggle' (1988: 114).

Notes

1 A special thanks to Giovanni Picker, Noa K. Ha, pê feijó, Rita Ávila Cachado and Silvia Rodríguez Maeso for their attentive and critical observations on earlier versions of this chapter.
2 This despite the fact that there is still no public data collection on the grounds of racial/ethnic origins in Portugal (Ba et al., 2019).
3 For further considerations and debate on the (double) silencing and erasure of the contributions of women of colour to academic knowledge production see Navarro et al. (2013).
4 I could also find the work of the Black Afro-Brazilian author Nilton Santos, *A arte do efêmero: Carnavalescos e mediação cultural no Rio de Janeiro* (2009).
5 The masters and doctoral programmes on Urban Studies emphasise the importance of interdisciplinarity to study and intervene in contemporary cities.
6 For example, the Centre for Sociological Studies (UNL), the Centre for Research and Studies in Sociology (ISCTE-IUL) or the Centre for Socioeconomic and Territorial Studies (ISCTE-IUL).

7 Displaced people produced by the increasing armed conflict in the region.
8 *Antropologia Urbana: Cultura e Sociedade no Brasil e em Portugal.*
9 *Viver (n)a Cidade.*
10 *Etnografias Urbanas.*
11 'Descobertos mas não "Descobridos": mecanismos de (des)integração dos imigrantes africanos em diáspora - leitura sociológica de um caso de intervenção'.
12 'Cidades e Diversidade: Perspectivas de Desenvolvimento em Antropologia Urbana'.
13 'Processos de integração da imigração'.
14 'Etnicidade e socialibilidade dos guinenses em Portugal'.

References

Agier, M. (1999), *L'invention de la ville: banlieues, townships, invasions and favelas* (Paris: Éditions des Archives Contemporaines).

Agier, M. (2002), *Aux Bords du Monde, Les Réfugies* (Paris: Editions Flammarion).

Agier, M. (2009), *Esquisees d'une anthropologie de la ville* (Louvain-la-Neuve: Bruylant-Academia).

Agier, M. (2011), *Antropologia da cidade: lugares, situações, movimentos* (São Paulo: Editora Terceiro Nome).

Agier, M. (2013), *La condition cosmopolite* (Paris: Édititons La Découverte).

Agier, M. (2015), Do refúgio nasce o gueto: antropologia urbana e política dos espaços precários. In Birman, P. et al. (eds) *Dispositivos urbanos e trama dos viventes: ordens e resistências* (Rio de Janeiro: FMG Editora), pp. 33–54.

Alves, A. R. (2013), Para uma compreensão da segregação residencial: o Plano Especial de Realojamento e o (Anti-)Racismo. Masters dissertation (Migrations, Inter-ethnicities and Transnationalism), Faculdade de Ciências Sociais e Humanas, UNL Lisboa.

Alves, A. R. (2016), (Pré)Textos e Contextos: Media, Periferia e Racialização. *Revista de Ciências Sociais Política & Trabalho* 44: 91–107.

Alves, A. R. and R. Falanga (2019), Desencontros entre Academia e Política: Conhecimento, Engajamento e Habitação em Portugal. *CIDADES, Comunidades e Territórios* 38: 14–19.

Alves, J. A. (2018), *The Anti-black City: Police Terror and Black Urban Life in Brazil* (Minneapolis, MN: University of Minnesota Press).

Araújo, M. and S. Rodríguez Maeso (2015), Eurocentrism, political struggles and the entrenched will-to-ignorance: an introduction. In Araújo, M. and S. Maeso (eds) *The Contours of Eurocentrism: Race, History, and Political Texts* (Lanham, MD: Lexington Books).

Araújo, M. and S. Rodríguez Maeso (2016), *Os Contornos do Eurocentrismo: Raça, história e textos políticos* (Coimbra: Almedina).

Ascensão, E. (2013), A barraca pós-colonial: materialidade, memória e afecto na arquitectura informal. In Domingos, N. and E. Peralta (eds) *Cidade e Império: dinâmicas coloniais e desdobramentos pós-coloniais* (Lisboa: Edições 70), pp. 425–473.

Ba, M., C. Roldão and M. Araújo (2019), Recolha de dados étnico-raciais nos Censos 2021: um passo à frente no combate ao racismo. *Público* (16 April), 21. Available at www.publico.pt/2019/04/16/sociedade/opiniao/recolha-dados-etnicoraciais-censos-2021-passo-frente-combate-racismo-1869349?fbclid=IwA R3pH4TcTZutRfpTlxQjlOmM8EF7X9f0ke2IY1qoa5f4C3vhtMFsWZD2b24.

Bastos, C. (2017), Utopias, portais e antropologias urbanas: Gilberto Velho em Lisboa. *Análise Social* 222, LII (1.º): 162–174.

Bhambra, G. (2014), A sociological dilemma: race, segregation and US Sociology. *Current Sociology Monograph* 62(4): 472–492.

Biondi, K. (2010), *Junto e misturado: Uma etnografia do PCC* (São Paulo: Editora Terceiro Nome).

Boal, F. W. (ed.) (2000), *Ethnicity and Housing: Accommodating Differences* (London and New York: Routledge).

Bourgois, P. (2003), *In Search of Respect: Selling Crack in El Barrio* (Cambridge: Cambridge University Press).

Bulmer, M. (1984), *The Chicago School of Sociology: Institutionalization, Diversity, and the Rise of Sociological Research* (Chicago, IL: University of Chicago Press).

Butler, J. (2009), *Frames of War: When Is Life Grievable?* (London and New York: Verso).

Cachado, R. (2012), *Uma Etnografia na Cidade Alargada. Hindus da Quinta da Vitória em processo de realojamento* (Lisboa: Fundação Calouste Gulbenkian e Fundação para a Ciência e a Tecnologia).

Cachado, R. (2018), A Etnografia Urbana em Portugal e suas redes com o Brasil. In Gonçalves, R. and Ferro, L. (eds) *Cidades em Mudança. Processos Participativos em Portugal e no Brasil* (Rio de Janeiro: Mauad Editora), pp. 41–56.

Castro, C. and J. O'Donnell (2012), Gilberto Velho (1945–2012) – In Memoriam. *Estudos Históricos* 25(49): 5–7.

Chaves, M. (1999), *Casal Ventoso: da gandaia ao narcotráfico. Marginalidade Económica e Dominação Simbólica em Lisboa* (Lisboa: Imprensa de Ciências Sociais).

Cordeiro, G. I. (1997), *Um Lugar na Cidade. Quotidiano, Memória e Representação no Bairro da Bica* (Lisboa: Publicações Dom Quixote).

Cordeiro, G. I. (2003). A Antropologia Urbana entre a tradição e a prática. In Cordeiro, G. L., V. Baptista and A. Firmino da Costa (eds) *Etnografias Urbanas* (Lisboa: Celta Editora), pp. 3–34.

Cordeiro, G. I., C. Afonso and M. B. Fernandes (1983), O Fado: um canto na cidade. Uma entrevista a Joaquim Pais de Brito. *Etnologia* 1: 149–184.

Cordeiro, G. I., L. V. Baptista and A. Firmino da Costa (eds) (2003), *Etnografias Urbanas* (Lisboa: Celta Editora).

Damasceno, I. et al. (2010), As cidades da antropologia: Entrevista com Michel Agier. *Revista de Antropologia* 53(2): 811–842.

Du Bois, W. E. B. (1899), *The Philadelphia Negro: A Social Study* (Philadelphia, PA: University of Pennsylvania).

Du Bois, W. E. B. (1994 [1903]), *The Souls of Black Folk* (New York: Dover Publications).

Duneier, M. (2016), *Ghetto: Invention of Place, the History of an Idea* (New York: Farrar, Straus and Giroux).

Eames, E. and J. Goode (1977), *Anthropology of the City. An Introduction to Urban Anthropology* (New Jersey: Prentice-Hall).

Emerson dos Santos, R. (org.) (2012), *Questões Urbanas e Racismo* (Rio de Janeiro: DP et Alii Editora).

Fanon, F. (2008 [1952]), *Black Skin, White Masks* (London: Pluto Press).

Ferro, L. and R. Gonçalves (2018), Etnografias urbanas: explorando as cidades contemporâneas – Introdução. *Etnográfica* 22(2): 305–310.

Firmino da Costa, A. (1999), *Sociedade de Bairro: Dinâmicas Sociais da Identidade Cultural* (Lisboa: Celta Editora).

Frúgoli, H. et al. (2014), Antropologia urbana (em língua) portuguesa: entrevista com Graça Índias Cordeiro. *Revista de Antropologia* (January): 449–484.

Gilmore, R. W. (2007), *Golden Gulag: Prisons, Surplus, Crisis, and Opposition in Globalizing California* (Berkeley, CA: University of California Press).

Green, D. S. and E. D. Driver (1976), W. E. B. Du Bois: a case in the sociology of sociological negation. *Phylon* 37(4): 308–342.

Hannerz, U. (1980), *Exploring the City: Inquiries toward an Urban Anthropology* (New York: Columbia University Press).

Hannerz, U. (1989 [1969]), *Soulside: Inquiries into Ghetto Culture and Community* (New York: Columbia University Press).

Harrison, F. (1988), Introduction: an African diaspora perspective for urban anthropology. *Urban Anthropology and Studies of Cultural Systems and World Economic Development* 17(2/3), Black Folks in Cities Here and There: Changing Patterns of Domination and Response, pp. 111–141.

Harrison, F. (1992), The Du Boisian legacy in anthropology: W. E. B. Du Bois and anthropology. *Critique of Anthropology* 12(3): 239–260.

Harrison, F. (2012), Dismantling anthropology's domestic and international peripheries. *World Anthropology Network e-Journal* 6: 87–110.

Harrison, F. (ed.) (2010 [1991]), *Decolonizing Anthropology: Moving Further toward an Anthropology for Liberation* (Arlington, VA: American Anthropological Association).

Henriques, I. C. (2009), *A Herança Africana em Portugal* (Lisboa: CTT Correios Portugal).

Hesse, B. (2007), Racialized modernity: an analytics of white mythologies. *Ethnic and Racial Studies* 30(4): 643–663.

Lamphere, L. (ed.) (1992), *Structuring Diversity: Ethnographic Perspectives on the New Immigration* (Chicago, IL: University of Chicago Press).

Lepetit, B. and C. Topalov (eds) (2001), *La ville des sciences sociales* (Paris: Belin).

LNEC (1991), *Colóquio Viver (n)a Cidade. Comunicações* (Lisboa: LNEC).

Low, S. M. (ed.) (1999), *Theorizing the City: The New Urban Anthropology Reader* (New Brunswick, NJ: Rutgers University Press).

Lutters, W. and M. Ackerman (1996), An introduction to the Chicago School of Sociology. *Interval Research Proprietary* 2(6): 1–25.

Machado, F. L. (2003), Etnicidade e socialibilidade dos guinenses em Portugal. In Cordeiro, G. et al. (eds) *Etnografias Urbanas* (Lisboa: Celta Editora), pp. 131–142.

Morris, A. (2015), *The Scholar Denied: W. E. B. Du Bois and the Birth of Modern Sociology* (Oakland, CA: University of California Press).

Navarro, T., B. Williams and A. Ahmad (2013), Sitting at the kitchen table: fieldnotes from women of color in anthropology. *Cultural Anthropology* 28(3): 443–463.

Park, R. (1968 [1915]), The city: suggestions for the investigation of human behavior in the city environment. *The American Journal of Sociology* 20(5): 577–612.

Park, R. E. and E. W. Burgess (1921), *Introduction to the Science of Sociology* (Chicago, IL: University of Chicago Press).

Peirano, M. (1998), When Anthropology is at home: the different contexts of a single discipline. *Annual Review Anthropology* 27: 105–128.

Pereira, P. (2013), O Parque das Nações em Lisboa: uma montra da metrópole à beira-Tejo. PhD dissertation (Sociology), Faculdade de Ciências Sociais e Humanas, UNL Lisboa.

Pires, R. P. (2003), Processos de integração na imigração. In Cordeiro, G. et al. (eds) *Etnografias Urbanas* (Lisboa: Celta Editora), pp. 63–74.

Rabaka, R. (2010), *Against Epistemic Apartheid. W. E. B. Du Bois and the Disciplinary Decadence of Sociology* (United Kingdom: Lexington Books).

Raulin, A. (2001), *Anthropologie urbaine* (Paris: Armand Colin).

Razack, S. (ed.) (2002), *Race, Space and the Law: Unmapping a White Settler Society* (Toronto: Between the lines).

Repak, T. A. (1995), *Waiting on Washington: Central American Workers in the Nation's Capital* (Philadelphia, PA: Temple University Press).

Santos, N. (2009), *A arte do efêmero: Carnavalescos e mediação cultural no Rio de Janeiro* (Rio de Janeiro: Apicuri).

Sennet, R. (1994), *Flesh and Stone. The Body and the City in Western Civilization* (London: Faber and Faber).

Signorelli, A. (2000), *Antropologia urbana: introduzione alla ricerca in Italia* (Milano: Guerini Studio).

Southall, A. (1998), *The City in Time and Space* (Cambridge: Cambridge University Press).

Sullivan, M. (1989), *'Getting Paid': Youth Crime and War in the Inner City* (Ithaca, NY: Cornell University Press).

Suttles, G. D. (1968), *The Social Order of the Slum: Ethnicity and Territory in the Inner City* (Chicago, IL: University of Chicago Press).

Tanenbaum, S. (1995), *Underground Harmonies: Music and Politics in the Subways of New York* (Ithaca, NY: Cornell University Press).

Tembo, A. (2014), The Rhodes-Livingstone Institute and interdisciplinary research in Northern Rhodesia (Zambia), 1937–1964. *Strategic Review for Southern Africa* 36(1): 90–99.

Toscano, M. (1991), Descobertos mas não 'Descobridos': mecanismos de (des) integração dos imigrantes africanos em diáspora em – leitura sociológica de um caso de intervenção. In *Colóquio Viver (n)a Cidade. Comunicações* (Lisboa: LNEC), pp. 73–90.

Varela, P., O. Raposo and L. Ferro (2018), Redes de sociabilidade, identidades e trocas geracionais. Da 'Cova da Música' ao circuito musical africano da Amadora. *Sociologia Problemas e Práticas* 86: 109–132.

Vargas, J. C. (2010), *Never Meant to Survive: Genocide and Utopias in Black Diaspora Communities* (Maryland: Rowman & Littlefield Publishers).

Velho, G. (1989 [1973]), *A Utopia Urbana: um estudo de antropologia social* (Rio de Janeiro: Jorge Zahar Editora).

Velho, G. (1999), *Antropologia Urbana: Cultura e Sociedade no Brasil e em Portugal* (Rio de Janeiro: Jorge Zahar Editor).

Velho, G. (2008), *Rio de Janeiro: Cultura, Política e conflito* (Rio de Janeiro: Jorge Zahar Editor).

Wilson, E. (1991), *The Sphinx in the City: Urban Life, the Control of Disorder, and Women* (Berkeley, CA: University of California Press).

Wirth, L. (1998 [1928]), *The Ghetto* (New Brunswick, NJ: Transaction Publishers).

Wright II, E. (2002a), Using the master's tools: the Atlanta Sociological Laboratory and American Sociology, 1896–1924. *Sociological Spectrum* 22(1): 15–39.

Wright II, E. (2002b), The Atlanta Sociological Laboratory, 1896–1924: a historical account of the first American school of Sociology. *Western Journal of Black Studies* 26(2): 165–174.

Wright II, E. (2006), W. E. B. Du Bois and the Atlanta University Studies on the Negro, revisited. *Journal of African American Studies* 9(4): 3–17.

Wright II, E. (2012), Why, where, and how to infuse the Atlanta Sociological Laboratory into the Sociology curriculum. *Teaching Sociology* 40(3): 257–270.

Wright II, E. (2014), W. E. B. Du Bois, Howard W. Odum and the sociological ghetto. *Sociological Spectrum: Mid-South Sociological Association* 34(5): 453–468.

Zaluar, A. (1985), *A máquina e a Revolta: as organizações populares e o significado da pobreza* (Sao Paulo: Brasiliense).

Zaluar, A. (2004), *Integração Perversa: pobreza e tráfico de drogas* (Rio de Janeiro: Editora FGV).

Zaluar, A. and M. Alvito (eds) (1998), *Um século de Favela* (Rio de Janeiro: Editora FGV).

Znaniecki, F. and W. Thomas (1984 [1918–20]), *The Polish Peasant in Europe and America* (Chicago, IL: University of Illinois Press).

9

Between hope and despair: how racism and anti-racism produce Madrid

Stoyanka Eneva

Introduction

In Spain racism is frequently understood as an ideology that comes mainly from far-right groups and parties. This has contributed to the lack of recognition of racism as a priority issue in various left-wing spaces, both institutional ones and autonomous social movements, which assume that they are non-racist by default (Gil-Benumeya Flores, 2018). This approach has led to a blind spot about racism within the practices and claims of social movements, which in many cases do not take into account the specific demands of their racialised and migrant members and/or sympathisers (Gonick, 2015; Johansson, 2017). As Arribas Lozano (2014; 2017) states, the agency of migrants and historically marginalised minorities and their ability to articulate their own anti-racist position are frequently underestimated.

However, as Angela Davis has remarked, in a statement that became popular in Spain after her last visit in 2018, 'In a racist society, it is not enough to be non-racist, we must be anti-racist'.[1] In the last three years, some feminist and anti-fascist groups, neighbourhood and squatting collectives, which are mostly organised in urban contexts and around different struggles for the right to the city, have undergone a transition from an evasion on the issue of racism to an incipient awakening of interest in anti-racism as an idea and practice. At the same time, they have been trying to approach racialised and migrant people as anti-racist allies.

In this process, cities have been especially relevant as spaces of organisation of different social movements as well as objects of urban struggles. Focusing on the different forms of representation of Spain's capital, this chapter presents an analysis of Madrid as an unequal city in which segregation, displacement and persecution due to racial profiling take place. Drawing on recent debates in Urban Studies, the chapter aims to answer two mutually related research questions: Are historical social movements being transformed by the incorporation of anti-racist discourse and practices? And what are the relationships between transformations of social movements and transformations of a city? How, in other words, are racism and anti-racism shaping Madrid?

This approach is relevant because there is a certain disconnection between the fields of Racial and Urban Studies. Violence and racial discrimination are often studied within national and supranational contexts but not so much on an urban scale, while urban problems at a global level – such as inequality, exclusion, displacement and domination – are underresearched in relation to racialisation and racism (Picker et al., 2018). This is why it is worth noting the work of scholars who focus on 'racial urbanities' like Giovanni Picker, Noa Ha or Manuela Boatcă.

My aim is to foreground the role of racism and anti-racism in producing urban spaces such as the two neighbourhoods I empirically focus on, Lavapiés and Usera. After providing analysis at the urban level, I will further develop the concept of the neighbourhood as a territory of possibilities to build identity, belonging and anti-racist political demands. I will discuss the concept of *'barrionalismo'* ('neighbourhoodism') from different perspectives: as it appears in academic research (Limón López, 2015), in the press (Delgado, 2018), in essays (de la Cruz, 2018) or in neighbourhood activist blogs (Suárez, 2012). Although this concept has been widely claimed to describe the sense of belonging, of shared identity and the struggle for certain urban rights, these have not explicitly included the migrant and racialised people who live in the neighbourhood, their identities and claims, their activism and their position as political subjects. The chapter therefore represents a critique of the way in which the imaginary of *barrionalismo* has failed to incorporate the racial dimensions of urban problems such as housing, police repression and urban inequality.

Through the analysis carried out in the chapter, I argue that, despite the will to incorporate an anti-racist perspective in some groups that seek to be anti-racist allies, there are different and polarising perceptions regarding everyday and institutional racism and the way in which these determine the lives of racialised people. It is important to research these issues precisely because the current moment is one of disputes over the meaning of racism, anti-racism, urban and neighbourhood activism in a context of prevailing nationalism in Europe, reinforced surveillance, maximised urban borders and advancement of policies that segment human rights. Although these debates have previously taken place in other European countries where postcolonial emigration has a far longer trajectory, in the case of Spain these are discussions that are still very difficult to open. Thus, the intentions of the chapter are to provide a better understanding of the racism/anti-racism scenario in Madrid and to contribute to the conversation that is ongoing in both academia and activism about the (im)possibility of alliances and mixed spaces between anti-racist and other urban activisms.

Defining racism: a contested terrain

A relevant debate about the approach to racism is the division between political and social understandings of the problem of racism. The former point of view, represented in Spanish academic literature from the 1990s until now (Alvite, 1995; Gil-Benumeya Flores, 2019), targets the way that political parties and discourses, together with governmental policies, contribute to the production and reproduction of institutional racism, but can neglect the practices of 'everyday racism' (Essed, 1991). As in academic disputes, on the activist terrain the discursive battle is between the definition of racism as an institutional, structural and systemic problem and its definition as a social, moral and individual one, related to personal characteristics, ideas and attitudes. However, both positions refer to the political, academic, social consensus that links racism in Spain to the beginning of large-scale international migration in the 1990s.

This perspective ignores, on the one hand, the long history of the slave trade, colonialism and anti-gypsyism in Spain (Garcés, 2018; Van Dijk, 2005) and, on the other, the discrimination that is faced by racialised persons who are born in the country (even as many of them are deprived of citizenship rights because of the 'jus sanguinis' principle).

Recently, scholars from different disciplines have been challenging this vision. Rodríguez Maeso and Cavia (2014) show that focusing on tolerance, interculturalism and the integration of migrants is not the same as exposing racism as a structural, institutional and political problem that is related not only to discrimination but also to the privileges of the dominant society. Mahdis Azarmandi (2016a; 2016b; 2017) points out the discontinuity between the colonial heritage of Spain and the current understanding of racism. In her work, Azarmandi relates this kind of collective amnesia to Mills's concept of 'white ignorance' (Mills, 2007). In this regard, it is important to mention the emerging work of migrant and racialised scholars, activists and artists in Spain who are producing important research targeting racism/anti-racism from a decolonial perspective. It is worth noting the work of Colectivo Ayllú[2] and the lecture series 'Program oriented to subaltern practices'. Another important author is Helios Garcés (2018), who is researching anti-gypsyism in Spain, drawing on the work of black Marxists such as Cedric Robinson and decolonial scholars such as Ramón Grosfoguel.

From an Afrocentric perspective, the doctoral thesis of Antumi Toasijé (2019) is dedicated not only to documenting the African presence since prehistoric times in the territory of present-day Spain but also to researching the absence of this physical presence in the collective memory, the archives or the schoolbooks. Other relevant recent works are *Cuando somos el enemigo* ('When we are the enemy'; 2019) by Jeffrey Abe Pans, focused on documenting the history and memory of Afrocentric activism in Spain and *La radicalización del racismo. Islamofobia de Estado y prevención antiterrorista* ('The radicalization of racism. State Islamophobia and anti-terrorism prevention') by Anhoa Douhaibi and Salma Amazian (2019).

Anti-racism in Spain: a historical overview

This section aims not only to situate the research in the existing theoretical and activist debates but also to highlight the characteristics that make Spain's and Madrid's cases different in terms of context and forms of transformation of anti-racism. Some of the specific characteristics are related to the current influence of decolonial theory at a time when the descendants of the first generation of migrants are beginning to gain prominence as anti-racist activists.

As shown in the previous section, the meaning of racism is still a contested terrain. In a similar way, in Spain, 'the framing of anti-racism involves moving boundaries between racism, tolerance, migration and other related terms in political action and public opinion' (Gómez-Reino Cachafeiro, 2006: 2).

In this sense, anti-racist activism in Spain and Madrid and, especially, alliances between groups of white and racialised people, have gone through different stages, discourses and actions. In the framework of the No Borders struggles (Alldred, 2003), it is important to mention some collectives that have been active in the 2000s and early 2010s. The activities and working groups that arose from collaborations between migrants and white activists during that period were based on mutual support and learning, mainly in the form of cooperation with migrants who experience difficulties navigating daily interactions with different institutions. The functioning of such collectives is rooted in a complex understanding of reality that combines the experiences of everyday racism (Essed, 1991) with analysis of the functioning of institutional racism and the elaboration of strategies to circumvent/survive it. This type of anti-racism not only focuses on the discrimination suffered by racialised people, but also tries to prioritise an understanding of white people's privileges and put them at the service of racialised people. Examples of this type of collective are Ferrocarril Clandestino (Underground Railroad), Brigades for the Observation of Human Rights (BVODH) and immigration working groups within different social centres (Escudero, 2013). This model of empowerment-accompaniment has been assessed as an especially positive experience, but it has also received some criticisms, especially related to the lack of leadership and positions of responsibility occupied by migrants and racialised people.

Another type of strategy has been followed by groups such as BVODH. Diego, a former activist (personal interview, 3 April 2020), explains that human rights discourse was used as a way of calling attention to institutional racism from the perspective of a term that appeals not only to the universal, but also to the supranational, and therefore offers the possibility of questioning the actions of the state that reproduce racism.

Currently, anti-racist activism in Spain is in a stage of transformation not only due to the existence of a 'second generation' – that is, children of migrants who have been born or/and socialised in Spain and have better access to resources, information, education and networks – but also due to the recent visibility of demands from immigrants themselves. These demands no longer focus only on basic needs, but also on demands for recognition, redistribution and reparation. Organisations such as the Union of Ambulant Street Vendors or the Centre of Empowerment of Domestic and Care Workers do not limit themselves to aspirations for better labour conditions. These organisations themselves represent the intersectionality between race, class and gender and their demands point directly to the institutional, structural and systemic racism that affects them in their condition as workers, immigrants and racialised men/women.

However, there are still problems regarding intersectionality or access of migrants and racialised people to spokespersons and leadership in different housing movements, feminist or labour rights collectives. There is a dividing line between migrant struggles and 'struggles for all'. In the housing or labour movements, the presence and work of migrants and racialised people are recognised, but not their leadership. A relevant example is the questioning of the right of street vendors to call themselves workers, to call their association a union and to claim public space as their workplace (Zepeda, 2017).

Methodology

The chapter is based on data obtained through the ongoing fieldwork of the author's doctoral thesis, which aims to carry out an ethnography of various anti-racist activisms in Madrid. This is qualitative research based on ethnographic methodology using as its main research techniques participant observation, semi-structured in-depth interviews and netnography.

The part of the fieldwork used for this chapter involves extended participant observation in three activist spaces with different proportions of racialised and white persons: SOS Racismo Madrid, based in the neighbourhood of Lavapiés, Juventud Antirracista de Usera (JAU), based in the district of Usera, and 8th March, in Madrid metropolitan area. I have observed and documented seven assemblies and three workshops in Lavapiés, five assemblies of JAU Usera and three assemblies of the feminist commission 8M Madrid. I have also observed three preparatory assemblies for the organisation of the annual anti-racist march 17N and the proper 17N march for two consecutive years. Fifteen interviews with anti-racist activists have been conducted in the period from June 2018 to January 2020, where some of the main topics have been the neighbourhood, the problems of racism, the possibility of building alliances and militancy from the neighbourhood.

Is Madrid a racist city?

Owing to its long history of national and international immigration, Madrid is often seen as an open and cosmopolitan city. But the narrative of a metropolis that is easily absorbing and integrating newcomers is contested by a great amount of literature that explores the contrasts, inequalities and segregation patterns that shape a map of uneven urban development (Chasco, 2018; Díaz-Orueta et al., 2018).

The urban development of the Spanish capital has been characterised by the growth of multinational companies' headquarters, financialisation of housing, gentrification, attraction of conference tourism and multiple attempts to attract mega-events such as the Olympic Games (Eneva and Abellán, 2018; Observatorio Metropolitano, 2007). At the same time, the income gap is increasing, creating a 'global class' and an army of workers at its service in different sectors that the former demands (domestic employees, retail trade, hotel and catering industry, personalised services). This division is expressed not only at the levels of income and sociocultural capital but also in an ethno-racial way where the worst working conditions correspond to the top three jobs occupied by migrants (Comunidad de Madrid, 2016).

Even if there is enough data to analyse the economic and ethnic division of Madrid, is it possible to analyse urban inequalities in the city in terms of racial segregation? In Spain, it is impossible to measure how the lives of racialised people are affected by different types of discrimination because self-determination in terms of race is banned for any type of data gathering, something that follows European trends in which mentioning race as a social reality is a taboo (El-Tayeb, 2010). What can be detected, then, is how the mentioned inequalities affect immigrants.

The map of urban vulnerability and the census of foreigners in the city, both based on data from 2018, show a similar pattern that is extremely concerning. The parameters used to calculate the ranking of each district and neighbourhood on the first map are: socio-economic status, economic activity, urban development and welfare needs, which show how foreign-born citizens are much more vulnerable to poverty, unemployment, poor housing conditions and poorer quality of public services and education. In the following sections, my aim is to analyse some of these issues in detail, using the data available from municipal and regional statistics.

Residential segregation as a consequence of racism is produced through the opportunities and conditions for housing access. The 2008 economic crisis had a strong impact on the migrant population in terms of housing: the data available from 2016 shows that 53.1 per cent live in a rented flat compared with 48.9 in 2014. Also, the number of immigrants who own a house in the Community of Madrid has decreased from 11.9 per cent in 2014 to 7.9 in 2016. It is also evident that immigrants need to rely on family networks, if available, since 19.6 per cent live with family/friends compared with 15.8 in 2014. The statistics are relevant because there is widespread discrimination in the housing market: only 51 per cent would rent their flat to foreigners. There is a huge inequality in terms of average salary (€18,155.05 per year in 2017 for immigrants in the Community of Madrid v. €27,903.10 for Spanish citizens during the same year). Owing to the restrictions and conditions of the Alien Act, immigrants are forced to endure some of the worst working conditions and keep their jobs at all costs in order to renew their residence permits. Therefore, immigrants face a situation of multiple vulnerabilities, created by economic inequality and normalised job and housing discrimination.

Although all non-EU migrants face multiple inequalities and discriminations, these differ according to their nationality and the degree of otherness attributed to them on an ethno-racial or religious basis. Research on police raids and imprisonment rates show that Africans and people of African descent represent a disproportionate share of the victims of detention, internment and deportation. Migrants from the former Spanish colonies, especially from Latin American countries, have some advantages in the possibilities of entering and remaining in the country (Brandariz García and Fernández Bessa, 2017) and there are certain more favourable conditions for accessing nationality. However, these small postcolonial concessions do not entail socio-economic equality or an absence of racism, either socially or institutionally. In this sense, Pardo's work (2014) shows a diachronic vision of the processes of racialisation through which the perception of Latin American migration in Madrid changes. Throughout the 1980s, the predominant profile of Latin American migrants was white people with a certain cultural and educational capital who had the capacity, in terms of both law and labour, to settle down. In the 1990s, however, the arrival of a growing number of racialised Dominican women transformed the category 'Latin American' in the eyes of Madrid's citizens, as they came to place Dominican women in a cultural and racial category that brought them closer to Senegalese and Gambian migrants who had also increased their numbers at this time. It was precisely during this period that racist aggressions in Madrid increased, a context in which the murder of the Dominican Lucrecia Pérez – the first hate crime motivated by racism that was judicially recognised in the country – took place. Finally, racial stratification and hierarchisation continue to be operative, as shown in the work of Cea D'Ancona and Martínez Vallés (2016) where participants in focus groups placed people with an indigenous appearance in a greater degree of otherness, without nationality being a decisive variable.

Thus, despite legal advantages and being recognised as culturally closer than other ethno-racial groups, racial discrimination against Latin Americans continues to be reproduced. Moreover, these postcolonial concessions are made at the costs of further securitisation and militarisation of the southern border and of the expulsion of migrants who are seen as culturally and racially distant. The relative benefit for some is constructed in opposition to the elimination of rights for others. The relatively easy entry of migrants through airports, on the other hand, is a secondary effect of the preferential treatment received by mass tourism, which accounts for 11.7 per cent of GDP in 2018.

Although this type of discrimination occurs at the national level, the case of Madrid is especially relevant. Based on data from the Ministry for Home Affairs' annual report on hate crime, it is evident that the Community of Madrid is the largest hub of racism/xenophobic crimes: 123 of the 531 cases reported in the country during 2018 are concentrated in Madrid (Ministerio del Interior, 2018). Racism constitutes a third of the hate crimes in the country in a stable manner over the last few years. This is a worrying trend. For example, in 2017 70 of the 524 hate crimes of a racist nature were committed in Madrid, while in 2016 there were 68 out of 416, in 2015 85 out of 505 and in 2014 45 out of 475. 2013 was the year with the highest proportion of serious incidents, 136 out of 381.

Anti-racist resistance and struggles from neighbourhood perspective

Before analysing empirically the two neighbourhoods I focus on, I will sketch an overview of social movements and their attachments to localities in Madrid. The concept of neighbourhood is a powerful symbol for social movements in Madrid since the 1970s when residents started organising, mainly claiming better housing and infrastructure, basic services and equipment in the peripheral neighbourhoods. These neighbourhood organisations inspired the concept of 'urban social movements', coined by the sociologist Manuel Castells (1977). During the 1980s and 1990s Madrid became famous for its squatted social centres (Martínez López, 2017) and autonomous anarchist collectives, closely related to their respective neighbourhoods. Another moment that has contributed to the resurgence of neighbourhoods as spaces of mobilisation and collective identity, and as places of struggle for social and political rights, has been the decentralisation of the 15M movement through neighbourhood assemblies in 2011 (Corsín Jimenez and Estalella, 2017).

From this perspective, the potential of the concept of *barrionalismo* (Limón López, 2015) should be highlighted. It represents the neighbourhood from the perspective of the lived experience, the common characteristics of its inhabitants and the possibilities of collective organisation. The neighbourhood does not form part of the administrative division of the city. However, the legitimacy of being recognised as a territorial unit lies in the very symbolic value given to the neighbourhood by its inhabitants. The neighbourhood represents a type of social relation in constant transformation, a set of power relations, changing alliances and conflicts. It is a space that is safe, recognisable, but on the other hand collective and quite unpredictable. It is a space between home and the city (Certeau et al., 1994). However, the dimension of a collective neighbourhood identity regardless of neighbours' nationality, and therefore with an anti-racist potential, is underresearched. As an exception, Luis de la Cruz (2018) mentions this possibility, defining *barrionalismo* as the other side of the coin of nationalism, as an opportunity to build alliances and inclusive struggles based on day-to-day shared experiences on a local scale.

The scholar-activist collective Carabancheleando also uses this concept in their 'Dictionary of the peripheries' (2017), though not only according to its positive meaning: while they agree that *barrionalismo* can be the expression of a common identity based on the use-value of the city (as opposed to the exchange value), they warn that the concept contains in itself a potential for exclusion, that coexistence does not automatically mean 'living together'. In this sense, it is important to mention Bourdieu (1999), who shows how social mixture is sometimes counter-productive for social justice struggles, since mixture sometimes can be rejected and even abhorred from the position of privilege as a hateful obligation to have to mix with people who are considered inferior. In this regard, the research of Barnor Hesse (1997) examines the concept of 'racial harassment', analysing from a postcolonial perspective how the national and nationalist imaginary is transferred to the urban space. In other words, the concepts of neighbourhood and neighbourhoodism, sometimes idealised in the imaginary of white social movements and activisms, can be discriminatory for migrants and racialised people. Living in the same place, sharing certain problems that affect everyone in the same territory, does not always create a feeling of communion and shared belonging.

This, however, does not mean that migrant and racialised people in Madrid do not have feelings of belonging or attachment to their neighbourhoods. In this sense, new voices in the research of racialisation and territorial roots have recently emerged not only from academia but also in a particularly valuable way from journalism. A relevant example is Lucía Mbomío, an Afro-Spanish journalist who publishes a weekly column called 'Barrionalismos' in one of the most read newspapers at the national level, *El País*. Mbomío's articles treat topics like everyday life in the metropolis periphery, her own memories of growing up as one of the few Afro-descendant persons in the neighbourhood and the micro-spaces of resistance in Alcorcón, the suburb where she lives. The plural of Barrionalismos indicates that there is no single way to live and understand the neighbourhood. Another relevant racialised columnist in *El País* is Chenta Tsai, who writes about the intersection between racialisation and sexual dissidence in Madrid.[3] In his articles, as well as in the weekly radio programme he used to host, Tsai often reflected on the (im)possibility of finding safe spaces for the racialised community in Madrid. Their voices also make visible from a new perspective a long-lasting problem: the stigmatisation of peripheral neighbourhoods, of the sociability and leisure of young people and migrants as 'uncivilised' ways of living in the city and using the public space.

The previous paragraphs show two versions of Madrid: the first one represents the neighbourhood as a safe space, as a territory of belonging and shared collective identity and a place for political organisation. This image is usually projected through some predominantly white leftist movements and collectives. At the same time, from the imaginaries of migrants and their descendants, the picture is not so idyllic. The neighbourhood is still recognised as an everyday space of belonging, memory, solidarity and mutual support, but public space is also problematised as an unsafe space where racialised people are hyper-visible and lose the right to anonymity, one of the fundamental urban rights (Delgado, 1997).

Neighbourhoods

So far I have discussed scholarly debates on racism and anti-racism in Spain and their connections to urban transformations in Madrid. The data presented above connects with the trajectory of anti-racist activism in both case studies: the neighbourhoods of Lavapiés and Usera have a high percentage of migrant and racialised population, low incomes and poor housing conditions. Likewise, both have a strong neighbourhood identity and collectives with anti-racist sympathies, although with very different mobilisation traditions.

Regarding Lavapiés I will focus on two very characteristic problems of the neighbourhood: the first is gentrification and the lack of awareness of questions of race when studying urban displacement; the second is the police racial profiling raids, which have been taking place in the public space with various levels of severity over almost a decade. Finally, a review of the strategies employed by different anti-racist groups to oppose them will be offered. In the case of Usera, I will focus on the emerging alliance between anti-fascist movements, anti-racist movements and feminist movements and the attempts of a recent neighbourhood collective to implement the mentioned alliance in its ideas and practices.

Lavapiés

The central zone of Lavapiés has been a historical epicentre of activism and political struggles, including pro-migrant and No Border ones, for more than two decades. Many NGOs and activist collectives are based in the neighbourhood, together with a high proportion of immigrants who work, live and/or are involved in different organisations in the area. The neighbourhood is highly stigmatised as a place of chaos, dirt, danger and crime and, at the same time, romanticised as a territory of activism and resistance (Bonfigli, 2014). Yet it is exoticised through both discourses and products of multiculturalism ready for consumption. This mix of positive and negative images, narratives and sensations acts as a powerful mechanism of both attraction and rejection. For racialised persons Lavapiés is simultaneously a safe and an extremely hostile place: a space where informal jobs can be found, information is circulating and co-ethnic solidarity is a must, but also a space of constant surveillance where police raids, racial profiling and police abuse are constantly happening.

Airbnb apartments, expensive flats owned by hedge funds and new fancy cafes are part of the current facade of Lavapiés. But even as gentrification and touristification have long been topics of discussion in the neighbourhood, they have rarely been researched in connection with race. Displacement associated with gentrification has been studied from the perspective of economic and symbolic violence (Sequera, 2013; Sorando and Leal, 2019), but not in relation to institutional racism and police violence against migrant and racialised people who inhabit the area. The case of Lavapiés is a clear example that displacement and permanence cannot be assessed only through access to housing. Although it has been proven that residential discrimination represents a serious problem, it is not the only difficulty, nor is it the only strategy of the migrant and racialised population for appropriation of the neighbourhood. The intense use of public space, related to leisure, informal activities, the exchange of information and survival strategies, represents some of the essential forms of permanence of the racialised community in the neighbourhood. Many people, even the ones sleeping rough, seek to spend a large part of their time in the neighbourhood. Most gentrification studies deal with displacement as a class problem and relate it to the subaltern position that migrant communities occupy on both a social and an urban scale. In this sense, it is important to insist once again that the racialised community of Lavapiés is not only an enemy and a target of displacement, but rather acts simultaneously as a factor of rejection and attraction – that is, as alien to the neighbourhood and as characteristic of its current picturesque image and marketable multiculturalism. This simultaneous exoticisation and rejection acts as a factor in the construction of the urban imaginary (Gil-Benumeya Flores, 2018).

There are several groups that pay special attention to the problems of displacement and gentrification of the neighbourhood, such as Lavapiés, ¿dónde vas?[4] (Lavapiés, where do you go?, which is an obvious reference to displacement), or Bloques en lucha[5] (Blocks in struggle). The campaign Bloques en lucha emerged through a concrete case where several Roma families who had been living in the neighbourhood for more than twenty years were evicted. Despite the fact that the Roma community is the most discriminated against in terms of housing (only 28.8 per cent would rent their flat to a Roma person according to a representative survey carried out in 2017 by the Centre of Sociological Research on a national level), this issue was not made public. Instead, the anti-eviction campaign focused on creating an image of neighbourhood unity. In many similar cases, there is a clear racial component in the housing problems and struggles, but not much importance is given to this fact. Instead, displacement and lack of housing are presented as universal problems that affect everybody (Gonick, 2015; 2016). The political subject who represents the resistance to gentrification is '*la vecina*' (a female neighbour). An endearing figure of an elderly white woman in a combative attitude, *la vecina* is one of the symbols that appear most often on posters and social network campaigns dedicated to raising awareness of the neighbourhood situation.[6] This image complements the analysis of *barrionalismo* in the previous section where the image of the neighbourhood and the collective identity, although described as something universal, actually includes a very narrow memory and identity of the neighbourhood. Several of the interviewees defended their attempt to universalise the struggle for housing. They recognised the presence of migrants and racialised people in the collectives of housing struggles, yet they insisted that what unites them is the problem of housing and evictions. Ethnic-racial belonging was secondary.

Another relevant example is the closure of the Baobab restaurant and the Prinoy pension in the heart of Lavapiés, both Senegalese-owned businesses that had been in the neighbourhood for twenty years. The landlord's refusal to renew the rent contract and his intention to sell the whole building to a hotel entrepreneur generated a series of meetings in a local squatted centre to discuss a possible resistance strategy. However, it focused on the fact that a hotel chain was to be opened in the place of these two small businesses and not on the displacement as a racial problem. This is something that the anarchist collective Incendiary Roots (a racialised non-mixed collective) drew attention to in their talk on 'Decolonize white anarchism at Madrid' on 1 March 2020. The members of the collective mentioned the difficulty of being heard by white movements when analysing the racial dimension of both gentrification and police violence in Lavapiés.

Regarding the latter, the moment of effervescence of the 15M movement in 2011, when more than a hundred people spontaneously intervened in a racist raid and expelled the police from the neighbourhood, is now very far away. Besides this moment of collective strength, the strategies to confront racist raids in the city and, above all, in the Lavapiés neighbourhood have changed over the years and have been adapted to the ways in which the police act. Raids increased between 2006 and 2009, when the annual number of countrywide arrests was 99,547, 74,894, 92,730 and 90,500. In 2005, prompted by a trip to the Ceuta wall on the southern border after the death of five people, the Ferrocarril Clandestino (Underground Railroad) collective was created. It operated in the neighbourhood until 2011. Blanca, Mariluz and Pedro, former members of the collective, described how going to the police station or to the Foreigners' Internment Centre in search of a detained person who was part of the support network had become part of their daily lives. The Human Rights Observation Brigades, another collective against police raids, were organised in a slightly different way during the peak of their time of action, 2009–14. In pairs or small groups, they observed and attempted to obstruct detention and to document control proceedings, while also speaking to passers-by and informing them what a racist raid was. However, this way of operating began to become inefficient, according to Lorena (personal interview, 19 June 2018). As she explains, the police and the detention methods have become so sophisticated and intensified that it was very difficult to oppose an arrest through direct action in public space. Given this situation, along with the complexity of contradictory hyper-regulations in which migrants are involved, one of the new strategies to defend the neighbourhood became the legal field (Pérez et al., 2019).

The current strategy of the Legal Committee on SOS Racismo Madrid fits in with this new way of operating. SOS Racismo is a nongovernmental organisation that over several decades has operated on issues from moral anti-racism to colonial amnesia (Azarmandi, 2017). However, the arrival of racialised people at its branch in Madrid, their parallel organisation in non-mixed spaces, the growing influence of decolonial discourses and the transformation of the legal work – from a focus on individuals to a focus on community defence of the neighbourhood of Lavapiés – have managed to transform it completely. Based on participant observation of assemblies and participation in working committees from September 2019 to March 2020, it has been concluded that SOS Racismo's connection and attachment to the neighbourhood are currently articulated from a singular vision: denunciation of structural racism, analysis of the vulnerability of migrants and racialised people in relation to public policies, institutional racism and intersectionality. This is due not only to the internal transformation of the association through the arrival of racialised people with an agenda of political anti-racism but also to the transformation of the strategies of stigmatisation, repression, persecution and racial displacement that have contributed to the shift in the panorama of resistance in the neighbourhood.

Usera

Usera is a peripheral district with the biggest presence of immigrants after the central district in which Lavapiés is located. Apart from its multicultural character, Usera also has a long tradition of associations of different ethnic-racial groups. The activities organised by different immigrant associations in Usera are often related to traditional dances and celebrations. This does not mean that they are limited to folklore, but that mobilisation around the reproduction of cultural celebrations and traditions is also a form of resistance, reclaiming and revitalising a practice that used to be stigmatised in western cities (Wence Partida, 2015).

As an example of a peripheral, working-class neighbourhood with a long organisational tradition in both the Spanish and migrant populations, it is worth exploring the possibility of alliances in the struggle against racism rooted in Usera.

In 2018, Rommy Arce, the first female district councillor of foreign origin, was harassed and her agenda was boycotted during several weeks by different organised groups. Also, several racist attacks took place in the district during the same period. This encouraged a group of youngsters, familiar with discourses and practices coming from anti-fascist organisations, to act. They were also alarmed by the appearance of racist posters and stickers that linked the presence of migrants to degradation, dirtiness and increased criminality. After analysing the situation that they were facing, the youngsters concluded that what they framed by default as 'far-right' or 'fascist' discourse and behaviour was, in fact, a specifically racist one. As previously mentioned, in Spain racism is frequently understood as an ideology that comes mainly from far-right groups and parties. This is why the new organisation was inspired by anti-fascist youth collectives, with whose repertoire young people from different left and anarchist backgrounds are familiar. This is why they started an anti-fascist collective but soon changed its denomination to anti-racist (Juventud Antirracista de Usera: JAU).

The data presented in this section is supported by two in-depth interviews with members of the collective and observation of four assemblies, as well as conversations in the group's public chat. This section will also use information from a group interview that was conducted with the Antipatriarchal Command, a feminist and anti-fascist collective, on 8 December 2019. Although the group is not related to a specific neighbourhood, the discourse of its members is quite consistent with the statements of the two Usera interviewees and, therefore, the information will be used to illustrate current trends in the connection between feminist anti-fascism and anti-racism in youth collectives in Madrid. All the interviewees agreed that the extreme right groups, parties and ideologies constituted a primary oppression that encompasses others, such as racial or patriarchal oppression.

For Fernando, a member and one of the founders of the JAU collective, anti-racism and anti-fascism have been related since the rise of the movement in the 1990s when collective organisation became necessary in the face of a multitude of aggressions, many of them suffered by migrants and racialised people. However, as Fernando states in our interview, 'the people who had the most abilities to remain in the movement are those who currently represent the stereotype of the anti-fascist militant: male, young, white, able to participate in street mobilisations and frequently in confrontations with the police'. Fernando considers that the re-connection between anti-fascism and anti-racism is extremely necessary nowadays: 'currently all anti-fascist movements have incorporated, at least at the discursive level, anti-racism'.

A mixture of young persons with and without foreign background, the collective is building alliances with neighbour organisations, NGOs, migrant and feminist associations from a strong identity of Madrid's periphery. JAU bases its political position on anti-capitalism, local and neighbourhood identity, abolitionist feminism and anti-racism understood as 'a collective defence'. Their collective represents the imaginary of the combative periphery, of the working-class neighbourhoods and of anti-fascism as an idea and practice.

The presence of racialised people in this type of collective is still scarce. However, the JAU's approach to the reality of migrants and racialised people is produced by different referents of the anti-racist movement. The female interviewees mentioned Lucrecia Pérez, bell hooks or Angela Davis as one of their first referents in anti-racism. These female figures draw attention to another interesting fact: in the last few years, feminism has been incorporated in a relevant way into the values and practices of anti-fascism. A particularly interesting intersection, although still not very common in today's social movements in Madrid, is the one between anti-fascism, anti-racism and feminism among collectives of young women in the peripheral neighbourhoods.

One of the relevant points in the interviews is the way in which the interviewees, young white women, describe their experience, ideas and practices as feminists as an essential point for understanding racial oppression. For them, it is possible to empathise with migrants and racialised people by means of the personal experience of another oppression that affects them and places them in the position of subordinate subjects. Thus, the emerging feminism within the anti-fascist movement has the will to lead to a broadening of demands and views using a set of oppressions as lenses through which to expand anti-racist efforts.

Feminism has a long history of struggle in Madrid, but it has become even more prominent since the last three mass demonstrations on 8 March. As a social movement that powerfully reclaims the public space, it has enormous potential but also many internal disputes, specifically around sex work. This is a conflict on a national level and of considerable magnitude, as can be seen in the article by Andrea Momoitio (Momoitio, 2019) describing the harassment to which the magazine was exposed after tweeting a chronicle of a debate where both abolitionist and regulationist approaches were represented.

These disputes affect the way anti-racism and feminism articulate. This is because a line of division between abolitionism and decriminalisation of sex work is beginning to become a racial one. By no means do I want to affirm that all migrants are pro-sex work, but that within the most vocal groups defending the rights of sex workers some of the most visible faces are those of migrant and racialised women. The 8th March organisation that structures the feminist movement in Spain does not have an official position on sex work precisely because there is no consensus within the organisation, but the abolitionist voices represent a considerable group, with visibility and mobilisation capacity.

From the abolitionist approach and on a neighbourhood level, a war has been declared against sex work advertising in public spaces. The widely distributed flyers are understood not only as female oppression, but as public space contamination and stigmatisation of the working-class neighbourhood. In the context of this conflict, it is easier to understand why one of the public actions of the JAU collective was to hold an open contest for 'taking prostitution advertisements off the street' (carried out between June and September 2019). The argument of the collective to do so is the connection between anti-racism and abolitionist feminism expressed through the rejection of objectification of racialised women whose pictures are exposed and 'invading' the public space of Usera. The information about the contest is collected through participant observation of the contest's presentation, of a route of withdrawal of advertising from the streets with members of the collective and of the contest's award ceremony.

The latter was held in the local retail market with the collaboration of some of the market vendors and other neighbourhood associations. It consisted of gathering the collected advertising that each team had brought in bags, baskets and boxes, weighing it and finally pouring it into a shopping cart to show its considerable volume. This is how the contest's award ceremony was transformed into a public exhibition of the collective's position on sex work through an unintentional performance of the market itself by making an allegory of the act of purchase in the market and the trade of woman's bodies. A manifesto was read, incorporating an anti-racist critique of the advertisements as racist and fetishist.[7] JAU expressed also their idea of what the neighbourhood should(not) look like: 'This doesn't happen in rich neighbourhoods', the manifesto stated, relating the advertisement to dirt, degradation and the practice of displacing unwanted activities to working-class neighbourhoods.

Avoiding the word prostitution, the manifesto expressed the young people's rejection of mafias, pimps and sexual exploitation of racialised women, taking for granted that the sex workers in the area were victims of traffic. However, the document did not incorporate an explicit criticism of laws like the Alien Act, which restricts the rights and freedom of movement of migrant women, nor did it allow the possibility for dissent or agency from racialised sex workers.

Connections and dis-connections between neighbourhoods and struggles

In the previous sections, emphasis was placed on the way in which white movements are trying to incorporate anti-racism into their discourses and practices. In this last section, however, I will focus on the agency and organisation of racialised people through the organisation of the annual anti-racist march held in Madrid on 17 November 2019. The purpose of this focus is to make visible the agency and struggles of racialised and migrant people and their forms of organisation and to pay attention to the connection between the march's organisation and the two previously analysed neighbourhoods. The data for this section was gathered through participant observation of three preparatory meetings and of the march itself.

The annual demonstration, which has been organised and led by racialised people since 2017, is one of the most visible anti-racist events of the year. The 2019 demonstration took place under the slogan 'Anti-racist memories', honouring the existence of activism, struggles and references in the past of Spain that serve as an example to young anti-racist activists. As in previous years, the organisation was run by racialised people, though not without attempts by white people with experience and contacts to take control. Collaboration was sought from allies, but with constant insistence on the importance of keeping in the background.

The first assemblies were held in the local office of the Street Vendors Union in Lavapiés. In addition to its central location, this obeys a spatial logic that situates Lavapiés as a natural habitat of activisms, assemblies and preparation of mobilisations. However, since the union shares the premises with other collectives, the second set of assemblies had to be moved and took place in the district of Usera in the recently inaugurated Centre for the Empowerment of Domestic and Care Workers, in which a multitude of activities are carried out. In this way, the places themselves, managed by migrants and racialised people, acquire their value not only as architectural and logistical facility but also as small territories of anti-racist resistance connected to the neighbourhoods. In this sense, the places for meeting and organisation represent a kind of archipelago (Stavrides in G. García and Ávila, 2015). The archipelagos as neighbourhoods or safe spaces are surrounded by 'the urban sea' that represents the surveillance, the hyper-vigilance and the daily dangers in the urban public spaces for racialised people.

Thus, three main conclusions can be drawn. First, anti-racist activism led by racialised persons is undergoing a process of transformation and creating new discourses. However, it is still difficult to escape from the shadow of the catch-all NGOs. Second, anti-racism is framed as 'complementary' of several neighbourhood movements whose members are mostly white and which work mainly through the lens of class, ignoring the importance of race in shaping hierarchies and inequalities. The willingness of white activists to collaborate and unite against racism often begins with theory, readings of postcolonial and decolonial authors, attending workshops and conferences of racialised activists. In practice, however, alliances are still not running very smoothly. Finally, the importance of being rooted in the territory needs to be mentioned. Urban frontiers are situated between neighbourhoods and non-neighbourhoods, between one's own neighbourhood and that of others. Evidence of this was the final message of the 17N demonstration that ended in the very centre of Madrid, in the Puerta del Sol square located less than 1km from Lavapiés but, at the same time, very distant from it. Sol can be called a non-place, a space of passage, of tourist photography. It is a hyper-surveilled place where the police usually chase the street vendors who do not fit the image of a tourist in a global city. On 17N, the final words before turning off the microphones and before the police approached to check the permits were 'Let's gather in front of the stage if someone does not feel safe and let's go back together to Lavapiés'.

Conclusion

This chapter has connected three themes that are usually studied separately in the European context (see the Introduction to this volume): racism, social movements and the transformation of urban space. The text has been based on two main concerns: firstly, how some social movements transform their discourses and practices by incorporating anti-racism as part of their ideas and repertoires of action and, secondly, how racism and anti-racism contribute to shaping Madrid and some of its neighbourhoods.

Through systematic analysis of the current debates on the varieties of racism and on the types of anti-racist activism, I have contextualised and discussed the field in which the social movements in question are trying to orient themselves. As has been pointed out, this is a contested terrain for defining what both racism and anti-racism are. The absence of debates concerning racism in Spanish public and media space means that each collective needs to relate the definitions or references given by anti-racist movements to other oppressions they suffer or know more about in order to understand what racism is and how it works. In this way, the ideas about the form that an anti-racist agenda should take proliferate and, in certain cases, such as housing and anti-gentrification struggles, lead to some strategic disagreements that can produce the invisibility or silencing of anti-racism in favour of other struggles that have the possibility of gathering more support or legitimacy by being presented as universal.

Regarding the urban dimension, as shown throughout the chapter, there is once again a 'false' universalisation of the neighbourhood, which portrays it as a territory for all with a unique capacity to create community and collective identity and to serve as a basis for joint struggle. As has been pointed out in the section on *barrionalismo*, both white people from diverse social movements and racialised people can identify with their neighbourhood and with the collective identity that it projects. However, it is essential to take into account that simple experiences, such as moving through public space, having the possibility of being part of the neighbourhood (owing to housing discrimination, among other things) and being given a space for a voice of one's own within the neighbourhood movements, are not taken for granted for everybody.

Finally, it is necessary to remember that, as was shown throughout the chapter and especially in the section on Lavapiés, institutional and economic urban violence takes very different expressions for white Spaniards and for migrant and racialised people and affects them in very different ways in their life trajectories and struggle for living with dignity in the neighbourhood.

Notes

1 Angela Davis en Madrid: 'El feminismo será antirracista o no será' (Angela Davis in Madrid: Feminism will be antirracist or won't be), *YouTube*, 26 October 2018, www.youtube.com/watch?v=1zBDpGI9RTw [accessed 14 April 2021].
2 A sample of their work is an exhibition and a book, both called *Give Us Back the Gold*: www.mataderomadrid.org/ficha/9630/devuelvannos-el-oro.html [accessed 14 April 2021].

3 'Chenta Tsai', *El País* [authors], https://elpais.com/autor/chenta_tsai_tseng/a [accessed 14 April 2021].
4 Website of the neighbourhood initiative 'Lavapiés, ¿dónde vas?' (Lavapiés, where do you go?), https://lavapiesdondevas.wordpress.com/ [accessed 14 April 2021].
5 Madrid Tenant's Union, calendar of events related to housing struggles in Lavapiés, www.inquilinato.org/calendario/bloques-en-lucha-lavapies/ [accessed 14 April 2021].
6 Poster that shows the described image of 'la vecina', Lavapies ¿dónde vas? *Twitter*, 2 July 2019, https://twitter.com/lavapiesdondeva/status/1146073518750294017 [accessed 14 April 2021].
7 Most of the advertisements were presenting Asian and Latina women.

References

Alldred, P. (2003), No borders, no nations, no deportations. *Feminist Review* 73(1): 152–157.
Alvite, J. P. (1995), *Racismo, antirracismo e inmigración* (Donostia: Tercera prensa).
Arribas Lozano, A. (2014), Formas de hacer. Experimentación y prácticas emergentes en los movimientos sociales. PhD dissertation, Universidad de Granada.
Arribas Lozano, A. (2017), Migraciones, acción colectiva y colonialidad del saber en el campo académico español: los y las migrantes como sujetos políticos invisibles/invisibilizados. *Tábula rasa* 29: 367–385.
Azarmandi, M. (2016a), Colonial continuities. *Peace Review* 28(2): 158–164.
Azarmandi, M. (2016b), Commemorating no-bodies – Christopher Columbus and the violence of social-forgetting. *Somatechnics* 6(1): 56–71.
Azarmandi, M. (2017), Colonial continuities – a study of anti-racism in Aotearoa New Zealand and Spain. PhD dissertation, University of Otago.
Bonfigli, F. (2014), Lavapiés: Seguridad urbana, activismo político e inmigración en el corazón de Madrid. Sortuz. *Oñati Journal of Emergent Socio-legal Studies* 6(2): 61–77.
Bourdieu, P. (1999), Efectos de lugar. In *La miseria del mundo* (Madrid: Akal), pp. 119–124.
Brandariz García, J. Á. and C. Fernández Bessa (2017), 'Perfiles' de deportabilidad: el sesgo del sistema de control migratorio desde la perspectiva de la nacionalidad. *Estudios Penales y Criminológicos* 37: 307–347.
Castells, M. (1977), *Movimientos sociales urbanos* (Madrid: Siglo XXI).
Cea D'Ancona, M. A. and M. Vallés (2016), Evolución de la discriminación en España. Informe de las encuestas IMIO-CIS de 2013 y 2016. Ministerio de Sanidad, Servicios Sociales e Igualdad [Evolution of discrimination in Spain. Report of the IMIO-CIS surveys of 2013 and 2016. Ministry of Health, Social Services and Equality].
Certeau, M. de, L. Giard and P. Mayol (1994), *La invención de lo cotidiano. 2. Habitar, cocinar* (México: Universidad Iberoamericana).
Chasco, S. R. (2018), Madrid, de norte a sur: análisis sociológico de las barrios de Lavapiés y Salamanca. PhD dissertation, Universidad Complutense de Madrid.

Comunidad de Madrid, Consejería de Servicios Sociales e Integración Social [Community of Madrid, Regional Department of Social Services and Social Integration] (2016), *Encuesta regional Inmigración* [Regional Inmigration Survey], http://webcache.googleusercontent.com/search?q=cache:PlJ_cJtN9ScJ:www.madrid.org/bvirtual/BVCM014015.pdf+&cd=1&hl=es&ct=clnk&gl=es [accessed 4 January 2021].

Corsín Jimenez, A. and A. Estalella (2017), Political exhaustion and the experiment of street: Boyle meets Hobbes in Occupy Madrid. *Journal of the Royal Anthropological Institute* 23: 110–123.

de la Cruz Salanova, L. (2018), *Barrionalismo* (Madrid: Editorial Decordel).

Delgado, M. (1997), Racismo y espacio público. Nuevas formas de exclusión en contextos urbanos. *Acciones e investigaciones sociales* 7: 23–30.

Delgado, M. (2018), 'Barrionalismo'. El barrio como fuente de identidad individual y colectiva. *El País* (24 January), https://elpais.com/elpais/2018/01/14/seres_urbanos/1515932437_091211.html [accessed 14 April 2021].

Díaz-Orueta, F., M. L. Lourés and M. Pradel-Miquel (2018), Transforming growth and cohesion models: changes in the governance of Barcelona and Madrid. *Eure* 44(131): 173–191.

El-Tayeb, F. (2010), *European Others: Queering Ethnicity in Postnational Europe* (Minneapolis, MN: University of Minnesota Press).

Eneva, S. and J. Abellán (2018), *EL MADRID PREVIO AL AYUNTAMIENTO DEL CAMBIO. Políticas públicas y modelo de gobernanza urbana durante el período 1995–2015*. Contested Cities working paper series, http://contested-cities.net/working-papers/2018/el-madrid-previo-al-ayuntamiento-del-cambio/ [accessed 14 April 2021].

Escudero, L. (2013), Brigadas Vecinales de Observación de Derechos Humanos, reivindicando el derecho a la ciudad. *Educación social: Revista de intervención socioeducativa* 55: 74–82.

Essed, P. (1991), *Understanding Everyday Racism: An Interdisciplinary Theory* (London: Sage).

Garcés, H. F. (2018), Capitalismo racial y narrativas de liberación: una aproximación a Cedric J. Robinson desde el Estado Español. *Tábula rasa* 28: 123–137.

García García, S. and Ávila Cantos, D. (2015), *Enclaves de riesgo. Gobierno neoliberal, desigualdad y control social* (Madrid: Traficantes de sueños).

Gil-Benumeya Flores, D. (2018), Viejas políticas y nuevos racismos. La izquierda frente a la islamofobia. *Revista de estudios internacionales mediterráneos* 24: 49–70.

Gil-Benumeya Flores, D. (2019), Islamofobia, racismo e izquierda. Discursos y prácticas del activismo en España. PhD dissertation, Universidad Complutense de Madrid.

Gómez-Reino Cachafeiro, M. (2006), Weak, disorganised and fragmented: anti-racist mobilisation in Spain. Working paper online series, UAM, https://bit.ly/2Q2veKY [accessed 14 April 2021].

Gonick, S. (2015), Indignation and inclusion: activism, difference, and emergent urban politics in postcrash Madrid. *Society and Space* 34(2): 209–226.

Gonick, S. (2016), From occupation to recuperation: property, politics and provincialization in contemporary Madrid. *International Journal of Urban and Regional Research* 40(4): 833–848.

234   *Provincialising the (urban) political*

Hesse, B. (1997), White governmentality: urbanism, nationalism, racism. In Westwood, S. and J. Williams (eds) *Imagining Cities. Scripts, Signs, Memories* (New York: Routledge), pp. 295–330.

Johansson, S. (2017), The involuntary racist. MA thesis, Linköping University.

Limón López, P. (2015) Un barrio para gobernarlos a todos: gentrificación, producción de globalidad y barrionalismo en Hortaleza y Poblenou. PhD dissertation, Universidad Complutense de Madrid.

Martínez López, M. A. (2017), Squatters and migrants in Madrid: interactions, contexts and cycles. *Urban Studies* 54(11): 2472–2489.

Mills, C. (2007), White ignorance. *Race and Epistemologies of Ignorance* 247: 26–31.

Ministerio del Interior (2018), *Anuario estadísitico 1985–2019* [Ministry of Home Affairs, Statistical Yearbook], www.interior.gob.es/web/archivos-y-documentacion/anuario-estadistico-de-2018 [accessed 7 January 2021].

Momoitio, A. (2019), Vale ya, joder. *Pikara* (13 November), www.pikaramagazine.com/2019/11/vale-ya-joder/ [accessed 14 April 2021].

Observatorio Metropolitano (2007), *Madrid: ¿la suma de todos?: globalización, territorio, desigualdad* (Madrid: Traficantes de sueños).

Pardo, F. (2014), Enfrentando las políticas de integración y de ciudadanía: migrantes latinoamericanos en la ciudad europea. *Revista Mexicana de Ciencias Políticas y Sociales* 220: 295–316.

Pérez, M., A. A. Rubio, D. Ávila and S. G. García (2019), Fronteras interiores. *Revista CIDOB d'Afers Internacional* 122: 111–136.

Picker, G., K. Murji and M. Boatcă (2018), Racial urbanities: towards a global cartography. *Social Identities* 25(1): 1–10.

Rodríguez Maeso, S. and Cavia, B. (2014), Esquivando el racismo: el paradigma de la 'integración' en las sociedades europeas y vasca contemporáneas. In Irazutza, I. and M. Martínez (eds) *De la identidad a la vulnerabilidad. Alteridad e integración en el País Vasco contemporáneo* (Barcelona: Bellaterra), pp. 151–193.

Sequera, J. (2013), Las politicas de la gentrificacion en la ciudad neoliberal. Nuevas clases medias, produccion cultural y gestión del espacio público. El caso de Lavapies en el centro historico de Madrid. PhD dissertation, Universidad Complutense de Madrid.

Sorando, D. and J. Leal (2019), Distantes y desiguales: el declive de la mezcla social en Barcelona y Madrid / Distant and unequal: the decline of social mixing in Barcelona and Madrid. *Revista Española de Investigaciones Sociológicas* 167: 125–148.

Suárez, K. (2012), Barrionalismo. *Periódico Vecinal Hortaleza* (1 November), www.periodicohortaleza.org/barrionalismo/ [accessed 14 April 2021].

Toasijé, A. (2019), Presencia e influencia africana y africano-descendiente denominada negra en la historia y prehistoria de España, frente a la desafricanización y ultraeuropeización en la construcción del pasado. PhD dissertation, Universidad Complutense de Madrid.

Van Dijk, T. (2005), Discourse and racism in Spain. *Apac* 53: 19–25.

Wence Partida, N. E. (2015), Trincheras transnacionales. Experiencias de luchas urbanas de la población migrante de origen boliviano. PhD dissertation, Universidad Autónoma Metropolitana.

Zepeda, H. E. (2017), El mercadillo rebelde de Barcelona. Prácticas antidisciplinarias en la ciudad mercancía. *Quaderns-e de l'Institut Català d'Antropologia* 22(1): 67–87.

10

Theorising Hamburg from the South: racialisation and the development of Wilhelmsburg

Julie Chamberlain

Introduction

The neighbourhood of Hamburg-Wilhelmsburg used to have 'a very bad reputation', long-time resident Casim told me over coffee in the spring of 2017. The island neighbourhood in the Elbe river to the south of Hamburg city centre had for decades been called all sorts of names in media and policy documents: 'the Bronx of the North', a 'problem neighbourhood', a 'neighbourhood in crisis' and a 'social hotspot' (see for example Adanalı, 2013; Brinkbäumer, 2000; Hohenstatt and Rinn, 2013; Twickel, 2011). Until a spate of new planning policies and projects was introduced in the mid-2000s to attract the white, German middle class to the island, people from other parts of Hamburg had often never set foot in Wilhelmsburg, though it is located just two stops away from the city's central train station. Indeed some Hamburgers 'jumped three steps backward in horror' when they met someone who lived in Wilhelmsburg, as resident organiser Barbara Kopf (2012: 102; my translation)[1] put it in a volume on local activism.

The dominant planning narrative at present traces the island's stigmatisation back to an unfortunate but apparently natural process. According to the narrative, the island emerged as a 'problem neighbourhood' after a period of planning indecision and treatment of it as the city's 'backyard' and 'dump' (see IBA Hamburg, 2011; Schultz and Sieweke, 2008). Garbage was dumped there along with loud and dirty industry, which triggered a 'downward spiral' and an increase in the population of so-called 'socially weak' and 'foreign' residents as the German middle class fled (Zukunftskonferenz Wilhelmsburg, 2002). The result, according to the narrative, was that the island was not perceived as part of the city of Hamburg, but rather as a distant '*terra incognita*' (Hellweg, 2010: 115).

In this chapter, and in contrast to this dominant narrative, I will theorise Wilhelmsburg's development 'from the South'. Following Ananya Roy (2018), I approach the South as a 'structural relation of space, power and knowledge, produced and maintained in the crucible of racial capitalism on a global scale'. I will demonstrate that Wilhelmsburg has a long history as a devalued space shaped by the logics of colonialism and the racialised labour systems and environmental racism that are part and parcel of racial capitalism (Melamed, 2015; Pulido, 2017; Robinson, 1983). I will illustrate that the neighbourhood's 'bad reputation' as a supposedly non-German and non-European migrant 'ghetto' aligns with its longer-term construction as a devalued geography of racialised working bodies.

Theorising Wilhelmsburg from the South in this way disrupts the dominant narrative by challenging the 'amnesia' of spatial disciplines like urban planning regarding 'their role in producing racialised landscapes of expulsion and exclusion' (Roy, 2018). Black German scholars and German scholars of Colour have argued for years that the relations of racial devaluation and exploitation forged in European colonialism continue to unfold in and on German urban landscapes (Ha, 2014; 2017; Della et al., 2018). This is reflected in the discourse and materiality of certain urban spaces: Wilhelmsburg is a unique neighbourhood, but is also one of many neighbourhoods that have been racialised and produced as 'ghettos' and 'problem neighbourhoods' in Germany's cities.

By theorising Wilhelmsburg from the South, I enter into conversation with the literature on the European city. Scholarship on so-called ghettos suggests that the production of such 'other' supposedly 'non-European' spaces plays a key role in the stabilisation of Germanness and Europeanness (Stehle, 2006; 2012; El-Tayeb, 2011; 2012; Tsianos, 2013). Yet the concept of 'the European city' appears unable to grapple with this production of racialised inequality as part of the city's normal functioning. Instead, as the Introduction to this volume demonstrates, texts such as sociologists Hartmut Häußermann's (2001) 'Die europäische Stadt' ('The European City') and Walter Siebel's (2004) introduction to an edited volume of the same name (and many other books about the 'European city') remain silent on the roles of 'race' and colonialism in the city. They address 'otherness' as a question of migrant v. non-migrant (see Siebel, 2004 for example), and thus reinforce the whiteness of the imagined city-dweller. Race and racism appear only in the American comparator to the European city, as if race were not in fact 'native to European thought,' as Fatima El-Tayeb (2011: xv) puts it, and as though the racial ghetto was not a European practice that travelled to the US and back again (Stehle, 2006). The location of race and racialisation elsewhere is typical of how racism functions in Germany today (Barskanmaz, 2012; El-Tayeb, 2016; Haritaworn, 2005). As a result, I deliberately draw on European scholarship and voices, particularly writing about the German context, alongside some of the international literature on racial capitalism, to underscore that race-critical European urban scholarship is not only possible, it already exists.

In this chapter, I draw on ethnographic interviews and archival research conducted in 2016–2018 in Hamburg-Wilhelmsburg to demonstrate that racialisation and racial capitalism have been crucial factors in the development of the neighbourhood.[2] Wilhelmsburg falls into a gap in the European city typology, into the silence about race and racism. I conclude by suggesting that a race-critical analysis of the concept and scholarship of the European city is necessary. Either space must be made within the 'history' that Siebel and Häußermann argue is part of the European city typology, or the notion should be jettisoned in favour of a concept that can grapple with race as a structuring logic of Hamburg and other European cities.

In the following section, I introduce my theoretical frame, defining racial capitalism, racialisation in the German context, and the racialisation of space. At the centre of my analysis of Hamburg-Wilhelmsburg are the notions of the ghetto and the problem neighbourhood as racialised spaces in reference to which the European city and supposedly European values are produced and reproduced. I then go on to discuss analyses of Hamburg-Wilhelmsburg's stigmatisation that have been produced by racialised long-time residents, before introducing the view of the island 'from the North' (of the Elbe river) – that is, from the perspective of recent city-state planning. This slightly unconventional narrative structure reflects my attempt to centre the interpretive authority of racialised residents first, in keeping with anti-racist methodological principles (Dei, 2005), rather than reproducing the dominant narrative that I, together with the residents, problematise. In this regard, I theorise Wilhelmsburg from the South both after Roy (2018) and in the literal sense: from the perspective of racialised residents speaking northwards towards the centre of power and planning in Hamburg.

Racial capitalism and the racialisation of urban space

In a 2018 lecture on racial banishment and American cities, urban scholar Ananya Roy argues for theorising cities from the South as a means of pushing the limits of Euro- and North American-centric urban theory, and of pinpointing the ways in which 'difference produced and spatialised in the context of colonialisms is constitutive of urban political economy.' The South, in this case, is not necessarily the Global South as a geographical location, but rather a 'structural relation of space, power and knowledge, produced and maintained in the crucible of racial capitalism on a global scale' (Roy, 2018). The term 'racial capitalism' was introduced by Cedric Robinson to capture how racism, and specifically the racisms of Europe, have always been crucial to the basic functioning of the capitalist system. Put simply, capitalism *is* racial capitalism (Robinson, 1983). It requires disposability and unequal differentiation of human value to produce profit, and 'racism enshrines the inequalities that capitalism requires … displacing the uneven life chances that are inescapably part of capitalist social relations onto fictions of differing human capacities, historically race' (Melamed, 2015: 77; see also Hall, 2018). Building on Robinson's insights, scholars in Geography, International Relations, Critical Ethnic Studies and Urban Studies have applied the concept to analyse the production of urban racialised social and spatial inequalities (Danewid, 2019; Dorries et al., 2019; Melamed, 2015; Pulido, 2016; 2017). Geographer Laura Pulido argues that as racial capitalism depends upon the racialised devaluation of lands and bodies to produce value, it also produces environmental racism as part of its everyday functioning (Pulido, 2016; 2017). The devaluation of racialised bodies is secured and maintained through racialised systems of labour and access to land that enable the production of more power and profit than could otherwise be the case (Pulido, 2016).

As capitalism thus depends upon racialisations (Danewid, 2019), an analysis of racial capitalism advocates attention to the origins and reproductions of racialisations along with capitalist wealth, and to the persistent legacies of processes of colonialism, imperialism and enslavement in these origins (Melamed, 2015; Pulido, 2017). Racialisations articulate with capitalism and with class in distinct, historically specific ways in different times and places (Hall, 2018). Racialisation refers to the varied and context-specific process through which racial categories are produced and fixed (Mirchandani et al., 2011). In her work on racialisation in the German context, Fatima El-Tayeb defines racialisation as 'the attribution of collective quasi-biological and or/cultural qualities that allow the perception of certain groups as not belonging, even when they are already part of society' (El-Tayeb, 2016: 34; my translation).[3] The definition of some people as non-German takes place on the basis of names, skin colour, hair colour, religion, immigration status or indeed the migration history of parents and grandparents, regardless of whether they themselves were born and raised in Germany (Ahyoud et al., 2018; Sanyal, 2019). The products of this process are categorisations that masquerade as cultural, religious or legal categories, but that adhere to particular bodies and are acquired by birth. Once fixed, they 'render groups of people as inferior, thereby justifying their marginalisation and exploitation' (Mirchandani et al., 2011: 120). El-Tayeb (2016) demonstrates that the constant definition of racialised 'un-German' others against which Germanness is defined has been quite consistent across the country's history, in relation in particular to Roma and Sinti, Jews, Muslims and Black people. Yet German public discourse and urban research have long been characterised by race evasion, a concept that Jin Haritaworn (2005) coined in their work on whiteness in queer theory, in which the socially constructed nature of race justifies the minimisation of racism (see also Barskanmaz, 2012).

The racialisation of *space* is the process through which spaces come to be associated with particular categorisations of people and naturalised as their supposedly 'correct place' (James, 2012; Razack, 2002). 'The ghetto', as a concept that has historically signified that part of the city to which racialised people are confined (Stehle, 2006), is a quintessential example of a racialised urban space. The compulsory and unequal separation of groups in city space has been practised in Europe since at least the Middle Ages, in service of elite accumulation of power and wealth (Nightingale, 2012). The ghetto concept and practice travelled from Europe to the United States and back again, maintaining its core meaning although the specific discourses about racial segregation changed and shifted over time and space (Stehle, 2006), particularly picking up anti-Black racist connotations.

Drawing on tropes of violence, lawlessness and social decay, references to the ghetto have been taken up in Germany in recent years to communicate fear and desire to control racialised people in and through the neighbourhoods in which they live (Stehle, 2006).[4] The notion of the 'problem neighbourhood' is a frequent companion to the ghetto discourse in Germany in particular; a problem neighbourhood is similarly 'wicked, dangerous, and foreign' (Keller, 2015; my translation),[5] and like the ghetto 'is constructed as a patriarchal, violent, and non-European space in the centre of Europe … a space that is "a problem" that "we" need to deal with' (Stehle, 2006: 61). Since 9/11, anti-Muslim racism has particularly driven urban moral panics in which supposedly self-segregating communities are framed as presenting a threat to 'European values' (El-Tayeb, 2012; Haritaworn, 2015; Tsianos, 2013). 'Anti-Muslim urbanism', a term coined by Vassilis Tsianos (2013) in reference to Hamburg, is fuelled by the notion of Muslim men as threats to women and LGBTQ people. Tolerance and equality get framed here as though they are essential European values, which obscures homophobia and gender-based oppression that is perpetrated by the dominant population (El-Tayeb, 2012; Haritaworn, 2015). This draws on a longer history in which 'Europe has long pointed to the inferior position of "Oriental women" in Muslim societies as a way of asserting its own civilisational superiority' (Yildiz, 2009: 471; drawing on Yeğenoğlu, 1998), and underscores how racialisation operates in 'complex and shifting interactions' with other systems of oppression (El-Tayeb, 2011: 125).

European cities are thus important sites of definition of who and what is European and who and what is not (Stehle, 2012; see also El-Tayeb, 2012; Picker, 2017). Crucially, 'Europe' is itself an unstable concept, the modern version of which is a product of the European Enlightenment, its racial theories and colonialism (Arndt, 2005). Stuart Hall (2002) argues that the myth of Europe depends upon repressed history and internal and external others. He argues in particular that Europe has 'constantly, at different times, in different ways, and in relation to different "others," tried to establish what it is – its identity – by symbolically marking its difference from "them"' (Hall, 2002: 60). Europe, then, is continually (re)made through a racialised process that plays out in and through cities (Stehle, 2006; El-Tayeb, 2011).

Racialised residents' views of a 'bad reputation'

Racialisation and the imagination of the neighbourhood as a non-European space have played a critical role in the development of Hamburg-Wilhelmsburg for quite some time. The 35 square kilometre island is the largest of the Elbe Islands, the largest river island in Europe and home to 55,000 people (Statistisches Amt für Hamburg und Schleswig-Holstein, 2018). Its population is quite heterogeneous in comparison to other parts of the city (Hohenstatt and Rinn, 2013). As Umut, who grew up on the island, put it to me: 'it's what really makes Wilhelmsburg: that there are people who live side by side and who do not understand each other – not only linguistically, even culturally – but live together peacefully' (Umut, interview, 2017).[6] The island is home, for example, to Hamburg's only officially settled Sinti community, which traces its presence on the island back hundreds of years (Journalisten der Henri-Nannen-Schule, 2014). In the most recent statistics, 34 per cent of Wilhelmsburgers are listed as 'foreigners' (with a passport other than German) and 60.4 per cent are counted as 'people with migration back-grounds', which is a racialising concept that is used in the census and in everyday life to identify some people as not fully German (Ahyoud et al., 2018; Sanyal, 2019). For youth under 18 years of age, the percentage with migration backgrounds is 78.9 per cent (Statistisches Amt für Hamburg und Schleswig-Holstein, 2018). Income in Wilhelmsburg is on the lower end of the city average, and neighbourhood residents live in a range of housing forms, including single-family homes, apartments and subsidised housing (Statistisches Amt für Hamburg und Schleswig-Holstein, 2017; 2018). These various forms of housing butt up against industrial and agricultural land that is also present in equal measure (Eckardt, 2017).

Despite the island's size and complexity, it had for many years quite a simplified and deeply negative image. The residents I interviewed in 2017 argued that people not from Wilhelmsburg tended to have warped perspectives on it that were the result of a lack of direct experience combined with racist media coverage. Özden described for example how a workmate at the airport had been afraid to go to Wilhelmsburg to visit a friend.

> He said: 'Can I go to Wilhelmsburg? Can I drive there?' I said, 'What do you mean by that?' 'Yeah, is it dangerous?' Look: a German didn't want to go to

Wilhelmsburg at that time, I'm talking about early 2001, 2002. Not so long ago. He was afraid to go to Wilhelmsburg ... So I died laughing, then I said: 'Wilhelmsburg is still part of Germany, and there are German police in droves. If something happens, you can get help, you don't need to worry' (Özden, interview, 2017).

The idea that Wilhelmsburg might not be safe for Germans was coming from media reports that characterised the neighbourhood as a 'ghetto' and 'problem neighbourhood'. Racialised residents considered this to be an outsider view, since their experiences were generally of Wilhelmsburg as a safe and welcoming home in the context of stigmatisation and exclusion. Gülhan, a counsellor in the neighbourhood, narrated for example the outside view that she had often encountered.

They see that this neighbourhood has a lot of migrants. And then there is also criminality, and unemployment, and that tends to be pinned on migrants. Migrants suffer because of that, although I don't have the feeling that in other neighbourhoods ... I don't know, Dammtor[7] or whatever, certainly also has the same thing, but because fewer migrants live there, it's not shown that way.... In the newspaper, when something happens, skin colour is immediately mentioned, and then migrants, and then underlined (Gülhan, interview, 2017).

Residents saw these kinds of depictions as a misreading of the neighbourhood based on the overwhelming influence of societal racism on perceptions of people who have dark hair, dark skin, wear a hijab, have a Muslim name or speak a language other than German. Gülhan's analysis refers to 'migrants' because this is how Wilhelmsburgers are often perceived and labelled, though 66 per cent of residents are German citizens (Statistisches Amt für Hamburg und Schleswig-Holstein, 2018). The discourse about the neighbourhood had only tenuous links to local reality; indeed when Özden's colleague was afraid to visit, the crime rate there was in fact lower than in the rest of Hamburg (Zukunftskonferenz Wilhelmsburg, 2002).

While residents lamented the dominant images of their neighbourhood, they also argued that it is a space in which racialised people, immigrants and people with low incomes were indeed concentrated: because the city-state had intentionally concentrated them there. As local researcher Zeynep Adanalı puts it (2013: 123; my translation), 'the city itself created the "social hotspot" of Wilhelmsburg'[8] through decades of planning policy. When I interviewed Arzu, who was born and raised and continues to live and work in Wilhelmsburg, I asked her what 'social hotspot' meant.

The underclass was settled here – knowingly, I think – so that people with fewer prospects simply accumulated, lived here. They call that a 'social hotspot' because then of course many people don't work, or become criminal, or things like that.... That was done, in my opinion, knowingly, controlled that way for years, decades, and now they're trying to shake it all up with this gentrification (Arzu, interview, 2017).

At the same time, Arzu and other residents argued that the neighbourhood had been given 'zero support' for decades. The reputation of the neighbourhood was thus linked to racist and classist notions of who lived there, along with material planning practices that had shaped the same. Consistent with other similarly racialised spaces, residents argued that low-income and racialised residents were themselves blamed for local conditions, though those conditions have been produced and reproduced by social, economic and spatial injustices that are systemic and structural in nature (see James, 2012).

The 'gentrification' to which Arzu refers involves the massive resources that the city-state of Hamburg has recently put into attempting to change Wilhelmsburg's image: 'hyping' it, as another interviewee put it (Mohammed, interview, 2017). Since 2005, planning has been aimed at the 'social mixing' of the island, through policies and projects to attract white, middle-class Germans. Subsidies have been introduced to encourage students to take over the larger apartments and houses on the island (Hamburgische Investitions- und Förderbank, n.d.), and a social mixing directive in public housing allocation favours people who do not have so-called 'migrant backgrounds' (see Adanalı, 2013). Two massive development-events also culminated in 2013: the International Garden Show and the Hamburg International Building Exhibition (IBA Hamburg). IBA Hamburg comprised over 60 building projects, €120 million in public investment, and €1 billion in private investment (IBA Hamburg, 2018; Vogelpohl and Buchholz, 2017). It was the latest in a 100-year tradition of IBAs in German urban planning and architecture, which are large-scale projects to transform built space and intervene in what are considered pressing urban issues that are otherwise difficult to address (Hellweg, 2010). I explore the details of these planning and development strategies and residents' critical engagement with them elsewhere (see Chamberlain, 2020a; 2020b).

The dominant planning narrative about Wilhelmsburg's issues – *why* it needs to be socially mixed – is that it has historically been planned as a space for work and for waste. In 1920, not long before Wilhelmsburg became administratively part of the city, Hamburg architect and Head of Urban Planning Fritz Schumacher famously said that 'Geest land is for living, and marshland is for working' (quoted in Zukunftskonferenz Wilhelmsburg, 2002: 5; my translation).[9] With this formulation, Schumacher argued in effect that the marshland that included the Elbe islands was best suited to industrial and harbour-related land uses rather than to 'living.' Schumacher's thinking remained influential long beyond his tenure.

The second piece of the dominant narrative holds that the deadly flood of 1962 was a turning point beyond which the city treated Wilhelmsburg as nothing more than a backyard dump (see IBA Hamburg, 2011). In February of 1962, a storm surge from the North Sea broke through dykes at several points in northern Germany. Flooding in the middle of the night killed 300 people, 200 of them in Wilhelmsburg, many of whom were living in makeshift housing in a low-lying area (Paech, 2008). After the flood, Hamburg moved to abandon housing in the northern part of the island, and was stopped only by extensive and successful protests by residents who wanted to stay (IBA Hamburg, 2011). Parts of the island were nonetheless declared unfit for anything but industrial and manufacturing uses, and the city later called an official halt to all renovation and investment in housing (Paech, 2008). As many as 10,000 people moved away after the flood, or as one planner puts it: 'everybody who could afford to do so' (Kai Dietrich, quoted in Rowe, 2015: 40). Those who stayed experienced an acceleration in the siting of 'undesirable elements from the city of Hamburg' (Schultz and Sieweke, 2008: 139), which over time included space-eating logistics centres and container yards, expanded highways cutting through the landscape, sewage treatment and a toxic waste dump (Hellweg, 2010; Humburg and Rothschuh, 2018).

The process of ongoing disinvestment and white flight that ensued tends to be characterised as unfortunate but natural. Yet at the same time that they halted investment and renovation, the city continued to allocate housing specifically to immigrants (Adanalı, 2013; Paech, 2008), and from the 1970s it also concentrated social housing on Wilhelmsburg (Eckardt, 2017). This is the process to which Arzu refers in her analysis above. The city-state deliberately produced conditions of environmental racism in Wilhelmsburg: the siting of undesirable city functions alongside people who were also considered undesirable (Gosine and Teelucksingh, 2008). While the flood is frequently depicted by media and planning publications as the beginning of a downward spiral for Wilhelmsburg that city planning now attempts to correct, it must also be understood as a precursor to decades of organised racial abandonment of the island (to borrow a phrase from Danewid, 2019).

Theorising Wilhelmsburg from the South: the longer history of the 'problem neighbourhood'

For Hanseatic people this was never the place to live. This is where money was made.
(Zukunftskonferenz Wilhelmsburg, 2002: 5; my translation).[10]

The racialised devaluation of Wilhelmsburg in fact traces back even further in time. While the dominant narrative locates the neighbourhood's devaluation in twentieth-century planning, I trace it back over a century, through the historical record and scholarship on Hamburg's colonial history. Hamburg has been called 'Germany's colonial metropolis' (Zimmerer, in Deutschland-funk Kultur, 2020; my translation) [11] because its investments in European colonial trade and governance made it what it is today, in terms of its wealth and its relationship to its 'others' (Della, in Della et al., 2018; Seukwa, in Schepers, 2018). Black and People of Colour activists and scholars in Hamburg have been arguing for decades that the city's colonial legacy is present in the space and everyday life of the city, and that it must be confronted (Della, in Della et al., 2018).

Though Hamburg's colonial legacy is rooted in various institutions, it is the port that has historically been most central to the city's identity and to its urban planning priorities. For centuries, urban development and port development were fundamentally the same thing; the city-state always tried to anticipate and respond to the needs of the port (Meyer-Lenz, 2016). Those needs depended upon expropriation and extraction from colonised lands. Through the shipping, trade and processing of products such as rubber, palm oil, cocoa and enslaved people, Hamburg merchants, ship owners and industrialists extracted value through the devaluation of lands and people (Zimmerer, quoted in Norddeutscher Rundfunk, 2018). At the end of the eighteenth century, Hamburg was also the European centre for sugar cane processing and cotton finishing (Todzi, 2018), and from the mid-nineteenth century, some Hamburg merchants operated plantations in Africa themselves, using slave labour to produce raw materials for trade (Norddeutscher Rundfunk, 2018).

As Mbakumua Hengari (in Hengari et al., 2018) puts it, colonialism is like a mega-project: the infrastructure built for it persists well beyond the project's nominal 'end', and the benefits and the costs continue to accrue. In Hamburg, the infrastructure of colonialism persists in the ongoing centrality of extractive and violent trade to the production of wealth (see Klij, 2019), and in monuments and buildings that honour colonial criminals and idealise colonial relations (see for example afrika-hamburg.de, n.d.; Mancheno, 2016; OvaHerero et al., 2018). It also persists in the spatialised, racialised inequality of the city in general. Currently, Hamburg has the highest per capita income in Germany and the most millionaires per capita (Handelskam-mer Hamburg, n.d.). In 2018 the city saw record sums change hands for residential real estate, with houses going for as much as €7.5 million in the wealthiest neighbourhoods (Preißler, 2019). Yet the average income of the city's poorest neighbourhood is less than 11 per cent of the richest, and the poorest neighbourhoods tend also to be those with the highest percentage of racialised residents (see Statistisches Amt für Hamburg und Schleswig-Holstein, 2017: 5, together with 2018: 12). Hamburg frequently ranks highest in Germany in levels of economic segregation, and low-income households are generally being pushed out of the inner city (Güntner, 2013).

The persistent logic of colonialism is fundamentally that some people are worth more than others (Adjei, in Della et al., 2018). I find that this logic underwrites what Moritz Rinn (2018; my translation) has called the 'urbanism of inequality'[12] in Hamburg, which accepts and cultivates inequality as a norm. This is evident if one looks at the long history of Wilhelmsburg, as residents urged me to do throughout my research. When Schumacher declared it a space for work rather than for living, 33,000 people were already living in Wilhelmsburg (Behörde für Schule und Berufsbildung, n.d.). The population was almost exactly the same proportion of the city's total as it is today. However, Wilhelmsburg had by that time already become a significant immigrant neighbourhood, comprised largely of workers who were not considered to be citizens of Germany, let alone subjects of urban planning.

The devaluation of racialised labour was a defining feature of industry and of life in Wilhelmsburg from the early days of industrialisation. In the late nineteenth century, Hamburg was engaged in an aspirational expansion of its port for overseas trade (Meyer-Lenz, 2016), tied to the advocacy of merchants and ship-owners for the establishment of German colonies in Africa (Todzi, 2017). As the port expanded, so did shipbuilding and oil industries in Wilhelmsburg, and by 1891 Wilhelmsburg was being called the 'most ideal industrial area in the German Empire!' (Geschichtswerkstatt Wilhelmsburg und Hafen, 2008: 2; my translation).[13] Hamburg businessmen actively recruited Polish-speaking peasants in Prussian-occupied Posen, and the people who came were driven by deep poverty, marginalisation and unemployment in what is now Poland (Geschichtswerkstatt Wilhelmsburg und Hafen, 2008; 2018). Once in Wilhelmsburg, they faced dire conditions, as they were recruited to do the most difficult and dangerous work for starvation wages. This was often skilled work that was devalued as menial or as 'women's work', such as in the wool factory (Geschichtswerkstatt Wilhelmsburg und Hafen, 2018).

The local historical record and the labour migration policy of the German Reich both reflect the racialisation of Polish-speaking workers at the time. Polish workers were considered to be inherently less intelligent than Germans and to be natural manual labourers (Ha, 2007), and were treated as fundamentally different and inferior because of their language, religion (Catholicism) and 'lack of education' (Geschichtswerkstatt Wilhelmsburg und Hafen, 2008). This racialisation, which aligned with the colonial framing of German national formation at the time as a service to its supposedly under-developed neighbours (Kopp, 2010), was reflected in policy that claimed that the country recruited foreign workers to do what Germans were 'too culturally advanced' to do, and that this was a healthy and 'hygienic' means of developing inherently different peoples (Geschichtswerkstatt Wilhelmsburg und Hafen, 2008: 4). Yet labour migration policy was also explicitly planned to maximise German profits by developing a workforce so precarious that it would be flexible to the whims of industry. In contrast to a workforce of citizens, who might make demands if they were unemployed and hungry, foreign workers 'could simply be discarded' in the case of any industrial decline (Prussian ministry of trade, quoted in Geschichtswerkstatt Wilhelmsburg und Hafen, 2008: 5; my translation).[14]

The history of Polish-speaking people in Wilhelmsburg remains part of the social and spatial fabric of the island today. The early industries are reflected in street names such as Bei der Wollkämmerei (referring to the wool processing factory), and at the base of Veringstrasse you can still attend Bonifatiuskirche, a Catholic church that was built by the Polish community in 1895. The Wilhelmsburg History Workshop suggests that over time Polish-speakers were no longer judged to be outsiders on the island, and that today their descendants consider themselves Wilhelmsburg's 'natives' (Geschichtswerkstatt Wilhelmsburg und Hafen, 2018). This underscores that racialisation is indeed a process that shifts and changes over time.

Yet the racialisation of people and of Wilhelmsburg as a space continued. The descriptions of working and living conditions for Polish-speaking immigrants and the logic of German labour migration policy could easily have been written seventy years later, about the migration of the so-called 'guest worker programme', in which migrant workers were recruited, particularly from impoverished areas of Southern Europe, West Asia and North Africa, to do dangerous and dirty work in German industries (Chin, 2007; 2009). There was, again, a lot of this kind of work in Wilhelmsburg's factories and in the neighbouring portlands, as well as in construction and the railway on the island, this time particularly for skilled tradespeople, and many migrant workers settled themselves and eventually their families in Wilhelmsburg (Dietz, 2008; Geschichtswerkstatt Wilhelmsburg und Hafen, 2008).[15] This remains the migration with which Wilhelmsburg is most associated, though the neighbourhood is in fact quite diverse. According to a recent report, 43 per cent of Wilhelmsburgers have roots in Germany, 22.4 per cent in Turkey, followed by Poland, Macedonia, Bulgaria, Serbia/Montenegro, Afghanistan, Portugal and Ghana (Bezirksamt Hamburg-Mitte, 2015). This is to name just the top-listed countries, and indeed to ignore for a moment how a focus on ties to elsewhere migrantises some of the 66 per cent of Wilhelmsburgers who are German citizens.

Much of what was considered unacceptable for the average German in terms of work, pay, safety and housing was treated as sufficient for so-called guest workers. In Wilhelmsburg, workers were often housed in low-quality, company-built housing, including in barracks with inadequate space, sanitation and basic facilities (Dietz, 2008; Geschichtswerkstatt Wilhelmsburg und Hafen, 2008). Though the 'foreign' populations changed, the fundamental logic of the labour regime remained consistent: increase profits for German companies by bringing in workers who are considered 'cheap and willing' (Chin, 2009) and easily discarded (Chin, 2007; 2009; Ha, 2003; 2007). The status of 'guest' meant lower wage entitlements and subjection to separate laws and employment standards from the German population (Chin, 2009). This differential status is emblematic of how racialised devaluation 'creates a landscape of differential value which can be harnessed in diverse ways to facilitate the accumulation of more power and profit than would otherwise be possible' (Pulido, 2016: 1).

Between the two periods I detail here, Germany attempted to 'eradicate its minorities' (Chin, 2007: 10), including precisely through work. The labour of prisoners of war, prisoners from concentration camps, people deported from Eastern Europe and people who were imprisoned locally was used by many companies in Hamburg and in Wilhelmsburg during World War II (Landeszentrale für Politische Bildung Hamburg, 2007). As just one example, Emil Weiss, who was head of the Wilhelmsburg Sinti community until he passed away in 2018, was forced as a 13-year-old to work in a factory (Journalisten der Henri-Nannen-Schule, 2014). The Langer Morgen 'Work Education Camp' was also located on the outskirts of Wilhelmsburg from 1943 to 1945. The purpose of the camp was to punish and 'retrain' defiant or uncooperative enslaved people, as well as people who were considered anti-social, 'work-shy,' criminals, quitters or sex workers. Eighty per cent of the people imprisoned there were non-Germans, and most were from Eastern Europe (Frank, 1997).

Discussion

This brief history illustrates that racialisation and devaluation are long-standing themes in how Wilhelmsburg has been approached by the city-state of Hamburg, industry and other levels of government. The island's 'bad reputation' and its stigmatisation as a 'problem' are rooted in its long-term planning as a location for racialised people and work that was considered fundamentally non-German, though it produced value for German companies. This does not contradict the dominant planning narrative, but fills gaps and silences, and historicises the island's stigmatisation more fully than is often the case both in local planning and in research that simply accepts the dominant narrative as fact. Theorising Wilhelmsburg and the city more broadly from the South in both of the senses I have used here illuminates, as

Roy (2018) suggests, that urban planning in Hamburg has played a direct and intentional role in the creation of the island as a racialised landscape. As residents indicate, the image of the island as a problem neighbourhood and ghetto flows from racist discourse and from uninformed outsider views, but also from concrete practices that have shaped Wilhelmsburg over more than a century. The differential treatment of the 'non-German' is a central theme in this history. Özden reassured his workmate that Wilhelmsburg is still part of Germany, because the dominant sense had long been that it was not, and that it therefore was not as valued or valuable as other parts of the city.

The limited accountability of Hamburg urban planning for this pattern, which is so evident in the dominant narrative's silence about the realities of racialisation, is consistent with the 'amnesia' that Roy attributes to the planning discipline, but also with the more widespread race evasion (Haritaworn, 2005) that has been endemic to German public discourse and urban research. In the amnesiac city described by Roy, it is possible for planning strategies and frameworks that aim to control racialised urban dwellers to appear somehow new (see Chamberlain, 2020b). To theorise from the South means approaching this, and the racialisation of space, as an aspect of the normal functioning of the city and of urban space within racial capitalism. Yet the European city typology does not account for racialisation of urban space at all, and instead reproduces the externalisation of racialised people from Europe. I find as a result that this externalisation, including the discourses and practices that treat Wilhelmsburg and neighbourhoods like it as somehow 'outside of Germany', are in fact integral to the European city. The European city, like Europe itself, is defined in relation to internal and externalised 'others'.

In conversation with Roy, this chapter offers a proposal for disruption of this process in knowledge production, theorising cities from the South to ensure that the European city is contextualised within global and local structures of power and inequality in which it is directly invested. A concept of the European city that could fully comprehend the development of Hamburg-Wilhelmsburg would be one in which racialisation was explicitly named, and in which there was self-awareness of the production of 'European' and 'non-European' through its conceptualisation. This kind of analysis would acknowledge the scholarly work and activism of Black Germans and German People of Colour in Hamburg that I have cited above, as well as the analysis of racialised Wilhelmsburgers regarding the stigmatising gaze and systematic devaluation that has marked the neighbourhood for transformation.

In a European city that is defined against racialised 'others', planning views large parts of the urban community – in Hamburg and elsewhere – as not properly belonging to the city, nor the city as properly belonging to them. The result is a planning landscape that favours the white, German middle class, and that attempts to shape the future of the city in their image (see Rinn, 2018 for more on this in Hamburg). This kind of planning landscape disregards the extensive, valuable achievements of racialised city residents who have created and maintain rich and interesting neighbourhoods, like Wilhelmsburg, through struggle and against multiple and intersecting forms of exclusion.

The racialised Wilhelmsburgers I interviewed resisted exclusion from German-ness both in our conversations and in their everyday lives. They value the island differently than the dominant discourse and contest the meanings of current urban planning strategies. I demonstrate elsewhere that they framed the island as a *Heimat,* a space of warmth, belonging and identification in the context of societal exclusion as 'migrants' and therefore as supposedly 'un-German'. The historical devaluation of Wilhelmsburg plays a conflictual role in this different valuation of the space and place. Without it, this *Heimat* would not exist in its present, beloved form. Yet it is predicated on the racialisation and marginalisation of people who are at home there. I also demonstrate elsewhere that this theme continues in the logic of 'social mix' as it is implemented in Wilhelmsburg. Though the explicit terms in which it takes place have changed, racialisation and the valuing of some people more than others continues to be central to planning on the island.

Conclusion

In this chapter, I have drawn from a study of Hamburg-Wilhelmsburg to analyse it 'from the South', and thus demonstrate the salience of racialisation and racial capitalism to the development of the neighbourhood. Based on archival research and interviews with racialised residents, as well as politicians and planners, I described the development of Wilhelmsburg as a racialised, devalued space and demonstrated the construction of the space and people who live there as non-German and non-European in the context of a city shaped by the long-standing processes and logics of colonialism. I framed this as theorising the city from the South in two senses: after Roy (2018) as a structural relation produced and maintained by racial capitalism, and literally from the South of the city, from the perspectives of residents of Wilhelmsburg. Viewed from the South, the ghetto/problem neighbourhood emerges as a German and European production that is external to the European city only insofar as it reproduces imagined non-European spaces as part of its normal functioning and self-definition. I proposed that any concept of a European city must contend with the production of racialised, devalued spaces as a norm. Only on this basis might the concept of the

European city prove useful to scholarship that engages with the realities of racialised urban lives and spaces.

Notes

1 'In den 90er Jahren traten die Leute noch vor Schreck drei Schritte zurück, wenn ich sagte, dass ich in Wilhelmsburg wohne' (Kopf, 2012: 102).

2 My research included nineteen interviews with racialised residents who had lived in Wilhelmsburg for at least ten years, and eight interviews with local politicians and planning professionals. Archival research drew from the archives of the Geschichtswerkstatt Wilhelmsburg und Hafen, the online historical archives of the city of Hamburg, German media reporting on Wilhelmsburg from 2000 to the present and from government documents that were identified by interviewees.

3 'Die Zuschreibung kollektiver quasi-biologischer und/oder kultureller Eigenschaften, die die Wahrnehmung bestimmter Gruppen als nicht-zugehörig erlaubt, auch wenn sie bereits Teil der Gesellschaft sind' (El-Tayeb, 2016: 34).

4 There is also a significant debate about the ghetto and racialised segregation in France; for varying perspectives see Kipfer (2013) and Wacquant (2008).

5 'Das Image der Verruchten, Gefährlichen und Fremden…' (Keller, 2015)

6 All quotations from interviews are translated from German by the author.

7 An area of central Hamburg where the main University of Hamburg campus is located.

8 'Die Stadt hat sich sozusagen den sozialen Brennpunkt Wilhelmsburg selber geschaffen' (Adanalı, 2013: 123).

9 'Die Geest ist zum Wohnen, die Marsch zum Arbeiten da' (Zukunftskonferenz, 2002: 5).

10 'Für Hanseaten war dies nie der Ort zum Wohnen. Hier wurde Geld verdient' (Zukunftskonferenz, 2002: 5).

11 'Hamburg ist die koloniale Metropole Deutschlands' (Zimmerer, in Deutschlandfunk Kultur, 2020).

12 'Ein Urbanismus der Ungleichheit' (Rinn, 2018).

13 'Wilhelmsburg ist das idealste Industriegebiet des Deutschen Reiches!' (Geschichtswerkstatt Wilhelmsburg und Hafen, 2008: 2).

14 'Beschränke man die Industrie auf inländische Arbeiter, so würde bei einem Rückgang der Industrie eine größere Anzahl von Arbeitern brotlos und vermehrten sie dadurch die unzufriedenen Elemente. Dagegen könne man ausländische Arbeiter in solchem Falle ohne weiteres abstoßen' (Geschichtswerkstatt Wilhelmsburg und Hafen, 2008: 5).

15 I have not been able to find data on the precise number of people who migrated to Wilhelmsburg in this period. Dietz (2008: 102) indicates that there were around 54,000 migrant workers in Hamburg in 1971, along with 10,642 children under 14. This is a relatively small number in comparison to other parts of West Germany, which underscores that stigmatisation is not contingent upon the number of racialised people who are present in a certain space.

References

Adanalı, Z. (2013), Türkischstämmige Migranten auf dem Hamburger Wohnungsmarkt: Am Beispiel des Stadtteils Wilhelmsburg. Masters dissertation, HafenCity Universität.

afrika-hamburg.de. (n.d.), www.afrika-hamburg.de/index.php [accessed 9 February 2019].

Ahyoud, N., J. K. Aikins, S. Bartsch, N. Bechert, D. Gyamerah and L. Wagner (2018), *Wer nicht gezählt wird, zählt nicht: Antidiskriminierungs- und Gleichstellungsdaten in der Einwanderungsgesellschaft – Eine anwendungsorientierte Einführung* (Berlin: Vielfalt entscheidet – Diversity in Leadership, Citizens for Europe).

Arndt, S. (2005), Weißsein: Die verkannte Strukturkategorie Europas und Deutschlands. In Eggers, M. M., G. Kilomba, P. Piesche and S. Arndt (eds) *Mythen, Masken und Subjekte: Kritische Weißseinsforschung in Deutschland* (Münster: Unrast), pp. 24–28.

Barskanmaz, C. (2012), Critical race theory beyond German exceptionalism. Critical Race Theory Europe Symposium, Humboldt University, Berlin, 16 June, https://vimeo.com/66955298 [accessed 6 December 2021].

Behörde für Schule und Berufsbildung (n.d.), Harburg/Wilhelmsburg: Stadtteile Harburg und Wilhelmsburg in der NS-Zeit. *hamburg.de*, www.hamburg.de/clp/dabeigewesene-begriffserklaerungen/clp1/ns-dabeigewesene/onepage.php?BIOID=782 [accessed 12 February 2019].

Bezirksamt Hamburg-Mitte (2015), *Sozialraumbeschreibung Wilhelmsburg* (Hamburg: Bezirksamt Hamburg-Mitte: Fachamt Sozialraummanagement).

Brinkbäumer, K. (2000), Er machte alle kalt. *Der Spiegel* (3 July), www.spiegel.de/spiegel/print/d-16810637.html [accessed 6 December 2021].

Chamberlain, J. (2020a). At home in Hamburg-Wilhelmsburg: racialized long-time residents' perspectives on urban development and social mix planning. Doctoral dissertation, York University.

Chamberlain, J. (2020b). Experimenting on racialized neighbourhoods: IBA Hamburg and the urban laboratory in Hamburg-Wilhelmsburg. *Environment and Planning D: Society and Space* 38(4): 607–625.

Chin, R. (2007), *The Guestworker Question in Postwar Germany*. Cambridge: Cambridge University Press.

Chin, R. (2009), Guestworker migration and the unexpected return of race. In Chin, R., H. Fehrenbach, G. Eley and A. Grossman (eds) *After the Nazi Racial State: Difference and Democracy in Germany and Europe* (Ann Arbor, MI: University of Michigan Press), pp. 80–101.

Danewid, I. (2019), The fire this time: Grenfell, racial capitalism and the urbanisation of empire. *European Journal of International Relations* 26(1): 289–313.

Dei, G. J. S. (2005), Critical issues in anti-racist research methodology: an introduction. In Dei, G. J. S. and G. Johal (eds) *Critical Issues in Anti-racist Research Methodology* (New York, Washington DC/Baltimore, Bern, Frankfurt am Main, Berlin, Brussels, Vienna, Oxford: Peter Lang), pp. 1–28.

Della, T., M. Adjei, J. Zimmerer and N. Kamaṭuka (2018), Quo vadis, Hamburg? Zum Stand städtischer, postkolonialer Erinnerungspolitik. Panel at *Quo Vadis, Hamburg?*

Der Genozid an den Ovaherero und Nama und die Hamburger Kolonialgeschichte. *2. Transnationaler Herero und Nama Kongress*, MS Stubnitz, Hamburg, 6 April, www.youtube.com/watch?v=_HzJGurdukg [accessed 6 December 2021].

Deutschlandfunk Kultur (2020), Geschichte einer Hansestadt – 'Hamburg ist die koloniale Metropole Deutschlands'. *Deutschlandfunk Kultur* (21 February), www.deutschlandfunkkultur.de/geschichte-einer-hansestadt-hamburg-ist-die-koloniale.1001.de.html?dram:article_id=470797 [accessed 9 April 2021].

Dietz, A. (2008), Fremdarbeiter, Gastarbeiter, Einwanderer – Migration in Geschichte und Gegenwart. In Geschichtswerkstatt Wilhelmsburg Honigfabrik e.V. and Museum Elbinsel Wilhelmsburg e.V. (eds) *Wilhelmsburg – Hamburgs große Elbinsel* (Hamburg: Medien-Verlag Schubert), pp. 97–112.

Dorries, H., D. Hugill and J. Tomiak (2019), Racial capitalism and the production of settler colonial cities. *Geoforum*. DOI: https://doi.org/10.1016/j.geoforum.2019.07.016.

Eckardt, F. (2017), Architecture and the 'right to the city': the IBA Hamburg as a case for critical Urban Studies. In Mendes, M., T. Sá and J. Cabral (eds) *Architecture and the Social Sciences: Inter- and Multidisciplinary Approaches Between Society and Space* (n.p.: Springer), pp. 171–190.

El-Tayeb, F. (2011), *European Others: Queering Ethnicity in Postnational Europe* (Minneapolis, MN: University of Minnesota Press).

El-Tayeb, F. (2012), 'Gays who cannot properly be gay': queer Muslims in the neoliberal European city. *European Journal of Women's Studies* 19(1): 79–95.

El-Tayeb, F. (2016), *Undeutsch: Die Konstruktion des Anderen in der postmigrantischen Gesellschaft* (Bielefeld: transcript Verlag).

Frank, T. (1997), *Das Arbeitserziehungslager Wilhelmsburg: Ein beitrag zum nationalsozialistischen Lagersystem* (Hamburg: Geschichtswissenschaft der Universität Hamburg).

Geschichtswerkstatt Wilhelmsburg und Hafen (2008), Einwanderer – Einwohner – Einheimische? Begleittext zur gleichnamigen Ausstellung. *Geschichtswerkstatt Wilhelmsburg & Hafen*, www.geschichtswerkstatt-wilhelmsburg.de/geschichte-wilhelmsburgs/ [accessed 9 April 2021].

Geschichtswerkstatt Wilhelmsburg und Hafen (2018), *Wo bin ich zu Hause? Die Geschichte der Elbinsel Wilhelmsburg – Band 2* (Hamburg: Geschichtswerkstatt Wilhelmsburg und Hafen).

Gosine, A. and C. Teelucksingh (2008), *Environmental Justice and Racism in Canada: An Introduction* (Toronto: Emond Montgomery Publications).

Güntner, S. (2013), Kalkulierbare Segregation? Drei Perspektiven auf die sozialräumliche Polarisierung in Hamburg. In Pohl, G. and K. Wicher (eds) *Hamburg: Gespaltene Stadt? Soziale Entwicklungen in der Metropole* (Hamburg: VSA: Verlag), pp. 34–53.

Ha, K. N. (2003), Die kolonialen Muster deutscher Arbeitsmigrationspolitik. In Steyerl, H. and E. Gutiérrez Rodríguez (eds) *Spricht die Subalterne Deutsch? Migration und postkoloniale Kritik* (Münster: Unrast), pp. 56–107.

Ha, K. N. (2007), Koloniale Arbeitsmigrationspolitik im Imperial Germany. In Ha, K. N., N. Lauré al-Samarai and S. Mysorekar (eds) *Re/visionen: Postkoloniale perspektiven von People of Color auf Rassismus, Kulturpolitk and Widerstand in Deutschland* (Münster: Unrast-Verlag), pp. 65–71.

Ha, N. K. (2017), Zur Kolonialität des Städtischen. In Zwischenraum Kollektiv (ed.) *Decolonize the City!* (Münster: Unrast), pp. 75–87.

Ha, N. (2014), Perspektiven urbaner Dekolonisierung: die europäische Stadt als 'Contact Zone'. *sub\urban. zeitschrift für kritische stadtforschung* 2(1): 27–48.

Hall, S. (2002), 'In but not of Europe': Europe and its myths. *Soundings: A Journal of Politics and Culture* 22(Winter): 57–69.

Hall, S. (2018), Race, articulation, and societies structured in dominance (1980). In Morley D. (eds) *Essential Essays* (Durham, NC: Duke University Press), pp. 172–221.

Hamburgische Investitions- und Förderbank (n.d.), *IFB Hamburg: Wohnen für Studierende und Auszubildende*, www.ifbhh.de/wohnraum/stadtteilentwicklung/quartiersentwicklung/wohnen-fuer-studierende-und-auszubildende/ [accessed 12 January 2019].

Handelskammer Hamburg (n.d.), Hamburg: a key financial centre. *Handelskammer Hamburg*, www.hk24.de/en/produktmarken/financial-economy/hamburg-key-financial-centre/1147600 [accessed 7 December 2018].

Haritaworn, J. (2005), Am Anfang war Audre Lorde: Weißsein und Machtvermeidung in der queeren Ursprungsgeschichte. *Femina Politica – Zeitschrift für feministische Politikwissenschaft* 14(1): 23–35.

Haritaworn, J. (2015), *Queer Lovers and Hateful Others: Regenerating Violent Times and Places* (London: Pluto Press).

Häußermann, H. (2001), Die europäische Stadt. *Leviathan* 29(2): 237–255.

Hellweg, U. (2010), Projects for the future of the metropolis: IBA Hamburg 2013. In Lütke Daldrup, E., P. Zlonicky and Federal Ministry of Transport, Building and Urban Affairs (eds) and J. Lutes (trans.) *Large Scale Projects in German Cities: Urban Development 1990–2010* (Berlin: Jovis Verlag), pp. 114–119.

Hengari, M., K. Murangi and T. Mancheno (2018), Kolonial Amnesie: Hamburg als Profiteur deutscher Kolonialpolitik im heutigen Namibia. Panel at *Quo Vadis, Hamburg? Der Genozid an den Ovaherero und Nama und die Hamburger Kolonialgeschichte. 2. Transnationaler Herero und Nama Kongress*, University of Hamburg, 7 April, www.youtube.com/watch?v=YW3Mrf17FMQ&list=PLmnAZlzZZovKp-RxC9 BVbOG59VXPEscos&index=5 [accessed 10 December 2021].

Hohenstatt, F. and M. Rinn (2013), Festivalisierte Problemarbeitung: Die bevölkerungspolitische Strategie der IBA Hamburg, die Abwesenheit Sozialer Arbeit in Stadtentwicklungspolitik und die Effekte auf Wohnverhältnisse in Wilhelmsburg. *Widersprüche* 127(1): 23–38.

Humburg, M. and M. Rothschuh (2018), Wenn die Kommune verschwindet... Bürgerengagement und Bürgerbeteiligung in Wilhelmsburg – Einem Hamburger Stadtteil ohne eigene Verwaltung und politische Vertretung. *Netzwerk Bürgerbeteiligung* (March 2018).

IBA Hamburg (2011), The great flood and its consequences. History of the Elbe islands: Twelve leaps in time. *IBA Hamburg*, www.iba-hamburg.org/en/01_entwuerfe/5_schauplatz/schauplatz_historie_1962.php [accessed 1 January 2021].

IBA Hamburg (2018), *IBA Hamburg – Seven Years on the Island*. IBA Hamburg, www.iba-hamburg.de/intro.html [accessed 1 January 2021].

James, C. (2012), *Life at the Intersection: Community, Class and Schooling* (Halifax, NS: Fernwood).

Journalisten der Henri-Nannen-Schule (2014), Sinti in Hamburg: Emils Ring. *Die Zeit* (6 May), www.zeit.de/zeit-magazin/leben/2014-07/sinti-hamburg-emil-weiss [accessed 10 December 2021].

Keller, C. (2015), Problemviertel? Imageproduktion und soziale Benachteiligung städtischer Quartiere. *Bundeszentrale für politische Bildung*, www.bpb.de/politik/innenpolitik/gangsterlaeufer/202834/problemviertel-image-und-benachteiligung [accessed 10 December 2021].

Kipfer, S. (2013), Urbanisation et racialisation: desegregation, emancipation, hegemonie. In Buclin, J. Daher, C. Georgiou and P. Raboud (eds) *Penser l'émancipation: Offensives Capitalistes et Résistances Internationals* (Paris: La Dispute), pp. 111–129.

Klij, A. (2019), *Die Wege des Stahls: Deutsche Waffen im Orient*, www.phoenix.de/sendungen/dokumentationen/die-wege-des-stahls-a-1294365.html [accessed 1 April 2019].

Kopf, B. (2012), Warum ich gern in Wilhelmsburg lebe – Und nicht ganz woanders. In Zukunft Elbinsel Wilhelmsburg (ed.) *Eine Starke Insel mitten in der Stadt* (Hamburg: Zukunft Elbinsel Wilhelmsburg e.V.), p. 102.

Kopp, K. (2010), Gray zones: on the inclusion of 'Poland' in the study of German colonialism. In Perraudin, M. and J. Zimmerer (eds) *German Colonialism and National Identity* (Florence, KY: Taylor & Francis), pp. 33–41.

Landeszentrale für Politische Bildung Hamburg (2007), *Zwangsarbeit in der Hamburger Kriegswirtschaft 1939–1945*, www.zwangsarbeit-in-hamburg.de/ [accessed 10 December 2021].

Mancheno, T. (2016), Das postkoloniale Erbe der Hafencity. Lecture given in the series *Deutschlands Tor zur kolonialen Welt: Über den Umgang mit einem schwierigen Erbe*, University of Hamburg, 29 June, www.kolonialismus.uni-hamburg.de/2016/07/04/video-tania-mancheno-universitaet-hamburg-das-postkoloniale-erbe-der-hafencity/ [accessed 10 December 2021].

Melamed, J. (2015), Racial capitalism. *Critical Ethnic Studies* 1(1): 76–85.

Meyer-Lenz, J. (2016), Hafenentwicklung: Entwicklung des Hamburger Hafens zum modernen Überseehafen. *Geschichtsbuch Hamburg*, https://geschichtsbuch.hamburg.de/epochen/kaiserreich/hafenentwicklung/ [accessed 10 December 2021].

Mirchandani, K., R. N. Coloma-Moya, S. Maitra, T. Rawlings, H. Shan, K. Siddiqui and B. Slade (2011), The entrenchment of racial categories in precarious employment. In Glenday, D. and N. Pupo (eds) *The Shifting Landscape of Work* (Toronto: Nelson Educational), pp. 119–138.

Nightingale, C. H. (2012), *Segregation: A Global History of Divided Cities* (Chicago, IL: University of Chicago Press).

Norddeutscher Rundfunk (2018), Hamburg arbeitet koloniales Erbe auf. *Norddeutscher Rundfunk: Hamburg Journal* (2 April).

OvaHerero, Mbanderu and Nama Genocides Institute (2018), Letter to Dr Carsten Brosda, Senator of the Free and Hanseatic City of Hamburg, 9 May, http://theongi.org/?p=1194 [accessed 10 December 2021].

Paech, F. (2008), 'Die ganzen menschlichen Geschichten': Die Hamburger Sturmflut von 1962 im Bewusstsein der Wilhelmsburg Bevölkerung. In Geschichtswerkstatt Wilhelmsburg Honigfabrik e.V. and Museum Elbinsel Wilhelmsburg e.V. (eds) *Wilhelmsburg – Hamburgs große Elbinsel* (Hamburg: Medien-Verlag Schubert), pp. 161–174.

Picker, G. (2017), *Racial Cities: Governance and the Segregation of Romani People in Urban Europe* (London: Routledge).

Preißler, S. (2019), Rekord: Einfamilienhäuser in Hamburg für 1,7 Milliarden verkauft. *Hamburger Abendblatt* (28 February), www.abendblatt.de/wirtschaft/article216546193/Rekord-Einfamilienhaeuser-fuer-1-7-Milliarden-Euro-verkauft.html [accessed 10 December 2021].

Pulido, L. (2016), Flint, environmental racism, and racial capitalism. *Capitalism Nature Socialism* 27(3): 1–16.

Pulido, L. (2017), Geographies of race and ethnicity II: environmental racism, racial capitalism and state-sanctioned violence. *Progress in Human Geography* 41(4): 524–533.

Razack, S. (2002), When place becomes race. In Razack, S. (ed.) *Race, Space and the Law: Unmapping a White Settler Society* (Toronto: Between the Lines), pp. 1–20.

Rinn, M. (2018), Ein Urbanismus der Ungleichheit: 'Neue soziale Stadtpolitik' in Hamburg als Strategie der Verbürgerlichung. *Sub\urban. Zeitschrift Für Kritische Stadtforschung* 6(1): 9–28.

Robinson, C. (1983), *Black Marxism: The Making of the Black Radical Tradition* (Chapel Hill, NC: University of North Carolina Press).

Rowe, M. (2015), Building a future. *Geographical* (February): 38–43, http://geographical.co.uk/magazine/issues/item/690-february-2015 [accessed 10 December 2021].

Roy, A. (2018), At the limits of urban theory: racial banishment in the contemporary city. Talk at London School of Economics, 13 February, www.lse.ac.uk/lse-player/home.aspx [accessed 10 December 2021].

Sanyal, M. (2019), Zuhause. In Aydemir, F. and H. Yaghoobifarah (eds) *Eure Heimat ist unser Albtraum* (Berlin: Ullstein Buchverlage), pp. 101–121.

Schepers, L. (2018), Leichen im Keller – Hamburgs koloniales Erbe. *FINK.HAMBURG*, https://fink.hamburg/snowball/hamburg-als-drehscheibe-des-kolonialismus/ [accessed 6 December 2021].

Schultz, J. and J. Sieweke (2008), *Atlas IBA Hamburg: Wilhelmsburg neu vermessen* (Salenstein: Verlagshaus Braun).

Siebel, W. (2004), Einleitung: Die europäische Stadt. In *Die europäische Stadt* (Frankfurt am Main: edition suhrkamp), pp. 1–50.

Statistisches Amt für Hamburg und Schleswig-Holstein (2017), *Lohn- und Einkommensteuerstatistik in Hamburg 2013: Grosse Unterschiede zwischen den Hamburger Stadtteilen* [Spezial VIII/2017; Statistik Informiert…] (Hamburg: Statistisches Amt für Hamburg und Schleswig-Holstein).

Statistisches Amt für Hamburg und Schleswig-Holstein (2018), *Hamburger Stadtteil Profile – Berichtsjahr 2016* (Hamburg: Statistikamt Nord).

Stehle, M. (2006), Narrating the ghetto, narrating Europe: from Berlin, Kreuzberg to the banlieues of Paris. *Westminster Papers in Communication and Culture* 3(3): 48–70.

Stehle, M. (2012), White ghettos: the 'crisis of multiculturalism' in post-unification Germany. *European Journal of Cultural Studies* 15(2): 167–181.

Todzi, K. S. (2017), Kolonialismus und Imperialismus. In Urbanski, S. (ed.) *Digitales Hamburg Geschichtsbuch*, www.geschichtsbuch.hamburg.de/epochen/kolonialismus/hamburg-und-die-kolonien/ [accessed 9 April 2021].

Todzi, K. S. (2018), Hamburg's first globalization. In Kokott, J. and F. Takayanagi (eds) *Erste Dinge. Rückblick für Ausblick/ First Things. Looking Back to Look Forward* (Hamburg: Museum am Rothenbaum, Kulturen und Künste der Welt), pp. 166–170.

Tsianos, V. (2013), Urbane Paniken: Zur Entstehung des antimuslimischen Urbanismus. In Gürsel, D., Z. Çetin and Allmende e.V. (eds) *Wer MACHT Demo_kratie?* (Münster: edition assemblage), pp. 23–43.

Twickel, C. (2011), Krisenviertel Hamburg-Wilhelmsburg: Einstürzende Neubauträume. *Spiegel Online* (25 March), www.spiegel.de/kultur/gesellschaft/krisenviertel-hamburg-wilhelmsburg-einstuerzende-neubautraeume-a-753127.html [accessed 6 December 2021].

Vogelpohl, A. and T. Buchholz (2017), Breaking with neoliberalization by restricting the housing market: novel urban policies and the case of Hamburg. *International Journal of Urban and Regional Research* 41(2): 266–281.

Wacquant, L. (2008), *Urban Outcasts: A Comparative Sociology of Advanced Marginality* (Cambridge and Malden, MA: Polity).

Yeğenoğlu, M. (1998), *Colonial Fantasies: Towards a Feminist Reading of Orientalism* (Cambridge: Cambridge University Press).

Yildiz, Y. (2009), Turkish girls, Allah's daughters, and the contemporary German subject: itinerary of a figure. *German Life and Letters* 62(4): 465–481.

Zukunftskonferenz Wilhelmsburg (2002), Zukunftskonferenz Wilhelmsburg: Wilhelmsburg – Insel im Fluss – Brücken in die Zukunft. Bericht der Arbeitsgruppen Mai 2001 bis Januar 2002, Zukunftskonferenz Wilhelmsburg.

Coda: toward urban provisioning

AbdouMaliq Simone

What to do with the city. With its conceptual and empirical traps. With its reified, truncated distillation of urbanization. With its accelerated implosions into intensely surveilled spaces promising to exist at the level of the 'world', and thus must be protected from the morass of parochialisms, messy encounters, and increasingly desperate improvisations that characterize its surrounds. Weighted down with the infrastructures of exclusivity and exclusion, somnambulant in the torpor of accumulated theft and exhausted from the obligation to produce incessant spectacle, what passes for the penultimate city is forced to retreat more and more into hyper-abstraction in order to render any image of efficacy. Not merely an apparatus for reconsolidating the salience of whiteness, it seems indifferent to anyone or any body specifically. Or perhaps more precisely, it aims to make use of anything that exists in any form, wounded, flourishing, capacitated or traumatized. It doesn't matter. Any condition becomes a hedge, a matter of arbitrage, a maneuver of variables whose value is only in terms of the derivatives or combinations to which they can be subjected. In plenitude or vacancy, the penultimate city, stopping just short of its ultimate disappearance and collapsing under its own leverages and sunk costs, confirms the irrelevance of inhabitation. The city is not a place of settlement, by anybody.

The work of this book is important in that it documents the extent to which the traditional categories of neighborhood, conviviality, multiculturalism, community organization and participation are insufficient either in accounting for the claimed capacities of European cities to ensure a modicum of spatial justice or as elements for an imaginary of the dissipation of coloniality and the rectification of anti-blackness. The entrenchment of white supremacy and the materialization of imperial extraction as the fundamental substrate of urban economies has not only institutionalized precarity as the predominant mode of inhabitation for peoples of color but undermined the potentialities of urbanization itself to produce multiple dispositions of well-being. Through the depletion of urban capacity, whiteness itself is inevitably destined to implode.

As cities hold the vulnerabilities of those structurally marginalized they have been twisted and turned through the multiple strategies of everyday survival. In many European cities where 'migrants' were often unable to attain formal work, education and health services, entire parallel worlds were forced into existence, often brutal and precarious, but nevertheless acted both as an affront to and revelator of the prevailing presumptions of urban modernity. By forcing people of color to the margins, the hegemonic imaginaries and operating procedures themselves become increasingly marginal to the 'real city'. For even if the pretensions of liberty and modernity were always held together by the avarice and power-hungry deal-making of political elites and all those who tried to become elites, the work needed to maintain racial assemblages demonstrated the extent to which multiple forms of violence – police, bureaucratic, institutional neglect – were at the heart of urban governmentality.

Europe clearly is not what it thinks it is. There are countervailing narratives always already in front of us. There are spaces between exclusive inclusion and inclusive exclusion that cities will always deem problematic, but from which they cannot dissociate. They cannot dissociate because such spaces simultaneously perpetuate problems that are used to legitimate particular forms of rule, provide spaces where problems can be worked out always temporarily without ruling regimes having to acknowledge responsibility, and posit specific propositions of urbanities that those same regimes do not have any idea about what to do with.

Despite its most recent postmodern instantiation, Stazione di Napoli Centrale and its surrounds are exemplars of both a more anachronistic and vital notion of the city. What more could you ask for? The profusion of thousands of games of chance and tactical proficiency. The intricate chore-ographies of tacitly coordinated bodies operating as mobile collectives in transactions of all kinds, and whose performances are adorned with constantly invented vernaculars. Here blackness is a gravitational field that pulls in all kinds of curiosities, vulnerability, interdiction and joy. Markets come and go instantaneously or are entrenched through detailed and mutating arrange-ments of 'local authorities' who all have difficulties recognizing themselves let alone each other. Gritty, parasitical, generous, transgressive and systematic, blackness here is fundamentally multivalent, and while constantly pissed off about the arbitrariness of municipal rule as applied to it, is also not all that interested in the tropes that pass for spatial justice.

It is nearly impossible to imagine what European cities would be without blackness. Without its sound ecologies, fashion statements, visceral maneuvers and collective intelligence. While of course forged under intensive racial oppression and within the ligatures of infrastructures designed to operational-ize the extraction of bodily and mental capacities and resources of all kinds, blackness, or rather its sacrifice, has positioned itself as the only salvation. Even if such a position approximates a rejuvenated enslavement, or the obdurate entanglements of boundary-making and conviviality, it is a critical element of the incomputable that extends urbanization beyond its city-centric capture. For only in such an extension is there a production of spaciousness contingent, not on the rolling out of a specific logic of growth, but on the intersection of multifaceted territories of operation, logics of appearance, and seemingly incompatible forms of life. Granted, this formulation skirts the constitution of abstract blackness as an endlessly malleable form operating, as Zakiyyah Iman Jackson (2020) points out, simultaneously across all register. Nevertheless, the white instrumentalization of malleability, according to its needs and fantasies, and in circumvention of the constitution of a milieu of mutual enactment and shaping of form, cannot define the scope of its use.

As such, justice cannot be 'served' on the platter of the city-form; it is not a matter of accommodation, of availing real and resourced opportunities on the part of the oppressed to define what they want the city to be, but rather its very abolition. For at its very core, the city was the locus for inhabitation based on the continuous evolvement of reflexivity about that very inhabitation – an economy of time and labor that required the proximity of those to whom that position and capacity were denied. The abolition of the city is not then the dismemberment of its densities and agglomerations but its constitutive narrative of articulation, the ability to subsume that which is made dense to a linear trajectory of interminable development, while occluding all the mechanisms of violence that are entailed in securing this geometry. It restores to urbanization an ambiguation, even indeterminacy of temporality that upends the capture of diverse experiences and bodies in the formatting of what counts, what is valuable.

Genericity

Rather than mobilizing the apparent heterogeneity of the city either in calculations of equilibration that ensures a judicious balance among inhabitants or in proliferating niche spaces and built environments capable of representing the self-valorized ways of life of the heretofore excluded, the abolition of the city is an upending of proportionality. It is the upending of all of those attempts to curate niche styles and built environments, which seek to blend judicious proportions and mixtures of functions, populations and capacities in favor of genericity. By genericity I mean an extensiveness, an extension of urbanization, and a production of spaciousness through a compression of differences that occludes the determinacy of a hierarchy of valuation.

Analogous to a black hole, the generic here, instead of a homogenization of difference or an empty abstraction, enables the operations of anything – where, for example, it is impossible to tell what is formal or informal, legal or illegal, and so forth.

Perhaps more important than Europe's monuments, neighborhoods of enduring antagonisms and gentrifying spaces are the vast swathes of seeming featureless spatial products – fractal housing blocks, storage spaces, warehouses, under-utilized industrial estates and transport nodes; all of those facets of the built environment, usually across the sprawling peripheries of metropolitan areas that elicit little attention. All of these seemingly generic spaces whose actual functions and uses remain or can remain largely unknown. In the fourth season of Italy's most popular television series, *Gomorrah,* these urban domains become a main character, as they are repurposed into a fabric of accumulation for Gennaro, having been stripped of everything, upon his return to Naples to start anew. Industrial bakeries on the verge of collapse, abandoned ports, tracts of suburban housing seemingly in the middle of nowhere, the *terroir vague* of underpasses, abandoned service roads, food processing centers shuttered for violations, and commercial storage spaces become essential infrastructure collapsing just enough of the minimal sustenance of their intended purposes with a circulation of varying provisional uses.

For generic spaces, it is nearly impossible to determine where they are headed and how, and so keep open the question as to who cities are for, and begin to undo the historical answer, which was for 'whites'. It restores the uncertainty as the role of 'dirty industries' and 'dirty populations' that, on the one hand provide a critical economic substrate but are rendered 'subaltern', a polluting of modernity. Here the conundrum has always been the capture of urbanization by and through technical apparatuses capable of rendering inhabitation beyond corporeal excess, of harnessing physical metabolisms to output, to the volumetric *expansions* of space and potentiality. Such expansion is opposed to the production of *spaciousness* through the intersections of wayward practices of settlement and unsettlement, which always entailed *dirty business* – processes that could never be stabilized within the terms of the furtherance of well-being, health and individual potential and, as such, meant both the predictable and unpredictable ramifications of *exposure* to slow death or enduring uncertainties.

Here, Fred Moten's (2017) notions of lateral agency are important: an agency that is not characterized by the furtherance of human development or the prolongation of life, but life in its priority, as that beyond linear steerage; something that veers off in all kinds of dimensions; that steals away from either being an object of theft or an asset whose value is to be maximized. In the ordinary duress of racialized cities, of the bodies of 'strangers' – no matter how long they have been around – being immobilized and exposed to constant interdiction, there remains the indistinction between surviving immanent threat and the costs of that surviving; that a focus on endurance may simply constitute a theft of an engagement with life, right here, right now.

This is not to obviate the importance of genealogies about how we got to where we are, about the structuring operations that as Dionne Brand (2010) says introduced terror into the world. And it is not that such genealogies lack the capacity to specify methods of transformation or offer imaginations of what freedom might look like. But no matter what genealogies are developed, they cannot account for all of the leakages, inexplicable circumventions, all of the life lived on the 'side' or 'besides' that has no unequivocal meaning, that measures no degrees of freedom or viability. These are the affective and practical extensions of urban inhabitation; they extend off the grid, off the normative trajectories of sustainable development, and are mute in face of grand pronouncements or major events.

While the specters of racialized trauma will always come back to haunt, and are materialized in the very infrastructures of European cities, there is something else besides these living memories that come to inhabit, which add 'new impossibilities' to the world – both in terms of capture and liberation as they are conventionally understood. Parading around as the most facile and digestible of forms, the generic also embodies the impossibilities of the coexistence of the irreconcilable outside the protocols of domination. Compressed into a proximity with forms of life, use and inhabitation otherwise deemed antithetical, the residues of the colonial are frozen in an uncertainty of their authority. As it was the surfeit of confidence beyond reason acting as reason that underpinned this authority, abolition eventually could care less about what of coloniality's materialization remains or not.

Beyond extraction

Decoloniality also puts in play the *technical* dimensions of the relationalities of urbanization that come from all over the place, and work in different degrees, proportions and manifestations that come to be associated with it but also do not intrinsically belong to it. This is because there is no essential overarching characterization attributable to urbanization outside of its profusion of technical relationalities – its capacity to continuously repeat everything we might know about it, and upend itself at the same time. This is not simply a matter of machines, calculative instruments, architectural plans or social media, but points to the ways in which processes of 'affecting and being affected' far exceed the deliberative mechanisms of planning, policy or sectoral protocols.

They entail constantly oscillating circuitries of reciprocal impact, reshaping and rearrangement emerging from the intersections of metabolisms, sensory systems, discourses and physical performance. They entail all of the ways in which gathering takes place, all of the ways in which infrastructures work on each other and all of the ways in which images and sounds 'address' each other, thus generating possibilities of spaciousness which no apparatus of control or mediation knows quite what to do with, even as it misrecognizes or obscures them. The technical concerns the range of organizing mechanisms that articulate materials, spaces and expressions with varying intensities generating constellations of livability that make up the virtual repertoires of the urban. What and how decisions are made to attend to specific constellations are a matter of politics, but politics do not bring into being this virtuality, to which the labor, expressive lives and practices of care and endurance of the oppressed have substantially contributed. In other words, the technical elaboration of the urban already embodies the incipience of multiple forms potentially constitutive of 'freedom'.

It is critical then to proliferate aesthetic forms and experiences that amplify the presence of such techno-poetics and facilitate investment in maximizing the resourcefulness, instead of vilification, of social arrangements that may have emanated from the positions of enduring catastrophe but which exemplify more just forms of urban existence. Just as the book has practiced a gathering of literatures over time, it is important to continue assembling an archive of all of those gatherings that rework the operative notions of household, home, collective and livelihood. This is in addition to the continuous reframing of the financialized city as systematic theft, and shifting the locus of economy away from *expansive reproduction*, with its logistical systems centered on maximizing the extraction of something from everything, to *extended social reproduction*, where childcare, marking, schooling, health, provisioning, calculating and working become the *conjoint* and coordinated responsibilities of multiple and intertwined institutions.

References

Brand, D. (2010), *Ossuaries* (London: Penguin).
Jackson, Z. I. (2020), *Becoming Human: Matter and Meaning in an Antiblack World* (New York: New York University Press).
Moten, F. (2017), *Black and Blur* (Durham, NC and London: Duke University Press).

Index

EU authorised representative for GPSR:
Easy Access System Europe, Mustamäe tee 50,
10621 Tallinn, Estonia
gpsr.requests@easproject.com

www.ingramcontent.com/pod-product-compliance
Lightning Source LLC
Chambersburg PA
CBHW051955270326
41929CB00015B/2665